International Criminal Justice Series

Volume 2

Series editors

Gerhard Werle, Berlin, Germany
Lovell Fernandez, Bellville, South Africa
Moritz Vormbaum, Berlin, Germany (Managing Editor)

Series Information

The *International Criminal Justice Series* aims to create a platform for publications in the whole field of international criminal justice. It, therefore, deals with issues relating, among others, to:

– the work of international criminal courts and tribunals;
– transitional justice approaches in different countries;
– international anti-corruption and anti-money laundering initiatives;
– the history of international criminal law.

The series concentrates on themes pertinent to developing countries. It is peer-reviewed and seeks to publish high-quality works emanating from excellent scholars, in particular from African countries.

Editorial Office

Prof. Dr. Gerhard Werle
Humboldt-Universität zu, Berlin
Faculty of Law
Unter den Linden 6,
10099 Berlin, Germany
gerhard.werle@rewi.hu-berlin.de
moritz.vormbaum@rewi.hu-berlin.de

More information about this series at http://www.springer.com/series/13470

Sosteness Francis Materu

The Post-Election Violence in Kenya

Domestic and International Legal Responses

Sosteness Francis Materu
Faculty of Law
University of Dar es Salaam
Dar es Salaam
Tanzania

ISBN 978-94-6265-040-4   ISBN 978-94-6265-041-1   (eBook)
DOI 10.1007/978-94-6265-041-1

Library of Congress Control Number: 2014954347

Published by T.M.C. ASSER PRESS, The Hague, The Netherlands www.asserpress.nl
Produced and distributed for T.M.C. ASSER PRESS by Springer-Verlag Berlin Heidelberg

Springer is part of Springer Science+Business Media (www.springer.com)

To my parents, Francis Mlang'a Materu (R.I.P.)
and Melania Msise Materu,
and
my siblings

Foreword

Although a familiar fixture for many of us, the nascency of the International Criminal Court (ICC) must be continually brought to our forethoughts. While it may stand alone as the world's only permanent international criminal tribunal, it stands there on the footing provided by all attempts to meet power with law and mete out a justice that ensures victims are entitled to see perpetrators brought to book, regardless of stature and position. That the ICC exists is an achievement of monumental importance; that the early years of the ICC have perhaps raised more questions than answers should equally be expected.

The Court's evolution will include steps forward, sideways, and every which way, as it encounters novel situations as a novel institution. The Court is in this Heraclitean dance with its partners: States Parties that have signaled to the world their rejection of impunity, those that participate from the sidelines, and those that may seek to undermine its operation. Each step yields a new understanding at every move, encountering new challenges and possibilities, undergirded by the promise of constant change. With one of the first contemporaneous studies of Kenya and its own fraught, ever-changing dance with the ICC, Sosteness Francis Materu gives us a lens to examine not only issues of importance to Kenya and Kenyans, but to all those with an eye on the Court and its relationships in the world, the region, and within itself.

As readers and learners, we glean many benefits from the author's own positioning. He is a highly skilled and qualified academic. I learned this first-hand through our interactions at the South African-German Centre for Transnational Criminal Justice, a partnership between the University of Western Cape in Cape Town and the Humboldt University in Berlin, where he was a student. This Centre supports the exploration of emerging transnational criminal issues from both African and International perspectives, an embrace that shines through in the author's own work.

The author displays a systematic approach to teasing apart the many facets of the issues in the Kenyan situation. While he offers a historically grounded socio-political analysis of the post-election violence that engulfed Kenya as 2007 became 2008, his study never loses sight of the procedural and substantive legal issues within Kenya and the ICC. He draws out the tensions in the evolution of accountability for international crimes, and, while maintaining distinctly national focus, is still able to highlight the overarching challenges of meeting power with law in a world of multi-level jurisdictions. He does all of this in a well-structured manner that is accessible for practitioners, academics, and those interested more broadly in the issues under study.

As he guides us first through the post-colonial genesis of fault lines in the Kenyan society and the dangers of imperial presidencies, we see how recurring episodes of unpunished electoral violence and a culture of impunity bred conditions ripe for exploitation. As Kenyans and the world watch the convulsions run across the country in the wake of the 2007 elections, there was also a belief, however tenuous, that the domestic system may yield the promised outcomes of justice and reconciliation. Materu neither holds false hope nor unwarranted cynicism for the restorative justice mechanisms that were brought in alongside the importance of recognizing the need for retributive justice in the agreements that flowed from the Kenyan National Dialogue and Reconciliation. The author shows us though that even the most promising attempts at creating a roadmap for accountability within Kenya were bedeviled by local politics. Again, we are returned to the persistent challenge of law meeting intransigent power.

Though Materu's analysis concludes there was the technical ability of the domestic Kenyan legal system to confront the crimes, he demonstrates the impossibility of that happening in the post-violence context. As his analysis moves to Kenya's dance with the ICC, which was initiated by the Prosecution's first exercise of the Office's *proprio motu* powers, we see how unwelcoming of a partner Kenya had become. Kenya's various attempts at ousting the Court's exercise of its complementarity jurisdiction are set out and examined, showing how a once willing state can foment discontent with institutions internally and regionally.

The Court's own engagement with the case quickly showed again the novelty of the situation. The Rome Statute's treatment of the contextual elements of crimes against humanity has given rise to divisive interpretations, no more clear than in the Kenyan cases. From the minority, we received the counterpoint to Pre-Trial Chamber II's majority both in authorizing the investigation into the situation in Kenya and subsequently their confirmation of charges against four of the original six who stood accused. As the author sets out, when examining the contested element of what constitutes "a State or organizational policy" from the minority we received an interpretation focused on the nature of the entity, an account that hues closer to our historically informed sense of international crimes. From the majority we get what Materu describes as a forward-looking account of the nature of crimes against humanity, one that focuses on the capacity of a group to commit heinous crimes and that appreciates the dynamic evolution of criminal actors. For a permanent institution, the author implores us to adopt this latter view and sets out cogent reasons for doing so. His legal analysis does not stop there and his treatment of the issues that have arisen in this situation continues to reflect his appreciation for the interplay between local, regional, and international regimes and actors.

At a time when the ICC is being critiqued from multiple angles, Materu's account helps us locate the institution's strengths and weaknesses. His treatment of the dance between the Court and Kenya is informed and balanced; neither escapes criticism. His recognition of the local limits for obtaining justice in Kenya should be a sound reminder to the Court's critics that it has a role to play and should be supported in bringing voice to victims of atrocities regardless of where they find themselves.

Berlin, Summer 2014   Prof. Dr. h.c. mult. René Blattmann
                                                                                  Visiting Professor,
                                                             Humboldt-Universität zu Berlin
                                                            Former Vice-President and Judge,
                                                             International Criminal Court

Acknowledgements

The research leading to this book was supported by the *Deutscher Academischer Austausch Dienst* (DAAD) with funds from the Federal Foreign Office of Germany. It was conducted under the auspices of the South African German Centre for Transnational Criminal Justice based on cooperation between the University of the Western Cape and Humboldt University of Berlin. I am very grateful to the DAAD and the Federal Foreign Office of Germany for this generous financial support. In addition, I owe a debt of gratitude to the following people whose contributions made this project a success.

My heartfelt gratitude goes to all the members of the South African German Centre for their support. I thank Professor Gerhard Werle of Humboldt University and Director of the Centre, who provided the main intellectual guidance throughout the research process. His trust and encouragement made me work harder and more enthusiastically to complete the project. Professor Lovell Fernandez of the University of the Western Cape and Co-director of the Centre provided intellectual advice on part of my research. He also assisted unreservedly in the final editing of the manuscript. Dr. Moritz Vormbaum, who is the Coordinator of the Centre, extended warm cooperation throughout my affiliation to the Centre. Anja Schepke from the Chair of Professor Werle at Humboldt University provided excellent administrative support that enabled my research to proceed smoothly. She diligently ensured that the research funds were secured and remitted to me both timely and conveniently. During my research stays in Berlin, she ensured that a decent and affordable accommodation was secured for me. Hazel Jeftha and Farieda Hendricks from the University of the Western Cape provided their invaluable administrative support during my research stays in Cape Town.

I am grateful to Professor Florian Jeßberger of Hamburg University and to Dr. Boris Burghardt, Senior Research Fellow at the Chair of Professor Werle at Humboldt University, for their useful insights into my research. Professor Palamagamba John Kabudi, former Dean of the Law Faculty, University of Dar es Salaam, deserves my sincere thanks. He not only encouraged me to seize the research opportunity at the South African German Centre, but also ensured that my employer, the University of Dar es Salaam, granted me a study leave for that purpose. I am also very grateful to Judge René Blattmann who, on a short notice, agreed to sacrifice his valuable time to write the Foreword.

I would like to thank my dear mother, siblings, relatives and friends for their constant love and support. I also thank my colleagues Dr. Juliet Okoth, Dr. Daniel Leslie, Dr. Charity Wibabara, Windell Nortje, Jean Phillipo, Marshet Tessema, Zainabu Mango, Arnold Gessase and Fatuma Silungwe for the moments and time we shared and spent together in Berlin and Cape Town as researchers affiliated to the South African German Centre. I thank Aziz Epik and Janosch Kunner from the Chair of Professor Werle for their cooperation in Berlin.

My very special thanks go to the staff of T.M.C. Asser Press and Springer for the cooperation extended to me throughout the publication process. I particularly thank Philip van Tongeren, Antoinette Wessels and Marjolijn Bastiaans in this regard.

Above all, I thank the Almighty God for His constant love and blessings. To Him be all the glory.

Contents

Abbreviations and Acronyms

AC	Appeals Chamber
AG	Attorney General
Art(s)	Article(s)
ASP	Assembly of States Parties
AU	African Union
Cap.	Chapter
CCL	Control Council Law (No. 10)
Cf.	Compare (*confer*)
CORD	Coalition for Reforms and Democracy
DPP	Director of Public Prosecutions
EAC	East African Community
EACJ	East African Court of Justice
ECOWAS	Economic Community of West African States
ed(s).	Editor(s)
edn.	Edition
EJIL	European Journal of International Law
eKLR	Electronic Kenya Law Reports
et al.	and others (*et alii*)
et seq.	and the following (*et sequens; et sequentes*)
G.N	Gazette Notice
i.e.	that is (*id est*)
ibid.	in the same place (*ibidem*)
ICC	International Criminal Court
ICD	International Crimes Division
ICTR	International Criminal Tribunal for Rwanda
ICTY	International Criminal Tribunal for (the Former) Yugoslavia
IMT	International Military Tribunal (at Nuremberg)
KADU	Kenya African Democratic Union
KANU	Kenya African National Union
KNDR	Kenya National Dialogue and Reconciliation
LDP	Liberal Democratic Party

MP(s)	Member(s) of Parliament
NAK	National Alliance (Party) of Kenya
NDP	National Development Party
NGO	Non-governmental Organization
ODM	Orange Democratic Movement
OTP	Office of the Prosecutor (of the ICC)
p, pp	page(s)
para(s)	paragraph(s)
PNU	Party of National Unity
PTC	Pre-Trial Chamber
R.E	Revised Edition (of the laws of Kenya)
s, ss.	section(s)
SCSL	Special Court for Sierra Leone
TC	Trial Chamber
TJRC	Truth, Justice and Reconciliation Commission (Kenya)
TRC	Truth and Reconciliation Commission
UN	United Nations

Chapter 1
Introduction

Abstract This chapter introduces the study and gives its general overview. It starts by situating the study within the context of the "duty to prosecute", being the basis for prosecuting crimes under international law allegedly committed in Kenya. The chapter also presents the background to the research problem, the objectives of the study and the outline of the book.

Contents

1.1 Preliminary Remarks

The Republic of Kenya is located in the eastern part of Africa. By 2009 its population was approximately 40 million people, spread over a land area of 580,000 km^2.[1] Like people in other African countries, Kenyans identify themselves, inter alia, by their ethnic groups (tribes), whose total number is 42, and which are distributed unevenly across the country.[2] Before the introduction of the county administration system in 2010, the country was divided into eight geographical-cum-administrative regions called provinces, which were controlled directly by the central government from the capital city, Nairobi.[3] In terms of

---

[1] See Kenya National Bureau of Statistics 2010, p. 20.

[2] See Jonyo 2003, p. 166.

[3] These are Nairobi, Nyanza, Eastern, Western, Coast, North-Eastern, Rift Valley and Central Provinces.

© T.M.C. ASSER PRESS and the author 2015

S.F. Materu, *The Post-Election Violence in Kenya*,
International Criminal Justice Series 2, DOI 10.1007/978-94-6265-041-1_1

economic development, Kenya is a developing country with the largest Growth Domestic Product (GDP) in Eastern and Central Africa (excluding Ethiopia), its capital city being the economic hub of the region.

Kenya was under effective British colonial rule between 1890 and 1963. The British colonialists introduced a settler economy which was accompanied by large-scale commercial farming.[4] By 1950, the white population, mostly settler coffee and tea farmers, was 80,000.[5] Today, the number of white population has dwindled, as most of the British settler farmers left after Kenya became independent. Until the general elections of 2007, which gave rise to the crimes dealt with in this book, Kenya had had three presidents, the third of whom, Mwai Kibaki, was seeking re-election.

1.2 Setting the Context

Crimes under international law differ from ordinary domestic crimes. Although some scholars argue that a *precise* definition of the former still remains controversial,[6] it is clear that such a controversy, if any, does not extend to their distinguishing features. Scholars agree on at least three most important features that make a criminal conduct a crime under international law. Firstly, apart from entailing individual criminal responsibility, the criminalization and punishment of such conduct must, as a matter of principle, arise directly under international law. Secondly, the aim of such criminalization must be to protect the interests of not just one or a few states, but of the international community as a whole. Thirdly, the official position of perpetrators of such crimes must not exonerate them from individual criminal responsibility, even if their national jurisdictions would ordinarily avail them such a privilege.[7]

Four "core crimes under international law" are recognized as such, namely genocide, war crimes, crimes against humanity and aggression.[8] This list presents the law as it stands today, but there is a possibility that it might be expanded in the future.[9] The four core crimes are said to be "the most serious crimes of international

---

[4] Library of Congress 2007, p. 2.

[5] Jonyo 2003, p. 166.

[6] See, e.g., Naqvi 2009, p. 21; Wouters 2005, pp. 17 et seq.

[7] Bassiouni 1986, p. 2; Cassese 2008, pp. 11–13; Damgaard 2008, pp. 56–60; Naqvi 2009, pp. 21–24; Schabas 2007, pp. 82–83; Werle 2009, p. 29.

[8] See Article 5 of the Rome Statute of the International Criminal Court, A/CONF.183/9, 17 July 1998 (hereafter "ICC, Statute"). See also Cassese 2008, pp. 11–13; Damgaard 2008, pp. 56–85; and Werle 2009, p. 29.

[9] See, e.g., ICC Statute, Article 123; Bassiouni 1986, pp. 1–2 (arguing that there are 22 "international crimes" in total). For more details see Triffterer 2008, pp. 40 and 59; and Zimmermann 2008, pp. 98–103.

concern",[10] because their effect not only transcends national boundaries, but also tends to threaten the peace, security and well-being of arguably the world as a whole.[11] In view of this, there is a global consensus that in the event that such crimes occur, the state on whose territory they are committed (state of commission) has a legal duty, arising directly under international law, to investigate, prosecute and punish the perpetrators.[12]

The duty to prosecute, which is imposed on the state of commission, exists alongside the right to prosecute availed to third states through universal jurisdiction. Pursuant to such a right, a third state may, in principle, prosecute a core crime even if it does not have any direct link with the perpetrator, the crime or the victims.[13] The right to prosecute exists solely on the basis of the *jus cogens* (customary) nature of the core crimes,[14] which makes them prosecutable by any state, irrespective of whether or not there is a treaty obligation to do so.[15]

Both the duty and the right to prosecute underscore one main point: impunity for the core crimes is not an option.[16] In addition, the right to prosecute is intended mainly to play a curative role, namely to fill a foreseeable impunity gap; it seeks to ensure that if the state of commission ignores or fails to discharge its duty to prosecute, then any third state which is committed to international criminal justice is able to do so.

However, if history is anything to go by, it proves amply that there is no guarantee that the state of commission will always discharge its duty to prosecute. A lacuna may arise in any of the following three scenarios. First, the state of commission may simply *ignore* its duty to prosecute (inaction). Second, it may *wish or even attempt* to prosecute, but fails to do so due to its inability to conduct effective investigations and/or prosecutions (inability). Third, it may *purport* to investigate or prosecute, but prove to be unwilling to carry out genuine investigations or prosecutions, sometimes with the intention to shield the perpetrators (shielding). Similarly, both history and practice show that in these three scenarios, even universal jurisdiction may not always be a reliable tool to fill the resulting lacuna. The reason being that in most

---

[10] ICC Statute, Preamble para 4 and Article 1.

[11] ICC Statute, Article 5 and Preamble, para 3; Werle 2009, p. 31.

[12] See Human Rights Watch 2009, pp. 10–17; International Committee of the Red Cross 2005; Jeßberger 2007, pp. 213–22; Scharf 1996, pp. 1 et seq.; Tomuschat 2002, pp. 315 et seq.; Werle 2009, pp. 69–70. On how the duty to prosecute is extended to third states by the principle of *aut dedere aut judicare* (prosecute or extradite), see generally Bassiouni and Wise 1995.

[13] Werle 2009, p. 64. See also generally Macedo 2004.

[14] Article 53 of the Vienna Convention on the Law of Treaties of 1969 defines a *jus cogens* as a "peremptory norm of general international law ... from which no derogation is permitted".

[15] Bassiouni 1996, p. 63 (noting, inter alia, that the *jus cogens* status of international crimes constitutes obligations *erga omnes* (owed to all mankind) which are non-derogable). See also Obura 2011, pp. 13–14.

[16] Cf. May 2005 (giving a theoretical and philosophical justification on why third states and international tribunals must exercise jurisdiction over *jus cogens* crimes when the state of commission fails or is unwilling to do so).

cases, third states do refrain from exercising their right to prosecute on account of, inter alia, diplomatic, political or practical considerations.[17]

If states fail or are unwilling to investigate and prosecute, there is a fallback: criminal accountability for at least those who bear the greatest responsibility for the core crimes can be sought before international courts and tribunals vested with jurisdiction. Currently, the most prominent institution vested with such jurisdiction is the permanent International Criminal Court (hereafter "the ICC" or "the Court"),[18] a treaty-based court for which a Statute (hereafter "ICC Statute") was adopted in 1998 and put to effect on 1 July 2002. The Court became fully operational in 2003.[19]

The ICC Statute reaffirms the duty of national jurisdictions to prosecute and punish the core crimes under international law, and reiterates that no impunity shall be tolerated in this regard.[20] As the Court officially commenced its activities, Luis Moreno-Ocampo, its first Chief Prosecutor, underscored the pivotal role of states in the fight against impunity with regard to these crimes through genuine utilization of their national courts. Ocampo stated that the ICC's efficiency would not be measured by the number of cases it prosecutes, but rather by the number of cases it *avoids* due to the proper functioning of domestic legal systems.[21] In line with this statement, the jurisdiction of the ICC is designed to be complementary (secondary) to that of national courts.[22] This arrangement rightly makes the

---

[17] Cf. Bassiouni 2001, pp. 81 et seq.; Macedo 2004, p. 44, Kissinger; 2001, pp. 86–96; and Werle 2009, pp. 67–68. A clear example of how sceptical the policies of states are with regard to the exercise of universal jurisdiction is to be found in State's argument in the judgment of the High Court of South Africa: *Southern African Litigation Centre and Another v. The South African National Director of Public Prosecutions and Three Others,* 8 May 2012, pp. 25–27. Also see the subsequent judgment of the South African Supreme Court of Appeal: *National Commissioner of the South African Police and another v. Southern Africa Litigation Centre and others* (485/2012) [2013] ZASCA 168 (27 November 2013). For critical analysis of these judgments see Kemp 2014; Werle and Bornkamm 2013, pp. 659 et seq.

[18] ICC Statute, Article 5(1). However, with regard to the crime of aggression, the ICC will only be able to exercise jurisdiction after 2017 upon meeting the specific conditions stipulated under Article 5(2) of the ICC Statute read together with Article 15 *bis* adopted in the first amendment to the Statute in 2010. For more details see Ambos 2010, pp. 463 et seq.; Clark 2009, pp. 1103–1115 and Manson 2010, pp. 417–443.

[19] For more information see "ICC at a glance" http://www.icc-cpi.int/en_menus/icc/about%20 the%20court/icc%20at.%20a%20glance/Pages/icc%20at.%20a%20glance.aspx. Accessed September 2014 See also Werle 2009, pp. 20–25.

[20] The Statute provides that in order to "put an end to impunity for perpetrators of these crimes and thus contribute to the prevention of such crimes…effective prosecution must be ensured by taking measures at national level". And therefore, "it is a duty of every State to exercise its criminal jurisdiction over those responsible for international crimes". See ICC Statute, Preamble, paras 4, 5 and 6.

[21] See Statement given at the ceremony for the solemn undertaking of the Chief Prosecutor of the ICC (June, 16 2003), p. 2 http://www.iccnow.org/documents/MorenoOcampo16June03.pdf. Accessed August 2014.

[22] See infra Sect. 6.5.

ICC "the ultimate executor of compliance to the duty to prosecute" and arguably "the main guarantor" of the same.[23]

In summary, therefore, a principle of international customary law exists which requires that commission of any of the core crimes under international law must not go unpunished. Similarly, the avenues or forums in which criminal account-ability for such crimes can be sought are clearly known and well established: In the first place, the state of commission is duty-bound to institute genuine prosecu-tions in its domestic courts, failing which last resort can be had to the ICC or to prosecution on the basis of universal jurisdiction.

One would expect that apart from their retributive purpose, the foregoing ini-tiatives would have also the effect of deterring the commission of crimes under international law. However, gross human rights violations resulting in the com-mission of these crimes remain a serious problem currently, especially in Africa. In the recent past, following the establishment of the ICC, several African coun-tries, including the Democratic Republic of the Congo, Central African Republic, Sudan, Ivory Coast, South Sudan, Nigeria, Mali, Libya and Egypt, have been affected by such violations in varying degrees.

Although most gross human rights violations in Africa have, in the past, been associated with civil wars, recent experience and trends show that terrorism and election-related violence are playing an increasing role. In addition, in some of the incidents where such violations occurred, particularly those related to election vio-lence, both national and regional actors, including the African Union, have focused more on political solutions, including, for example, urging the formation of so-called "governments of national unity".[24] In such cases, legal responses were not given priority, even where it was apparent that crimes under international law were or could have been committed. However, when similar gross human rights viola-tions occurred in Kenya, an agreement was reached that both political and legal responses would be pursued. This created the immediate impression that perhaps a positive step in the right direction was being made.

The background is that from 30 December 2007 to 28 February 2008 Kenya was plunged into a widespread violence following a highly contested and contro-versial presidential election.[25] In the course of this violence (hereafter "post-elec-tion violence"), atrocities such as murders, rapes, inflictions of grievous bodily injury, forceful evictions, malicious destruction of property, arson, pillaging, etc., were committed.[26]

A mediation process was carried out amidst the heightening violence (see infra Sect. 3.3). As a result, five important agreements were signed between the contest-ing political parties. The first agreement, which was signed on 28 February 2008,

---

[23] Valinas 2010, p. 269. Cf. Laplante 2010, p. 636.

[24] See generally Chigora and Guzura 2011; Mapuva 2013.

[25] BBC News, 31 December 2007.

[26] See Internews 2010 https://internews.org/sites/default/files/resources/2010-05_Kenya_ICC_5-Page_Briefing.pdf. Accessed September 2014.

concerned power sharing between the main contestants in the presidential election. This agreement de-escalated the violence immediately.[27] The second agreement pertained to the establishment of a commission of inquiry into the post-election violence which was mandated, inter alia, to identify and recommend "measures with regard to bringing to justice those persons responsible for crimes committed during the violence".[28] The third agreement pertained to the formation of a truth commission to look into, among other things, the human rights violations that occurred during and beyond the violence.[29] The fourth agreement pertained to "long-term issues and solutions", the most important issue being the creation of agencies for constitutional reforms and mechanisms for implementation of such reforms.[30] The fifth agreement related to the creation of an Independent Review Committee (IREC) to, among other things, do a review of the electoral legal framework and give recommendations for appropriate electoral reforms.[31]

The findings of the commission of inquiry formed pursuant to the second above-mentioned agreement suggested that gross atrocities constituting crimes against humanity had been committed. The commission gave, among others, two important recommendations on addressing criminal accountability in respect of those crimes. First, it identified the alleged main perpetrators and recommended that they be prosecuted by a local special tribunal that had to be created. Second, it recommended that should Kenya fail to prosecute the perpetrators domestically, then the intervention of the ICC would be invoked.

As the recommendation above had speculated, Kenya did not institute proceedings against the alleged main perpetrators within the set time frame. As a result, the commission of inquiry in conjunction with the mediators requested the ICC to intervene as it had been agreed.[32] Thus, on 6 November 2009, the ICC became officially seized with the matter,[33] and subsequently, indicted six Kenyans for crimes against humanity. The then ICC Prosecutor Luis Moreno-Ocampo noted that the ICC's intervention in Kenya was particularly important in order to "prevent the commission of [similar] crimes during the next elections."[34]

The Kenyan government was discontented with the intervention of the ICC and tried to halt the ensuing judicial process in at least four different ways. First, it made two unsuccessful attempts at requesting the United Nations Security Council

---

[27] See Kenya National Dialogue and Reconciliation 2008a.

[28] See Kenya National Dialogue and Reconciliation 2008b.

[29] See Kenya National Dialogue and Reconciliation 2008c.

[30] See Kenya National Dialogue and Reconciliation 2008d.

[31] See Kenya National Dialogue and Reconciliation 2008e.

[32] See ICC Press Release ICC-OTP-20090709-PR436, 9 July 2009.

[33] See Decision Assigning the Situation in Kenya to Pre-Trial Chamber II, ICC-01/09-1, 6 November 2009.

[34] ICC Press Release ICC-OTP-20090716-PR439, 16 July 2009.

to suspend the proceedings before the Court.[35] Second, it threatened to withdraw from the ICC Statute.[36] Third, it raised a legal challenge against the jurisdiction of the ICC over the alleged crimes, citing complementarity as a basis. This, too, failed. Fourth, it showed a keen interest in and actively pressed for the initiative to extend criminal jurisdiction to two regional courts in Africa, hoping that such a development would make the ICC "transfer" the cases back to Africa. This, too, did not work out.

Meanwhile, at the time of the post-election violence, Kenya had already ratified the ICC Statute, but was yet to domesticate it. Besides, the Kenyan government has not denied that crimes against humanity were or might have been committed on its territory during the violence. However, 6 years after the violence, Kenya has not instituted domestic proceedings against the alleged main perpetrators whose number is clearly more than the six suspects indicted by the ICC. Although the Kenyan Parliament blocked all attempts to create a local tribunal that would have prosecuted these perpetrators, it swiftly passed a law which established a truth commission with "non-retribution" as its main objective, and which contained some amnesty provisions.

Two main arguments have been advanced in the aftermath of the violence regarding Kenya's failure to institute domestic proceedings against the main perpetrators. The first argument is that the Kenyan government lacked (and still lacks) a political will to investigate and prosecute the perpetrators. The second argument is that even if it was to be assumed that Kenya had wanted to prosecute the prosecutors, it would not have succeeded, because it lacked a sufficient legal framework. One view that emerged domestically soon after the end of the violence was that the Kenyan substantive criminal law as it stood at the time of commission of the crimes was inadequate for the prosecution of core crimes under international law. According to this view, even though a law was enacted a year after the violence to domesticate the ICC Statute, it would not have been legally possible to use that law retrospectively to prosecute the perpetrators. It was further argued that even if, for argument's sake, one could assume that the existing Kenyan laws were sufficient, the Kenyan judicial institutions would still have been "unfit" to enforce such laws, the reason being that these institutions were not independent and credible enough to be entrusted with such a huge task. From these arguments, the predominant conclusion drawn was that the ICC or a tribunal which is completely independent of the Kenyan judicial system would be the best forum to address criminal accountability for the post-election violence.[37]

---

[35] See infra Sects. 6.6.1 and 6.7.4.

[36] See Daily Nation, 22 December 2010. A Motion to withdraw from the Statute was presented to the Parliament by Isaac Ruto (MP) on Thursday December 16, 2010. See Parliament of Kenya 2010, pp. 30 et seq.; For further discussion see infra Sect. 6.6.3.

[37] See Asaala 2010, pp. 377–406; Asaala 2012, pp. 119–143; Gathii 2010; Mohochi 2011; Musila 2009, pp. 445 et seq.; Nmaju 2009, pp. 78 et seq.; Okuta 2009, pp. 1063 et seq.; Sing'Oei 2010, pp. 5 et seq.

Even though there were consistent calls made on Kenya to institute domestic proceedings, several influential people who were named by official reports as being the masterminds or sponsors of the violence continued serving in the Kenyan Parliament and others in the government as ministers or senior civil servants. This includes almost all the individuals who were officially indicted by the ICC. Thus, these individuals continued to have both direct and indirect influence in respect of key government actions, decisions and policies, including those pertaining to the search for criminal accountability for the crimes that they themselves were accused to have masterminded. The climax of all this, which brought in a completely new dimension, was reached in March 2013, when two among those Kenyans indicted by the ICC were elected Kenya's President and Deputy President.

Moreover, since the ICC started exercising its jurisdiction over the Kenyan cases, several issues of interest, some of which entailing contentious legal issues, have emerged. The most contentious legal issue which deserves a mention at this stage emerged at the very inception of the ICC process, and for the first time in the jurisprudence of the ICC. It concerned the interpretation of the definitional elements of crimes against humanity under Article 7(2)(*a*) of the ICC Statute, namely the phrase "State or organizational policy". A serious disagreement arose over whether this definitional threshold was met with regard to the criminal acts that occurred in Kenya so as to justify the ICC's intervention. In the end, both the judges of the ICC's Pre-Trial Chamber and scholars were left fundamentally divided (see infra Sect. 6.4.2.3). The ensuing debate[38] is far from settled, and this book adds more thoughts to it.

Apart from the legal issues that have arisen out of the ICC's proceedings, much more happened outside the courtroom. Most importantly, the fact that the ICC continued to exercise jurisdiction in respect of the persons who are now the Kenyan President and Deputy President fuelled a pre-existing "hostility" of the African Union (AU) towards the ICC, thereby compounding the perception held by the AU that the ICC is "targeting" African leaders.

1.3 Objectives

In view of the foregoing background, there is a need to take stock of what transpired during the post-election violence in Kenya and how the question of criminal accountability for the alleged crimes against humanity has been dealt with so far, both at the national and international level. In addition, there is a need to clarify a number of issues, ranging from socio-political and historical issues related to the violence; controversies, allegations, perceptions and demands which have arisen so far in connection with the ICC's intervention in Kenya. More importantly, there is a need to clarify and analyse the main legal issues and options arising at both

---

[38] See, e.g., Halling 2010, pp. 827 et seq.; Hansen 2011, pp. 1 et seq.; Kress 2010, pp. 855 et seq.; Werle and Burghardt 2012, pp. 1 et seq.

the domestic and international level in relation to accountability for the post-election violence. The main aim of this book is to carry out this task. It will do so by seeking to answer the following specific questions:

- To what extent is Kenya's political and historical background linked to the 2007–2008 post-election violence, and how has this background affected or how is it likely to affect the efforts to ensure criminal accountability for the alleged crimes against humanity?
- Pursuant to the agreed road map for domestic criminal accountability for the crimes linked to the violence, and in view of the currently available domestic legal framework, to what extent has Kenya discharged and can still discharge its duty to prosecute those who bear greatest responsibility for the crimes?
- To what extent are the non-prosecutorial mechanisms adopted in response to the post-election violence consistent with Kenya's duty to punish the alleged crimes against humanity? And given their design, could these mechanisms ultimately affect the search for criminal accountability for those responsible for the crimes?
- To what extent was the ICC's intervention justified, and what are the main legal issues of jurisprudential significance that have so far emanated from the Kenyan cases before the ICC?

1.4 Chapters Outline

To achieve the objectives above, the book is organised into seven chapters.

Apart from Chapter 1, which introduces the book and gives its general overview, Chapter 2 presents a concise political, sociological and historical background of the Kenyan politics prior to 2007. This chapter is meant to give the reader the impression of how the post-election violence links to Kenya's recent history. It also prepares the ground for understanding that such historical background has had a spill-over effect with regard to how Kenya has so far acted at the national level with regard to criminal accountability for the alleged crimes against humanity.

Chapter 3 is devoted for the post-election violence, describing its immediate trigger, patterns, magnitude and associated crimes. It also discusses the mediation process, focusing mostly on the political settlement, the agreed road map towards criminal accountability, the failed attempt to implement the road map and the consequences of such failure. Lastly, the chapter presents the general perception of Kenyans about the appropriate place or forum to prosecute the perpetrators.

Chapter 4 discusses the legal options for ensuring criminal accountability at the domestic level. It analyses Kenya's substantive criminal law as it stood at the time of commission of the alleged crimes against humanity and subsequent to their commission, with a view to establishing whether this legal framework could be used as an effective tool to prosecute the alleged crimes against humanity, taking into consideration the principle of legality, which prohibits imposition of retrospective punishment. In addition, the chapter examines to what extent Kenya has actually prosecuted the crimes under the available domestic legal framework; and whether by doing so Kenya can be said to have fulfilled its duty to prosecute those who bear major responsibility for the crimes.

Chapter 5 explores the alternatives and adjuncts to domestic prosecutions, with particular emphasis on the Kenyan truth commission. It outlines the background of the commission, its creation, composition and mandates, but the main focus is on the relationship between the commission and criminal accountability for the post-election violence. The chapter studies the relationship between the commission and the domestic judicial institutions, specific focus being on how such a relationship could impair or foster domestic criminal accountability for the alleged crimes.

Chapter 6 concerns the prosecution of the alleged crimes against humanity at the ICC level. It analyses the Kenya situation before the ICC, and covers selected legal issues of procedural and substantive nature arising from the pre-trial phase of the proceedings. These include, but are not limited to, the trigger mechanism, complementarity, and more importantly, the Pre-Trial Chamber's interpretation of the definitional elements of crimes against humanity under the ICC Statute. Other issues covered include the impact of the ICC's intervention on Kenya's 2013 general elections; the implications of the outcome of the 2013 presidential election on the ICC legal process; and the African Union's position with regard to the ICC's prosecution of Kenya's serving head of state and his deputy.

Lastly, Chapter 7 concludes with a summary of the book.

References

Ambos K (2010) The crime of aggression after Kampala. Ger Yearb Int Law 53:463–509
Asaala EO (2010) Exploring transitional justice as a vehicle for social and political transformation in Kenya. Afr Hum Rights Law J 10(2):377–406
Asaala EO (2012) The International Criminal Court factor on transitional justice in Kenya. In: Ambos K, Maunganidze OA (eds) Power and prosecution: challenges and opportunities for international criminal justice in Sub-Saharan Africa. Universitätsverlag, Göttingen
Bassiouni MC (1986) Characteristics of international criminal law conventions. In: Bassiouni MC (ed) International criminal law: crimes. Transnational Publishers Inc, New York
Bassiouni MC (1996) International crimes: *Jus cogens and obligatio erga omnes*. Law Contemp Probl 59(4):63–74
Bassiouni MC (2001) Universal jurisdiction for international crimes: historical perspectives and contemporary practice. Va J Int Law Assoc 42:81–134
Bassiouni MC, Wise E (1995) *Aut dedere aut judicare*: the duty to extradite or prosecute in international law. Martinus Nijhoff Publishers, London
Cassese A (2008) International law, 2nd edn. Oxford University Press, New York
Chigora P, Guzura T (2011) The politics of the Government of National Unity (GNU) and power sharing in Zimbabwe: challenges and prospects for democracy. Afr J Hist Cult 3(2):20–26
Clark RS (2009) Negotiating provisions defining the crime of aggression, its elements and the conditions for ICC exercise of jurisdiction over it. Eur J Int Law 20(4):1103–1115
Damgaard C (2008) Individual criminal responsibility for core international crimes. Springer, Heidelberg

Gathii JT (2010) Jurisdiction to prosecute non-national pirates captured by third states under Kenyan and international law. Loyola of Los Angeles International and Comparative Law Review. http://ssrn.com/abstract=1360981. Accessed August 2014

Halling M (2010) Push the envelope—watch it bend: removing the policy requirement and extending crimes against humanity. Leiden J Int Law 23:827–845

Hansen TO (2011) The policy element in crimes against humanity: lessons from and for the case of Kenya. George Wash Int Law Rev 43:1–41

Human Rights Watch (2009) Selling justice short: why accountability matters for peace. Human Rights Watch, New York

International Committee of the Red Cross (2005) Customary international humanitarian law, vol 1. Cambridge University Press, New York

Internews (2010) The International Criminal Court and post-election violence in Kenya. https://internews.org/sites/default/files/resources/2010-05_Kenya_ICC_5-Page_Briefing.pdf. Accessed Sept 2014

Jeßberger F (2007) Universality, complementarity and the duty to prosecute crimes under international law in Germany. In: Kaleck W et al (eds) International prosecution of human rights crimes. Springer, Berlin

Jonyo F (2003) The centrality of ethnicity in Kenya's political transition. In: Oyugi et al (eds) The politics of transition in Kenya. Heinrich Böll Foundation, Nairobi

Kemp G (2014) The implementation of the Rome Statute in Africa. In: Werle G et al (eds) Africa and the International Criminal Court. T.M.C. Asser Press, The Hague

Kenya National Bureau of Statistics (2010) The 2009 Kenya population and housing sensus, vol 1. file:///C:/Users/Materu/Desktop/Volume%201A-Population%20Distribution%20by%20Administrative%20Units.pdf. Accessed Sept 2014

Kenya National Dialogue and Reconciliation (2008a) Agreement on the principles of partnership of the coalition government. http://www.dialoguekenya.org/Agreements/14%20February%202008-Agreement%20on%20the%20Principles%20of%20Partnership%20of%20the%20Coalition%20Government.pdf. Accessed Aug 2014

Kenya National Dialogue and Reconciliation (2008b) Agreement on commission of enquiry on post-election violence. http://www.dialoguekenya.org/Agreements/4%20March%202008-Truth,%20Justice%20and%20Reconciliation%20Commission.pdf. Accessed Aug 2014

Kenya National Dialogue and Reconciliation (2008c) Agreement on the truth, justice and reconciliation commission. http://www.dialoguekenya.org/Agreements/4%20March%202008-Truth,%20Justice%20and%20Reconciliation%20Commission.pdf. Accessed Aug 2014

Kenya National Dialogue and Reconciliation (2008d) Agreement on the longer-term issues and solutions: constitutional review. http://www.dialoguekenya.org/Agreements/4%20March%202008-Long-Term%20Issues%20and%20Solutions_Constitutional%20Review.pdf. Accessed Aug 2014

Kenya National Dialogue and Reconciliation (2008e) Agreement on the independent review commission terms of reference. http://www.dialoguekenya.org/Agreements/Independent%20Review%20Committee.pdf. Accessed Aug 2014

Kissinger HA (2001) The pitfalls of universal jurisdiction. Foreign Aff 80(4):86–96

Kress C (2010) On the outer limits of crimes against humanity: the concept of organization within the policy requirement: some reflections on the March 2010 ICC Kenya Decision. Leiden J Int Law 23:855–873

Laplante LJ (2010) The domestication of international criminal law: a proposal for expanding the International Criminal Court's sphere of influence. John Marshall Law Rev 43:635–680

Library of Congress (2007) Country profile: Kenya. http://lcweb2.loc.gov/frd/cs/profiles/Kenya.pdf. Accessed Aug 2014

Macedo S (ed) (2004) Universal jurisdiction: national courts and the prosecution of serious crimes under international law. University of Pennsylvania Press, Pennsylvania

Manson RL (2010) Identifying the rough edges of the Kampala conference. Crim Law Forum 21(3–4):417–443

Mapuva J (2013) Governments of national unity (GNUs) and the preponderance of the incumbency: case of Kenya and Zimbabwe. Int J Polit Sci Dev 1(3):105–116

May L (2005) Crimes against humanity: a normative account. Cambridge University Press, Cambridge

Mohochi SM (2011) Prosecuting perpetrators of injustice is the best method of dealing with the past atrocities—the case of Kenya http://papers.ssrn.com/sol3/papers.cfm?abstract_id=1847470. Accessed Aug 2014

Musila G (2009) Options for transitional justice in Kenya: autonomy and the challenge of external prescriptions. Int J Trans Justice 3:445–464

Naqvi YQ (2009) Impediments to exercising jurisdiction over international crimes. T.M.C. Asser Press, The Hague

Nmaju MC (2009) Violence in Kenya: any role for the ICC in the quest for accountability? Afr J Legal Stud 3:78–95

Obura K (2011) Duty to prosecute international crimes under international law. In: Murungu C, Biegon J (eds) Prosecuting international crimes in Africa. Pretoria University Law Press, Pretoria

Okuta A (2009) National legislation for prosecution of international crimes in Kenya. J Int Crim Justice 7:1063–1076

Parliament of Kenya (2010) Official Hansard reports. Doc. Hansard 16.12.110A. Nairobi

Schabas WA (2007) An introduction to the International Criminal Court, 3rd edn. Cambridge University Press, New York

Scharf MP (1996) Swapping amnesty for peace: was there duty to prosecute international crimes in Haiti? Tex Int Law J 31(1):1–41

Sing'Oei AK (2010) The ICC arbiter in Kenya's post-election violence. Minn J Int Law Online 19:5–20

Tomuschat C (2002) The duty to prosecute international crimes committed by individuals. In: Cremer HJ et al (eds) Tradition und Weltoffenheit des Rechts. Springer, Berlin

Triffterer O (2008) Preliminary remarks: the permanent International Criminal Court—ideal and reality. In: Triffterer O (ed) Commentary on the Rome Statute of the International Criminal Court: observers' notes article by article, 2nd edn. Nomos Verlagsgesellschaft, Baden-Baden

Valinas M (2010) Interpreting complementarity and interests of justice in the presence of restorative-based alternative forms of justice. In: Stahn C, Van den Herik L (eds) The future perspectives of international criminal justice. T.M.C. Asser Press, The Hague

Werle G (2009) Principles of international criminal law, 2nd edn. T.M.C. Asser Press, The Hague

Werle G, Bornkamm PC (2013) Torture in Zimbabwe under scrutiny in South Africa: the judgment of the North Gauteng High Court in SALC v. National director of public prosecutions. J Int Crim Justice 11(3):659–675

Werle G, Burghardt B (2012) Do crimes against humanity require the participation of a state or a "State-Like" organization? J Int Crim Justice 9:1–20

Wouters J (2005) The obligation to prosecute international law crimes. The need for justice and requirements for peace and security, Collegium, 32nd edn. College of Europe, Bruges

Zimmermann A (2008) Article 5: crimes within the jurisdiction of the court. In: Triffterer O (ed) Commentary on the Rome Statute of the International Criminal Court: observers' notes article by article, 2nd edn. Nomos Verlagsgesellschaft, Baden

Part I
Historical Roots of Ethnic Violence in Kenya

Chapter 2
Background to the Post-Election Violence

Abstract Literature indicates that the violence accompanying the 2007 general elections in Kenya was a spill-over effect of the country's previous history, hence the need to scrutinize the historical antecedents to these elections. This chapter identifies and analyses five factors, namely negative ethnicity, dictatorship, political alliances, criminal gangs and impunity, which, prior to the 2007 elections, had characterized the Kenyan politics. The chapter reveals that in view of the five factors, feelings had developed in Kenya, already before the 2007 elections, that certain ethnic communities had been deliberately marginalized since independence, while others had been highly privileged or favoured in different ways. This gave rise, inter alia, to a number of historical fears and grievances, mostly in relation to land. It is shown that this state of affairs became a recipe for election violence accompanying all the multi-party elections prior to 2007, and since the grievances were not addressed, and in view of the previous trend of election violence, it indeed became certain that even the 2007 general elections would not be free from violence.

Contents

© T.M.C. ASSER PRESS and the author 2015   15
S.F. Materu, *The Post-Election Violence in Kenya*,
International Criminal Justice Series 2, DOI 10.1007/978-94-6265-041-1_2

2.1 Introductory Remarks

Sometimes due to historical connectedness of events, the present may not be fully comprehended unless the past is brought into perspective. By the same token, it may also be impossible to divorce completely the future from both the present and the past. And usually, the link between the past, the present and the future becomes even more relevant when one wishes to analyse a current event which in reality is a culmination of preceding historical state of affairs. Locating such a link becomes particularly crucial if the intention is, inter alia, to address the aftermath of such an event and project what the future may hold. Any study, whether legal or otherwise, relating to the post-election violence in Kenya will, by and large, befit this context.

A narrow view would associate the violence with the problem of power transfer which faces most African countries after an election process. Usually, this problem occurs when, after the poll count, it transpires that a ruling party or an incumbent president seeking re-election has lost the election and must hand power over to the opposition. The narrow view would explain why, for instance, the general perception in the run-up to the 1992 and 1997 multi-party elections in Kenya was that a smooth transition from the then ruling party, KANU (in case it lost) to an opposition party (in case any won) was a myth and almost infeasible. This perception existed only because in these two elections, the incumbent President Daniel Arap Moi was seeking re-election.[1] But as this chapter will reveal, this view, although not entirely dismissible, is too narrow to wholly depict the real situation in Kenya. Indeed the problem goes beyond mere electoral politics.

A broad view would indicate that it is inappropriate to describe the post-election violence in Kenya merely as sporadic events attributable only to the 2007 electoral process. On the contrary, this view would describe the violence as a climax of cumulative historical factors or, as it has been described, as "a volcano that had long been waiting to erupt".[2] The reference to a "volcano" in this regard describes long-standing grievances and several unresolved issues pertaining to social, political and economic relations among Kenyans that had hitherto not been adequately addressed.[3]

The preceding remarks should, however, not be taken as suggesting that this study is the work of a historian. The inclusion of this historical account is only intended to bring into perspective the causal and factual links between Kenya's previous historical, socio-political background and the 2007–2008 post-election

---

[1] See Troup and Hornsby 1998, p. 2.

[2] Biegon 2008, p. 34.

[3] Cf. Kenya Truth Justice and Reconciliation Commission Report 2013, Vol. IV, para 263.

violence. Such a picture is considered crucial here, because it will prepare a ground for a better understanding of the political paradigms or undertones surrounding the proposed domestic criminal accountability measures to punish the perpetrators of the crimes related to the violence.

To that effect, five factors unfold as generally being the most prominent features that have singly or jointly characterized Kenya's politics at a time since independence. These are entrenched negative ethnicity,[4] ethno-political alliances, dictatorship, hired violence (criminal gangs) and entrenched "culture" of impunity. This chapter gives a brief but reasonably fair account of these aspects of the Kenyan history.

2.2 Historical Role of Negative Ethnicity in Kenyan Politics

2.2.1 Transition from Colonialism to Independence

The earliest indicators that negative ethnicity would adversely affect the post-colonial Kenya were evident during the last days of the struggle for independence from the British. The problem of negative ethnicity is an impress of the colonial legacy, having been reinforced by the British ruling system. The British introduced a divide-and-rule system in Kenya as they also did in their other African colonies. This was a system that entailed a purposeful stratification of the colony's population in a number of ways, including along ethnic lines, mostly for ease of ruling and exploitation.[5]

By 1950 Kenya was already divided by economic differentiation between the minority white population and the majority local population. This differentiation was evident in, among other aspects, the allocation of massive land to the white settler farmers, which land was alienated from the indigenous population.[6] The Kikuyus were the most affected ethnic community. The land

---

[4] Negative ethnicity refers to the use of tribes or tribal affiliations to further the interests of one ethnic group against those of other similar groups or at the expense of national unity, peace and security. It is contrasted from "positive ethnicity" whereby ethnicity is used to mirror group's identity in terms of its customs, traditions and culture. Thus, whereas positive ethnicity, in the African context, is good for the nations that are ethnically diverse, negative ethnicity could become disastrous. For greater detail see *generally* Wamwere 2003a, b.

[5] Cf. Kenya Truth, Justice and Reconciliation Commission Report 2013, Vol. IV, paras 259–263. The divide-and-rule system created both a physical and social distance among the colonial subjects. It was implemented through, inter alia, dividing the colonial territory into smaller geographical-cum-administrative regions, in order to decentralize and consolidate ruling at the grass root level. It was used as a formal separation of the colonial population according to their ethno-regional origins to facilitate exploitation of each. It also entailed an indirect rule system in which the tribal leaders (chiefs) received favours and privileges from the colonial government, and consequently, were used as instruments/puppets of that government. For more details see Christopher 1988, pp. 233 et seq.

[6] Troup and Hornsby 1998, p. 7.

issue was one of the underlying reasons which triggered a long war of liberation, the *Mau Mau* movement, between 1952 and 1960.[7] The earliest impact of
the divide-and-rule policy manifested itself during this war. The majority of the
members of the other big ethnic groups, mostly the Luo, the Luhya, the
Kalenjin and the Coastal people, remained as bystanders, having refused to
rally behind the Kikuyu leadership.[8] Thus, *Mau Mau* was in some way considered as a Kikuyu affair, and was brutally suppressed by the colonial state in the
late 1950s.

Apart from this armed struggle, ethnic interests continued to shape most
events, even those which concerned or seemed to affect the collective interests
of the Kenyan people as a whole. For instance, in the early days of negotiations
for independence, specifically in the famous 1962/1963 Lancaster Conferences
in London,[9] ethnicity took precedence, and strongly shaped the demands of the
Kenyan participants. The fear that "big tribes" would dominate the "small
tribes" after independence was taken seriously by some of the participating
members of the Kenyan delegation. There was an informal division among the
Kenyan delegation which, to a great extent, was informed by tribal affiliation of
the delegates. Two parties, namely, the Kenya African National Union (KANU)
and the Kenya African Democratic Union (KADU) participated in the conference, apparently representing ethnic demands of their respective members.[10] As
the following section will show, the difference between these parties also
entailed an ideological dimension which, in a way, had a link to the tribalistic
dimension. This pertained to the structure of the constitution which should be
adopted at independence. The said ideological dimension remained one of the
key issues dominating Kenyan politics throughout, including during the 2007
elections and beyond.

---

[7] The *Mau Mau* was not only a rebellion against the British colonial government, but also as
a civil war among the Kikuyus. They set against their own chiefs, the ambitious commercial
farmers and local Christians who were supportive of the colonial system. See Troup and Hornsby
1998, p. 7.

[8] Ibid., pp. 7–8.

[9] Three Lancaster conferences held between 1962 and 1963 were part of the Great Britain's
programme for empire dissolution by relinquishing its political domination over overseas territories. In respect of Kenya, the conference brought together the existing Kenyan political parties
to agree on the form of government and the structure of the constitution to be adopted after full
political independence. See Manner 1962, p. 8; Ogot 1995, pp. 73–76.

[10] KANU was predominantly of Kikuyu and Luo membership, the largest and second largest
ethnic groups, respectively. On the other hand, KADU's membership comprised the smaller
tribes of the Abaluya, the Kalenjin, the Maasai and Coast people. See Manner 1962, p. 9. The
remaining small tribes, if taken singly, were not a "threat", because their population was insig-
nificant. Since independence, these tribes have always showed allegiance to the political affiliations of whichever big tribes they think would best protect and advance their interests. See Lamb
1969, p. 538.

2.2.2 The Regionalism and Centralism Ideologies

In the early 1960s, after the British had shown interest in decolonization, party politics in Kenya took a new dimension, as they became dominated by two different themes. In 1961, the main issue was the release of Jomo Kenyatta, a Kikuyu hero and first President of independent Kenya.[11] This was followed, between 1962 and 1963, by the argument or theme already alluded to above—the structure of the government to be adopted at independence. It is within the context of the second theme that the 1963 first general elections were dominated by two quasi-ideological arguments, namely *centralism* versus *regionalism*.

From the onset, the two political parties, KANU and KADU, wanted a constitutional structure which, as a matter of priority, would benefit the tribal interests of their members. This placed the expected independent Kenya in a latent problem of tribalism and nepotism. KANU strongly wanted an independence constitution based on centralism (unitary state), while KADU strived for regionalism or federalism. KANU's centralism envisioned a constitutional structure with three main features: an administration of the country done by a central government in Nairobi; a state-driven economy; and a free competition for resources.[12] Apparently, this had a strategic reason: to ensure that its members, predominantly Kikuyu and Luo, would perform relatively better in this set-up. KADU, which claimed to protect the interests of the minority ethnic communities, was in the phobia of "domination" by the two big tribes in the structure proposed by KANU. For this reason it campaigned for *majimbo*[13] (Swahili word for regional governments) in which different federal "states", apparently based on ethno-regional demarcations, would have the autonomy to decide their own affairs, more importantly the question of ownership of land and other resources found in their *majimbo*.[14]

---

[11] Jomo Kenyatta was the first president of independent Kenya. In 1952, following a declaration of a state of emergency by the British colonialists, he and other Kenyan nationalists were arrested and charged with "managing and being members" of an illegal movement, the *Mau Mau*. He was sentenced to 7 years imprisonment and remained under restriction, even after serving his sentence, until 1961. See "African History: Jomo Kenyatta" http://africanhistory.about.com/od/biography/a/bio-Kenyatta01.htm. Accessed August 2014.

[12] Troup and Hornsby 1998, p. 9.

[13] Originally, this is traceable to the formation of the Federal Independence Party (F.I.P), a political party formed by white farmers in Kenya in 1954. The F.I.P had foreseen that political independence in Kenya was inevitable, and that it would place control into the hands of an African central government. They wanted to seal off the "white highlands" from the reach of a Black central government, so as to ensure that the great wealth of these areas remained in the hands of those who had been responsible for developing it. They would then establish a local self-government (white state) in the area, and so would the Africans in other states to be demarcated. Therefore, the original ambition of the F.I.P. was that Kenya would become a federation of several states. See Sanger and Nottingham 1963, p. 10.

[14] Troup and Hornsby 1998, p. 9. For more details on the *majimbo* ideology see Anderson 2005, pp. 547 et seq.

It was in this context that during the independence negotiations at the Lancaster Conference, KADU's delegation carried the slogan "regionalism or death". In a meeting before departing for London, the party leaders had assured their members that they were prepared to negotiate for *majimbo* constitution at any cost, even if it meant bloodshed.[15] The party secretary even told KADU members that the "Abaluhya, Kalenjin, Maasai and Coast people" would declare their independence if regionalism were not adopted at the Lancaster Conference.[16] Eventually, the framework constitution agreed upon in London, and which was operational at independence, was based on *majimbo* system.[17] This was the case despite the fact that there was a misconception about the framework actually adopted, each party claiming to have triumphed in having its ideology adopted.[18]

The Lancaster arrangement led to the first general elections in 1963. In these elections, more divisions were witnessed, whereby tribalism and the phobia of "big tribe domination" manifested themselves clearly. The so-called "small tribes" did not trust KANU's candidate, who was also Kenya's independence hero, Jomo Kenyatta. They accused him of having sided with a group of Kikuyu elites which was allegedly planning on how their tribe should receive awards commensurate with their suffering in the *Mau Mau* war of liberation. Leaders of the "KADU tribes", specifically the Maasai, Abaluya and the Kalenjin, feared that without regionalism their land would be grabbed by the "KANU tribes", for Kenyatta was nothing but allegedly a "Kikuyu tribalist".[19] As a result, the election campaigns assumed a tribal trend at all levels. In the areas inhabited by the "small tribes" the decision on who to vote for was not necessarily based on candidates' leadership qualities, but rather on their ethnic affiliations.[20]

Eventually, KANU won the majority seats in the elections, the fact which enabled it to form an autonomous internal government. Jomo Kenyatta became Kenya's first Prime Minister.[21] For a short period of time, Kenya became a

---

[15] Manners 1962, p. 9; Sanger and Nottingham 1963, p. 12.

[16] Manners 1962, p. 9.

[17] See Ndengwa and Letourneau 2004, p. 85.

[18] While KADU came out of the negotiation confidently claiming that the *majimbo* structure had been adopted, KANU refuted this claim as a misconception. Instead KANU was confident that the draft which had just been adopted kept intact the centralism structure that was being used by the departing colonialists. See Sanger and Nottingham 1962, pp. 8–9.

[19] Ibid., p. 11.

[20] Ibid., pp. 16–17, indicating, for example, that in Kericho East constituency, the KADU's political advisor said that he would resign his seat in protest should a non-Kipsigis candidate be elected as he had too strong feelings against "foreigners". In the Coast the campaign slogans for KADU, on which it won, were "*Wabara kwao*" (literally meaning upcountry people to their own home) and later "*Kila mtu kwao*" (meaning each man to his own home).

[21] Results for the House of Representatives were: KANU (83 seats), KADU (33 seats) and African People's Party, APP (8 seats). For the Senate, the results were: KANU (18 seats), KADU (16 seats), APP (2 seats), Independents (1 seat), and the Nyanza Province African Union, NPUA (1 seat). See Electoral Institute for the Sustainability of Democracy in Africa (EISDA) at http://www.eisa.org.za/WEP/ken1963results.htm and http://www.eisa.org.za/WEP/ken1963results2.htm. Accessed August 2014. See also Sanger and Nottingham 1963, p. 36.

Dominion State pending official declaration of independence. In this transitional arrangement, the British monarch remained the Head of State[22] and the Prime Minister became the Head of Government. Independence was officially declared on 12 December 1963, and on 1 June 1964, Kenya became a Republic, Jomo Kenyatta being its first Executive President. Having won the elections, KANU was determined to use its overwhelming majority in Parliament to diffuse the *majimbo* system, as it claimed that such a system was "unnecessary and expensive, and that it constrained its (KANU's) rightful power emanating from its electoral supremacy".[23]

2.3 The Rise of Monopartysm and Consolidation of Dictatorship

2.3.1 From De Jure *Multipartysm to* De Facto *Monopartysm*

As pointed out earlier, Kenya was a *de jure* multi-party state at independence, KADU being the official opposition party after the 1963 elections. However, after KANU's victory in these elections, concentration shifted temporarily from the ideological differentiation of the two parties to the building of a new consensus, i.e. politics of *nation-building*. In this new focus, national stability and identity were heralded as the most important national priorities of the infant state.[24] KANU was successful in ensuring that a completely new argument emerged. The argument was that the new priorities of the infant nation could not be realized if the "confrontational electoral politics" envisaged by the Westminster-style democracy inherited from the departing colonialists was emphasized.[25] Apparently, the new "consensus", the paramountcy of nationhood over party ideologies, was put to experiment when the first cabinet was formed. KANU's "determination" to the consensus seemed to have been confirmed when Kenyatta created a "tribal ruling coalition" within the KANU government by bringing in members of the small or "KADU tribes".[26] This, to some extent, eased the tension, overcame the fears of big tribe domination and, more importantly for KANU, appeared to render KADU's "protective" ideology of regionalism completely redundant.[27]

---

[22] Constitution of Kenya of 1963, Article 72.

[23] See Ndengwa and Letourneau 2004, p. 85.

[24] Troup and Hornsby 1998, p. 12.

[25] Ibid.

[26] In order to balance the tribes and factions within KANU, Kenyatta co-opted his long-time Luo rivals, Jaramogi Oginga Odinga and Tom Mboya. These were given portfolios of equal standing. All the regions were found a minister and all big and small tribes had their member in the government. See Sanger and Nottingham 1963, pp. 37–38.

[27] Troup and Hornsby 1998, p. 12.

The tribal-regional balance achieved in the Kenyatta's first cabinet, together with the new perception, namely that competitive party politics was detrimental to the development of the infant state, had a serious impact on the continued existence of KADU. First, KADU's strong supporters of *majimbo* vanished from the scene, as the ideology seemed to lose its strength drastically. This paved the way for Kenyatta's new ideology, *harambee* (working together).[28] Secondly, KADU was significantly weakened by defections, as most of its members started to cross the floor in the National Assembly to join KANU having been lured by promises of more funds from the government for the development of their communities.[29] Apparently, this was a tactic by KANU to have KADU dissolved.[30] Shortly thereafter KADU actually dissolved itself voluntarily in December 1964, thereby rendering Kenya a de facto single-party state.[31] KADU's key leaders, including Daniel Arap Moi (a Kalenjin), joined KANU, and were soon appointed to key ministerial positions in the KANU government.[32]

2.3.2 Emergence of Factions Within KANU (1964–1966)

The amalgamation of KADU into KANU did not save the purpose for which it was intended. Instead, it brought the old ideological differences into KANU, and even created more others from within it. The reason being that before the fusion of the two parties, already there were two groups of radicals and moderates within both KADU and KANU.[33] For instance, while on the one hand the radicals advocated for, among other things, a total shift from pure capitalist economic policies inherited from the departing colonialists to socialist policies similar to those that were later adopted in neighbouring Tanzania, the moderates, on the other hand, preferred to continue with the *status quo*. Thus, upon the fusion of the two parties, a number of other radicals and moderates such as Daniel Moi moved from KADU to KANU to add to the numbers. This consolidated the existing factional groups. As a result, KANU experienced an internal threat of stability. A deliberate campaign was launched to eliminate all the followers of the radical faction. It was achieved through rigged party elections, allegedly engineered by President Kenyatta and his moderate allies.[34] This was then followed by the demotion of Jaramogi Oginga Odinga, a radical, from vice presidency at the party conference in Limuru. His seat was taken by Daniel Arap Moi, a moderate, who, later in

---

[28] Anderson 2005, p. 547.

[29] Odhiambo-Mbai 2003, p. 61.

[30] Ibid., p. 60.

[31] Troup and Hornsby 1998, p. 12.

[32] Odhiambo-Mbai 2003, p. 61.

[33] Troup and Hornsby 1998, p. 12.

[34] Ibid., p. 13.

January 1967, was named Vice President. This happened after the eliminated radicals—a group of 29 KANU MPs led by Jaramogi Oginga Odinga—did party hopping; they crossed the floor and found a new party, the Kenya People's Union (KPU), in 1966.[35] Thus, from 1966 Kenya resumed its *de jure* multiparty status.

2.3.3 Suppression of Opposition Parties (1966–1982)

KANU's strategy had always been to remain the sole political party in the Kenya's politics, even where Kenya was *de jure* a multiparty state. The formation of the KPU was viewed as a hindrance to the realization of this ambition. As a result, between 1966 and 1969 there was a serious suppression of political opposition. Firstly, immediately after the KPU's formation, KANU engineered an *ex post facto* constitutional amendment which forced all KANU MPs who had "crossed the floor" to re-contest their seats. Only six of them were re-elected. Secondly, the KPU's political activities were suppressed, including registration of new branches, which was refused or deliberately delayed. Thirdly, constitutional amendments and other draconian laws targeting the opposition were enacted. Such laws banned independent candidates and empowered the President to order preventive detentions.[36] The climax of this suppression was reached in 1969 when the KPU was banned and its leaders, including Jaramogi Oginga Odinga, were arrested and detained without trial.[37] Kenya became once again a de facto single party state.

2.3.4 From Kenyatta to Moi: Tyrannical Rule Consolidates

The banning of the opposition parties was never lifted throughout the remaining tenure of Kenyatta, who remained president until 1978 when he died. The then Vice President Daniel Arap Moi, a Kalenjin, took over the presidency, despite the disapproval of the Kikuyus in KANU.[38] Having assumed power, Moi promised to follow the *nyayo* (footsteps) of the "old man" (Kenyatta).[39] The *nyayo* politics, for sure, saw to it that the dictatorial state originally crafted by the "old man" was perfected. Moi's regime became relatively more tyrannical and self-centred

---

[35] Odhiambo-Mbai 2003, p. 62.

[36] Mueller 1984, pp. 407–418.

[37] Ibid., 417.

[38] When Kenyatta died, the Kikuyu, through the then powerful association, the Gikuyu, Embu and Meru Association (GEMA), strived to retain the political power within their tribes. These efforts became futile as the transition went smoothly in favour of Moi. For more details see Asingo 2003, pp. 20–24; Kimundi 2011, p. 81; Steeves 2006, pp. 211–212; Tamarkin 1979, pp. 21–33.

[39] Biegon 2008, p. 37.

compared to Kenyatta's.[40] For example, notwithstanding the ban against opposition parties, it is said that the Kenyatta regime had a higher level of tolerance for freedom of expression, dissent, criticism and independence of the judiciary than the Moi regime.[41] When Moi took over, ethnic tensions and mistrust grew stronger as attention was perceived to have shifted from the Kikuyus, who had relatively benefited under Kenyatta's rule, to the people of Rift Valley (Moi's home Province).[42] In the early 1980s, Moi is said to have made deliberate efforts to minimize the control of the Kikuyu elite in both public parastatal boards and civil service by replacing some of them with his loyal appointees.[43] The Moi regime continued to show all signs of authoritarian tendencies and concentration of powers in the presidency.

Two landmark events dominated the political scenes in 1982. First, through a motion moved by the then Vice President Mwai Kibaki,[44] the existing Constitution was amended by inserting the infamous section 2A that officially converted Kenya to a single party state.[45] It should be recalled that since 1969, when the opposition party, Kenya Progressive Union (KPU) was banned, Kenya had only remained a de facto single party state. The leaders of the banned KPU had, therefore, been rendered politically impotent, because they were denied any chance to contest any seats, even those who joined KANU. Once again, led by Jaramogi Oginga Odinga, they tried to form and register a new political party, the Kenyan Socialist Alliance, in order to challenge KANU's monopoly of political power. However, registration was refused, and immediately, the aforementioned constitutional amendment was promulgated to make Kenya a *de jure* mono-party state from 1982.[46]

The second event that dominated the political scene was an attempted *coup d'état* in August 1982, which was allegedly staged by low-rank members of the Air Force. It is not very clear which politicians were behind this attempt, although it is alleged that some of the senior Kikuyu members in KANU, the army and the police force were responsible.[47] Subsequent to this event, Moi strived more to

---

[40] See, generally Adar 2000, pp. 74–96.

[41] Troup and Hornsby 1998, pp. 26–27.

[42] Biegon 2008, p. 37; Troup 1993, p. 371.

[43] Troup and Hornsby 1998, pp. 30–31. This was done in order to deconstruct the Kenyatta hegemony. Two strategies are said to have been used to achieve this. The first strategy was the disengagement of influential politicians from the activities of civil society. The second strategy was the creation of strong patron-client networks within the civil society. In this way, the state was able to silence the opposition groups that were contained in the civil society. See Kanyinga 2003, p. 104.

[44] NB. During the 2007 elections, Mwai Kibaki was PNU presidential candidate who was vying for his second and last term. Apart from Vice Presidency, he also held various ministerial posts under KANU in both Kenyatta and Moi governments. He left KANU and joined opposition when multipartysm was re-introduced in 1991.

[45] See Otieno 2010.

[46] Kanyinga 2003, p. 102.

[47] Troup and Hornsby 1998, p. 31. For more details about the *coup* see Pal Ahluwalia 1996, pp. 129–148.

centralize power and perfect the repressive state. The operation of an "imperial presidency" became more evident than ever before. The separation between the three arms of state became blurred, as the Judiciary and Parliament are said to have been reduced to mere "appendages" of the all-powerful Executive.[48] The party (KANU) became the central focus of authority, while the Parliament assumed a subordinate status. Some voices of discontentment were still raised despite serious state intimidation. The clergy, for example, echoed their dissent from the pulpit, having seen that democracy was being trampled underfoot.[49]

Those who opposed Moi had a huge price to pay. The state agents implemented preventive detentions without trial, forcible exiles, political assassinations and extra-judicial killings.[50] Raila Odinga[51] was Kenya's longest serving political prisoner in this regard.[52] After the attempted *coup,* he was put under house arrest for 7 months, detained without trial for 6 years, and later, in 1988, tried for supporting an underground movement, the Kenyan Revolutionary Movement, which was demanding a reintroduction of multiparty system in Kenya.[53] The following paragraph, retrieved from a post-Moi government official report, summarizes how tyrannical the Moi State turned:

> The Moi government pursued an open policy of using naked state violence to suppress and vanquish the political opposition and pro-democracy campaigners, among them civil society, opposition political parties, journalists, students, the clergy, and any and every real or imagined political dissident. Opposition political rallies and meetings of government critics were frequently broken up, and violently so. Police and security forces have killed scores of reformers throughout the last two decades.[54]

In the 1990s, the Moi-KANU government, under the pretext of land clashes, allegedly instigated and, in some cases, directed an ignition and execution of inter-ethnic violence against the communities and zones which supported opposition against Moi.[55] In the Rift Valley and Coastal provinces, for instance, people from other provinces (tribes) were termed as "foreigners" or "land grabbers" and subsequently forced out of their land or, in some instances, killed instantly. This has even been equated to "attempted genocide by way of ethnic cleansing".[56]

---

[48] Kimundi 2011, p. 80; Mutua 2001, p. 98.

[49] Troup and Hornsby 1998, p. 37. Also see Kanyinga 2003, p 104.

[50] Kimundi 2011, p. 82. Also see Ajulu 2000, pp. 137 et seq; Londale, 2004, pp. 91 et seq; Muigai 1995, pp. 171 et seq.

[51] NB. Raila Odinga was the presidential candidate for the Orange Democratic Movement (ODM) in the 2007 elections. He is a son of Jaramogi Oginga Odinga, KADU's leader and the former KANU's Vice President, who, in a similar way, experienced the mighty hand of the tyrannical state under Kenyatta.

[52] Musila 2009, p. 447. Cf. Miguna 2012, p. 108.

[53] Kimundi 2011, p. 83; Musila 2009, p. 447. For more details see Odinga 2013.

[54] Republic of Kenya 2003, p. 31.

[55] Mutua 2001, p. 98.

[56] Kimundi 2011, p. 82; Musila 2009, p. 447; Republic of Kenya 2003, p. 31.

2.4   Resumption of Political Pluralism and Proliferation of Political Alliances

2.4.1   Resumption of Multipartysm

In December 1991, with Moi still in power, Kenya resumed its roots as a *de jure* multiparty state, thereby responding to the mounting pressure from within the country as well as from the international community, especially the donors.[57] The Constitutional provision establishing the mono-party state was repealed, and a constitutional restriction of the presidential seat to a maximum of two five-year terms was introduced.[58] Interestingly, despite its past suppression, the call for the *majimbo* (federalism) ideology resurfaced alongside the domestic pressure for resumption of multipartysm.[59]

The first two multiparty elections were conducted in 1992 and 1997, and in both elections KANU emerged victorious. The presidential term limit introduced with the resumption of multipartysm in 1991 was prospective in nature. Consequently, although the incumbent President Moi had already been in power since 1978, he was allowed, under this arrangement, to count his "first" term effectively subsequent to the date of the law establishing term limits. He thus contested as KANU's candidate in both the 1992 and 1997 presidential elections. The mere presence of Moi's name in the ballot paper diminished almost completely the chances for the opposition parties to win these two elections. The main reason for this pessimism was that, although the opposition was

---

[57] See Otieno 2010. For details on how this pressure was effective, see Brown 2001, p. 726; Klopp 2001, pp. 481–482; Oyugi 1997, pp. 45–47.

[58] See Kimundi 2011, p. 80; Otieno 2010.

[59] The call for *majimbo* mostly came from Rift Valley, the province where KANU had a strong hold. The aim seemed similar to the 1960 s idea of *majimboism*. As Klopp notes "[t]he attraction of such a model for Kenya's patronage bosses was that, even if they should lose control of the central government, they could bargain with the new leaders on the basis of their political strength in ethnic enclaves where their grip on local politics would ensure their dominance". See Klopp 2001, pp. 483–487. Subsequently, the *majimbo* discussion (pro and against) featured again prominently towards the adoption of Kenya's 2010 Constitution. See The Standard 29 March 2010; The Standard, 28 March 2010; The Standard 26 March 2010; The Standard, 19 March 2010; Daily Nation, 28 September 2010 and Daily Nation, 16 September 2010. Although the advocates of *majimbo* did not succeed by a 100 %, the new constitution of Kenya of 2010 settled on a county system of governance. It established a dual system of government, consisting of 47 county governments and the national government. In this new structure, the county governments were given semi-autonomous powers of legislation and implementation of governance of their respective plans without prejudice to the control exercised by the National Government. The President was given powers to dissolve any county under prescribed conditions in Part 6 of Chapter Eleven, read *in tandem* with the Fourth Schedule to the Constitution. It is said that the county system is more of a compromise between those who favoured a purely federal/regional system and those who favoured a purely unitary system. See Daily Nation, 31 March 2010; Mugoya, 2010, pp. 1 et seq.

generally too weak and divided to triumph over KANU, Moi, being the head of state seeking re-election, had an added advantage: he had at his disposal all the loyal state agents and machinery which he could use—and which he allegedly used—to manipulate the whole process.[60] What else could one expect from a framework where the incumbent President was the discretionary appointing (and firing) authority of the officials charged with the task of managing the elections? As will be shown shortly, the opposition parties had to wait until 2002 for them to win against KANU. This time, however, Moi was no longer eligible to contest having exhausted his two-term limit.

2.4.2 Politics of Alliances and Party Hopping

Since its inception, the multiparty system in Kenya has exhibited a constant trend of mergers, alliance forging and pact signing among the parties. The immediately conceivable rationale for this practice could be the need for strength-building in the environment characterized by proliferation of political parties.[61] These alliances have exhibited two characteristics. Firstly, in all cases, they have been ad hoc in nature, emerging only as temporary vehicles for political elites angling for post-election posts. They have hardly lasted after elections, even in the first case in which an opposition alliance won the presidential election in 2002. The composition of the alliances changes frequently due to "party hopping" i.e. the tendency of individual members to constantly change their party affiliations. This tendency has been described sarcastically as "political nomadism",[62] and one that makes most political parties in Kenya "indomitable lions".[63] Secondly, ethno-regional interests have remained the common denominator in almost all the party alliances, specific focus being on power and access to state resources.[64]

The following parts describe some of the major party alliances in which the aforementioned features manifest themselves clearly. One notable thing is that most alliances emerged towards the 2002 and 2007 elections.

---

[60] Troup and Hornsby 1998, p. 2.

[61] For instance, at the time of general elections in 2007, there were about 300 registered political parties, out of which 117 nominated candidates for the National Assembly. This number had significantly reduced to 47 parties by March 2010 following the enforcement of a new law, the Political Parties Act of 2007, which was introduced to check on the proliferation of parties. See the information by the Electoral Institute for Sustainability of Democracy in Africa (EISA) http://www.eisa.org.za/WEP/ken2010parties.htm.and   http://www.eisa.org.za/WEP/kenparties2.htm. Accessed September 2014.

[62] Tsuda 2010, p. 12.

[63] Keverenge (undated), p. 14.

[64] Ibid., p. 36.

2.4.2.1 The Rise and Fall of the "New KANU" Alliance

Having won the first two multiparty elections in 1992 and 1997, Moi was constitutionally barred from seeking re-election in the 2002 elections. The pre-conceived fear that he would engineer a constitutional change to enable him extend his term limit was rebutted by Moi himself.[65] Therefore, towards the 2002 elections, the transition in respect of the occupier of the presidential seat became clear. This gave rise to yet another cloud of uncertainty and speculations, which dominated the period preceding the elections. This uncertainty pertained to whether, apart from the transfer of the presidency from Moi to a new individual, the transition would also entail a transfer of the presidency from the long ruling party, KANU, to another political party. Apparently, Moi himself was engulfed in this uncertainty. He, like all other Kenyans, could not predict with certainty how the ethno-regional dynamics in the Kenyan voting patterns would affect this election, especially now that the "professor of politics" (Moi as he was known) would no longer be running for president. This caused fear that KANU's candidate might fail to acquire the 25 per cent vote threshold required under the existing Constitution.[66] Only a political alliance was the way out. Moi worked on one.

2.4.2.1.1 Courting Alliance with Odinga's NDP

To reduce uncertainties and increase KANU's chances of victory, Moi decided, as the 2002 election approached, to solicit a merger with Raila Odinga's opposition party, the National Development Party (NDP). It was ironical that Moi sought to ally with Raila Odinga who had previously been a victim of torture and preventive detention by the Moi regime for almost a decade. Odinga had an overwhelming support of his tribe (Luo), one of the biggest tribes in Kenya. So the immediate question was whether these former antagonists would be able to work together in good faith, or whether their "political marriage" was merely one of convenience.

The KANU-NDP collaboration started as a parliamentary alliance on the basis of parliamentary seats each party had won in the 1997 elections.[67] It culminated into a full merger in March 2002, whereupon NDP leaders, including Raila Odinga,

---

[65] This fear had intensified because, among other things, Moi did not show any interest in the Vice President, Professor George Saitoti, as the elections drew near. The public had expected that Saitoti would be groomed as Moi's successor. See Asingo 2003, p. 32.

[66] The law required that for a presidential candidate to be declared President, he or she must, among other things, garner a minimum of 25 % of the valid votes cast in at least five out of the eight provinces of Kenya. See Constitution of Kenya, 1963 (R.E 2009), Article 5(3)(f).

[67] In the 1997 elections, KANU won the majority in the parliament only by a small margin of 4 seats over the combined opposition parties. Thus, a parliamentary alliance with one of the opposition parties was considered inevitable in order to have a comfortable majority for assurance. See Odhiambo-Mbai 2003, p. 70.

were elevated to ministerial positions.[68] The resulting alliance was named "New KANU". The underlying aim of this alliance, in Moi's perspective, was to widen KANU's voter-strength by securing the vast NDP support in Nyanza Province, which was predominantly of Odinga's Luo ethnicity.[69] Following the merger, Moi believed that KANU was now stronger than ever, because it had brought on board each of the five big ethnic groups[70] by having one of "their persons" as party leader.[71] As Moi was preparing to finish his second term (1997–2002) and leave office, this was part of his broad but hitherto undisclosed succession plan.

2.4.2.1.2   Effect of Moi's Succession Plan: Project Uhuru

After the KANU-NDP successful merger, it appeared that Moi had managed to play the "ethnic cards" well, because the resulting alliance had a strong fusion of ethnic forces. However, as soon as the secret of his succession plan became known, the merger that Moi had created turned sour and became a source of great discomfort for him. A perception emerged that Moi's succession plan was crafted deliberately to enable him continue ruling Kenya indirectly even after his formal retirement. The reason was that the party constitution that was adopted during the merger allocated extraordinary powers to the Chair (Moi), such as powers to approve cabinet appointments and a veto over major government policy decisions, that is, if the alliance won and formed the government.[72] Moi was aware that if this was to be achieved, his successor had to be someone who was loyal to him—an individual who, even as president, could be controlled easily from behind the curtain. Moi, therefore, imposed the 41-year old Uhuru Kenyatta, the son of Kenya's first president Jomo Kenyatta, as New KANU's presidential candidate. Moi told the nation:

> I have chosen Uhuru to take over leadership when I leave. This young man Uhuru has been consulting me on leadership matters. I have seen that *he is a person who can be guided*. If there are others who are chosen then it will depend on the people.[73]

---

[68] Elischer 2008, p. 19.

[69] Asingo 2003, p. 115.

[70] There are at least five most influential ethnic groups the support of which any politician would strive to win in any presidential election in Kenya, if he or she is to increase the chances of victory. Their importance lies in their composition of the total national population. These are: Kikuyu (21 %), Luhya (14 %), Luo (12 %), Kalenjin (12 %) and Kamba (11 %). See Elischer 2008, p. 1.

[71] With this vision, the party leadership structure was changed to create five vice chairmanship positions, apparently to cater for each of "the big five". Four Vice Chairmen elected were: Uhuru Kenyatta (a Kikuyu), Musalia Mudavadi (a Luhya), Kalonzo Musyoka (a Kamba) and Noah Katanangala (a Mijikenda). Moi (a Kalenjin) remained Chairman, while Raila Odinga (a Luo) was elected Secretary-General. See Odhiambo-Mbai 2003, p. 71. Cf. Steeves 2006, p. 217.

[72] Steeves 2006, p. 218.

[73] Daily Nation 29 July 2002 (emphasis added). See also Odhiambo-Mbai 2003, p. 77.

This imposition was met with a strong, open and unprecedented defiance of Moi. The defiance was orchestrated by Raila Odinga, supposedly due to his "intoxicating influence and his aggressive and uncompromising pursuit of what he believes to be right".[74] Consequently, despite Moi's preference of Kenyatta, five other individuals in the New KANU alliance, including Odinga, also declared their interests to be nominated as the alliance's presidential candidates.[75] They formed a faction within the New KANU alliance and named it a "Rainbow Alliance". The aim of this faction was to push for democratic nominations, opposing the imposition by the Uhuru-Moi faction of an "unpopular" candidate. However, seeing that they were unlikely to defeat Moi, the Rainbow Alliance transformed itself into a political party, the Liberal Democratic Party.[76] This event happened coincidently with the endorsement of Uhuru Kenyatta as KANU's candidate at Kasarani on 14 October 2002.[77] This marked the end of the short-lived New KANU political marriage. Meanwhile, the other opposition parties were also strategizing on their own political alliances.

2.4.2.2 Advent of the Rainbow Coalition as a Winning Opposition Alliance

The formation of the short-lived New KANU alliance had sent signals to the opposition parties that if they resorted to contesting individually in the 2002 elections, they would lose. The fragmented opposition had lost the two preceding multiparty elections supposedly due to lack of unity.[78] As a strategy for unity towards the 2002 general elections, two opposition alliances were formed a few weeks before the general elections with a view to competing against KANU in the presidential election. The first alliance was the Liberal Democratic Party (LDP), which, as already explained in the preceding section, originated from the Rainbow Alliance that had severed itself from the New KANU. The second alliance was the National Alliance (Party) of Kenya (NAK) that started as an alliance of three political parties,[79] but which would later admit more parties to become an alliance of 13 political parties.

---

[74] Asingo 2003, p. 34.

[75] The others were Moi's Vice President Professor George Saitoti, Kalonzo Musyoka, Noah Katanangala and Musalia Mudavadi. However, Moi was able to persuade and co-opt Katanangala and Mudavadi, who abandoned their interests in the presidency and supported Kenyatta. The other three could not be "deceived" by Moi to abandon their interests. See ibid., p. 34.

[76] Steeves 2006, p. 220.

[77] Asingo 2003, p. 34.

[78] For instance, in the 1997 elections, KANU candidate won by 41 % although the four opposition candidates got 59 % of all the presidential votes in the aggregate. Individually, however, only one opposition party, the DP, got 31 %. See Kanyinga 2003, pp. 108–111.

[79] This alliance brought together the Democratic Party (DP) under Mwai Kibaki, the National Party of Kenya (NPK) under Charity Ngilu and the Forum for Restoration of Democracy-Kenya (FORD-Kenya) under Michael Wamalwa. See Odhiambo-Mbai 2003, p. 79.

On 22 October 2002 the two alliances above, the LDP and the NAK, decided to merge into one opposition alliance, the National Rainbow Coalition (NARC) (hereafter "Rainbow Coalition"). Thus, the Rainbow Coalition was an *alliance of alliances*—a grand alliance. Its origin was in two agreements (i.e. memoranda of understanding) signed on 21 October 2002 between the LDP and the NAK. The first agreement, which was made public, was based on policy commitments and the principles of power-sharing in a coalition government in the event that the Rainbow Coalition won the elections. The second agreement was signed secretly between the leaders of the parties to the Rainbow Coalition, and was never made public. However, it later came to light that in the secret agreement the parties had agreed on a detailed power-sharing formula which would be adopted after winning the elections.[80] Indeed the Rainbow Coalition was able to win both the presidential and parliamentary elections by an overwhelming majority. Its presidential candidate Mwai Kibaki was declared the winner, thereby defeating KANU's candidate, Uhuru Kenyatta.[81]

Therefore, the 2002 presidential election in Kenya goes down in history for being the first time that KANU, the party which had been in power since independence, was ousted from power by an opposition alliance, the Rainbow Coalition. But as the next section shows, this particular alliance, too, was another "indomitable lion"; it did not last long.

2.4.2.3 Towards the 2007 Elections: Disintegration of the Rainbow Coalition and Advent of PNU and ODM Alliances

2.4.2.3.1 Rainbow Coalition: A Fragile Alliance

The Rainbow Coalition was a unity whose cohesion remained largely dependent on a *bona fide* implementation of the memoranda of understanding signed among its members. As indicated earlier, the emergence of factions within political parties leading to break aways had become a common feature in Kenya's politics before and after the advent of political pluralism. This explains the early prediction that, even though it had won the 2002 presidential election, the Rainbow Coalition, too, was a fragile alliance which was prone to disintegration at any time.[82]

The Rainbow Coalition was *prima facie* a fragile entity for one main reason: It was an *umbrella alliance.* Unlike an ordinary political party whose membership comprises individuals (natural persons), the Rainbow Coalition admitted *political*

---

[80] Nyong'o 2007, p. 116. Also see Kanyinga 2003, p. 122.

[81] New York Times, 30 December 2002. Statistically, NARC won the presidential votes by 62.2 % against 31.3 % earned by KANU and 6 % by FORD People. In the parliamentary results, while NARC won the majority by 125 seats, KANU got 64 seats and FORD People got 14 seats. See Troup 2003a, pp. 4–7. See also Bakari 2002, p. 284; Nasong'o 2007, pp. 98–100.

[82] Cf. Wanyande 2003, p. 151; Ndengwa 2003, pp. 157–158.

parties as members (partners). The parties that acceded to the Coalition retained their
identities and own members. As a result, although individuals contested the election
carrying the Coalition's flag, their respective parties did not abandon their party interests, such as economic and ethnic demands, nor did they dissolve themselves upon
acceding to the coalition.[83] This posed an obvious 'danger' that the political parties
forming the Rainbow Coalition could withdraw from the alliance any time if a disagreement occurred among them. Indeed this is exactly what happened.

The road to the disintegration of the Rainbow Coalition started with the failure
to honour the objectives and principles agreed upon in the agreements creating it.
One such principle was that the two sub-alliances forming the Coalition, the LDP
and the NAK, would be "equal partners", and for that reason, the cabinet positions
would be shared equally between them.[84] According to the formula that had been
agreed upon, a cabinet of 23 members, composed of 11 members from the two
sides, with Kibaki as the chair, would be created. However, Kibaki is accused to
have breached this agreement by appointing more members from his own side,
NAK, and also by disregarding many other aspects of the agreement.[85] This elicited criticism, caused frustration, dissatisfaction and feelings of betrayal and, more
detrimentally, led to the emergence of factions within the Rainbow Coalition.[86]
Responding to the criticisms raised, Kibaki's side, allegedly made of "impenetrat-
able aides" nicknamed the "Mt. Kenya Mafia",[87] argued that the President was
exercising legitimate constitutional powers which could not be curtailed by political or "secret agreements among power-hungry leaders".[88] This untrustworthiness
was the biggest fracture to befall the Rainbow Coalition's foundation. The
Coalition's actual disintegration followed in 2005 as described below.

2.4.2.3.2 Effect of the 2005 Constitution Making Process

The ultimate fall of the Rainbow Coalition was triggered by the 2005 attempt at initiating a constitution making process. The parties to the Coalition had agreed, inter
alia, that if they won the elections, they would see to it that a much needed new constitution was adopted within 6 months.[89] The background to this commitment is that
prior to the 2002 elections, a statutory body known as the Constitution of Kenya
Review Commission (CKRC)[90] had done a survey and recommended an adoption

---

[83] Elischer 2008, p. 20.
[84] See Troup 2003b, p. 4. See also Kadima and Owuor 2006, pp. 179, 189 and 211.
[85] Steeves 2006, pp. 230–231.
[86] Ibid.
[87] Ibid., p. 230.
[88] Nyong'o 2007, pp. 116–117.
[89] NARC's Memorandum of Understanding, General Principle 11.
[90] It was established under the Constitution of Kenya Review Act of 2000.

of a new constitution in Kenya.[91] When the Rainbow Coalition was formed in 2002, its members agreed wholeheartedly that if they won the upcoming elections, they would pursue this agenda to its conclusion.[92] In fact, this is believed to have been the *only* policy issue which had bound the Rainbow Coalition together.[93]

Therefore, the expectation remained that the constitutional draft which was supported widely by all Coalition members, as endorsed by them at Bomas of Kenya (Bomas draft), would be subjected to a referendum. On the contrary, instead of the Bomas draft, President Kibaki, through the then Attorney General Amos Wako, endorsed an alternative draft, the Wako Draft, and put it to a national referendum in 2005.[94] The Bomas draft and the Wako draft differed fundamentally on several critical aspects in respect of which Kenyans and members of the Rainbow Coalition in particular had originally demanded reforms.

One such difference is that the Bomas draft had proposed an introduction of a parliamentary system in which the president would only be the head of state, while a prime minister with executive powers would be the head of government accountable to the parliament. In contrast, the Wako draft proposed that the existing presidential system be retained, and consequently, the president would continue to be head of both state and government. In addition, under the Wako draft, the prime minister would be an appointee of the president and merely the head of government business in parliament, but without any executive powers. Another key difference between the two drafts is that the Bomas draft provided for a bicameral legislature i.e. one with an upper house (senate) and a lower house (national assembly). The Wako draft, on the other hand, provided for a unicameral legislature.[95]

Few months preceding the constitutional referendum witnessed an irreparable disintegration of the Rainbow Coalition and a birth of new alliances. Both the Rainbow Coalition and KANU, which was now an opposition party, experienced inner-party factions (camps within the parties), which have been described as "pro-reform forces" and "anti-reform forces".[96] The pro-reform and anti-reform camps, respectively, opposed or supported the Wako draft Constitution which the government decided to subject to a YES/NO referendum on 21 November 2005. The "no" camp[97] (pro-reformists), which was led by Raila Odinga, used an orange as their

[91] See Report of the Constitution of Kenya Review Commission 2002.

[92] The reforms proposed and highly demanded included, inter alia, the introduction of an executive Prime Minister, demotion of the presidency to a mere ceremonial post, establishment of two chambers in the National Assembly and implementation of a county government structure. See Constitution of Kenya Review Commission 2002, pp. 44–75.

[93] Elischer 2008, p. 22.

[94] Steeves 2006, p. 231.

[95] For more details on the two drafts, see Chr. Michelsen Institute 2006.

[96] See Tsuda 2010, p. 9.

[97] The "No" camp brought together the LDP side of the NARC government, one faction of KANU (under William Ruto) and the National party of Kenya (NPK) under Charity Ngilu. See Elischer 2008, pp. 22–23.

symbol to campaign strongly against the government constitutional draft. The Kibaki's "yes" camp[98] (anti-reformists), which used a banana as their symbol, campaigned in favour of the referendum. In the end, the oranges ("no" camp) succeeded. The government draft constitution was, therefore, rejected by the Kenyans.[99]

Thus, the constitutional reform agenda was not successfully accomplished as it had been expected; it was put in further abeyance. But the constitutional referendum signified a stamp on the death certificate of the Rainbow Coalition. The reason is that subsequent to the referendum, and shortly before the 2007 elections, the two camps in the referendum campaigns, the banana and orange camps, transformed themselves into new political parties. Odinga's "no" camp became the Orange Democratic Movement (ODM), while Kibaki's "yes" camp became the Party of National Unity (PNU).[100] It is these two political parties, the ODM and the PNU, which, 2 years later, were principal participants in the 2007 presidential election, Odinga and Kibaki being their respective candidates. And as will be shown in Chap. 3, the two parties were at the centre of the ensuing post-election violence, the main focus of this book.

2.5   Criminal Gangs, Election Violence and Impunity

2.5.1   Use of Criminal Gangs for Political Purposes

Apart from political alliances, the use of violence in the form of militias or criminal gangs is another relatively recent feature of the Kenyan politics since 1980s. Subsequent to the re-introduction of political pluralism in 1991, politicians resorted to sponsoring, creating or manipulating the already existing criminal gangs to achieve their political ends through violence during each election. This practice was first allegedly authored by KANU, being part of its so-called "ethnic crusade" to eliminate or weaken opposition.[101] Mueller observes:

> In most cases these gangs were formed, aided, or abetted by the state's security apparatus and the provincial administration. Gangs of youth were organized by key KANU politicians who were identified by names in both human rights reports and reports produced by a government commission.[102]

---

[98] The "Yes" camp comprised Kibaki's side of the NARC government (i.e. the NAK) which teamed up with other parties, the Democratic Party (DP), FORD-Kenya, FORD-People and one faction of KANU under Uhuru Kenyatta. See ibid.

[99] See Kenya GN No. 9510, 23 November 2005. The "no" vote won by 58 % while the "yes" vote got 42 %. See "Kenya: 2005 Constitutional referendum results" http://www.eisa.org.za/WEP/ken2005results.htm accessed May 2011), also see "Elections in Kenya" http://africanelections.tripod.com/ke.html. Accessed August 2014.

[100] Elischer 2008, p. 23.

[101] Branch and Cheeseman 2008, p. 15.

[102] Mueller 2008, p. 190.

Mungiki (a Kikuyu word for masses or multitude of people) is the largest and most written about criminal gang. It started in the late 1980s under the disguise of a Kikuyu religious movement,[103] before it later assumed diverse cultural, political and socio-economic dimensions.[104] In terms of organization, the *Mungiki* has been described as a "mafioso-style shakedown gang" with reliable sources of income, a requirement for membership and a defined organizational structure.[105] In the 2002 elections it was allegedly "co-opted in a patron-client relationship" by KANU and worked for the Kikuyu KANU's presidential candidate, Uhuru Kenyatta.[106] After the ouster of KANU in 2002, the *Mungiki* movement rose to a full-fledged criminal gang increasingly engaging in violent activities.[107] Although in 2002 it was banned and its members were declared *persona non grata,* the gang never disappeared from the scene, nor did the government succeed in dismantling it.[108]

There are other gangs which have emerged in various towns, being more active during election periods. These include *the Taliban* (a Luo militia), Baghdad boys, *Jeshi la Mzee* (the elder's battalion), *Jeshi la Embakasi* (Embakasi battalion), Kaya Bombo Youth, *Chionkororo, Amachuma, The Rwenjes* Football Club, *the Jeshi ya King'ole,* and *Jeshi la Mbela, Jeshi la Darajani, Bukhungu* (Luhya militia) *Ghetto* and Huruma Youth Group.[109]

It is in this context that in the 2007 post-election violence some of these gangs, especially the *Mungiki* and the *Luo Taliban,* were allegedly used by politicians in support of the Orange Democratic Movement (ODM) and Party of National Unity (PNU), respectively.[110]

---

[103] Claiming likeness to the *Mau Mau* movement, the Mungiki organization rejects Christianity and advocates a restoration of the traditional African (Kikuyu) beliefs and practices. It administers oath to its members. See Land Info 2010.

[104] Ibid., pp. 5–6.

[105] Mungiki became a gang for hire allegedly available to "the highest bidder", politicians inclusive. Literature shows that the relationship between Mungiki and the Moi-KANU regime developed strongly from mid 1990s on a *quid pro quo* basis. E.g., the gang offered its support to the KANU candidate in the 2002 elections allegedly in exchange for arms and aid from the state security forces and allocation of transport routes in the *matatu* (mini-buses for public transport) business in Nairobi. The "bandit economy" of the gang was estimated to be USD 3.8 million per year in 2004, mostly derived from, among other sources, the resale of hijacked cars and USD 58,000 per month from member subscriptions. See Katumanga 2005, pp. 512–515; Mueller 2008, pp. 192–193. It is estimated to have more than one million members. See Immigration and Refugee Board of Canada 2006–2007.

[106] See Kagwanja 2005, p. 59; Katumanga 2005, p. 513. For more details on the role of Mungiki during Moi's era, see Kagwanja 2007, pp. 25 et seq; Rasmussen 2010, pp. 435 et seq.

[107] See Kagwanja 2005, pp. 65–66. Also see Frederiksen 2010, pp. 1065 et seq.

[108] Mueller 2008, p. 193. See also Atieno 2007 p. 527.

[109] Branch and Cheeseman 2008, p. 15; Katumanga, 2005, pp. 512–513; Kenya National Commission on Human Rights 2008, p. 47, para 161; Mueller 2008, pp. 193–194.

[110] Kenya National Commission on Human Rights 2008, paras 159–216.

2.5.2 Trends of Election Violence

It can be asserted that the 2007–2008 post-election violence was not a total surprise to Kenyans. The preceding multiparty elections were also characterized by politically and ethnically sponsored violence.[111] It is alleged that during his presidency Moi and his ruling party KANU actively aided such kinds of violence to fulfil Moi's "prophecy" that the re-introduction of multipartysm would increase tribal animosity, polarize the nation and destroy peace and co-existence. To prove this, KANU is accused of having applied deadly tactics in different parts of the country, including incitement to ethnic cleansing through stereotyping people from certain ethnic communities.[112] Human Rights Watch uses the title "echoes of Rwanda" in trying to describe what usually happened. This is not, however, to equalize Kenya to Rwanda, but simply to point out the parallelism and close resemblance between the tactics employed to bring to fruition the 1994 Rwandan genocide and those used to cause violence in Kenya mostly during elections. For instance, as regard the violence that followed Kenya's 1997 general elections, Human Rights states:

> As in pre-1994 Rwanda, Coast politicians [in Kenya] exploited ethnic divisions to preserve and expand their own power. They blamed a group of perceived outsiders whose ethnic identity was taken as an indicator of their support for the political opposition….politicians mobilized supporters to carry out acts of targeted violence….They began with political attacks … to kill the designated "enemy." The killers … depended on guidance from their political leaders, as well as the expertise of highly trained and well-armed military leaders. Their ability to target and wipe out their victims was greatly increased by the use—even the mere possession—of firearms. In essence, the strategy of the Coast killings, as well as the Rwanda slaughter, hinged on two factors: the manipulation of ethnic divisions into ethnic hatred for political ends and the organization and arming of groups of supporters who could execute or orchestrate widespread killings.[113]

The violence accompanying *all* multiparty elections prior to those of 2007 had, apart from its general political dimension, assumed ethno-regional patterns.[114] The land ownership is among the factors that played (and continues to play) a central role in these incidents of violence. Land disputes, which had been there since independence, worsened with the animosity instigated by politicians playing the ethnic card. People with political connections, mostly the allegedly "over-privileged Kikuyus", were (and still are) accused of corruptly obtaining and holding huge pieces of land, mostly in the Rift Valley Province, which is not their ancestral

---

[111] Human Rights Watch 2008, p. 11.

[112] Kiage 2004, p. 106.

[113] Human Rights Watch 2002, p. 4.

[114] Kenya National Commission on Human Rights 2008, p. 47, para 159. Also see Orvis 2001, p. 8 (describing the Kenyan politics as arguably the "most ethnic in Africa").

land.[115] For example, it is alleged, although this could be an exaggeration, that the family of Kenya's first President Jomo Kenyatta alone owns more than 30 per cent of all the land in Kenya.[116]

A commission of enquiry formed after the 2002 elections (Ndung'u Commission) found that "most illegal allocations of public lands took place before or soon after the multiparty general elections of 1992, 1997 and 2002".[117] This finding, therefore, makes the timing of the ethnic violence in Kenya noteworthy: it occurred in the period immediately preceding or following general elections. The reason is that although the issue of land pressure caused by the so-called "land grabbing" raises genuine complaints, it has, over time, been used (abused?) by politicians as a campaign tool, and in so doing, it has caused or intensified hatred of local people towards people from other ethnic groups owning land in their areas, considering them as "invaders" and accusing them of benefiting from land which originally or traditionally did not belong to them.[118] Campaigning on the land question usually gives the impression to the local people that if such politicians are elected, they could help the traditional inhabitants in the areas to reclaim their land from the "invaders" or "grabbers" from other ethnic communities.

On the basis of the foregoing historical context, it has been stated that even the approaching 2007 elections were also expected to "reshape national space, and to create ethnically cleansed regions".[119] Katumanga describes this as the desire of the political elite "to act, manoeuvre and manipulate social formations against each other that enhance [their] freedom of choice in deciding who to back or displease".[120] This desire did not start with the 2007 elections. Prior to and after the first multiparty general elections in 1992, a widespread violence orchestrated by the Kalenjin in the Rift Valley province targeted members of other ethnic communities, mostly the Luo, Kikuyu, Luhya and Kisii, who were perceived as opposing president Moi and his ruling party KANU.[121] The aim of the attackers was to expel the so-called "hostile

---

[115] Human Rights Watch 2008, pp. 12–15. It is said that while the Kikuyus migrate largely for commercial farming and business purposes, thereby breaking links with their original homes, the other communities migrate mainly as workers while maintaining links with their rural homes. Arguably, this nature of the Kikuyu has made them "obvious candidates for discrimination and detestation by those whose property or territory (land in particular) they have been accused of "invading". See Oucho 2002, p. 58.

[116] See Kenya Today, 27 February 2013. NB. When asked this question in a televised presidential debate in 2013, Uhuru Kenyatta, the presidential candidate for the Jubilee Alliance, did not expressly accept or deny this allegation. Instead he only insisted that all the land that the Kenyatta family owns was acquired legally on a "willing-buyer-willing-seller basis". See second presidential debate [full video], NTV Kenya, published 25 Feb. 2013 http://www.youtube.com/watch?v=DoBo86ttZCo. Viewed September 2014.

[117] As quoted verbatim in Southall 2005, pp. 142–151.

[118] Human Rights Watch 2008, p. 14.

[119] Taussig-Rubbo 2011, p. 65.

[120] Katumanga 2005, p. 506.

[121] Kenya National Commission on Human Rights 2008, para 45.

tribes" from the Rift Valley area.[122] Specifically, it was demanded that "those Kikuyu settled in the Rift Valley [were "invaders", and] would have to pack up and return to Central Province".[123] Similarly, during the 1997 elections, widespread attacks occurred in a more organized fashion. Apart from the Rift Valley Province, this particular violence spread to the Coastal Province and other areas.[124]

Estimates by Africa Watch indicate that during the 1992 election violence, about 1,500 people died and about 300,000 others were internally displaced.[125] These figures pertain to the Rift Valley Province only, and do not include considerable incidents of retaliatory attacks against the Kalenjin in other areas.[126] Similarly, estimates by Human Rights Watch indicate that during the 1997 elections the accompanying violence claimed at least 2,000 lives and displaced over 400,000 people countrywide.[127] Literature further indicates that the 2002 elections, too, were accompanied by some violence on a smaller scale (when compared to the previous two elections), but no exact figures or estimates could be found.

Based partly on the foregoing, the Kenyan National Commission on Human Rights (KNCHR) is of the view that one of the factors that differentiated the 2007–2008 post-election violence from the violence that occurred in the preceding three general elections was its magnitude and level.[128] This could be correct in terms of the scale of destruction of property, sexual crimes and geographical widespreadness. But from the figures given above, one can conclude that regarding loss of life and displacement of people, the election violence of 1992 and 1997 had comparable dimensions with the 2007–2008 post-election violence.[129] Nevertheless, the 2007–2008 violence remains unique in that it received a particular attention beyond Kenyan borders, as it was the first time in the history of Kenya that an election violence attracted external intervention, particularly in the form of the AU's mediation process and the intervention by the ICC.

2.5.3 Commissions of Enquiry and Culture of Impunity

If history is anything to go by, then it would not be wrong to contend that to most Kenyans the 2008 Commission of Inquiry into the Post-Election Violence[130] was not necessarily expected to be a panacea for impunity at the domestic level. There

---

[122] Ibid., para 44. See also National Christian Council of Kenya 1992, p. 3.

[123] Klopp 2002, p. 274; Oucho 2002, pp. 86–89.

[124] Kenya National Commission on Human Rights 2008, para 46.

[125] Ibid., para 45. See also Africa Watch 1993, p. 1.

[126] Africa Watch 1993, pp. 27–37.

[127] Human Rights Watch 2002, p. 21 Kiage 2004, p. 107.

[128] Kenya National Commission on Human Rights 2008, para 43.

[129] See infra Sect. 3.2.2 in relation to the magnitude of the 2007–2008 violence.

[130] See infra Sect. 3.4.1.

are historical explanations to this contention. Prior to this particular Commission, the Kenyan government had set a bad precedent, portraying Kenya as state that was indifferent about or condoned commission of serious crimes to encourage impunity. Whenever serious human rights violations occurred, the government would form commissions of enquiry to look into them, mostly due to public outcry for accountability. For example, from 1963 to 2008, a total of 25 commissions of inquiry or bodies similar to them were established to deal with a broad range of issues of great concern to Kenyans.[131] Mostly, such issues included land grievances, murders, political assassinations, political/election violence, grand corruption, politically-instigated ethnic cleansing and other incidents of gross human rights violations.[132] For purposes of this study, the most relevant commissions are those that looked into political, ethic or election violence during which serious violations of human rights occurred.

For example, the parliamentary select committee (famously known as the Kiliku Committee) was formed after the 1992 elections to investigate ethnic clashes accompanying these elections. In its final report, the Committee concluded that the violence in the Rift Valley Province, for example, had been instigated and sponsored by senior politicians from the ruling party KANU and Moi's government.[133] A similar finding would later be made by a fact-finding mission deployed to Kenya by the United Nations Office of the High Commissioner for Human Rights which concluded that the 1992 election violence was organized under a central command involving local administrative and security officers.[134] The Kiliku inquiry was followed by a judicial commission of enquiry (famously known as the Akiwumi Commission) formed after the 1997 election violence to inquire again into the tribal clashes in Kenya. This commission, too, made similar findings like those of the Kiliku Committee.[135]

In their findings, these commissions made accusations by identifying and expressly naming individuals, including high-profile politicians and government officials, who, allegedly, were responsible for funding, supporting or committing the crimes. The commissions recommended further investigations and prosecution of the individuals so adversely mentioned.[136] Despite all these findings and recommendations, neither political nor criminal accountability followed. Most of the politicians accused in the commissions' reports enjoyed state protection, as they

---

[131] Africa Centre for Open Democracy 2007; Kisemei and Kimani 2010.

[132] See Kituo cha Katiba 2007.

[133] Republic of Kenya 1992. Also see Kenya National Commission on Human Rights 2008, para 46.

[134] UN Office of the High Commissioner for Human Rights 2008, p. 6.

[135] For its report, see Republic of Kenya 1999.

[136] E.g. see Appendix "G" of the Akiwumi Commission Report which contains a list of 189 persons adversely mentioned and notified as suspects of ethnic violence in various places. For a long list of names of people expressly accused by various commissions as perpetrators of various crimes, including economic crime, murder, political assassinations, etc., see Kisemei and Kimani 2010, pp. 6–26.

continued to serve in the Moi's and later Kibaki's governments.[137] Instead of taking legal measures, the Moi regime is alleged to have labelled the violence as "ordinary insecurity". This, according to the Kenyan National Commission on Human Rights, was nothing but state's effort to subsume crime into the political violence, apparently in order to justify impunity.[138] That is why even a few people arrested in connection with these incidents of violence were soon released unconditionally.[139]

Given the tendency above, ordinary citizens, as well as politicians, usually consider such commissions as toothless dogs which do not bite. For example, the Waki Commission formed to look into the 2007–2008 post-election violence (see infra 3.4.1) reported that many of its respondents expressly stated that the commission, just like all other commissions formed before it, was "a waste of time and resources", because its recommendations "would never be implemented".[140] The paragraph quoted below echoes similar views, underscoring how, prior to the 2007 elections, impunity had already become the rule rather than the exception in Kenya. The paragraph is reproduced from the contribution of Ms Esther Murungi Mathenge, MP for Nyeri Town constituency, during the parliamentary debate on the Motion for the establishment of yet another commission, the Truth, Justice and Reconciliation Commission[141] so established also in response to the 2007–2008 post-election violence. The MP lamented:

> We have had the same incidents, although not of the same magnitude. One was in 1992, another in 1997, a minor one in 2002 and the major one in 2007. In the past, after such incidents occurred, we formed commissions. We formed the Akiwumi Commission. However, what did we do with it? We put it under the carpet. We also formed the Ndung'u Commission … What did we do with the Ndung'u Commission Report? We also put it under the carpet.[142]

Thus, prior to 2007, the culture of impunity had already grown roots to become, one could contend, an entrenched feature in Kenya, especially in relation to crimes committed in connection with grand corruption or gross human rights violations, including those accompanying election violence. It is due to this nurtured and deep-rooted impunity that, in 1998, the Law Society of Kenya (Bar Association) wrote a letter to the then UN Secretary-General, Kofi Anan, calling for an independent UN-led investigation and establishment of an ad hoc tribunal to punish the perpetrators of "genocide and crimes against humanity" that had allegedly occurred in Kenya.[143] This, however, did not materialize. At this juncture, it suffices to say that had Mr. Anan foreseen that 10 years later he would be asked to

---

[137] Kisemei and Kimani 2010, p. 10.

[138] Kenya National Commission on Human Rights 2008, para 47.

[139] UN Office of the High Commissioner for Human Rights 2008, p. 6.

[140] Republic of Kenya 2008, p. 18.

[141] See Chap. 5.

[142] See Parliament of Kenya 2008. For similar sentiments by expressed in Parliament by other MPs, see Parliament of Kenya 2010.

[143] Kiage 2004, p. 107.

mediate in a similar violence in Kenya (see infra 3.3), this time not in his capacity as UN Secretary-General, but as the head of AU's mediation team, he would have probably reacted to the request differently.

2.6 Chapter Summary

In this chapter the historical and sociological dynamics of Kenyan politics prior to the 2007 general elections have been presented. The chapter has shown that, under the first two Presidents (Kenyatta and Moi), the Kenyan politics was dominated by authoritarianism. And since the resumption of multiparty democracy in 1991, the politics became dominated by proliferation of political parties, short-lived political alliances and use of criminal gangs for political gains. At all times negative ethnicity has been the common denominator. Consequently, negative ethnicity has been one of the main reasons for the recurring ethno-political violence, mostly during elections. A pattern of electoral violence, entailing the commission of serious gross human rights violations, can be clearly established with regard to the multiparty elections of 1992, 1997 and 2002. The fact that no accountability measures were ever taken against the main perpetrators (mostly politicians) of such violence in the past was a precursor of the violence that would happen in the upcoming 2007 general elections. What had not been foreseen, however, was the fact that the violence accompanying the 2007 elections would, unlike the one accompanying the previous elections, greatly attract the attention of the international players, particularly the AU and the ICC.

References

Adar KG (2000) The internal and external contexts of human rights practice in Kenya: Daniel Arap Moi's operational code. Afr Sociol Rev 4(1):74–96
African Centre for Open Democracy (2007) A study of commissions of inquiries in Kenya. First AfriCOG Report. http://www.africog.org/reports/Commissionsofinquirypaper.pdf. Accessed Aug 2014
Africa Watch (1993) Divide and rule: report on state-sponsored ethnic violence in Kenya. Human Rights Watch, New York
Ajulu R (2000) Thinking through the crisis of democratization in Kenya: a response to Adar and Murunga. Afr Sociol Rev 4(2):133–157
Anderson DM (2005) Yours in struggle for Majimbo: nationalism and party politics of decolonization in Kenya 1955–64. J Contemp Hist 40(3):547–564
Asingo PO (2003) The political economy of transition in Kenya. In: Oyugi WO et al (eds) The politics of transition in Kenya: from KANU to NARC. Heinrich Böll Foundation, Nairobi
Atieno A (2007) Mungiki, "Neo-*Mau Mau*" & the prospects for democracy in Kenya. Rev Afr Polit Econ 34(113):526–531
Bakari M (2002) Kenyan elections 2002: the end of Machiavellian politics? Turkish J Int Relat 1(4). http://www.alternativesjournal.net/volume1/number4/bakari.htm. Accessed Aug 2014
Biegon J (2008) The advent of unholy alliances? Coalition governments in the aftermath of disputed elections and electoral violence in Africa: a case study of Kenya. LL.M Dissertation, University of Pretoria

Branch D, Cheeseman N (2008) Democratization, sequencing and state failure in Africa: lessons from Kenya. Afr Aff 108(430):1–26

Brown S (2001) Authoritarian leaders and multiparty elections in Africa: how foreign donors help to keep Kenya's Daniel Arap Moi in power. Third World Q 22(5):725–739

Chr. Michelsen Institute (2006) Kenya constitutional documents: a comparative analysis. CMI Report 2006:5. Chr. Michelsen Institute, Bergen

Christopher AJ (1988) Divide and rule: the impress of British separation policies. Area 20(3):233–240

Constitution of Kenya Review Commission (2002) The People's choice: report of the Constitution of Kenya Review Commission (Short Version). CKRC, Mombasa

Elischer S (2008) Ethnic coalitions of convenience and commitment: political parties and party systems in Kenya. GIGA Working Paper No. 68 http://papers.ssrn.com/sol3/papers.cfm?abstract_id=1114123. Accessed Aug 2014

Frederiksen BF (2010) Mungiki, vernacular organization and political society in Kenya. Dev Change 41(6):1065–1089

Human Rights Watch (2002) Playing with fire: weapons proliferation, political violence, and human rights in Kenya, ISBN: 1-56432-275-0. Human Rights Watch, New York

Human Rights Watch (2008) Ballots to bullets: [Report on] organized political violence and Kenya's crisis of governance, vol 20, No. 1 (A). Human Rights Watch, New York

Immigration and Refugee Board of Canada (2006–2007) Kenya: the Mungiki sect; leadership, membership and recruitment, organizational structure, activities and state protection available to its victims. http://www.unhcr.org/refworld/docid/4784def81e.html. Accessed Aug 2014

Kadima D, Owuor F (2006) The national rainbow coalition: achievements and challenges of building and sustaining a broad-based political party coalition in Kenya. In: Kadima D (ed) The politics of party coalitions in Africa. Electoral Institute for Sustainable Democracy in Africa, Johannesburg. Accessed Sept 2014

Kagwanja MP (2005) Power to Uhuru: youth identity and generational politics in Kenya's 2002 elections. Afr Aff 105(418):51–75

Kagwanja MP (2007) Facing mount Kenya or facing Mecca? The *Mungiki,* ethnic violence and the politics of the Moi succession in Kenya, 1987–2002. Afr Aff 102:25–49

Kanyinga K (2003) Limitations of political liberalization: parties and electoral politics in Kenya. In: Oyugi WO et al (eds) The politics of transition in Kenya. Heinrich Böll Foundation, Nairobi, pp 1992–2002

Katumanga M (2005) A city under siege: banditry and modes of accumulation in Nairobi, 1991–2004. Rev Afr Polit Econ 196:505–520

Kenya National Commission on Human Rights (2008) On the Brink of the precipice: a [Report on] human rights account of Kenya's post-2007 election violence. CRC, Nairobi

Kenya Truth, Justice and Reconciliation Commission (2013) Final report of the Kenyan truth, justice and reconciliation commission, vols I, IIA, IIB, IIC, III and IV. TJRC, Nairobi

Keverenge SK (undated) Political party formation and alliances: a case of Kenya. Final PhD Proposal Atlantic International University. http://citeseerx.ist.psu.edu/viewdoc/download?doi=10.1.1.371.1977&rep=rep1&type=pdf. Accessed Sept 2014

Kiage P (2004) Prosecutions: a panacea for Kenya's past atrocities? East Afr J Hum Rights Democracy 2(104):104–119

Kimundi E (2011) Post election crisis in Kenya and the implications for the International Criminal Court's development as a legitimate institution. Eyes ICC 7(1):79–109

Kisemei MG, Kimani JW (2010) Impunity and the politics of commission of inquiry in Kenya. ICCP Publications. http://www.icpcafrica.org/site/index.php?option=com_content&view=article&id=201:impunity-and-the-politics-of-commission-of-inquiry-in-kenya&catid=3:our-reports&Itemid=117. Accessed July 2011

Kituo cha Katiba (2007) Revisiting transitional justice: a non-partisan and non-governmental engagement. http://www.kituochakatiba.org/index2.php?option=com_docman&task=doc_view&gid=408&Itemid=36. Accessed Nov 2011

Klopp JM (2001) Ethnic clashes and winning elections: the case of Kenya's electoral despotism. Can J Afr Stud 35(3):473–517

Lamb GB (1969) The political crisis in Kenya. World Today 5(12):535–544

Land Info (2010) Kenya: Mungiki: abusers or abused? Report of the country of information centre (Land Info) to the Norwegian Directorate of Immigration Norway's Immigration Appeals Board and the Norwegian Ministry of Labour and Social Inclusion, Oslo

Londale J (2004) Moral and political argument in Kenya. In: Berman et al. (eds) Ethnicity and democracy in Africa. James Currey Publishers, Oxford

Manner RA (1962) New tribalism in Kenya. Afr Today 9(8):8–10 + 14

Miguna M (2012) Peeling back the mask: a quest for justice in Kenya. Gilgamesh Africa, London

Mueller SD (1984) Government and opposition in Kenya, 1966-9. J Modern Afr Stud 22(3):399–427

Mueller SD (2008) The political economy of Kenya's crisis. J East Afr Stud 2(2):185–210

Mugoya BC (2010) Devolution and conflict resolution: assessing the potential role and capacity of county governments in enhancing local peace in Kenya. Institute of Federalism. http://www.federalism.ch/files/FileDownload/956/CONRAD%20BOSIRE.pdf. Accessed April 2011

Muigai G (1995) Ethnicity and the renewal of competitive politics in Kenya. In: Glickman H (ed) Ethnicity, conflict and democratization. African Studies Association Press, Oxford

Musila G (2009) Options for transitional justice in Kenya: autonomy and the challenge of external prescriptions. Int J Trans Justice 3:445–464

Mutua M (2001) Justice under siege: the rule of law and judicial subservience in Kenya. Hum Rights Q 23(1):96–118

Nasong'o SW (2007) Political transition without transformation: the dialectic of liberalization without democratization in Kenya and Zambia. Afr Stud Rev 50(1):83–107

National Christian Council of Kenya (1992) The cursed arrow: a report on organised violence against democracy in Kenya, vol 1. NCCK, Nairobi

Ndengwa SN, Letourneau RE (2004) Constitutional Reform. In: Kaiser PJ, Okumu FW (eds) Democratic transitions in East Africa. Ashgate Publishing Limited, Aldershot

Nyong'o PA (2007) A leap into the future: a vision for Kenya's socio-political and economic transformation. Afr Res Res Forum, Nairobi

Odhiambo-Mbai C (2003) The rise and fall of the autocratic state in Kenya. In: Oyugi WO et al (eds) The politics of transition in Kenya. Heinrich Böll Foundation, Nairobi

Orvis S (2001) Moral ethnicity and political tribalism in Kenya's Virtual democracy. Afr Issues 29(1):8–13

Otieno I (2010) Kenya's quest for a new constitution: the key constitutional moments. Institute for Security Studies. http://www.polity.org.za/article/kenyas-quest-for-a-new-constitution-the-key-constitutional-moments-2010-07-29. Accessed Sept 2014

Oucho JO (2002) Undercurrents of ethnic conflict in Kenya. Koninklijke Brill NV, Leiden

Oyugi WO (1997) Ethnicity in the electoral process: the 1992 general elections in Kenya. Afr J Polit Sci 2(1):41–69

Pal Ahluwalia D (1996) Post-colonialism and the politics of Kenya. Nova Science Publishers, New York

Parliament of Kenya (2008) Official Hansard reports. Doc. Hansard 19.03.10A. Nairobi

Parliament of Kenya (2010) Official Hansard reports. Doc. Hansard 08.10.10A. Nairobi

Rasmussen J (2010) Outwitting the professor of politics? Mungiki narratives of political deception and their role in Kenyan politics. J East Afr Stud 4(3):435–449

Republic of Kenya (1992) Report of the Parliamentary Select Committee to investigate ethnic clashes in western and other parts of Kenya. Republic of Kenya, Nairobi

Republic of Kenya (1999) Report of the judicial commission appointed to inquire into the Tribal clashes in Kenya Nairobi. Republic of Kenya, Nairobi

Republic of Kenya (2003) The report of the Task Force on the Establishment of the Truth, Justice and Reconciliation Commission. Government Printer, Nairobi

Republic of Kenya (2008) Report of the Commission of Inquiry into Post-election Violence (CIPEV). Government Printer, Nairobi

Sanger C, Nottingham J (1963) The Kenya general election of 1963. J Mod Afr Stud 2(1):1–40

Southall R (2005) The Ndung'u report: land & graft in Kenya. Rev Afr Polit Econ 32(103):142–151

Steeves J (2006) Presidential succession in Kenya: the transition from Moi to Kibaki. Commonwealth Comp Polit 44(2):211–233

Tamarkin M (1979) From Kenyatta to Moi: the anatomy of a peaceful transition of power. Afr Today 3:21–37

Taussig-Rubbo M (2011) Pirate trials, the International Criminal Court, and Mob justice: reflections on post-colonial sovereignty in Kenya. Int J Hum Rights Humanitarianism Dev 2(1):51–74

Troup DW (1993) Elections and political legitimacy in Kenya. J Int Afr Inst 63(3):371–396

Troup DW (2003a) Kibaki's triumph: the Kenyan general elections of December 2002. Royal Institute of International Affairs Briefing Paper No. 3

Troup DW (2003b) The Kenya general election: December 27, 2002. Africa Notes No 14 2003. http://csis.org/files/media/csis/pubs/anotes_0301b.pdf. Accessed Sept 2014

Troup DW, Hornsby C (1998) Multi-party politics in Kenya: the Kenyatta and Moi States and the Triumph of the system in 1992 election. James Currey Publishers, Oxford

Tsuda M (2010) The experience of the national rainbow coalition (NARC): political parties in Kenya from 1991 to 2007. IDE Discussion Paper No. 222. http://ir.ide.go.jp/dspace/bitstream /2344/871/1/222.pdf. Accessed Sept 2014

United Nations Office of the High Commissioner for Human Rights (2008) Report from OHCHR Fact-finding Mission to Kenya, 6–28 Feb 2008

Wamwere K (2003a) Negative ethnicity: from bias to genocide. Seven Stories Press, New York

Wamwere K (2003b) Towards genocide in Kenya: the curse of negative ethnicity. MvuleAfrica Publishers, Nairobi

Wanyande P (2003) Alliance building in Kenya: the search for opposition unity. In: Oyugi WO et al (eds) The politics of transition in Kenya. Heinrich Böll Foundation, Nairobi

Part II
Post-Election Violence, Domestic Legal Options and Responses

Chapter 3
The Post-Election Violence and Immediate Aftermath

Abstract In the aftermath of the 2007 general elections in Kenya, widespread violence erupted. Subsequent inquiries by various commissions concluded that serious human rights violations, some of which amounting to crimes against humanity, had been committed, and that Kenya was duty-bound to investigate, prosecute and punish those responsible. This chapter describes the various aspects of the violence, and analyses the findings and recommendations of such inquiries, the main focus being the nature of the ensuing crimes and the agreed road map for domestic criminal accountability. It shows that the attempts to create a special tribunal for Kenya, which was at the core of the aforementioned road map, failed, and that such a failure resulted mainly from the lack of a political will at the domestic level. Most of the political elite favoured impunity, thereby frustrating the initiatives to implement the road map. However, the perception of the Kenyan civil society organizations and ordinary citizens remained that the crimes must not go unpunished, and that to achieve this, the masterminds of the violence, mostly politicians, must be prosecuted by an externally controlled judicial process, preferably the ICC.

Contents

© T.M.C. ASSER PRESS and the author 2015
S.F. Materu, *The Post-Election Violence in Kenya*,
International Criminal Justice Series 2, DOI 10.1007/978-94-6265-041-1_3

3.1 Introductory Remarks

Kenya's fourth multi-party general elections were held on 27 December 2007.[1] Three presidential candidates, namely Mwai Kibaki, Raila Odinga and Kalonzo Musyoka, commanded significant popular support,[2] mostly from their respective ethnic communities.[3] The management of the electoral process was entrusted to the then Electoral Commission of Kenya[4] whose members had been appointed by the President.[5] As it prepared to manage the 2007 elections, the electoral commission had significantly lost the confidence and trust of many Kenyans.[6] This mistrust resulted partly from the fact that President Kibaki, who himself was not only a candidate in the elections but also a leader of a contesting political party, had a *de jure* discretion in appointing the members of the commission.[7] Therefore, even prior to the election date, scepticism and suspicion had already started to mount.

---

[1] These were presidential, parliamentary and civic elections. In total, there were nine presidential candidates, 2,548 candidates contesting for 310 parliamentary seats and 15,332 candidates contesting for 2,500 civic local authority seats. See Commonwealth Secretariat 2008, p. 28.

[2] Kibaki and Odinga had almost equal amount of support. Two weeks before the elections, opinion poll showed that the two were "virtually tied", commanding 44 and 43 % of support, respectively. See East African Standard, 19 December 2007; Gallup, 17 December 2007.

[3] See United Nations High Commissioner for Human Rights 2008, p. 7. E.g., a poll revealed that "93 % of registered Luo voters planned to vote for Odinga, a Luo; 92 % of Kikuyus to vote for Kibaki, a Kikuyu; and 78 % of Kambas were for Musyoka, a Kamba". See Gallup, 21 November 2007.

[4] See Constitution of Kenya of 1963, Article 41.

[5] No legal criteria were laid down for the President to follow in appointing of commissioners, save for the Chairman and Vice Chairman who were only supposed to be individuals with qualifications equal to those of High Court or Court of Appeal Judges. The President could also cancel the appointment of any commissioner by forming a five-member tribunal of his choice to advise him accordingly. See Ibid.

[6] E.g., such confidence had dropped from 60 % in 2006 to only 24 % in 2008. See Gallup 30 October 2008.

[7] See Kenya National Commission on Human Rights 2008, para 57; Republic of Kenya 2008b, pp. 30 and 31.

3.2 The Violence

3.2.1 Immediate Trigger

Prior to the election date, during the campaigns, some isolated incidents of violence had occurred, which reportedly claimed the lives of 70 people and displaced 2,000 others.[8] But the "post-election violence" per se commenced on 30 December 2007, the day on which the Kenya Electoral Commission announced Mwai Kibaki the winner of the just concluded presidential election.[9] Following this announcement, tensions arose, as allegations emerged that there had been large-scale rigging of the election, mostly levelled against the Party of National Unity (PNU), Kibaki's party alliance.[10]

Two main factors stirred the tensions. The first factor was the controversy contained in the utterances of the Chairman of the electoral commission, Samuel Kivuitu. He declared publicly that although it was he who had announced the presidential results, he "could not say for sure if Kibaki had won fairly".[11] He said that he announced the results "under pressure"[12]; and that he did not have "full control" of the electoral commission.[13] The second factor that intensified the tensions is the reports of different domestic and international official election observers. These observers stated categorically that the presidential vote counting and tallying processes were flawed or had been tempered with.[14] As a consequence, the general public also perceived the whole presidential election as dishonest.[15] As part of this uproar, different demands and calls were made, including, for example, calls for a ballot re-count.[16] Also, there was a demand by the Kenya Law Society (Bar Association) that Kibaki should step down immediately for lack of legitimacy.[17]

---

[8] See Kenya National Commission on Human Rights 2007, p. 6.

[9] According to the official results of the Electoral Commission, in the presidential election, Kibaki garnered 4,584,721 votes (46 %), Raila Odinga 4,352,903 votes (44 %) and Kalonzo Musyoka (ODM-Kenya) 879,903 votes (9 %). In the parliamentary elections, the ODM got 99 seats, PNU (43 seats), the ODM-K (16 seats) and KANU (14 seats). See International Republican institute 2007, pp. 41–50.

[10] E.g., see BBC News, 8 January 2008; BBC News, 31 December 2007.

[11] BBC News, 8 January 2008; Lynch 2009, p. 1.

[12] African Press International, 12 January 2008; The Standard, 2 January 2008.

[13] The Citizen, 30 December 2011.

[14] See, e.g. East African Community Observer Mission 2008; European Union Election Observation Mission 2008; International Republican Institute 2008, pp. 31–34; Kenya Elections Domestic Observation Forum 2007; Kenya Human Rights Commission 2008; Kenyans for Peace with Truth and Justice 2008; Pan-African Parliament 2008; Republic of Kenya 2008b, pp. 115–138.

[15] See Gallup, 30 October 2008.

[16] See Kanyinga 2011, p. 97.

[17] See Law Society of Kenya 2008.

Somehow Odinga's party, the Orange Democratic Movement (ODM), which had lost the election marginally, capitalized on the allegations made by these neutral observers to justify and consolidate its own claim that its victory had been "stolen". The Kenyan Constitution had a clear legal mechanism which could be used to challenge the announced presidential results in the High Court,[18] but the ODM denounced this mechanism publicly, alleging that the existing judiciary was not capable of rendering "impartial justice".[19] Instead, the ODM resorted to a "mass action" strategy, envisioning protests and demonstrations country wide. As part of this strategy, they also threatened to swear in Raila Odinga as the "people's president" if Kibaki did not agree to a re-run.[20]

These events led to confrontations between the supporters of the two parties, which escalated into ethnic clashes that plunged a big part of the country into the bloody violence.

3.2.2 Extent, Organization and Nature

The extent and magnitude of the physical violence was formidable. The violence took the form of attacks on civilians, involving acts which were *prima facie* crimes under the laws of Kenya. Official figures indicate that 1,133 people were murdered, 3,000 were raped and 350,000 others were internally displaced. Moreover, there were 3,561 incidents of grievous bodily injuries and 117,216 incidents of destruction of properties, including 41,000 houses.[21] Six provinces, namely Rift Valley, Nyanza, Central, Western, Nairobi and Coastal provinces, were most affected, but in varying degrees.[22] About 66 % of the deaths occurred in Rift Valley, 12 % in Nyanza and 11 % in Nairobi.[23]

Initially, the violence manifested itself merely as demonstrations to protest against the results which had just been announced. This was partly the immediate response to the "mass action" strategy called for by Odinga's party.[24] As such, it

---

[18] See Articles 10 and 44 of the Constitution of Kenya of 1963, read together with ss. 19–23 and 28–30 of the National Assembly and Presidential Elections Act (R.E 2009).

[19] Specifically, Odinga's party, ODM contended that it was "not possible to receive justice from a partisan judiciary that was known to subvert justice in electoral matters"; and that President Mwai Kibaki's appointment of new judges 2 days before the elections was done in "preparation for a biased consideration of the anticipated election petitions". See Kenya National Commission on Human Rights 2008, para 58; Republic of Kenya 2008b, p. 59. For a critical examination of the appointment and functioning of the then Kenyan judiciary see Mutua 2001, pp. 96 et seq.

[20] See Kenya National Commission on Human Rights 2008, paras 78 and 121.

[21] Republic of Kenya 2008a, pp. 345–352; Roberts 2009, p. 2.

[22] Kenya National Commission on Human Rights 2008, p. 34.

[23] See Republic of Kenya 2008a, p. 341. Also see UN Office of the High Commissioner for Human Rights 2008.

[24] Republic of Kenya 2008a, pp. 346 and 347.

involved either confrontations between PNU and ODM demonstrators, or between the demonstrators of these two parties and the Kenyan police, for example, in the Nairobi slums, Kisumu and Nakuru.[25]

However, subsequently, the violence soon acquired a pattern of massive attacks and retaliatory attacks directed against specific groups of people or their properties, the basis being, inter alia, victims' real or perceived political inclination, or their regional or ethnic origin or affiliation. This included, for instance, prior issuance of warnings to the victims; mobilization, acquisition, transportation and distribution of weapons;[26] barricading of roads in order to identify, kill or generally attack travellers from the "enemy" communities;[27] and taking of oath by youths to fight and kill, which oath was administered by tribal elders.[28] In some areas, such as Rift Valley, there was, allegedly, a prior marking or identification of specific homes and premises belonging to non-Kalenjins. The prior identification aimed at ensuring that the subsequent unleashing of attacks would only be directed against the properties of the "enemy" communities (non-Kalenjins) in that area.[29]

The underlying cause of the tribal violence was a clear nexus with long-time unresolved tribal land issues and negative ethnicity which had always been used by politicians to incite more divisions.[30] It was also fuelled by the general perception that since independence certain ethnic communities had been marginalized in various aspects because, among other things, they had not had their tribesman to lead the country. For instance, in the Rift Valley Province, a stronghold of the ODM during the 2007 elections, the violence targeted the "unwanted" communities, the Kikuyu (Kibaki's tribe) and other non-Kalenjin communities or groups, which were or were perceived to be PNU supporters.[31] Allegedly, the local political and traditional leaders, who were partly interested in settling their communities' long-standing grievances pertaining to land and other real and (or) perceived discrimination against the targeted victims, were largely involved.[32]

In retaliation, in the Central Province and Nairobi, which were PNU's strongholds, the Kikuyus, through their militia gang, *Mungiki,* attacked the Luos (Odinga's tribe) and Kalenjins, who were or were perceived to be ODM supporters.[33] Similarly, the armed *Mungiki* carried out attacks in Nakuru against "enemy" communities, inter alia, by beheading Luo men or forcefully circumcising them by using *pangas* and

---

[25] See Republic of Kenya 2008a, p. 96; UN Office of the High Commissioner for Human Rights 2008, pp. 8 and 9.

[26] Republic of Kenya 2008a, p. 347.

[27] Kenya National Commission on Human Rights 2008, para 4.

[28] Ibid., paras 214, 307, 331, 523 and 537.

[29] Ibid., para 204.

[30] See Ibid., pp. 16–27. Also see Human Rights Watch 2008a, pp. 11–20; Republic of Kenya 2008a, pp. 20–36; UN Office of the High Commissioner for Human Rights 2008, pp. 5–7.

[31] Republic of Kenya 2008a, pp. 92 and 97.

[32] UN Office of the High Commissioner for Human Rights 2008, pp. 9 and 10.

[33] Ibid., p. 3.

broken bottles.[34] In preparation for these attacks, prior plans had reportedly been in place, including one for allegedly recruitment of 300 new members into the *Mungiki* specifically for this task. Moreover, intelligence reports revealed that local leaders and Kikuyu businessmen in Nakuru had conducted fund-raising meetings to raise money for financing the revenge or attacks against the Luo, Luhya and Kalenjin.[35]

Not all atrocities in this violence resulted from civilians attacking fellow civilians. The role of the police during the violence is noteworthy. It has been reported that, generally, the role of the police in this respect oscillated between being praiseworthy and blameworthy. For example, it is said that in Rift Valley, the outbreak of the violence was so sudden that it caught the police "totally unprepared", and that they were consequently "overwhelmed" by the number of Kalenjin attackers.[36] The reaction of the police in this area has been described as "chaotic"—one in which *some* police officers joined the attackers, while others "bravely saved lives".[37]

However, evidence points to the police being implicated in some of the atrocities. It is common knowledge that the principal function of the police in any jurisdiction is to ensure the safety of citizens and their properties. On the contrary, some of the members of the Kenyan police force are accused of having participated directly in the commission of crimes during the violence by, inter alia, using excessive force. They also allegedly participated by omission, which indirectly encouraged the civilian perpetrators to commit the atrocities.[38] As it has been rightly noted, this has cast doubt on the contention that "the post-election violence was a citizen-to-citizen violence".[39]

For example, the Waki Commission (see infra Sect. 3.4.1) found that about 80 % of all deaths through gunshots in Nyanza and Western Provinces were caused by the police.[40] Although there were claims that guns had been acquired and distributed to the ordinary citizens for the purposes of the violence, the Commission concluded that country wide, *all* recorded gunshots leading to deaths or injuries were reported to have come from the police.[41] Members of the police force were also allegedly involved directly in sexual violence, 26 % of all reported rape cases against women having been allegedly committed by police officers.[42]

Furthermore, both Human Rights Watch and the Waki Commission made three serious allegations against the police in connection with the post-election violence. First, it is alleged that there was an unofficial "shoot to kill" policy that was being

---

[34] Republic of Kenya 2008a, pp. 102 and 106.

[35] Ibid., pp. 105, 106 and 117.

[36] Ibid., p. 89.

[37] Ibid., p. 76.

[38] See Ibid., pp. 89–91; UN Office of the High Commissioner for Human Rights 2008, pp. 10 and 11.

[39] Republic of Kenya 2008a, p. 346.

[40] Human Rights Watch 2008a, p. 27; Ibid., pp. 342–343.

[41] Republic of Kenya 2008a, p. 346.

[42] See Human Rights Watch 2011a, p. 22. For detailed information on members of the security agencies as perpetrators of sexual violence, see Heinrich Böll Stiftung 2009; Republic of Kenya 2008a, pp. 252–257.

implemented; second, that there was a manifestation of politicized commands which entailed, inter alia, non-interference whenever pro-government mobs committed crimes against the opposition (suggesting that the leadership of the police force was pro-PNU); and third, that there was "inaction" on the part of the police whenever complaints from victims were received in Molo, Naivasha and Eldoret, where the police allegedly sided with the perpetrators.[43] Allegedly also, the police did not take any pre-emptive action in Nakuru, even though they had prior information of some planned attacks.[44] In the Coastal province, the police allegedly engaged in a kind of a "loot-but-don't-kill policy", inferred from their failure to intervene, allegedly even when they were "clearly available and present".[45]

All the atrocities committed during the post-election violence were indisputably shocking and horrendous. However, some specific incidents that occurred have been referred to as "most tragic" or "most terrifying", while others have specifically been most cited in the literature or widely reported by the media. This is due to the gruesome manner in which these particular incidents were carried out, the number or type of victims involved, etc.

One such incident happened in Kiambaa area in Rift Valley province. On 31 December 2007, between 200 and 3,500 armed Kalenjin members raided and torched the Kiambaa settlement area in Eldoret, predominantly inhabited by Kikuyus. The residents were forced to flee. Some of them sought refuge in a church building in the locality, the only place they considered safe in the circumstances. On New Year's Day 2008, the raiders set the church on fire. About 35 people, mostly women and children, died in the fire, 50 were severely wounded, and seven others, who tried to escape, were hacked to death.[46] A similar incident happened on 27 January 2008 in Naivasha. Some organized members of the *Mungiki*, targeting Luo properties, burnt a house belonging to a Luo in which 19 people, including women, children and two infants, died.[47] Another incident involved a catholic priest, Michael Kamau (a Kikuyu), who was killed by Kalenjin attackers on 26 January 2008 at a road block. The priest was travelling from Nandi to Nakuru and on the way helped two persons who were fleeing the violence by giving them a lift in his car.[48]

There were many other well-documented incidents of a similar nature that involved shocking civilian-to-civilian violence.[49] But what is indisputably clear is that this violence was "more than a mere juxtaposition of citizen-to-citizen

---

[43] Human Rights Watch 2008a, p. 25. Cf. Republic of Kenya 2008a, p. 421.

[44] Republic of Kenya 2008a, pp. 108–112 and 424.

[45] Ibid., p. 424.

[46] See Human Rights Watch 2008a, p. 41 and Kenya National Commission on Human Rights 2008, paras 237–243.

[47] See Human Rights Watch 2008a, pp. 45–47.

[48] Ibid., p. 94.

[49] See Ibid., pp. 35–56; Kenya National Commission on Human Rights 2008, Chapter 4 (see esp. illustrative text boxes at pp. 44, 55, and 87); Republic of Kenya 2008a, Chapters 3–6.

opportunistic assaults". Rather, it entailed coordinated or organized attacks on civilians "based on their ethnicity and political leanings".[50] Thus, the ethnic or political affiliations of both the perpetrators and the victims mattered.

3.2.3 Incitement to Violence

Various incidents and statements that were *prima facie* incitement to violence were reported, mostly in the Rift Valley and Central provinces. Similarly, attempted ethnic cleansing (see infra Sect. 3.4.3.1) was reported. In the Rift Valley province, whose original inhabitants are Kalenjins, the Kikuyus and non-Kalenjins in general were (still are) viewed as "invaders" on the land.[51] Among other reasons, most Kalenjins in this area supported the ODM in the 2007 elections apparently believing that its victory would enable them reclaim their "stolen" land.[52] As a result, hate speech from local politicians, tribal leaders and a section of the media dominated against the "alien" tribes in the area, mostly against the Kikuyu. The Kalenjin local leaders allegedly told their people to "remove the roots", and that they had "a snake (Kikuyus) to get rid of".[53] Allegedly, high-profile ODM leaders, including Raila Odinga and William Ruto, once asked the Kalenjin community to remove all "madoadoa" (stains) from "Rift Valley".[54]

One should not at all ignore the role of vernacular radio stations (broadcasting in tribal languages) in inciting the violence. Arguably, their role could be similar to that of the Kigali-based Radio, *Télévision Libre des Milles Collines*, which was used in inciting the Hutus against the Tutsis during the Rwandan genocide of 1994.[55] Reference to vernacular radio stations here excludes the mainstream national media, which comprise newspapers, radio and television stations broadcasting in English and Kiswahili, Kenya's official languages. This category of media, the English and Kiswahili media, is usually not aimed for listeners or readers from one specific ethnic group or region. Thus, media in this category has been absolved from accusations of any negative role in the violence.[56]

The role of four vernacular radio stations, namely *KASS FM* (Kalenjin station), *Inoor* and *Kameme* (Kikuyu stations) and *Lake Victoria FM* (Luo station), was particularly most notorious in spreading the hate speech. These stations did not

---

[50] Republic of Kenya 2008a, p. vii.

[51] Kenya Truth, Justice and Reconciliation Commission Report 2013, Vol. IV, para 264.

[52] But note that Kenya had been under a Kalenjin President (Moi) for 23 years, but the Kalenjins had not been able to "reclaim" their "invaded" land.

[53] Human Rights Watch 2008a, p. 36.

[54] See Republic of Kenya 2008a, p. 92.

[55] IRIN News, 22 January 2008.

[56] See Fackler et al. 2011 for a detailed analysis of the role of the Kenyan media during the violence.

necessarily disseminate hate speech directly through their presenters. Rather, they are blamed for having indirectly sanctioned or condoned the hate speech by recklessly or intentionally *failing to prevent* their guests or calling listeners from doing so.[57] For example, KASS FM is accused of having aired several appeals by Kalenjin callers carrying connotative implications for "people of the milk" (the Kalenjin) to "cut grass" (i.e. clear the land by removing the Kikuyus) and "reclaim our land".[58] In its call-in programmes, callers also referred to the Kikuyus in the Rift Valley province as "settlers", "mongoose [that] has come and stolen our chicken"; and also talked about the need to "get rid of the weeds". The Luo station, Lake Victoria FM, is alleged to have played a song with a metaphorical reference to the "leadership of baboons", insinuating the leadership by Kikuyus (Kibaki). *Kameme FM* on its part played a derogatory Kikuyu song about "the beasts from the west", connoting the tribes from Western and Nyanza provinces, including Luos.[59]

Other means were also used to disseminate hate speech and incitement to persecute the targets. For example, text messages and leaflets were distributed in Western Province urging all the "Mount Kenya mafia"[60] to leave the area. One quoted leaflet read:

> Notice to all landlords. Please take note that no Mount Kenya Mafia is your tenant lest you face the consequences. Avail quit notices to them immediately with no hesitation. Comply immediately![61]

A text message which allegedly circulated among the Kikuyus in Nairobi in mid-January 2008 incited retaliatory attacks. It partly read:

> We say no more innocent kikuyu blood will be shed. We will slaughter them right here in the capital city. For justice, compile a list of all Luos and Kaleos [slang for kalenjins] you know at work, your estate, anywhere in Nairobi, plus where and how their children go to school. We will give you a number to text this info.[62]

It is believed that the hate speech so disseminated partly contributed and shaped the pattern of the violence in various parts of Kenya whereby the incited ethnic groups targeted each other.

---

[57] Human Rights Watch 2008a, p. 36.

[58] Ibid., p. 37; IRIN News, 22 January 2008.

[59] IRIN News, 22 January 2008 (noting that similar hate speeches from vernacular radio stations dominated also during the 2005 constitutional referendum as a result of which KASS FM was temporarily suspended on allegations that it was inciting violence). Cf. Republic of Kenya 2008a, p. 41.

[60] This refers to the closely intertwined Kikuyu, Embu and Meru people who inhabit Kenya's Central Province, who are known for their Gikuyu, Embu and Meru Association (GEMA), an influential ethnic association in politics, and allegedly very close to Kikuyu-backed presidents, Jomo Kenyatta and Mwai Kibaki. See BBC News, 14 April 2006. This is reportedly comparable to the KAMATUSA (Kalenjin, Maasai, Turkana and Samburu) association that backed Moi's rule. See Republic of Kenya 2008a, pp. 25–26.

[61] See IRIN News, 22 January 2008.

[62] Ibid.

3.3 Mediation Process

In order to stop the humanitarian crisis in Kenya, the African Union (AU) brokered a mediation process[63] through the Panel of African Eminent Personalities, under the chairmanship of the former UN Secretary General Kofi Anan.[64] On 29 January 2008, the Panel managed to engage the PNU and ODM in this process which was carried out within a framework called the Kenya National Dialogue and Reconciliation (KNDR). This initiative entailed, inter alia, a series of negotiations and agreements aimed at, first and foremost, implementing an immediate "cease-fire" before setting a long-term programme to secure lasting peace, stability, justice and reconciliation.[65] To this effect, on 1 February 2008, the negotiating parties arrived at the annotated agenda items and the timetable for implementation,[66] and subsequently, issued public Statements on specific agreed measures to be taken on each agenda.[67] As part of the Dialogue, three possibilities, namely a court petition to challenge the results, a ballot re-count and a rerun, were discussed, but were all dismissed as being unsuited in the circumstances to resolve the disputed presidential results.[68] Since the bone of contention was known to be the fight for political power, the mediators suggested a political compromise as an immediate solution to achieve "ceasefire". As part of this compromise, the PNU and ODM agreed to let bygones be bygones—to leave the presidency to Mwai Kibaki, regardless of the controversy surrounding his victory, and work together in a coalition government.[69]

The agreement on the formation of a coalition government was signed by Raila Odinga and Mwai Kibaki on behalf of their parties on 28 February 2008.[70] The agreement entailed two things: First, they agreed on the amendment of the existing Kenyan

---

[63] See further Lindenmayer and Kaye 2009.

[64] Other members were Benjamin Mkapa, former President of the United Republic of Tanzania and Graça Machel, former First Lady of Mozambique. See Kofi Anan Foundation 2009, p. 1.

[65] Each party appointed a negotiating team of five members. See KNDR Negotiating Team at http://www.dialoguekenya.org/index.php/negotiating-team.html. Accessed September 2014.

[66] See KNDR, Annotated Agenda and Timetable. http://www.dialoguekenya.org/Agreements/1%20February%202008%20-Annotated%20Agenda%20for%20the%20Kenya%20Dialogue%20and%20Reconciliation.pdf. Accessed September 2014. Also see Kofi Anan Foundation 2009, pp. 2 and 3.

[67] See, e.g. KNDR Statements on: agreed security measures at http://www.dialoguekenya.org/Agreements/Agreed%20Statement%20on%20Security%20Measures.pdf; how to address humanitarian crisis http://www.dialoguekenya.org/Agreements/4%20February%202008-Agreed%20Statement%20on%20Measures%20to%20Address%20Humanitarian%20Crisis.pdf; and how to resolve the political crisis http://www.dialoguekenya.org/Agreements/14%20February%202008-Agreed%20Statement%20on%20How%20to%20Resolve%20Political%20Crisis.pdf. All links accessed September 2014.

[68] See agreed statement on how to resolve the political crisis at http://www.dialoguekenya.org/Agreements/14%20February%202008-Agreed%20Statement%20on%20How%20to%20Resolve%20Political%20Crisis.pdf. Accessed September 2014.

[69] Ibid.

[70] Kenya National Dialogue and Reconciliation 2008a.

Constitution to create the new posts of Prime Minister and two Deputies.[71] Second, they also agreed that the power-sharing deal was only a temporary arrangement[72] whose aim was to create a suitable environment for the implementation of the other agreed mechanisms aimed at achieving lasting justice, healing and reconciliation.[73] On the basis of this understanding, the coalition government was formed by amending the Constitution through the National Accord and Reconciliation Act of 2008.[74] Raila Odinga became its Prime Minister while Mwai Kibaki remained President.

3.4 Inquiries into the Violence and Road Map for Criminal Accountability

3.4.1 Commission of Enquiry into the Post-Election Violence

As part of the Kenya National Dialogue and Reconciliation negotiations, on 4 March 2008, the leaders of the coalition government agreed on the formation of an independent Commission of Inquiry into the Post-election Violence.[75] The commission was appointed accordingly,[76] and on 23 May 2008, three commissioners were appointed to work under the chairmanship of Kenyan Court of Appeal Judge, Philip Waki.[77] The commission (hereafter "Waki Commission") was mandated to investigate the 2007–2008 post-election violence and, as part of its broad mandate, to recommend measures aimed at "bringing to justice the individuals who committed criminal acts during the violence".[78] Being a quasi-judicial body, the commis-

---

[71] By this agreement, the leader of the party with majority in Parliament (ODM) would become Prime Minister, while an equal number of other cabinet ministers would be nominated from both sides of the coalition government through consultation. See Ibid., p. 1.

[72] It was agreed that the coalition government would be dissolved under the following three circumstances: When the Tenth Parliament (2007–2012 phase) was dissolved; or if the parties agreed in writing to dissolve the coalition; or if one partner in the government withdrew from the coalition. See Ibid., p. 2.

[73] Ibid., Preamble.

[74] Act No. 4 of 2008: commencement date: 20 March 2008.

[75] Kenya National Dialogue and Reconciliation 2008b.

[76] Commissions of enquiry in Kenya are regulated under the Commissions of Inquiry Act, Cap. 102 (R.E. 2009).

[77] Apart from Justice Waki, the two other commissioners were Gavin Alistair MCFadyen, a former Police Assistant Commissioner in New Zealand and Pascal K. Kambale, a lawyer from the Democratic Republic of the Congo. George Mong'are Kegoroas, an advocate of the High Court of Kenya and Kenyan Section Director of the International Commission of Jurists, was appointed as Secretary to the Commission, while David Shikomera Majanja, advocate of the High Court of Kenya, was appointed as Counsel to assist the Commission. See Kenya GN No. 4473, Vol. CX-No. 4, 23 May 2008.

[78] See Kenya GN No. 4474, Vol. CX-No. 41, 23 May 2008.

sion was also empowered to summon any person to testify on oath or to bring along any document, and to hold public or private hearings.[79] The commission took an oath of office to commence its work officially on 3 June 2008, compiled and published its final report ("Waki Report") on 15 October 2008.

3.4.2 Other Inquiries

There are other inquiries into the post-election violence which were conducted independently of the inquiry by the Waki Commission. Such inquiries mattered to the Waki Commission because, according to its terms of reference, the Waki Commission could (as it actually did), rely, inter alia, on the findings of "other inquiries" to corroborate its own findings.[80]

One such inquiry was conducted by the Kenya National Commission on Human Rights, an autonomous statutory body[81] which acts as a watchdog over the government in furtherance of the protection and promotion of human rights in Kenya.[82] One of the statutory mandates of the Kenya National Commission on Human Rights is "to investigate, on its own initiative or upon a complaint made by any person or group of persons, the violation of any human rights".[83] The inquiry into the post-election violence was conducted pursuant to this mandate, and was conducted simultaneously with that of the Waki Commission. A detailed final report was published on 15 August 2008, 2 months prior to that of the Waki Commission.[84]

Two other important inquiries into the violence were conducted under the auspices of the United Nations (UN). One such inquiry was that of the United Nations Office of the High Commissioner for Human Rights (UNHCHR), which looked into the violations of human rights in Kenya committed during the post-election violence. The inquiry was conducted during the currency of the violence, from 6 to 28 February 2008, and a final report was published accordingly.[85] Another UN-mandated inquiry was conducted by the UN's fact-finding mission between 16 and 25 February 2009, 1 year after the violence. It was conducted by the UN's Special Rapporteur on Extrajudicial Summary and Arbitrary Executions, Philip Alston. The scope of this inquiry covered, but extended beyond, the post-election violence. It also covered the killings by the police and the violence in the Mount Elgon District. The report of this inquiry was published on 26 May 2009.[86]

---

[79] Ibid.

[80] Ibid.

[81] See Kenya National Commission on Human Rights Act, No. 9 of 2002.

[82] More information about the Kenya National Commission on Human Rights can be found on its website http://www.knchr.org/. Accessed September 2014.

[83] Kenya National Commission on Human Rights Act, s. 16(1)(a).

[84] See Kenya National Commission on Human Rights 2008.

[85] See UN Office of the High Commissioner for Human Rights 2008.

[86] See UN General Assembly 2009.

Lastly, Human Rights Watch (HRW) conducted an inquiry into the violence through two missions between January and February 2008, in which 200 people, including the victims, witnesses, perpetrators, the police, politicians and other stakeholders, participated. A consolidated report was published on 16 March 2008.[87]

3.4.3 Findings of the Inquiries: Were Crimes Under International Law Committed?

The inquiries never hesitated to conclude outrightly that crimes under the domestic laws of Kenya had obviously been committed. What was not so obvious, however, was whether crimes under international law had also been committed. The following subsections present the considerations and findings of these inquiries with respect to the three core crimes of genocide, crimes against humanity and war crimes.

3.4.3.1 Genocide

When the post-election violence ended, some local and international commentators confusingly made reference to "genocide" as though it had just occurred in Kenya.[88] The Waki Commission, however, did not dwell on this subject at all. In fact, even the word "genocide" does not appear anywhere in the Waki Report. On its part, the Kenya National Commission on Human Rights made a specific inquiry into this matter and reached an unequivocal and non-contradictory conclusion that genocide did not occur.[89] However, both the Waki Commission and the Kenya National Commission on Human Rights made a finding that attempted "ethnic cleansing" took place in Kenya, for example, in Rift Valley.[90]

The literature correctly suggests that the current social relations among different communities in Kenya make the risk of genocide *against an ethnic group* very high.[91] This reality notwithstanding, those who made reference to "genocide" in the context of the post-election violence in Kenya confused the two related but different notions of "genocide" and "ethnic cleansing". The difference between these two notions lies, inter alia, in their nature and status under international law. While genocide *as such* is a crime under international law, ethnic cleansing is not. In fact, the latter is not even a legal concept yet, even though it is becoming increasingly common. In terms of definition, "ethnic cleansing" refers to acts or omissions

---

[87] See Human Rights Watch 2008a.

[88] See, e.g. Daily Nation, 1 December 2008; The Telegraph, 3 January 2008.

[89] Kenya National Commission on Human Rights 2008, para 634.

[90] Kenya National Commission on Human Rights 2008, para 553; Republic of Kenya 2008a, pp. 91–95.

[91] See, e.g. Sentinel Project for Genocide Prevention 2011; Wamwere 2003.

whose aim is to render an area "ethnically homogenous by using force or intimidation to remove from a given area persons of another ethnic or religious group".
More specifically, ethnic cleansing involves:

> A purposeful policy designed by one ethnic group to remove by violent and terror-inspir-
> ing means the civilian population of another ethnic group or religious group from certain
> geographical areas. To a large extent, it is carried out in the name of misguided national-
> ism, historic grievances and a powerful driving sense of revenge.[92]

Going by the definitions above, and in view of the patterns of events during the
post-election violence, one can agree to the contention that ethnic cleansing happened or was at least attempted in some parts of Kenya, especially in the form of
attacks and forceful removal of the non-Kalenjins from Rift Valley. Apparently, the
purpose of these attacks was twofold: (i) to create a homogenous voting bloc in
support of the candidates from the respective ethnic groups; and (ii) to force the
members of the targeted ethnic groups (considered as land "invaders") to leave
Rift Valley, so that the Kalenjins could exclusively occupy their ancestral land. But
as the Kenya National Commission on Human Rights stressed, there is no indication whatsoever that the attacks were done with a *genocidal intent.*[93] That is to
say, for that conduct to have qualified as "genocide", the attackers must have committed the criminal acts with the "the intent to destroy, in whole or in part, a
national, ethnical, racial or religious group, as such".[94] This intent cannot be
established with regard to Kenya.

In conclusion therefore, it can be stated that, *prima facie,* the attackers' conduct, which amounted to attempted ethnic cleansing, could possibly qualify as
crimes against humanity. It, however, does not fulfil the legal requirements for
genocide. Therefore, as far as Kenya's post-election violence is concerned, the
crime of genocide does not merit further consideration.

3.4.3.2 Crimes Against Humanity

Unlike genocide, crimes against humanity have received a deserved attention with
regard to Kenya's post-election violence. Barely a week into the violence, by 3
January 2008, the then Kenya's Attorney General, Amos Wako, had already
formed an opinion that until then the violence had been "very close to … crimes
against humanity".[95] Moreover, the findings from the aforementioned inquiries on

---

[92] See United Nations Security Council 1994, p. 33 (defining the concept in the context of the
conflict in the former Yugoslavia). Also see Hayde, 1996, p. 733; Ratner et al. 2009, p. 30 (discussing this definition).

[93] Kenya National Commission on Human Rights 2008, para 633.

[94] Cf. Rome Statute of the International Criminal Court, A/CONF.183/9, 17 July 1998 (hereafter "ICC, Statute"), Article 6; Convention on the Prevention and Punishment of the Crime of
Genocide, UNGA Res. 260 (III) A, 9 December 1948, Article II.

[95] Republic of Kenya 2008a, p. 303.

whether crimes against humanity happened in Kenya are overwhelmingly in the affirmative, but are not necessarily very straightforward.

Having scrutinized the legal requirements for crimes against humanity, the Kenya National Commission on Human Rights made two findings as regards the crime. On the one hand, it concluded that the criminal acts committed during the post-election violence *might not* qualify as crimes against humanity *under the ICC Statute*, because according to the Statute, such acts must have been committed as part of "state or organizational policy".[96] The commission was unable to conclude affirmatively whether the acts committed during the violence would meet this definitional threshold requirement.[97] On the other hand, the commission concluded affirmatively that the acts qualified as crimes against humanity *under customary international law,* because under customary law, crimes against humanity do not necessarily require a link to a "state or organizational policy"[98] (cf. infra Sect. 6.4.2).

On its part, the Waki Commission took a more cautious approach. First, unlike the Kenya National Commission on Human Rights, the Waki Commission did not expressly make separate conclusions about crimes against humanity under the ICC Statute and under customary international law. Generally, the Waki Commission *impliedly* found that there was *a strong indication* that crimes against humanity had been committed, although it refrained from positively asserting so *solely* on the basis of the evidence it had gathered.[99] It stated as follows:

> The evidence the Commission has gathered so far is not, in our assessment, sufficient to meet the threshold of proof required for criminal matters in this country: that it be "beyond reasonable doubt". It may even fall short of the proof required for international crimes against humanity.[100]

Despite the finding above, the Waki Commission went on to suggest affirmatively in one of its main recommendations that the prosecution of crimes, "particularly crimes against humanity relating to the 2007 General Elections in Kenya", must be carried out.[101] As it stands, this recommendation does not necessarily contradict the finding of the commission reproduced in the paragraph quoted above. For critics could argue that if, in the first place, the commission was not even sure whether crimes against humanity had been committed, why then did it go on to recommend emphatically that they be prosecuted? But one has to note that the only thing the commission suggested in the paragraph quoted above is that the evidence it had gathered might not be sufficient as *proof beyond reasonable doubt,*

---

[96] Kenya National Commission on Human Rights 2008, paras 638–648.

[97] Ibid., para 648.

[98] Ibid., paras 641 and 658.

[99] The Commission was criticized for this seemingly uncertain finding. See, e.g. Musila 2009, p. 454 and The Standard, 23 November 2008.

[100] Republic of Kenya 2008a, p. 17 (emphasis original).

[101] Ibid., p. 472 (emphasis added).

which is the evidentiary standard required for a conviction in a criminal trial.[102] Thus, the Commission was only being cautious and taking cognizance of the fact that a proper criminal trial would require a very high threshold of evidence. But by recommending concrete measures for prosecution of "crimes against humanity" as such committed during the post-election violence, the Commission sent the clear message that on the basis of its inquiry there existed *all reasonable grounds* for it to believe that such crimes had been committed.

All other literature reviewed generally finds affirmatively that the atrocities committed in Kenya do qualify as crimes against humanity. But at this point, it is worthy stating that whether they qualify as such under the ICC statute or under international customary law is not very relevant: What is more relevant is that whatever their nature, they must not go unpunished. For that reason, crimes against humanity are further dealt with in Chap. 6.

3.4.3.3 War Crimes

There have been allegations, especially by Human Rights Watch, that war crimes were committed in Kenya, specifically in Mount Elgon district. On that basis, Human Rights Watch has consistently called for domestic and ICC investigations and prosecutions of the crimes, stressing that violence that happened in Mount Elgon district "shares many of the hallmarks of the post-election violence".[103] Human Rights Watch even published a special report entitled "war crimes in Kenya's Mount Elgon."[104] It is alleged that the Kenyan army and a militia called the Sabot Land Defence Force (SLDF) committed "war crimes" during a "fighting" in this area.[105] Human Rights Watch alleges that:

> Since the beginning of the joint army-police operation in March 2008, fighting in Mt. Elgon appears to have risen to the level of an internal armed conflict under international humanitarian law (the laws of war). This law is applicable in situations of armed conflict that rise above internal disturbances and tensions such as riots or sporadic acts of violence. Relevant law includes Article 3 common to the 1949 Geneva Conventions and customary international humanitarian law.[106]

As an indispensable legal element, war crimes require a nexus with an armed conflict of either an international or non-international character.[107] The paragraph reproduced above is an attempt by Human Rights Watch to establish that nexus. But as the paragraph clearly shows, the alleged violence in Mount Elgon district

---

[102] Ibid., p. 17.

[103] Human Rights Watch 2011b, p. 29.

[104] Human Rights Watch 2008b.

[105] Human Rights Watch 2008c, 2011b, p. 39.

[106] Human Rights Watch 2008b, p. 6.

[107] Werle 2009, pp. 373–376.

might have acquired the character of an internal armed conflict only "in March 2008". It is noteworthy, however, that in its broad context, the violence in Mount Elgon occurred between 2006 and June 2008. It thus started before the 2007 elections and continued even after the official "ceasefire" of the ensuing violence. As such, the Mount Elgon violence *partly* overlapped with the 2007–2008 post-election violence, specifically between December 2007 and February 2008. In other words, although the violence in Mount Elgon was partly subsumed in the post-election violence, the war crimes alleged by Human Rights Watch, assuming they occurred, were committed after 28 February 2008, which is to say that they fell outside the defined time frame of the 2007/2008 post-election violence.

The foregoing facts explain why the Waki Commission did not make any inquiry into or finding on war crimes. In fact, like the case is for the crime of genocide, the expression "war crimes" does not appear anywhere in the Waki Report. Apparently, this is due to the fact that the Waki Commission did not consider the violence in Mount Elgon as part of the "post-election violence" per se which it was specifically mandated to investigate. On its part, the Kenya National Commission on Human Rights stated that it decided not to inquire into war crimes, because "no credible allegations to that effect were ever made in relation to the post-election violence".[108]

Therefore, for purposes of the defined time frame for Kenya's post-election violence, i.e. 30 December 2007 to 28 February 2008, war crimes may be irrelevant. However, the violence in Mount Elgon will be revisited later in this book (see infra Sect. 6.3.3) because of its magnitude and in connection with the jurisdiction of the ICC. Here, the focus will go beyond the time frame of the post-election violence, in view of the broad and general temporal scope of ICC's investigation into the Kenya situation.

3.4.4 Agreement and Recommendations Pertaining to Criminal Accountability

The need and call for the prosecution of those who committed crimes during the post-election violence in Kenya permeates the literature. It emerges as the number one preferred accountability mechanism in comparison with other options such as a truth commission, reparations and amnesties, although these accountability mechanisms are not seen as mutually exclusive. Theoretically, prosecutions in the Kenyan context would serve two purposes. The first purpose is deterrence—to prevent similar violence in future. The second purpose is retribution—to break the tradition of impunity, especially for crimes associated with the political elite or the rich, who have previously been considered "too powerful" for the domestic courts to dare hold accountable for wrong doing.

---

[108] Kenya National Commission on Human Rights 2008, para 629.

During the mediation process, it was generally agreed that the criminal accountability issues would be determined according to the recommendations of what came to be the Waki Commission. The Waki Commission recommended that, first and foremost, domestic prosecutions of all the persons who took part in the organization, planning and direct perpetration of the violence must be done immediately after publishing its findings. To achieve this, the Commission specifically proposed an immediate creation of a Special Tribunal for Kenya (hereafter "Special Tribunal") that would "seek accountability against persons bearing the greatest responsibility for crimes, particularly crimes against humanity, relating to the 2007 General Elections in Kenya ... through the investigation, prosecution and adjudication of such crimes".[109] The Commission also proposed that the envisioned Special Tribunal make use of "all investigative material and witness statements and testimony collected and recorded" by the Commission for further investigations and prosecutions.[110]

It was recommended that the proposed structure and organization of the envisioned Special Tribunal be that of a "hybrid" nature. As such, it would entail an international component by way of inclusion of non-Kenyans in the positions of senior investigation and prosecution staff as well as judges.[111] In principle, it was agreed that the proposed Special Tribunal would apply the domestic laws of Kenya to prosecute the perpetrators of the alleged crimes. In order to make sure that the domestic legal framework was adequate for this purpose, the Waki Commission further proposed that the process of domestication of the ICC Statute, which had commenced before the violence but not completed, be fast-tracked so that the envisaged International Crimes Act could be applied retrospectively by the Special Tribunal.[112]

Moreover, as a prerequisite for effective investigation, prosecution and adjudication of the post-election violence cases, the Waki Commission proposed that several other legislative enactments be made in order to facilitate the work of the contemplated Special Tribunal. Firstly, it was recommended that potential witnesses must be assured of their protection through full utilization of Kenya's Witness Protection Act of 2006[113]; secondly, that the Freedom of Information Bill be drafted and enacted into law in order to facilitate full access to information by state and non-state actors, especially if such information might lead to arrest, detention and prosecution of the perpetrators[114]; and thirdly, that the existing Constitution of Kenya of 1963 be amended to entrench the Special Tribunal and give it constitutional legitimacy.[115]

---

[109] Republic of Kenya 2008a, p. 472.

[110] Ibid., p. 475.

[111] Ibid., pp. ix and 472.

[112] Ibid., pp. 472 and 476.

[113] Cap. 76 [R.E 2012].

[114] Republic of Kenya 2008a, p. 476.

[115] Ibid., p. 473.

The most potent recommendation of the Waki Commission was the one pertaining to the enforcement of its recommendation on criminal accountability. There are all indications that this specific recommendation was given with the view to ensuring that the Kenyan government would not view the report of the Waki Commission as yet another museum piece; or that the government would not give it yet another business-as-usual treatment. The reason for this observation is that when giving the recommendation, the Waki Commission was fully aware, as the Commission itself indicated, of the numerous previous similar reports and recommendations by other commissions of inquiry which had been disregarded and archived by the government without any implementation (see supra Sect. 2.5.3). The Waki Commission was, therefore, aware that in all those cases the government had deliberately chosen impunity in lieu of both criminal and political accountability.[116]

In order to circumvent this predicament which could in turn render its work nugatory, the Waki Commission cleverly fixed strict deadlines for the implementation of the recommendations, specifically those pertaining to criminal accountability of the perpetrators bearing major responsibility for the alleged crimes. Accordingly, an agreement on the formation of the Special Tribunal would be signed by the parties to the Agreement on National Accord and Reconciliation "within 60 days of the presentation of the Report of the Commission … to the Panel of Eminent African Personalities or the Panel's representative". Then a statute for the Special Tribunal would be enacted and put to effect "within further 45 days after the signing of the agreement". Lastly, the date of commencement and functioning of the Special Tribunal would be determined "within 30 days" after the statute of the Special Tribunal came to effect.[117]

The Commission articulated unequivocally the consequences that would flow from non-compliance with these strict deadlines. It stated:

> If either an agreement for the establishment of the Special Tribunal is not signed, or the Statute for the Special Tribunal fails to be enacted, or the Special Tribunal fails to commence functioning as contemplated …, or having commenced operating its purposes are subverted, a list containing names of and relevant information on those suspected to bear the greatest responsibility for crimes falling within the jurisdiction of the proposed Special Tribunal shall be forwarded to the Special Prosecutor [sic] of the International Criminal Court. The Special Prosecutor [sic] shall be requested to analyze the seriousness of the information received with a view to proceeding with an investigation and prosecuting such suspected persons.[118]

President Mwai Kibaki and Prime Minister Raila Odinga signed the *agreement for the implementation* of the recommendations of the Waki Commission on 16 December 2008.[119] This agreement was not merely a toothless dog that would not

---

[116] For extensive findings of the Commission on this aspect, see Ibid., pp. 443–454.

[117] Ibid., p. 473.

[118] Ibid.

[119] Kenya National Dialogue and Reconciliation 2008c.

bite: It was a document which was binding on the Kenyan government as part of the broad range of commitments made during the mediation process. The implementation of these recommendations was, for that matter, not an exclusive discretion of the Kenyan government or politicians, but rather, to a certain extent, externally controlled: It was partly in the hands of the AU mediation Panel, which was not only empowered but was actually prepared to invoke the intervention of the ICC if circumstances so dictated.

This arrangement earned the Waki Commission some praise. It was praised mainly for the good "innovation" that sealed all the possibilities of government opting for impunity. Bosire described it as "a coercive tactic to catalyze the domestic prosecutions".[120] The Kenyan *Daily Nation* (newspaper) described it as "clever" arrangement. The paper reported that, unlike the previous commissions of inquiry which, "always appealed to suspected perpetrators of crimes and their friends to investigate and prosecute themselves", the Waki Commission was not a waste of time and resources. The strength of the recommendation, according to the daily tabloid, lay in the fact that the Commission "went over its suspects' heads and roped in the international justice system over which the government had no control; and that in so doing, the Commission "showed astonishing ingenuity in anticipating and sealing every potential loophole that could serve as an escape hatch".[121]

3.5 The Proposed Special Tribunal for Kenya: An Overview

On 28 January 2009, the Kenyan coalition government drafted the Special Tribunal for Kenya Bill in order to "provide for the establishment, powers and functions" of the envisaged Special Tribunal.[122] In its Preamble, the Bill acknowledged the heinous nature of the crimes linked to the post-election violence.[123] While on the one hand the Bill reiterated that "such serious crimes should not go unpunished", it, on the other hand, affirmed that "these transgressions [could not] be properly addressed by [the ordinary Kenyan] judicial institutions due to procedural and other hindrances".[124] Thus, the expectation was that the envisioned Special Tribunal would be the best forum to address the crimes.

The Waki Commission had proposed that the Special Tribunal be "insulated from objections on constitutionality, and … [to] be anchored in the Constitution of Kenya."[125] The logical explanation for this proposal is that its implementation

---

[120] Bosire 2009.

[121] See Daily Nation, 1 September 2011.

[122] Special Tribunal for Kenya Bill, Preamble para 1.

[123] Ibid., Preamble para 2.

[124] Ibid., Preamble para 4.

[125] Republic of Kenya 2008a, p. 473, see specifically recommendation 6.

would give constitutional legitimacy to the Special Tribunal, for if it was not entrenched to the Constitution, the Tribunal would fall outside the constitutionally recognized hierarchy of courts in the Kenyan court system.[126] This would definitely make it prone to unconstitutionality attacks.

3.5.1 Salient Features of the Tribunal

3.5.1.1 Structure, Jurisdiction and Definition of Crimes

For reasons to be presented shortly, the proposed Special Tribunal for Kenya did not materialize. However, had its bill been passed into law, the resulting Tribunal would have had the following features.

It would have consisted of six organs: A Trial Chamber, an Appeals Chamber, Prosecutor, Registry, Defence Office and Special Magistrates.[127] Its composition would have included a minority of Kenyan judges and a majority of foreign judges[128]; a foreign Prosecutor and a foreign Registrar.[129] It would have exercised jurisdiction as follows: Its jurisdiction *materiae temporis* would have been limited to acts committed between 30 December 2007 and 28 February 2008 and, exceptionally, any act falling beyond this time frame, provided such an act had *a* nexus with the post-election violence[130]; its jurisdiction *ratione personae* would have been over both natural and legal persons; it would have enjoyed primacy of jurisdiction over the ordinary national courts; and would have had exclusive jurisdiction over the crimes connected to the post-election violence.[131] The Tribunal's jurisdiction *ratione*

---

[126] The Constitution of Kenya of 1963 provided for a two-tier court system. The first tier comprised a hierarchy of Kadhi's Courts (Article 66) with jurisdiction to "determine questions of Muslim law relating to personal status, marriage, divorce or inheritance in proceedings in which all the parties profess[ed] the Muslim religion" (Article 66(5).The second tier consisted of the Court of Appeal (highest) the High Court (second highest) and the Subordinate Courts plus Martial Courts (lowest, same level). See Constitution of Kenya of 1963, Articles 64, 60 and 65, respectively. The Parliament only had powers to establish subordinate courts that were subordinate to the High Court. Therefore, as the proposed Special Tribunal would fall outside this two-tier court system, there was a need to legitimize it by anchoring it in the Constitution. A similar step had been taken in 2008 when Article 60 of the 1963 Constitution was amended by the Constitution of Kenya (Amendment) Act No. 10 of 2008 (by adding Article 60A), thereby creating the Interim Independent Constitutional Dispute Resolution Court, whose role was to hear and determine matters arising from the Constitutional Review process which was in pipeline then.

[127] Special Tribunal for Kenya Bill, s. 3(3).

[128] This would have applied to the Trial and Appeals Chambers. See Ibid., ss. 16 and 17. The Special Magistracy would have been composed exclusively of Kenyan nationals.

[129] Ibid., ss. 30(3) and 31(3), respectively.

[130] Ibid., ss. 4, 5 and 6.

[131] Ibid., s. 7.

materiae would have been over four categories of crimes, namely "genocide", "gross violations of human rights", "crimes against humanity" and "other crimes".

Moreover, the Special Tribunal would have comprised three divisions: Special Magistrates, Trial Chamber and Appeals Chamber. The jurisdiction of the divisions would have been apportioned as follows: The Special Magistrates would have been responsible for trying the fourth category of crimes (in the list above), namely "other crimes". This category would have comprised all "ordinary" crimes under the domestic laws of Kenya, provided such crimes fell within the jurisdiction *ratione temporis* of the Tribunal.[132] The Trial Chamber would have been responsible for trying all persons bearing greatest responsibility for the first three categories of crimes, i.e. "genocide", "gross violations of human rights" and "crimes against humanity".[133] "Persons bearing the greatest responsibility" would have included those who were knowingly responsible for "planning, instigating, inciting, funding, ordering or providing other logistics which directly or indirectly facilitated the commission of the crimes." To determine whether a person fell within this category, the Special Tribunal would have had to consider "the leadership role or level of authority or decision-making power or influence of the person concerned and the gravity, severity, seriousness or scale of the crime committed".[134] Apart from its general appellate jurisdiction,[135] the Appeals Chamber would also have had jurisdiction to review its own judgements or those of the Trial Chamber.[136]

The definitions of some of the crimes were to be wider than those under customary or conventional international criminal law. For example, apart from the requirement that crimes against humanity be part of "a widespread or systematic attack against a civilian population", the Tribunal's definition would have further required the attack to have been done on national, regional, political, ethnical, racial, cultural or religious grounds. Neither the perpetrator's knowledge of the attack nor a state or organizational policy would have been a requirement for the crimes against humanity tried by the Special Tribunal. Moreover, the Tribunal would have prosecuted "harassment" and "destruction of property" as individual acts constituting crimes against humanity.[137]

---

[132] Ibid., s. 9(1)(ii).

[133] Ibid., s. 9(1)(a). As an exception, these categories of crimes would also be tried by the Special magistrates only if committed by people who did not fall within the Tribunal's definition of "persons bearing greatest responsibility". See s. 9(1)(b).

[134] Ibid., s. 2.

[135] Ibid., ss. 41(1) and 46(1).

[136] An application for review proceedings would be made if a new fact not known at the time of the closed proceedings was discovered and which apparently could have been a decisive factor in reaching a different decision. See Ibid., s. 42.

[137] The remaining acts would have been the same as those under Article 7 of the ICC Statute, except the crime of apartheid which was omitted. The included acts would have been murder, extermination, enslavement, deportation, deportation or forcible transfer of population, imprisonment, torture, rape and other forms of sexual violence, persecution and forced pregnancy.

Although violations of human rights are ordinarily imputed to state actors (through the actions of state agents, e.g. police), the Special Tribunal Bill implicitly recognized private actors (i.e. individuals acting in their personal capacities) as being able to commit such violations. Consequently, the category of "gross violation of human rights" tried by the Tribunal would have comprised six individual criminal acts the commission of which would have given rise to individual criminal responsibility. But interestingly, with only the exception of "enforced disappearance", the rest of the individual acts in this category would have overlapped with the individual acts falling under the category of "crimes against humanity". However, the only difference between the two categories would have been in the contextual elements: Unlike crimes against humanity, the act falling under the category "gross violations of human rights" would not have required proof of a "widespread or systematic attack".

As regards the crime of genocide, the definition proposed in the Bill was the same as the customary definition in the 1948 Genocide Convention.

3.5.1.2 Individual Criminal Responsibility

Individual criminal responsibility would have attached to any person who "planned, instigated, ordered, committed, or otherwise aided and abetted in the planning, preparation or execution of the crimes."[138] Furthermore, intentional contribution in "any other way" to the commission of the crimes by a group of persons with a common purpose or to individual criminality would also have given rise to individual criminal responsibility, provided that such contribution was made under any of the following three circumstances: (a) "with the aim of furthering general criminal activity, or purpose of the individual or group;" or (b) "with knowledge of the intention of the individual or group to commit the crime" or (c) if the contributor "ought to have known the intention of such individual or group".[139] Liability would also have arisen irrespective of the fact that the accused person acted in his official capacity or carried out superior or official orders.[140]

3.5.2 Evaluation

A hybrid tribunal for Kenya as a time-and-event-specific mechanism to prosecute crimes under international law would not have been a new phenomenon. Since 1993, about seven similar bodies have been formed as UN-mandated tribunals,

---

[138] Ibid., s. 14(1). Cf. ICC Statute, Article 25(3)(c).

[139] Special Tribunal for Kenya Bill, s. 14(2). Cf. ICC Statute, Article 25(3)(d).

[140] Ibid., s. 14(3), (4) and (5).

hybrid (internationalized) courts and others which were in a way "special" but non-internationalized.[141] As Bassiouni rightly observes, the "special" nature of such tribunals arises, inter alia, from their temporary existence and limited mandate to exercise jurisdiction over only specific crimes committed in a specific time frame.[142] Apart from the International Criminal Tribunal for Rwanda (ICTR) and International Criminal Tribunal for [the former] Yugoslavia (ICTY), which were established by the UN Security Council, tribunals of a nature similar to that of the proposed Special Tribunal for Kenya include the Special Court for Sierra Leone,[143] the Special Tribunal for Lebanon,[144] the Special Panels for Serious Crimes in East Timor,[145] the Extraordinary Chambers in the Courts of Cambodia,[146] the Special Panels for War Crimes in Bosnia and Herzegovina[147] and the Iraq's Special Tribunal for Crimes against Humanity.[148] Although the mode of establishment and their legal status under international law are not necessarily the same, one of their common denominators is the fact that all were formed to prosecute crimes committed prior to their creation.

As stated earlier, the Waki Commission had proposed that the domestication of the ICC Statute through the International Crimes Act (which was then at a bill stage) be fast-tracked in order to create a substantive law to be applied by the proposed Special Tribunal.[149] However, as already shown, the Kenyan authorities opted instead to include substantive law in the Special Tribunal Bill. This decision appears to have been the most correct approach for the following reasons.

The threshold for crimes against humanity in the proposed law for the envisioned Special Tribunal would have been potentially lower than that of the envisioned International Crimes Act of 2008, which, as will be seen later (see infra Sect. 4.3.2.2.2), applies the same standards, including the crime definitions of the ICC Statute. Consequently, more perpetrators would have been held liable under the Special Tribunal's statute than the case would have been if the Tribunal was to apply the fast-tracked International Crimes Act of 2008. One could take the definition of crimes against humanity as a clear example entailing a point of departure between the two. Unlike Kenya's International Crimes Act of 2008, the law of the Special Tribunal, as stated earlier, would not have required any knowledge of the

---

[141] See Bassiouni 2003, pp. 545–581; Romano et al. 2004; Werle 2009, pp. 26, 101–106.

[142] Bassiouni 5005, p. 364.

[143] For details see Cerone 2001–2002, pp. 379 et seq.; Cryer et al. 2001, pp. 435 et seq.; Dougherty 2004, pp. 311 et seq.; Frulli 2000, pp. 857 et seq.

[144] See Cockayne 2007, pp. 1–4; Jurdi 2007, pp. 1125 et seq.; Serra 2008, pp. 344 et seq.; Wierda et al. 2007, pp. 1065 et seq.

[145] See Cohen 2002; Dickinson 2003, pp. 295 et seq.; Suzzane 2003, pp. 245 et seq.

[146] See De Bertodano 2006, pp. 285 et seq.; Scheffer 2008; Williams 2004, pp. 227 et seq.

[147] See Bohlander 2003, pp. 59 et seq.; Garms and Pesche 2005, pp. 258 et seq.

[148] See Bassiouni 2005, pp. 327 et seq.; Heller 2006–2008, pp. 261 et seq. Newton 2005, pp. 863 et seq.; Tom 2005, pp. 899 et seq.

[149] Republic of Kenya 2008a, p. 476.

attack on the part of the perpetrator, nor would it have required the attack to have been made pursuant to a state or organizational policy. Also, as stated earlier, under the substantive law of the Special Tribunal statute, unlike the International Crimes Act, it would have been possible to prosecute "harassment" and "destruction of property" per se as specific acts constituting crimes against humanity.[150]

But given the magnitude of the post-election violence, and the need to fight impunity, it was paramount that a balance was stricken, at the domestic level, between two things. While on the one hand it was mandatory to prosecute (by abiding by due process requirements) the perpetrators of any conduct constituting core crimes under international law, it was, on the other hand, important to ensure that in doing so justice would not be hindered by procedural technicalities or sophistications entailed in the definitional requirements of the crimes. Apparently, in order to achieve this balance, it was pertinent that the thresholds of the crimes to be prosecuted by the contemplated special tribunal be lower, or that the scope of some of the crime definitions be made wider than that of the International Crimes Act of 2008, which, as stated above, adheres to the standards of the ICC Statute. In addition, the law for the special tribunal would have applied retroactively, while the International Crimes Act of 2008, as will be shown later (infra Sect. 4.3.2.2.4), is prospective in nature. Therefore, the former would have potentially covered crimes against humanity, war crimes and genocide, which were not expressly part of the Kenyan law when the violence erupted, but which were nevertheless crimes under customary international law.

At another level, the hybrid nature of the proposed special tribunal would have had two advantages over the use of Kenyan ordinary courts. First, it would have allowed foreigners with expertise and experience in the area of international criminal law to serve in the Kenya's judicial system. Second, the fact that the tribunal was to have its own staff and finances[151] would have expectedly fostered expeditious dispensation of justice in relation to cases specifically related to the post-election violence. Thus, with regard to trials carried out by the tribunal, the risk of diminishing the strength of the prosecution's case due to, for example, deaths of key witnesses, the fading of their memories, or loss of documentary evidence, would have been greatly mitigated. All this would not have been easily possible under the ordinary court system in Kenya where completion of cases, especially those involving serious criminal charges, takes very long time due to, among other factors, the backlog of cases.[152]

Lastly, being a hybrid court, the special tribunal would have probably commanded more credibility among Kenyans, especially the victims of the post-election

---

[150] Special Tribunal for Kenya Bill, s. 7.

[151] A Special Tribunal Fund receiving monetary support from the government and donors would have been created. See Ibid., ss. 58 and 59.

[152] According to Nancy Baraza, Deputy Chief Justice of Kenya, by the year 2011, there were cases where the accused persons had been in jail or remand for 15 or 20 years awaiting judgement. See Daily Nation, 13 October 2011. See also the Address by Chief Justice of Kenya at the Launch of the Judiciary Transformation Framework on 31 May 2012. http://kenyalaw.org/kl/index.php?id=156. Accessed August 2014.

violence, as compared to the ordinary courts. Even Justice Philip Waki, who himself was a senior member of the Kenyan Judiciary, acknowledged in his commission's report that prior to the post-election violence, the Kenyan Judiciary had "acquired the notoriety of losing the confidence and trust of those it must serve because of the perception that it [was] not independent as an institution even if *some* individual members were".[153] Also, as stated above, it was because of the same perception or reason that the ODM declined to challenge the 2007 presidential results in court and resorted to its "mass action" strategy.[154]

3.5.3 Failed Attempts to Establish Special Tribunal

At the Bill stage, the proposed Special Tribunal was already described as "the best option" which was more preferable than even "to a transfer of jurisdiction outside of Kenya."[155] Unfortunately, the Bill was not passed into law. The following part reveals why this was the case, and analyses its implications.

As proposed, the Kenyan government drafted the Constitution of Kenya (Amendment) Bill of 2009, which proposed insertion of Article 3A to the Constitution of Kenya of 1963 to empower the Parliament to establish the Special Tribunal. On 29 January 2009, two bills, one for the amendment of the Constitution and the other for the establishment of the Tribunal, were together introduced in Parliament. However, the two bills were both rejected by Parliament on 11 February 2009. Two new bills for the Tribunal prepared by the government did not reach Parliament, because they were rejected at cabinet level on 14 July 2009 and 30 July 2009, respectively. It has been said that even the first set of bills would not have reached Parliament had President Kibaki and Prime Minister Odinga not "directed" the cabinet members belonging to their respective parties to vote for it at the cabinet level.[156]

Two groups of MPs were against the proposed Special Tribunal and favoured the "The Hague option" for two completely different motives. The first and smaller group comprised the so-called "reform-minded parliamentarians" whose motive was also shared by the Kenyan civil society and public in general. This group genuinely believed that justice could only be rendered through an external process, namely the ICC, because national judicial processes could be easily manipulated by those with "vested interests".[157] The second and bigger group of

---

[153] See Republic of Kenya 2008a, pp. 460–601 (emphasis added). The lack of independence of the Kenyan judiciary was also acknowledged by Justice Jackton Ojwang of the Kenyan High Court. See Ojwang 2008–2010.

[154] Republic of Kenya 2008a, p. 461.

[155] Wainaina and Chepng'etich 2009.

[156] The Star, 12 March 2011 (pointing out that the two leaders wrote a letter to each of the Ministers and Assistant Ministers "directing" them to vote in favour of the bill).

[157] International Crisis Group 2012, p. 6.

MPs which was against the idea of a special tribunal was that of MPs who decided to play the political card. This group thought that a domestic tribunal would be too close in terms of time and geography. They conceived the ICC as a "remote threat" at the time, for they thought it would take protracted time for its processes to start, thereby giving them ample time to avoid accountability and to contest for political seats again in the 2013 elections.[158]

In rejecting both the Prime Minister's and Justice Minister's earnest calls for the Parliament to pass the Special Tribunal bill, Mr. Isaac Ruto (MP), supported by the other MPs in the second, bigger group, is on official record as having said to the Prime Minister: "Do not be vague, say Hague".[159] This statement indicated that those in this group were clear about their preference, though not genuinely so, for the "The Hague option". What is particularly interesting is that several cabinet members, including the former Education Minister, William Ruto, and Uhuru Kenyatta, the Deputy Prime Minister who doubled as Finance Minister, were among MPs who championed the "The Hague" option.[160] William Ruto, for example, is on record having expressly stated that "Kofi Annan should hand over the envelope that contains names of suspects to the International Criminal Court at The Hague so that proper investigations can start".[161] Apparently, the duo lobbied for The Hague option in ignorance of the fact that they themselves would be arraigned before the ICC shortly thereafter to be charged with crimes against humanity. To say the least, this ploy later proved to have been a serious miscalculation on their part, and their efforts to have it reversed when it backfired were futile.[162]

Subsequent to the abortive attempts by the government to establish the Special Tribunal, on 24 August 2009, a Member of Parliament, Mr. Gitobu Imanyara, privately drafted and introduced a new bill ("Imanyara bill") to Parliament.[163] This was yet another genuine attempt to resuscitate the idea of establishing a special tribunal. Like the government bills, the Imanyara bill was hamstrung by political considerations. The bill was not passed because the MPs boycotted it three times, resulting in a consistent lack of a quorum in Parliament.[164] The idea of the proposed Special Tribunal was thus blocked at this crucial moment.

---

[158] Cf. Asaala 2012, p. 131; International Crisis Group 2012, pp. 6 and 7.

[159] Parliament of Kenya 2010a, p. 36.

[160] International Crisis Group 2012, p. 6; The Star, 12 March 2011.

[161] See Daily Nation, 21 February 2009.

[162] International Crisis Group 2012, p. 7. When the two were named by the ICC Prosecutor as suspects, they reversed their stand about The Hague option. See Daily Nation, 26 March 2011.

[163] Constitution of Kenya (Amendment) Bill of 2009. For critical comments about the Imanyara bill, see Bosire 2009 (identifying critical flaws in the bill, including on the proposed jurisdictional relationship between the tribunal and the ICC, and which, if approved, would have made the resulting law of the tribunal inconsistent with the ICC Statute).

[164] See the Parliament of Kenya 2010b, Doc. Hansard 16.12.110P, p. 22–25. See also The Standard, 2 December 2009; The Star, 12 March 2011.

However, the possibility of creating a special tribunal did not necessarily die a permanent death. It remained a feasible option to resuscitate the idea, provided there was a political will. Subsequent to the failed attempt to create the proposed Special Tribunal for Kenya, the Kenyan government made several promises that it would create a "Special Division" in the High Court to prosecute the perpetrators of the post-election violence.[165] Admittedly, such a "Special Division" could, if genuinely utilized, serve the same purpose that would have been served by a special tribunal. In early 2013, Kenya's Chief Justice announced the creation of an "International Crimes Division" in the High Court of Kenya. But as it will be shown in the next chapter (see infra Sect. 4.3.1.5), this specific Division was not created specifically to address criminal accountability with respect to the post-election violence. In fact, there are all indications that it will never be used for that purpose.

3.6 Consequences of Failure to Create the Proposed Special Tribunal

According to the strict deadlines which had been agreed upon (supra Sect. 3.4.4), the Special Tribunal was supposed to have been formed by 1 February 2009. But when the initial efforts to create it failed, the Panel of African Eminent Personalities gave the Kenyan government an extension until the end of August 2009, to provide a second chance for Parliament to be re-engaged. Seeing that the August deadline, too, would not be met, the Kenyan government sought yet another extension. This time, however, a conditional extension was granted by the ICC Prosecutor, who was already in communication with the AU mediators.

In their meeting on 3 July 2009, the then ICC Prosecutor, Louis Moreno-Ocampo, and the leaders of the Kenyan coalition government agreed on the extension on the condition that Kenya would submit progress reports, the first one by the end of September 2009, as to the status of domestic investigations leading to the initiating of domestic proceedings, be it through a special tribunal or any other avenue, within a year.[166] Seeing that a new arrangement had been put in place between the Kenyan government and the ICC Prosecutor, on 9 July 2009, the AU mediation Panel, decided, as originally planned, to submit to the Office of the ICC Prosecutor a sealed envelope which contained until then undisclosed names of the alleged leading perpetrators of crimes against humanity, together with supporting materials which had been handed over to the Panel by the Waki Commission.[167]

---

[165] See BBC News, 30 July 2009.

[166] See Office of the Prosecutor 2009.

[167] See ICC Office of the Prosecutor, Weekly Briefing, 12–18 January 2010, Issue 20, pp. 4 and 5. See also Press Release ICC-OTP-20090709-PR436, 9 July 2009; BBC News, 9 July 2009; The Guardian, 9 July 2009; VOA News, 9 July 2009.

The matter was now in the hands of the ICC Prosecutor who would assess the materials and act on the information got out of it depending on how the implementation of his special arrangement with the Kenyan government turned out.[168]

The first progress report by the Kenyan government, which was submitted in September 2009, was enough to prove to the Prosecutor that Kenya would not prosecute any time soon.[169] The Prosecutor, therefore, met with President Kibaki and Prime Minister Odinga, and officially informed them of his opinion that crimes against humanity had been committed during the post-election violence. The Prosecutor made it clear to the two Kenyan leaders that since their government had not investigated or prosecuted as agreed domestically, and that since it had failed to do so even after the extension of time had been granted, he was now determined to officially trigger the ICC's jurisdiction. Interestingly, the two leaders expressed their support for the triggering of the ICC jurisdiction and committed themselves to full cooperation.[170]

Consequently, on 15 December 2010 the ICC Prosecutor took the first step by naming six high-profile individuals, commonly referred by the Kenyan media as "the Ocampo six", whom he would charge before the ICC.[171] This marked the commencement of the ICC process in respect of Kenya, which is dealt with extensively in Chap. 6.

3.7 Where to Prosecute the Big Fish? General Domestic Perceptions

Commendably, most Kenyans, including the so-called ordinary *wananchi* (citizens), remained well informed about each stage of the ongoing processes regarding efforts to address criminal accountability for the post-election violence, thanks to, among others, civil society organizations, the media and the Kenya National Commission on Human Rights. It is against this background that when the Prosecutor announced the invocation of the ICC process, a heated debate emerged as to the pros and cons of seeking accountability through the domestic courts or through an externally controlled court, the ICC.

The debate entailed perceptions about the most appropriate forum to prosecute the "big fish", namely those who allegedly bear greatest responsibility for the violence, especially the politicians. The perception in this regard was apparently influenced mainly by three factors: the lack of trust and confidence in the domestic

---

[168] See "Note on Handover of post-election violence Materials to the Prosecutor of the ICC" http://www.dialoguekenya.org/pressmedia/29-Jul-2009%20-%20Statement%20by%20the%20 Legal%20Advisor%20to%20the%20Panel%20of%20Eminent%20African%20Personalities.pdf. Accessed August 2014.

[169] International Crisis Group 2012, p. 7.

[170] ICC Office of the Prosecutor, Weekly Briefing, 12–18 January 2010, Issue No. 20, p. 4.

[171] BBC News, 15 December 2010. See more details in infra Sect. 6.1.

judicial and criminal justice system; the high expectations as regards the impact of the ICC on the culture of impunity in Kenya; and the ethnicization and politicization of justice, especially due to the composition of the "Ocampo six" list.

For example, Kenya's Catholic Church made it clear that it favoured the ICC route to justice only because "Kenyans had little faith in the local Judiciary".[172] Similarly, a renowned Kenyan expert in international criminal law and transitional justice issues, who was then the Director of the Nairobi-based African Centre for International Legal and Policy Research, Dr. Godfrey Musila, opined that it was not viable to try the perpetrators before a judiciary with a "tainted history". In Musila's view, the mere idea of proposing the creation of a hybrid special tribunal *with exclusive jurisdiction even over the lowest perpetrators* "was intended to bypass [the Kenyan] judiciary [which was] perceived by the general public [to be] corrupt and inept", and also to overcome the "huge rule of law deficit" in Kenya.[173]

The Kenyan judiciary was accused of past "depressing history of incompetence, corruption and subservience", as well as lack of independence on the part of the judges.[174] Related to this was also the concern about the incompetence on the part of the national authority responsible for criminal prosecutions.[175] Of specific concern in this regard was the alleged previous abuse of broad prosecutorial discretion given to the Attorney General as regards powers to enter *nolle prosequi*, i.e. the discretion to choose who and when to prosecute, and also to withdraw criminal cases at any stage of the proceedings without giving reasons.[176]

Independent surveys conducted immediately before and after the commencement of the ICC process clearly indicated that, generally, the overwhelming majority of the general public perceived the ICC as the most trustworthy, independent and reliable forum which could punish the perpetrators, especially the rich and powerful politicians.[177] Through a continuous monitoring, South Consulting, a research firm working for the African Panel of Eminent Personalities, issued periodic reports tracking the progress with regard to the implementation of the agreements reached during the mediation process, including the implementation of the recommendations pertaining to criminal accountability.

---

[172] See Daily Nation, 19 July 2009.

[173] Musila 2009, p. 456.

[174] Ibid. Also see Hansen 2011a. For a detailed discussion on the independence of judges and lawyers and allegations of and investigations of corruption against judges in Kenya see Mbote and Akech 2011, pp. 99–115.

[175] Further on these challenges see infra Sect. 4.3.1.5.

[176] Musila 2009, p. 455. For greater detail on *nolle prosequi* see infra Sect. 4.4.2.2.4.

[177] Alai and Mue 2011, p. 1232. For example, the survey conducted by Infotrack Research and Consulting in November 2009 showed that the public support was 62 % for the ICC trials and 2 % for trials under the proposed Special Tribunal. See Alai and Mue 2010. In September 2010, a poll by Synovate indicated that despite the judicial and legal reforms planned domestically, the public support for accountability measures was as follows: trial at the ICC (54 %), local trials (22 %), granting of amnesty (22 %). See Reuters, 27 September 2010. From another poll published by Synovate in April 2011, the results were: ICC trials (61 %) and a special tribunal (24 %). See Africa Review, 5 April 2010.

The report published in April 2011 presented the perception of Kenyans about the ICC. The survey found a "clear disconnect" between ordinary Kenyans and politicians in this respect.[178] It stated that while "the political elite appear[ed] to have a common interest in opposing accountability and other measures to end impunity ... there [was] a strong public mood against impunity".[179] As a result, most ordinary Kenyans strongly perceived the ICC as "the only concrete action to hold powerful people accountable for [the] post-election violence".[180]

The report released in January 2012 made a similar finding. Apart from breaking the tradition of impunity, the ICC was also strongly perceived to be the single most dependable forum to: bring justice to victims; establish the truth about the violence; and deter future violence, because the domestic courts could not be trusted and had not achieved this previously.[181] There was also a perception, especially strong among the victims of the post-election violence, that the Kenyan "government [would] unlikely conduct genuine investigations and prosecute the [ICC] suspects", even if it designed its own domestic mechanism to do so.[182] A victim of the violence then residing in one of the internally displaced persons' camps believed that:

> The ICC is the only option left to fight impunity in Kenya because the [domestic] institutions and the politicians have failed. Ocampo cannot fail. He must not fail. If he does, that will be the end of Kenya because there will be nothing left to fear anymore.[183]

To put this into a clearer perspective, the December 2010 survey indicated that the support for the ICC was at 78 % nationally,[184] and fluctuated between 60 and 82 % at provincial level.[185] The report released in 2012, including that of January towards ICC's decision on confirmation of charges against the Ocampo six (see infra Sect. 6.1), revealed that the public support for the ICC was still above 50 %.[186] In addition, many Kenyans wanted the prosecutions to go beyond the

---

[178] See Kenya National Dialogue and Reconciliation 2011, p. 25, para 60.

[179] Ibid., p. vi, para 9.

[180] Ibid., p. 8, para 26.

[181] Kenya National Dialogue and Reconciliation Monitoring Project 2012a, p. 52, para 133.

[182] Ibid., p. 57, para 142.

[183] As quoted *verbatim* in Kenya National Dialogue and Reconciliation Monitoring Report 2011, p. 25, para 59. See also International Center for Transitional Justice 2011, pp. 51–54.

[184] Kenya National Dialogue and Reconciliation Monitoring Project 2011, p. 9, para 27. In March 2011 the confidence was at 72 %. See p. 12, para 34.

[185] In December 2010, confidence in the ICC per province was: North Eastern (82 %), Western and Nyanza (75 %), Eastern (74 %), Rift Valley, where three of the ICC suspects hail from (60 %). See ibid., pp. 9–12, paras 28–33.

[186] Kenya National Dialogue and Reconciliation Monitoring Project 2012a, p. 51, para 132; Kenya National Dialogue and Reconciliation Monitoring Project 2012b, para 52–60 (indicating, e.g. at para 56, that by May 2012, up to 58 % of Kenyans were happy about the work of the ICC in Kenya).

"Ocampo six". About 77 % of them said that they would like to see the middle and lower level perpetrators also prosecuted and punished through local mechanisms. Of this number, 48 % preferred the Special Tribunal proposed by the Waki Commission, while only 29 % favoured the use of the ordinary domestic courts.[187]

It is also important to highlight the views of those who expressed anti-ICC sentiments, which generally embody a strong negative perception towards the "The Hague option". The empirical surveys mentioned above imply that this group is relatively small. However, the group must not be underestimated, given its composition. It was composed of mainly a section of the financially powerful political elite, who are also among the "sharks" of the Kenyan domestic politics, and who have tried to politicize and ethnicize the fight against impunity.[188] The group moved around the country telling the people that their six "sons" were being prosecuted by a "white man's court"; and that this was a "neo-colonialist ploy … taking them back to before independence".[189] Similarly, they described the ICC as an "imperialist imposition" dangerous to Kenya's sovereignty—"a Western colonial institution that is bent on re-colonizing Africa".[190]

More interesting is the fact that the negative perception gained greater momentum after the names of the Ocampo six were revealed. This time it became much stronger in the regions where the Ocampo six hail from, and especially among members of their ethnic communities, thereby echoing the strength of the negative ethnicity in Kenya. For example, part of the ethnic groups in Rift Valley started to be convinced that the ICC has "targeted the suspects and their respective communities."[191] The survey report of February 2013 indicated that although the general public support for the prosecution by the ICC was at 66 % national wide, it only remained strongest in Nairobi, Nyanza, Western, North Eastern, and Coastal provinces (from where no single ICC suspect came), while it was lowest in the Central Province and in Rift Valley, where the remaining four suspects (the number having been reduced from "Ocampo six" to "Ocampo four") hailed from.[192] Thus, although citizens in general showed more support for the ICC, the suspects and some members of their respective communities gradually started to ethicise the ICC process.

In April 2012, KAMATUSA, a controversial association that brings together the Kalenjin, Maasai, Turkana and Samburu ethnic groups, held a meeting in which they endorsed one of the ICC suspects, William Ruto, as their preferred presidential candidate for the upcoming 2013 general elections. The association claimed that "the entire Kalenjin community was on trial at the ICC by virtue of

---

[187] Kenya National Dialogue and Reconciliation Monitoring Project 2011, pp. 19 and 20, para 42.

[188] Ibid., p. v, para 6.

[189] See Drakard, 2011.

[190] See Jalloh 2010.

[191] Kenya National Dialogue and Reconciliation Monitoring Project 2012a, p. 57, para 142. Three of the suspects, namely, Kosgey, Ruto and Sang, come from this province.

[192] See Kenya National Dialogue and Reconciliation Monitoring Project 2013, para 75.

Ruto being a suspect".[193] What is particularly interesting is that the perception of this group was not necessarily that the allegations against the suspect were untrue. Rather, their perception was that the ICC was practising "selective justice". They believed, inter alia, that the people in the Ocampo list were used as "sacrificial lambs" to pay for the "sins" of "other known suspects", ostensibly from other ethnic communities, whom the ICC Prosecutor had deliberately opted not to indict.[194]

In a similar scenario, on 23 March 2012, the Central Kenya local leaders under the auspices of yet another controversial ethnic association, namely the Gikuyu (for Kikuyu), Embu and Meru Association (GEMA), issued a statement calling for the ICC to "postpone" the cases against the Kenyan suspects "to a period after the forthcoming [2013] general elections". Their argument was that by proceeding with the case against the suspects, specifically Uhuru Kenyatta, whom the association endorsed as its preferred presidential candidate, the ICC intended to "[deprive them] of their constitutional right to elect leaders of their choice in free, fair and all-inclusive elections". They even resolved that "their community" (tribes) would collect two million signatures on the basis of which to petition to the ICC to postpone the cases.[195] However, they seem to have been ignorant of the fact that legally speaking, this kind of "ethno activism" would not have had any effect in terms of deferral of the cases at the ICC.[196]

In another development, which is legal in character, the anti-ICC "movement" resulted in a local civil suit to which the ICC was included as a defendant. It is highly suspected that this case was instigated and sponsored by the political group touched or affected by the ongoing ICC process. The Constitutional Reference No. 12 of 2010 was filed in the High Court of Kenya at Mombasa in which the plaintiff, one Mr. Joseph Gathungu, asked the court to bar the ICC from conducting any activities in Kenya in relation to the post-election violence. The applicant asked the court for the following:

He asked for a declaration that "the involvement of the [ICC] … in the affairs of Kenya in general, and in particular in the investigations and possible prosecutions of the perpetrators of the post-2007 general-elections [violence] violate[d] … the Constitution of Kenya". In consequence thereof, he prayed that the ICC: (a) "be ordered not to involve itself in the investigations of post-2007 Kenyan general elections"; and (b) be ordered not to prosecute any Kenyan "on account of any acts or omissions resulting from the acts of violence perpetrated during and after the 2007 general elections in Kenya". The applicant also asked for an order that perpetrators of the post-election violence "be prosecuted in the constitutionally-established

---

[193] See The Star 3, April 2012.

[194] Kenya National Dialogue and Reconciliation Monitoring Project 2012a, p. 53, para 134.

[195] See Daily Nation, 24 March 2012. This move elicited a lot of criticism in Kenya. See, e.g. Daily Nation, 25 March 2012 (reporting that Justice Minister Mutula Kilonzo dismissed it as "the height of hypocrisy"); Daily Nation, 26 March 2012 (stating that the Immigration minister Otieno Kajwang' dismissed it as "dragging Kenya back to the dark old days of ethnicity by organising tribal meetings").

[196] On deferral of cases at the ICC see infra Sect. 6.6.1.

Courts in Kenya." Lastly, he also asked for a declaration that the ICC's "acts of investigating and threatened prosecutions of any Kenyan in the [ICC] contravene[d] the [Kenyan] Constitution and, as such, that such acts … [were] null and void and of no legal consequence", and that to allow the ICC to operate in Kenya "amount[ed] to surrender of the sovereignty of Kenya to foreigners which is totally untenable".[197]

However, the Kenyan High Court dismissed the arguments and prayers in this petition in their entirety. According to the High Court, the challenge to the operations of the ICC in the domestic courts of Kenya had no legal foundation, and the matter raised by the plaintiff was not justiciable. Thus, the anti-ICC forces received yet another blow in this respect.

3.8 Chapter Summary

This chapter has been presented both anecdotally and analytically, covering various aspects of the post-election violence and the important events in its aftermath. Specifically, the focus has been on what exactly happened during the violence; the inquiry into the violence; the nature of the crimes which were committed, the mediation process, the findings of the commissions of inquiry; the proposed criminal accountability measures; and the perception of Kenyans as regards these measures. As far as crimes under international law are concerned, only a preliminary scrutiny and observations have been made. In this respect, it has been shown that many indices exist pointing to the fact that crimes against humanity were committed during the violence. However, the question whether they were committed under both customary international law and the ICC Statute has been reserved for a subsequent discussion. It has also been shown that the proposed creation of a special tribunal as an effective avenue at domestic level to prosecute the alleged crimes against humanity was failed by political motivations, despite the considerable public support for the creation of the same, and that this failure prompted the trigger of the ICC intervention in Kenya as per a prior agreement.

Furthermore, the chapter has also revealed that the idea of using the ICC, which is, in principle, an externally managed justice mechanism, to prosecute those who bear the greatest responsibility for the alleged crimes, was received with mixed feelings in Kenya. On the one hand, the victims of the violence as well as the majority of ordinary citizens generally preferred the ICC option to the local mechanisms. On the other hand, an influential section of the political elite behaved like swinging pendulum bobs; they oscillated "between the various options, unsure which would safeguard their own agendas: trials in The Hague or local trials; trials before the Special Tribunal or national courts; and/or [a truth commission]".[198]

---

[197] *Joseph Kimani Gathungu v. Attorney General and 5 Others* (2010) eKLR.

[198] Musila 2009, p. 445. See also Hansen 2011b, pp. 8 and 9.

Falling in this category are partly the politicians who allegedly had, in the past, had the tendency and ability to manipulate the local judicial processes in their favour. This constant shift of interest on the part of the political elite was a signal that domestic accountability, especially with respect to the planners and financiers of the violence, would be affected by the dynamics of the domestic politics.

Lastly, the chapter has pointed out that the ICC identified the original list of only six individuals out of the many perpetrators who participated directly or indirectly in the commission of the alleged crimes. This is despite the longer list compiled by the Kenya National Commission on Human Right and that of the Waki Commission[199] in respect of people who allegedly bear the greatest responsibility for the violence. This indicated that, despite being generally perceived by Kenyans as the most credible forum, the extent to which the ICC could address impunity with regard to the post-election violence remained very limited. It was also an indication that the scope of the ICC process would probably not go beyond the six individuals initially investigated and officially charged.

The foregoing paragraph suggests that the prosecution of the majority of those alleged to have masterminded or executed crimes during the post-election violence can only be realized by the Kenyan domestic courts. This is the reality regardless of the fact that the attempt to create a special tribunal for that purpose failed; or that the majority of Kenyans may want all the cases to be tried by the ICC or any other external court. Given that domestic prosecutions are indispensable in this regard, it is important to explore other options which can guarantee positive results. The next chapter is devoted for this objective.

References

Allai C, Mue N (2010) Kenya: impact of the Rome Statute and the International Criminal Court. ICTJ Briefing. http://ictj.org/sites/default/files/ICTJ-Kenya-ICC-Impact-2010-English.pdf. Accessed Aug 2014

Alai C, Mue N (2011) Complementarity and the impact of the Rome Statute and the International Criminal Court in Kenya. In: Stahn C, El Zeidy M (eds) The International Criminal Court and Complementarity, vol II. Cambridge University Press, New York

Asaala EO (2012) The International Criminal Court Factor on transitional justice in Kenya. In: Ambos K, Maunganidze OA (eds) Power and prosecution: challenges and opportunities for international criminal justice in Sub-Saharan Africa. Universitätsverlag, Göttingen

Bassiouni MC (2003) Introduction to International Criminal Law. Transnational Publishers, New York

Bassiouni MC (2005) Legislative history of the International Criminal Court, vol 2. Transnational Publishers Inc., New York

Bohlander M (2003) Last exit Bosnia—transferring war crimes prosecution from the International Tribunal to Domestic Courts. Crim Law Forum 14:59–99

Bosire (2009) Misconceptions II—domestic prosecutions and the International Criminal Court. http://www.csls.ox.ac.uk/documents/Bosire2.pdf. Accessed Aug 2014

---

[199] See infra Sect. 4.3.1.4.1.

Cerone J (2001–2002) The Special Court for Sierra Leone: establishing a new approach to International Criminal Justice. ILSA J Int Comp Law 8(379):379–387

Cockayne J (2007) The special tribunal for Lebanon—a cripple from birth? Foreword. J Int Crim Justice 5:1–4

Cohen D (2002) Seeking justice on the cheap: is the East Timor tribunal really a model for the future? Asia Pacific Issues 61 http://scholarspace.manoa.hawaii.edu/bitstream/handle/10125/3790/api061.pdf?sequence=1. Accessed Aug 2014

Commonwealth Secretariat (2008) Kenya General Elections 27 December 2007: The Report of the Commonwealth Observer Group. http://humanrightsinitiative.org/programs/aj/police/intl/docs/report_of_cth_observer_grp_to_kenya_election.pdf. Accessed Aug 2014

Cryer R et al (2001) A "Special Court" for Sierra Leone? Int Comp Law Q 50(2):435–446

De Bertodano S (2006) Problems arising from the mixed composition and structure of the Cambodian Extraordinary Chambers. J Int Crim Justice 4(2):285–293

Dickinson LA (2003) The promise of hybrid courts. The Am J Int Law 97(2):295–310

Dougherty BK (2004) Right-sizing international criminal justice: the hybrid experiment at the special court for Sierra Leone. Roy Inst Int Aff 80(2):311–328

Drakard M (2011) International Criminal Court investigation of Kenyans is perceived as mixed blessing. The Cutting Edge, 11 April 2011

East African Community Observer Mission (2008) Report, Kenya General Elections December 2007. http://www.parliament.go.tz/bunge/docs/ealanews.pdf. Accessed Jan 2012

European Union Election Observation Mission (2008) Kenya: final report on the general elections of 27 December 2007 http://www.eods.eu/library/final_report_kenya_2007.pdf. Accessed Aug 2014

Fackler PM et al (2011) Media and post-election violence in Kenya. In: Fortner RS, Fackler PM (eds) The handbook of global communication and media ethics. Wiley-Blackwell, Oxford

Frulli M (2000) The Special Court for Sierra Leone: some preliminary comments. Eur J Int Law 11(4):857–869

Garms U, Pesche K (2005) War crimes prosecution in Bosnia and Herzegovina (1992–2002): an analysis through the jurisprudence of the human rights chamber. J Int Crim Justice 4(2):258–282

Hansen TO (2011a) How will International Criminal Court prosecutions impact Kenya's legacy of political violence? Toward freedom. http://www.towardfreedom.com/30-archives/africa/2288-how-will-international-criminal-court-prosecutions-impact-on-kenyas-legacy-of-political-violence. Accessed Aug 2015

Hansen TO (2011b) Transitional justice in Kenya? An assessment of accountability process in light of domestic politics and security concerns. Calif W Int Law J 42(1):1–35

Hayde RM (1996) Schindler's fate: genocide, ethnic cleansing, and population transfers. Slavic Rev 55(4):727–748

Heinrich Böll Stiftung (2009) Report on gender based violence in Kenya's post-election crisis. Heinrich Böll Stiftung Regional Office, Nairobi

Heller KJ (2006–2008) A poisoned chalice: the substantive and procedural defects of the Iraqi High Tribunal Case. W Res J Int Law 39:261–302

Human Rights Watch (2008a) Ballots to bullets: report on organized political violence and Kenya's Crisis of Governance, vol 20, no 1(A). Human Rights Watch, New York

Human Rights Watch (2008b) All the men have gone. War crimes in Kenya's Mt. Elgon conflict. Human Rights Watch, New York. ISBN:1-56432-363-3

Human Rights Watch (2008c) Kenya: punish war crimes in Mt. Elgon: account for disappeared, investigate torture and killings http://www.hrw.org/news/2008/07/28/kenya-punish-war-crimes-mt-elgon. Accessed Aug 2014

Human Rights Watch (2011a) Turning pebbles: evading accountability for post-election violence in Kenya. Human Rights Watch, New York. ISBN:1-56432-836-8

Human Rights Watch (2011b) Unfinished business: closing gaps in selection of ICC cases. Human Rights Watch, New York. ISBN:1-56432-810-4

International Center for Transitional Justice (2011) To live as other Kenyans do: a study of the reparative demands of Kenyan victims of human rights violations. http://www.ictj.org/sites/default/files/ICTJ-Kenya-Reparations-Demands-2011-English.pdf. Accessed Aug 2014

International Crisis Group (2012) Kenya: impact of the ICC proceedings. Africa Briefing no. 84. http://www.crisisgroup.org/en/regions/africa/horn-of-africa/kenya/b084-kenya-impact-of-the-icc-proceedings.aspx. Accessed Aug 2014

International Republican Institute (2008) Kenya presidential, parliamentary and local elections of December 27, 2007: election observation mission final report. http://www.iri.org/sites/default/files/Kenya's%202007%20Presidental,%20Parliamentary%20and%20Local%20Elections.pdf. Accessed Aug 2014

Jalloh CC (2010) Kenyan parliament endorses Ruto motion calling for withdrawal from ICC Statute. International criminal law in ferment blog. http://iclferment.blogspot.com/2010/12/kenyan-parliament-endorses-ruto-motion.html. Accessed Aug 2014

Jurdi N (2007) The subject-matter jurisdiction of the Special Tribunal for Lebanon. J Int Crim Justice 5(5):1125–1138

Kanyinga K (2011) Stopping a conflagration: the response of Kenyan civil society to the post-2007 election violence'. Politikon 38(1):85–109

Kenya Elections Domestic Observation Forum (2007) Preliminary press statement and verdict of 2007 Kenya's general elections. http://kenyastockholm.files.wordpress.com/2008/01/kedof-statement-31-12-07.pdf. Accessed Aug 2014

Kenya Human Rights Commission (2008) Violating the vote: a report on the 2007 general election. Nairobi

Kenya National Commission on Human Rights (2007) Still behaving badly. Second periodic report of the election-monitoring project, Nairobi

Kenyans for Peace with Truth and Justice (2008) Count down to deception: 30 hours that destroyed Kenya. http://www.kenyanpundit.com/2008/01/20/count-down-to-deception-30-hours-that-destroyed-kenya/. Accessed Aug 2014

Kenya National Commission on Human Rights (2008) On the brink of the precipice: a (report on) human rights account of Kenya's post-2007 election violence. Nairobi

Kenya National Dialogue and Reconciliation (2008a) Agreement on the principles of partnership of the Coalition Government. http://www.dialoguekenya.org/Agreements/14%20February%202008-Agreement%20on%20the%20Principles%20of%20Partnership%20of%20the%20Coalition%20Government.pdf. Accessed Aug 2014

Kenyan National Dialogue and Reconciliation (2008b) Agreement on commission of enquiry on post-election violence. http://www.dialoguekenya.org/Agreements/4%20March%202008-Commission%20of%20Post-election%20Violence.pdf. Accessed Sept 2014

Kenya National Dialogue and Reconciliation (2008c) Agreement for the implementation of the recommendations of the commission of inquiry into post-election violence. http://www.odm.co.ke/2012/01/the-agreement-signed-between-kibaki-raila-on-pev-suspects/. Accessed Feb 2012

Kenya National Dialogue and Reconciliation (KNDR) Monitoring Project (2011) Draft review report. Nairobi. April 2011

Kenya National Dialogue and Reconciliation (KNDR) Monitoring Project (2012a) First draft review report. Nairobi, Jan 2012

Kenya National Dialogue and Reconciliation (KNDR) Monitoring Project (2012b) Reforms and preparedness for elections. Second review report. Nairobi. May 2012

Kenya National Dialogue and Reconciliation (KNDR) Monitoring Project (2013) Kenya's 2013 general election: review of preparedness (report). Nairobi

Kenya Truth, Justice and Reconciliation Commission (2013) Final report of the Kenyan truth, justice and reconciliation commission, Vols I, IIA, IIB, IIC, III and IV. Nairobi

Kofi Anan Foundation (2009) The Kenya national dialogue and reconciliation: one year later: overview of events. http://kofiannanfoundation.org/sites/default/files/Microsoft%20Word%20-%20Overview%20of%20events%20note_0.pdf. Accessed Sept 2014

Law Society of Kenya (2008) Kenyan electoral crisis. Press statement. http://www.Marsgroupkenya.org/pdfs/2008/jan08/LSKSTATEMENT.pdf. Accessed Jan 2012

Lindenmayer E, Kaye JL (2009) A choice for peace? The story of forty-one days of mediation in Kenya. International Peace Institute, New York

Mbote PK, Akech M (2011) Kenya: justice sector and the rule of law. The Open Society Initiative for Eastern Africa, Nairobi

Musila G (2009) Options for transitional justice in Kenya: autonomy and the challenge of external prescriptions. Int J Trans Justice 3:445–464

Mutua M (2001) Justice under siege: the rule of law and judicial subservience in Kenya. Hum Rights Q 23(1):96–118

Newton MA (2005) Iraqi Special Tribunal: a human rights perspective. Cornell J Int Law 38:863–898

Office of the Prosecutor (2009) Agreed minutes of the meeting between prosecutor Moreno-Ocampo and the Delegation of the Kenyan government. http://www.icc-cpi.int/NR/rdonlyres/1CEB4FAD-DFA7-4DC5-B22D-E828322D9764/280560/20090703AgreedMinutesofMeetingProsecutorKenyanDele.pdf. Accessed Aug 2014

Ojwang JB, Otieno-Odek JA (1998) The judiciary in sensitive areas of public law: emerging approaches to human rights litigation in Kenya. Neth Int Law Rev 35:29–52

Parliament of Kenya (2010a) Official Hansard reports. Doc Hansard 16.12.110A. Nairobi

Parliament of Kenya (2010b) Official Hansard reports. Doc Hansard 16.12.110P. Nairobi

Ratner SR et al (2009) Accountability for human rights atrocities in international law: beyond the Nuremberg legacy, 3rd edn. Oxford University Press, New York

Republic of Kenya (2008a) Report of the Commission of Inquiry into Post-election Violence (CIPEV). Government Printer, Nairobi

Republic of Kenya (2008b) Report of the independent review commission on the general elections held in Kenya on 27 December 2007. Office of Public Communications, Nairobi

Romano CPR et al (eds) (2004) Internationalized Criminal Courts. Oxford University Press, New York

Scheffer D (2008) The extraordinary chambers in the courts of Cambodia. In: Bassiouni MC (ed) International Criminal Law, 3rd edn. Martinus Nijhoff Publishers, Leiden

Serra G (2008) Special Tribunal for Lebanon: a commentary on its major legal aspects. Int Crim Justice Rev 18:344–355

Sentinel Project for Genocide Prevention (2011) The risk of genocide in Kenya. http://www.genocidewatch.org/images/Kenya_11_09_XX_The_Risk_of_Genocide_in_Kenya.pdf. Accessed Sept 2014

Suzzane K (2003) Hybrid Tribunals: searching for justice in East Timor. Harvard Hum Rights J 16:245–278

Tom P (2005) Prosecuting Saddam: the coalition provisional authority and the evolution of the Iraqi Special Tribunal. Cornell Int Law J 38:899–910

United Nations General Assembly (2009) Report of the International Criminal Court to the United Nations for 2008/2009, UN Doc A/64/356, 17 Sept 2009

United Nations Office of the High Commissioner for Human Rights (2008) Report from OHCHR fact-finding mission to Kenya, 6–28 Feb 2008

United Nations Security Council (1994) Final report of the commission of experts established pursuant to security council resolution 780 (1992), UN Doc S/1994/674, 27 May 1994

Wainaina N, Chepng'etich P (2009) Special Tribunal enactment: why cabinet, MPs, are misleading Kenyans. Oxford Transitional Justice Research Working Paper series. http://otjr.crim.ox.ac.uk/materials/papers/44/Wainaina_Special_Tribunal_Enactment_final_OTJR.pdf. Accessed Aug 2014

Wamwere K (2003) Towards genocide in Kenya: the curse of negative ethnicity. MvuleAfrica Publishers, Nairobi

Werle G (2009) Principles of international criminal law, 2nd edn. TMC Asser Press, The Hague

Wierda M et al (2007) Early reflections on local perceptions, Legitimacy and legacy of the special Tribunal for Lebanon. J Int Crim Justice 55:1065–1081

Williams SA (2004) Cambodian extraordinary chambers—a dangerous precedent for international justice. Int Crim Law Q 53:227–245

Chapter 4
Criminal Accountability at Domestic Level

Abstract A state wishing to punish the core crimes under international law in its domestic courts can choose to follow two approaches. The first is to prosecute those crimes by relying on its ordinary domestic criminal law. The second approach is to prosecute them by relying on the structure of international criminal law as it is or as modified. The effectiveness of the first approach depends largely on how broadly or narrowly the domestic criminal law is structured, whereas that of the second approach depends, inter alia, on the practice followed in that state as regards domestication of international law norms so as to make them enforceable in the domestic courts. This chapter examines the two approaches in relation to the crimes against humanity allegedly committed in Kenya during the post-election violence, and evaluates whether Kenya has or could have utilized any of the approaches to effectively prosecute and punish the main perpetrators of these crimes. This discussion will provide a model for other jurisdictions, especially in the developing countries, that wish to address impunity for the core crimes in their domestic courts.

Contents

© T.M.C. ASSER PRESS and the author 2015
S.F. Materu, *The Post-Election Violence in Kenya*,
International Criminal Justice Series 2, DOI 10.1007/978-94-6265-041-1_4

4.1 Introductory Remarks

This chapter identifies legal frameworks on which Kenya could rely at the domestic level to prosecute the main perpetrators of the alleged crimes against humanity committed during the post-election violence. It examines broadly whether such legal frameworks could provide adequate alternatives to achieve the goals that could have been achieved by the Special Tribunal for Kenya which, as shown in the previous chapter, failed to materialize. The first option analysed is the ordinary-crimes approach. This entails a critical analysis of the Kenyan substantive criminal law (Penal Code) as *it stood at the time of the violence*, in order to establish whether it is adequate to punish the alleged crimes not as "crimes against humanity" as such but as "ordinary crimes" under the Penal Code. As a second option, the chapter analyses the legislative reforms adopted in Kenya *subsequent to the violence,* in order to establish whether the criminal acts could be prosecuted using their legal structure and labels under international law, i.e. as "crimes against humanity" as such without violating the principle of legality. This entails an examination of two sub-questions: whether prosecution could be based on Kenya's International Crimes Act of 2008, or whether it could be based directly on customary international law existing *at the time of commission* of the crimes.[1]

The main argument of this chapter is that the failure to pass the law for the proposed Special Tribunal for Kenya, or the fact that Kenya had not domesticated the ICC Statute at the time of commission of the crimes, does not per se deprive Kenya of sufficient legal frameworks to punish those crimes domestically, and that although Kenya has carried out a few prosecutions in its domestic courts, it lacks a political will to prosecute those who bear major responsibility for the crimes.

4.2 Legal Position Regarding Enforceability of Core Crimes in Kenya

At the time of the post-election violence, the Constitution of Kenya of 1963 was still in force.[2] Under this constitutional order, Kenya followed the dualist practice[3] of implementing international treaties. Accordingly, upon ratification of an international treaty, the treaty did not automatically create rights or obligations enforceable as such in Kenya's domestic courts, unless, as a matter of principle, the whole treaty or its relevant provisions were explicitly transformed into rules of domestic

---

[1] Cf. Kenyans for Peace with Truth and Justice and Kenya Human Rights Commission 2013, pp. 16–26.

[2] This Constitution was repealed on 27 August 2010.

[3] See generally Bradley 1999, pp. 529 et seq.; Collier 1989, pp. 924 et seq.; Ginsburg 2006, pp. 715–716.

legal order (i.e. were domesticated) through a piece of legislation.[4] In case of an inconsistency, the Constitution prevailed over "any other law", including international treaties.[5] Furthermore, the principle of legality (infra Sect. 4.3.2.2.4) was entrenched under Article 77(4) of the Constitution as follows:

> No person shall be held to be guilty of a criminal offence on account of an act or omission that did not, at the time it took place, constitute such an offence, and no penalty shall be imposed for a criminal offence that is severer in degree or description than the maximum penalty that might have been imposed for that offence at the time when it was committed.

Kenya signed the ICC Statute on 11 August 1999 and ratified it on 15 March 2005.[6] However, the Statute was domesticated into the Kenyan domestic legal order 1 year after the post-election violence. The domestication process was done via the International Crimes Act of 2008, which became operational *prospectively* from 1 January 2009. However, prior to the domestication of the ICC Statute, and more importantly, prior to the post-election violence, at least five other international criminal law conventions had already been domesticated in Kenya. The four 1949 Geneva Conventions, which together embody substantive criminal law on war crimes, had been domesticated since 1968.[7] The Convention on Non-Applicability of Statutory Limitations to War Crimes and Crimes against Humanity[8] had been domesticated since 1972.[9] The Genocide Convention of 1948 had not (and still has not) even been signed, let alone being domesticated.[10] On their part, crimes against humanity as such had not been domesticated, given that

---

[4] *East African Community v. Republic [1970] E.A; Okunda v. Republic [1970]* EA 453; *Pattni and Another v. Republic [2001] KLR 262.* Also see Ambani 2010, pp. 27–31; Ford 2008, p. 60; Isabirye 1980, pp. 63 et seq.; Kenya Parallel Report 2008, pp. 13–14; Ojwang and Otieno-Odek 1998, pp. 29 et seq.

[5] Constitution of Kenya of 1963, Article 2.

[6] See ICC Press Release ICC-CPI-20050316-93, 16 March 2005.

[7] See the Geneva Conventions Act of 1968. Note that Kenya was party to four other war crimes treaties, but had not domesticated them. These were: Protocols I and II Additional to the Geneva Conventions of 1977, the Convention on the Prohibition of the Development, Production, Stockpiling and Use of Chemical Weapons and on their Destruction of 1993 and the Protocol for the Prohibition of the Use in War of Asphyxiating, Poisonous or other Gases, and of Bacteriological Methods of Warfare of 1925. See "Kenya: International Treaties Adherence" http://www.geneva-academy.ch/RULAC/international_treaties.php?id_state=119. Accessed September 2014.

[8] UN General Assembly Res. 2391, 26 Nov. 1968.

[9] See "Kenya: International Treaties Adherence" http://www.geneva-academy.ch/RULAC/international_treaties.php?id_state=119. Accessed September 2014. However, this particular Convention does not codify substantive criminal law.

[10] See Genocide Convention ratification status (as at 3 September 2014) https://treaties.un.org/pages/ViewDetails.aspx?src=TREATY&mtdsg_no=IV-1&chapter=4&lang=en. Accessed September 2014.

prior to the adoption of the ICC Statute there had not been any convention or treaty codifying such crimes.[11]

Therefore, under the legal framework which existed in Kenya at the time of the post-election violence, it was only possible to prosecute "war crimes" as such, but not "genocide" or "crimes against humanity" in Kenya's domestic courts.

Does the foregoing mean that, legally speaking, Kenya did not at all have a possibility or mechanism of punishing the alleged crimes against humanity committed during the violence? There is a view that Kenya, like any other State Party to the ICC Statute, was not under any obligation to domesticate the substantive provisions of the Statute in order to be able to punish the core crimes therein (crimes against humanity in particular), since the Statute imposes such obligation expressly only in respect of "offences against the administration of justice" under Article 70 of the Statute, but not in respect of the core crimes.[12] However, there is yet another (second) view which suggests that domestication of the substantive provisions of the ICC Statute, including Article 7 which codifies crimes against humanity, was mandatory on the part of Kenya and other States Parties, even though the Statute itself may not have expressly imposed a duty to do so.[13] According to this view, the "duty to domesticate" the ICC Statute, specifically the core crimes and general principles therein, is implied or presupposed in the complementarity principle[14] under which the ICC operates.[15] Arguably, it would be impossible for the principle to operate if states were given the liberty to choose whether or not to implement or domesticate the Statute.[16]

Harmonizing the two views above, Werle rightly submits that although, in principle, domestication of the Statute is not mandatory, it is nevertheless desirable for the effective carrying out of the *intent and spirit* of the ICC Statute by any State Party,[17] namely ensuring that the "most serious crimes of concern to the international

---

[11] Bassiouni 2003, p. 139 (noting that between 1943 and 1993 this crime was regulated by eleven different instruments (see pp. 232–233), the earliest provisions being Articles 6(c) and 5(c) of the Nuremberg and Tokyo Charters, respectively. See generally Sadat 2011.

[12] See Kleffner 2003, pp. 90–94; Nouwen 2011, pp. 214–216; Triffterer 2000, pp. 24–25; Werle 2009, p. 27. NB. In this regard, the ICC Statute departs from other conventions that expressly impose such a duty on States Parties. See, for example, Convention against Torture and Other Cruel, Inhuman or Degrading Treatment or Punishment of 1984 (Article 4(1)); The Geneva Convention for the Amelioration of the Condition of the Wounded and Sick in Armed Forces in the Field of 1949 (Article 49); The Geneva Convention for the Amelioration of the Condition of Wounded, Sick and Shipwrecked Members of Armed Forces at Sea of 1949 (Article 50); and the Convention on the Prevention and Punishment of the Crime of Genocide of 1948 (Article V).

[13] See Ambos 2008, marginal no. 51; Bellelli 2010, p. 212; Burchasrds 2006, p. 329; Cryer 2005, p. 171.

[14] For details see infra Sect. 6.5.

[15] Duffy and Huston 2000, pp. 31–33.

[16] Cryer et al. 2007, p. 63.

[17] Werle 2009, p. 27.

community do not go unpunished".[18] It is the same spirit that seeks to enhance international cooperation by urging states to take "measures at national level" to ensure "effective prosecution" of crimes under international law.[19]

In summary, therefore, it can be stated that the decision by Kenya to domesticate the ICC Statute as a whole, even though it was not under any express obligation to do so, is commendable and welcome. But as it stands now, the resulting legislation is still not applicable to the crimes committed before it was enacted, including those linked to the post-election violence. However, this *does not* necessarily mean that domestication prior to the violence *is the only* legal framework that could have ensured that the alleged crimes against humanity were prosecuted and punished in the Kenyan courts. It would suffice if on the basis of any other available legal framework it could be possible to prosecute the *conduct* criminalized in the core crimes in any manner which is *largely consistent* with the intention of ending impunity for such crimes. It would not matter much whether or not the law used for such prosecutions has resulted from the domestication of the ICC Statute, or whether the conduct is prosecuted as "crimes against humanity" as such.[20] What matters most is whether the legal framework chosen can impose *adequate punishment* especially on the main perpetrators of the violence—those who bear the greatest responsibility. The following sections will explore such alternative possibilities.

4.3 Alternative Legal Frameworks for Domestic Prosecution of Crimes Linked to the Post-Election Violence

4.3.1 Prosecuting as Domestic "Ordinary" Crimes

4.3.1.1 Understanding the Ordinary-Crime Approach

Despite their legal classification, the core crimes under international law should not be viewed in isolation of the "ordinary" crimes found in the domestic laws. There are many substantial areas of convergence and only a few areas of divergence between the two sets of crimes. The main area of divergence is that, characteristically, crimes under international law as such entail two main additional elements which are not elements of purely domestic ordinary crimes. The first element is that, as a general rule, the core crimes entail a systematic or large-scale

---

[18] ICC Statute, Preamble para 4.

[19] Ibid., preamble para 5.

[20] Cf. Werle and Jeßberger 2002, p. 195.

use of force, mostly by a collective.[21] The second element is that individual acts, such as murder, rape, assault, etc., which are also found in the ordinary criminal law of Kenya, form what one may refer to as "predicate offences" for the core crimes under international law.

The predicate offences acquire an "elevated status" to become crimes under international law only if the manner in which they are committed exhibits certain additional *contextual elements* over and above the requirement for the ordinary crimes. For example, some ordinary crimes become crimes against humanity when committed in the context of a widespread or systematic attack on a civilian population; they become war crimes when committed in the context of an armed conflict; and genocide when committed with the intent to destroy a protected group in whole or in part.[22] Legally speaking, therefore, it is mainly *the absence* of these contextual (international) elements which brings about the "ordinariness" of the acts, thereby making them "ordinary" domestic crimes. Save for these elements, the conduct, whether criminalized as ordinary crime or as a crime under international law, is, by and large, *substantially* the same, regardless of its nomenclature, legal label or characterization.

Against the foregoing background, it can now be stated that the atrocious acts committed during the post-election violence in Kenya were, in the first place, obviously crimes contrary to the Kenyan domestic criminal law, particularly the Penal Code.[23] It was on this basis that the Kenyan National Commission on Human Rights (KNCHR) concluded that the criminal liability for these acts could sufficiently be established "under either domestic or international criminal law".[24]

However, in analysing these crimes, part of the literature fails to appreciate adequately this reality.[25] For instance, Okuta overlooks the fact that Kenya could still be discharging its duty to prosecute the core crimes under the ICC Statute even if these atrocities were prosecuted and punished not *qua* crimes under international law as such but *qua* domestic ordinary crimes. She asserts that at the time of commission of the alleged crimes "the Kenyan Penal Code, which lays down offences under Kenyan law, did not contain any provisions that defined or provided for penalties for international crimes".[26] On this ground, she concludes that Kenya "*did not have any laws* that would have enabled it to prosecute international crimes

---

[21] See Decision on the Confirmation of Charges, *Katanga and Chui* (ICC-01/04-01/07-717), PTC, 30 September 2008, para 501; ICTY Judgment, *Tadic* (IT-94-1-A), 15 July 1999, para 191. See also Drumbl 2005, pp. 570–571; Fichtelberg 2006, p. 167; Fletcher 2002, p. 1514; Swart 2009, p. 82; Werle 2009, p. 32.

[22] Werle 2009, p. 32.

[23] Cap. 63 of Laws of Kenya [R.E.] 2009.

[24] Kenya National Commission on Human Rights 2008, pp. 144–150, para 571. See also paras 572–623 for a detailed account of the specific ordinary crimes in the penal code that could be charged in this respect.

[25] See, e.g., Okuta 2009, pp. 1065–1066; Kenyans for Peace with Truth and Justice and Kenya Human Rights Commission 2013, pp. 21–22.

[26] Okuta 2009, p. 1065.

effectively, *since implementing legislation for the ICC Statute had not yet been passed into law*.[27] Similarly, it has been argued that in view of *mens rea* requirements, "crimes against humanity sets itself [sic] apart from the crimes punishable under the Kenyan law" at the time of the post-election violence, and therefore, to prosecute them "on the basis of provisions in the Kenyan Penal Code" might "contravene the principle of specificity".[28] These arguments put undue emphasis on the *labels* of the crimes as they appear in the ICC Statute or international customary law. They seem to disregard or underrate another (second) argument that in fulfilling state's duty to prosecute and punish the core crimes under international law, it is basically the prohibited conduct, and not the label of the crime, which should be given primary emphasis.

The first and second arguments above embody different schools of thought which Heller refers to as the "hard mirror" and "soft mirror" theories, respectively.[29] These theories concern the question how domestic substantive criminal law should be adapted by national jurisdictions which are discharging their duty to prosecute and punish the core crimes under the ICC Statute.

The hard mirror theory holds that prosecuting international crimes as ordinary domestic crimes does not adequately satisfy the duty to prosecute the core crimes under international law,[30] but is arguably an indication that the state of commission is unwilling or unable to prosecute those crimes.[31] Consequently, the proponents of this theory argue that the definitions of the core crimes in the ICC Statute must, apparently, be adapted *verbatim,* and also the crimes must be prosecuted in the domestic courts as they are appear under international law.[32]

On the other hand, the soft mirror thesis holds that punishing the core crimes under international law as ordinary domestic crimes cannot, by that mere fact, amount to unwillingness or inability to prosecute the crimes, unless it becomes clear that there is an intention to shield the perpetrators from criminal responsibility. Those who subscribe to this theory, including this author, agree that the

---

[27] Ibid. (emphasis added).

[28] See Kenyans for Peace with Truth and Justice and Kenya Human Rights Commission 2013, pp. 21–22.

[29] See Heller 2012, p. 203; Megret 2011, pp. 363 et seq.

[30] On the duty to prosecute, see supra Sect. 1.2.

[31] Heller 2012, p. 203. More on state's willingness or inability to prosecute see infra Sects. 6.5.1 and 6.5.2.

[32] Ibid., pp. 203–212. E.g., see Amnesty International 2000, pp. 5–6 (arguing that the definitions of the crimes in national law must be as broad as those in the ICC Statute and customary law); Ellis 2002–2003, pp. 224–225; Halling 2010, p. 839 (arguing that complementarity requires that states prosecute crimes as they are spelled out in the Rome Statute; the prosecutions have to be for "crimes against humanity", not the murders, rapes, and so on that underlie the charge of crimes against humanity."); Philippe 2006, pp. 390–391 (arguing that it is an "obvious requirement" that "the definition of international crimes in domestic legislation should be in line with their definition at the international level"); Sedman 2010, pp. 266 et seq.

ordinary-crime approach is, in principle, consistent with the ICC Statute, and that it was actually contemplated by the drafters of the Statute.[33]

Therefore, pursuant to the soft mirror theory, Kenya's substantive criminal law cannot be explained as "unavailable" merely because "crimes against humanity" as such could not be charged at the domestic level at the time of the violence. Mere absence of a piece of legislation expressly domesticating the ICC Statute, or non-inclusion of crimes against humanity *as such* (or the other core crimes) in the Penal Code, does not necessarily point to the total absence of domestic substantive criminal law to punish such crimes. Instead it can be stated that in the absence of such legislation, Kenya had de facto opted for the "ordinary-crime approach" (or "zero solution") of punishing the core crimes under international law at the domestic level. According to Werle, the zero solution approach entails the punishment of the *conduct* criminalized in the international core crimes as part of domestic *ordinary crimes,* without necessarily having to use the crime definitions, elements or titles as used under international law; or without having to rely on their direct citation.[34] Thus, the zero solution approach focuses entirely on the criminalized *conduct* rather than the *title or label* given to that conduct. Consequently, under the ordinary-crime approach, prosecuting "wilful killing" as "murder" under the Kenyan Penal Code would arguably save a *similar purpose* as prosecuting it as, for instance, "genocide" or "crime against humanity" under Articles 6 and 7 of the ICC Statute, respectively. The same reasoning applies in respect of most of the other individual acts such as rape, extermination, torture, persecution, etc., which are criminalized as "crimes against humanity" under the ICC Statute or customary international law.[35]

It is worth stating that the ordinary-crime approach is not entirely new in domestic courts. It was used successfully for the first time in Germany as a basis for the domestic prosecutions of genocide committed against the European Jews under the Nazi regime.[36] Furthermore, in 2005, Professor Bassiouni suggested that the same approach be used by the Iraq Special Tribunal, arguing that prosecuting the conduct criminalized in the Tribunal's statute in their titles as crimes under international law as such would be "an outright violation of the principle of legality envisaged in the Iraqi law".[37]

---

[33] Cf. Heller 2012, pp. 203, 213–223. Also see Jurdi 2011, pp. 52–53; Schabas 2010, p. 84 (arguing that it is "excessive [for] the Court to intervene where a state has conducted a serious prosecution for crimes against the person yet failed to label the act genocide, crimes against humanity, or war crimes in accordance with the Statute").

[34] For a detailed discussion see Werle 2009, pp. 116–122.

[35] Cf. International Center for Transitional Justice 2013, p. 4. Some States Parties to the ICC Statute have officially chosen to use this approach as their formal policy. Japan, e.g. announced officially that the ordinary crimes under its current Criminal Code are adequate to deal with the crimes in the ICC Statute, arguing that the Code "can punish them as homicide, assault, unlawful capture and confinement, and so forth". As a result, Japan does not deem it necessary to fully domesticate the ICC Statute. See Meierhenrich and Ko 2009, pp. 245–246.

[36] Werle 2009, p. 109.

[37] Bassiouni 2005a, pp. 376–377.

4.3.1.2 ICC's Jurisprudence Regarding Ordinary-Crime Approach

Hitherto the ICC's jurisprudence indicates clearly that the ordinary-crime approach is acceptable to the ICC as long as the aim and ultimate result of relying on such approach is to genuinely punish those who bear greatest responsibility for the crimes under the ICC's jurisdiction. Regardless of the nomenclature of the crime charged domestically, the underlying rule which has played a central role in the ICC's determination of admissibility of a case (see infra Sect. 6.5) is whether the domestic investigation or prosecution of an ordinary crime covers *the same person and the same conduct* which would have been prosecuted had the prosecution been instituted by the ICC itself.[38] This rule relates directly to the *ne bis in idem* principle (against double jeopardy) which is recognized both in the ICC Statute and Kenyan laws. The gist of the principle is that the domestic courts in Kenya, or the ICC for that matter, shall not try a person for a *conduct* for which he or she has been prosecuted by another court.[39] In a recent submission, the ICC Prosecutor has endorsed the ordinary-crime approach expressly as follows:

> There is no requirement that the crimes charged in the national proceedings have the same "label" as the ones before this Court…. National authorities are not necessarily required to charge the suspect under the exact same legal qualification. While the conduct itself must necessarily be the same, meaning the underlying acts and incidents concerned, the legal characterisation of such conduct may differ: it must be the same in substance.[40]

In addition, when applying for the issuance of summonses to appear in respect of the six Kenyan suspects, the ICC Prosecutor argued that "there [had] been no trial held before any competent national jurisdiction for the *conduct* that [was] the subject of the application".[41] Prior to this submission, Kenya had argued that the criminal *conduct* in respect of which the summonses were being sought was being investigated as part of ordinary crimes under its Penal Code with a view to prosecuting them domestically. As will be shown below (Sect. 6.5), Kenya's argument would have been accepted if the investigations claimed to have taken place had

---

[38] Batros 2011; Boas et al. 2011, pp. 75–76; Nouwen 2011, p. 213 (stating that mere "domestic qualification of a conduct as an ordinary crime instead of an international crime does not render a case admissible before the ICC").

[39] See Constitution of Kenya of 2010, Article 50(2)(o); ICC Statute, Article 20(2) and (3). Whereas subsection 2 of Article 20 of the Statute prohibits double jeopardy specifically in respect of the "crime" of genocide, war crime, aggression or crime against humanity, subsection 3 prohibits double jeopardy in respect of the "conduct" proscribed in the individual acts under Articles 6, 7 and 8 of the Statute. For more details, see Bassiouni 2005b, pp. 168–171; Carter 2010; Schabas 2007, pp. 192–193.

[40] Public Redacted version of Prosecution Response to Application on behalf of the Government of Libya, *Gaddafi and Al-Senussi* (ICC-01/11-01/11-167-Red), PTC, 5 June 2012, para 23.

[41] See, Prosecutor's Application Pursuant to Article 58 as to William Samoei Ruto, Henry Kiprono Kosgey and Joshua Arap Sang, *Situation in the Republic of Kenya* (ICC-01/09-30-Red 2), PTC, 15 December 2010, para 212 (emphasis added).

indeed encompassed the *same persons* charged before the ICC and for the *same conduct*.[42]

In this regard, Heller takes not only a precise but pragmatic position to which this author also subscribes. He maintains that even where the conduct is not substantially the same, or the ordinary crime is seemingly "minor", another decisive factor to judge whether the ordinary domestic criminal law is effective should be the *adequacy of the punishment* imposed or likely to be imposed upon conviction. Accordingly, the most important consideration is that the punishment imposed or expected to be imposed can be greater, equal, or even slightly lower than that of the international crime.[43] Based on the combination of these two factors, namely the substance of the ordinary crime charged and its gravity (determined by the severity of the sanction the crime attracts), it is now opportune to assess the adequacy of Kenya's domestic ordinary criminal law in light of the ICC Statute and, specifically, the conduct charged as "crimes against humanity" at the ICC.

4.3.1.3 Kenyan Penal Code Vis-a-Vis ICC Statute

4.3.1.3.1 Individual Acts and Sanctions

In the charges brought before the ICC, the Prosecutor alleged that during the post-election violence in Kenya a total of five individual acts potentially constituting crimes against humanity were committed, namely "murder", "forcible transfer of population", "persecution", "rape" and "other inhumane acts".[44] To establish whether the ordinary crimes in Kenya cover the conduct charged in these five acts, the ordinary crimes must be assessed in relation to the ICC's Elements of Crimes.[45] As shown below, such assessment indicates that the *conduct* charged before the ICC is covered substantially in the Kenyan Penal Code, and that for

---

[42] See Judgment on the Application by the Government of Kenya Challenging the Admissibility of the Case, *Muthaura, Kenyatta and Ali* (ICC-01/09-02/11-274), AC, 30 August 2011, para 39. For a further discussion on the same-person-same-conduct test see infra Sects. 6.5.3.2.1.3 and 6.5.3.2.2.

[43] Heller 2012, pp. 223–245 (expounding the theory of "sentence-based complementarity" which, he argues, is superior to the "traditional conduct-and-gravity theory". At p. 231 he argues that in order to determine the adequacy of the ordinary crime a comparison should be made "on the international side, ICC maximum and/or the average sentence imposed by international tribunals and on the other side average sentences and/or the actual sentence imposed in the case in question", and that "as long as the sentence for the ordinary crime is equal to the sentence for the international crime, the nature of the ordinary crime is irrelevant". Also see generally Olasolo 2012, pp. 74–101 (analysing complementarity in relation to national sentencing for ordinary crimes).

[44] See *Prosecutor v. William Ruto, Henry Kosgey and Joshua Sang*, Case No. ICC-01/09-01/11 and *Prosecutor v. Uhuru Kenyatta, Francis Muthaura and Mohammed Ali*, Case No. ICC-01/09-02/11.

[45] See ICC Elements of Crimes http://www.icc-cpi.int/NR/rdonlyres/9CAEE830-38CF-41D6-AB0B-68E5F9082543/0/ElementofCrimesEnglish.pdf. Accessed October 2011. The Elements of Crimes, adopted pursuant to Article 9 of the ICC Statute, are used by the ICC as aids to interpretation of the crimes under the Statute. For details see Dörmann et al. 2003, p. 8.

some individual acts, the Kenyan Penal Code is by far more punitive than the ICC Statute.[46]

Killing (homicide) is criminalized under Chapter XIX of the Kenyan Penal Code as "murder" and "manslaughter", and the two carry severe punishment of death and life imprisonment, respectively.[47] Murder is defined as causing death of another person "with malice aforethought".[48] In addition, attempted murder and conspiracy to commit murder are also criminalized as inchoate offences and punishable by life and 14 years imprisonment, respectively.[49]

Sexual offences, including rape, are criminalized as such and severely punishable. Before 2006, these crimes fell under the category of *offences against morality* under Chapter XV of the Penal Code of Kenya. The offences under this chapter have been re-characterized as *sexual offences* and are now comprehensively regulated by a specific piece of legislation.[50] This legislation makes "provision about sexual offences, their definition, prevention and the protection of all persons from harm from unlawful sexual acts, and for connected purposes".[51] It establishes, defines and punishes a wide range of sexual offences, ranging from rape, attempted rape, sexual assault, defilement and others.[52] The punishment levels for sexual offences are very severe, ranging mostly from 10 years to life imprisonment.[53] The scope of this legislation in terms of the offences is wide enough to adequately cover even the category "other sexual offences" in the ICC Statute.[54]

Furthermore, Chapters XXII and XXIV of the Penal Code contain other criminalized acts which, in their totality, are intended to protect life and health. The crimes provided for here cover several types of conduct which are also punishable before the ICC. One such conduct in the ICC Statute is the vague and open-ended crime of "other inhumane acts" which the ICC Prosecutor charged with respect to the Kenyan cases, and whose constituent or specific acts are not clearly provided in the ICC Statute. The ICC Prosecutor has alleged that the "other inhumane acts" committed

---

[46] A broad range of punishments can be imposed by Kenyan courts. These include death, imprisonment (including life imprisonment), detention, fine, forfeiture, and payment of compensation. See Kenyan Penal Code, Chap. 6.

[47] Ibid., ss. 202–205.

[48] Ibid., s. 203. "Malice aforethought" is defined extensively under s. 206.

[49] Ibid., ss. 220(a) and 224.

[50] See Sexual Offences Act of 2006.

[51] Ibid., Preamble.

[52] Ibid., ss. 1–29.

[53] E.g., severe sentences are imposed as follows: life imprisonment for rape (s. 3(3)), 10 years to life sentence for attempted rape and sexual assault (ss. 4 and 5(2), respectively); 15 years to life imprisonment for defilement of a child (s. 8); and 15 years to life imprisonment for gang rape (s. 10).

[54] The ICC Statute criminalizes the following conduct as crime against humanity of other sexual offences: "Rape, sexual slavery, enforced prostitution, forced pregnancy, enforced sterilization or any other form of sexual violence of comparative gravity". See ICC Statute, Article 7(1)(g).

during the post-election violence took the form of "very serious and life-changing injuries" resulting from "injuries inflicted by, or resulting from, sharp pointed objects, blunt objects, soft tissue injury, gunshots, arrow shorts, burns, and other assaults" in respect of 3,561 people.[55] Most of these acts could be punished under the Kenyan Penal Code, for example, "intentionally causing grievous harm to another person",[56] "common assault"[57] and "assault occasioning actual bodily harm"[58] They could also be prosecuted as attempts and be punished adequately.

Chapter IX of the Penal Code criminalizes and punishes offences related to unlawful assemblies, riots and other offences against public tranquillity. One offence here which could effectively cover the post-election violence is established under section 77(1). This provision criminalizes both as completed offences or inchoate offences (i.e. attempts and conspiracy, including mere preparation) any commission of any act or any utterance of words with "subversive" intention. Subversive intention is defined to include, inter alia, "incitement to violence or other disorder or crime",[59] "indicating, expressly or by implication, any connexion, association or affiliation with or support for, any unlawful society"[60] or intended or calculated to promote feelings or enmity between different races or communities in Kenya (hate speech).[61] Moreover, administering or taking or presence in an illegal oath to commit a crime is in itself a crime punishable by up to maximum of death penalty.[62]

It is notable that property crimes were widely committed during the post-election violence. As a result, offences against property, specifically looting, theft and destruction of property, were included as part of the indictment in the two Kenyan cases before the ICC, and it has been argued before the ICC's Pre-Trial Chamber that such acts constitute the crimes against humanity of "other inhumane act", "deportation or forcible transfer of population" or "persecution".[63] This conduct, too, is extensively covered under Division V of the Kenyan Penal Code as, for example, felonies of theft, armed robbery, house breaking and arson. They also

---

[55] See Prosecutor's Request for Authorisation of an Investigation, *Situation in the Republic of Kenya* (ICC-01/09-3), PTC, 26-November 2009, para 101.

[56] Kenyan Penal Code, ss. 231(a) and 234. Both provisions impose life imprisonment upon conviction.

[57] Ibid., s. 250.

[58] Ibid., s. 251.

[59] Ibid., s. 77(1)(b).

[60] Ibid., s. 77(1)(d).

[61] Ibid., s. 77(1)(e) See also s. 96(a) and (b), punishing a person who "utters, prints or publishes any words, or does any act or thing, indicating or implying at it is or might be desirable to do, or omit to do, any act the doing or omission of which is calculated to bring death or physical injury to any person or to any class, community or body of persons; or (*b*) to lead to the damage or destruction of any property".

[62] Ibid., ss. 60–65.

[63] See infra Sect. 6.4.1.1 on how property crimes committed during the post-election violence in Kenya have been treated during the confirmation of charges stage at the ICC.

attract a broad range of severe punishments, the maximum of which being death sentence for armed robbery.[64]

4.3.1.3.2 Modes of Criminal Liability

The question as to how criminal liability is apportioned to the perpetrator according to his or her contribution or mode of participation in the criminal act or omission is generally regulated by Sections 20 to 22 (Chapter V) of the Kenyan Penal Code under the caption "parties to offence".[65] From these provisions, individual criminal responsibility arises if a person participates in the commission of a crime in four ways which can be summarized as: (i) commission; (ii) aiding and abetting (assistance); (iii) encouragement; and (iv) conspiracy.[66]

4.3.1.3.2.1 Commission

Two forms of commission are provided for in the Kenyan Penal Code. These are direct commission (section 20(1)(a)) and joint commission (section 21). On the one hand, direct commission (or direct perpetration) creates liability when the conduct of the perpetrator was the immediate cause of the *actus reus* of the offence in question. It thus holds responsible "every person who actually does the act or makes the omission which constitutes the offence" in question.[67] On the other hand, joint commission (or co-perpetration) creates criminal liability for participation in a *common plan* involving a plurality of persons who have agreed to *jointly* commit a crime. It suffices that the crime committed was a probable consequence of the execution of such a purpose (*dolus eventualis*).[68]

According to the High Court of Kenya: (i) the common plan must not necessarily come into being prior to the commission of the crime: it can also develop in the course of the commission of the crime; (ii) the perpetrator must share with other

---

[64] E.g. Punishments are defined follows: 3–14 years imprisonment for theft (ss. 275–285); 5 years imprisonment to death sentence for robbery and related crimes (ss. 295–302); 5–15 years imprisonment for house breaking, burglary and similar offences (ss. 303–311); and 14 years to life sentence for arson or attempt thereof (ss. 332–333).

[65] In a few cases, other pieces of legislation provide for modes of participation specific for crimes established therein. See, for example, Geneva Conventions Act of 1968, s. 3.

[66] Cf. ICC Statute, Article 25(3), ICTY Statute, Article 7(1); ICTR Statute, Article 6(1). For a more detailed elaboration on modes of participation are under international criminal law, see Bantekas 2010, pp. 51–78; Cassese 2013, pp. 161–179; Damgaard 2008, Werle 2009, pp. 167–185; Werle 2007, p. 953 et seq. On joint criminal enterprise as a mode of participation before the ICTY see Judgment, *Tadic* (IT-94-1-A), 15 July 1999, para 190 et seq.

[67] Kenyan Penal Code, s. 20(1)(a).

[68] It reads: "When two or more persons form a common intention to prosecute an unlawful purpose in conjunction with one another, and in the prosecution of such purpose an offence is committed of such a nature that its commission was a probable consequence of the prosecution of such purpose, each of them is deemed to have committed the offence".

perpetrators of the crime a common intention to pursue a specific unlawful purpose which leads to the commission of the offence; (iii) the common intention may also be inferred from the actions of the accused persons; (iv) the accused must be aware of the common plan when he or she decided to participate in the joint criminal act; and (v) any offence committed by one of the implementers of the common plan, even when it falls outside the plan, creates liability to all other co-perpetrators, provided it was a natural and foreseeable consequence of realizing their common purpose.[69]

It is worth mentioning that the above-mentioned two forms of commission are largely comparable to what is contained under Article 25 of the ICC Statute. A third form of commission which is found under Article 25 i.e., commission through another person, is not contemplated by the Kenyan Penal Code.[70]

4.3.1.3.2.2 Aiding and Abetting (Assistance)

Assistance is another mode of participation which can be located in the provisions of section 20(1)(b) of the Kenya Penal Code. This provision creates liability for "every person who aids or abets another person in committing the offence", as well as "every person who does or omits to do any act for the purpose of enabling or aiding another person to commit the offence".[71]

4.3.1.3.2.3 Encouragement

Encouragement to commit a crime is a third mode of criminal liability established under section 20(1)(c) of the Kenya Penal Code. The section holds criminally responsible "any person who counsels or procures any other person to commit the offence".[72] The Penal Code provides expressly that encouragement can be charged alternatively as "individual commission", and in either way, the same consequences in terms of punishment flow.[73] Moreover, the Penal Code is clear that the offence actually committed and the manner in which it is committed need not be the same as that which was counselled. Also relevant is the fact that, like the case of a common plan, it is enough that the facts constituting the offence actually committed are a probable consequence of carrying out of the counsel.[74]

4.3.1.3.2.4 Conspiracy

Besides being targeted as an independent crime in itself under the Kenyan Penal Code, the common law conspiracy is also a mode of participation which is similar to,

---

[69] *Republic v. Kiprotich letting & 3 Others* (2009) eKLR, pp. 13–15.

[70] Cf. ICC Statute, Article 25(3)(a); Werle 2009, pp. 67–80.

[71] Cf. ICC Statute, Article 25 (3)(c); Werle 2009, pp. 182–184.

[72] Cf. ICC Statute, Article 25(3)(b); Werle 2009, pp. 180–182.

[73] Kenyan Penal Code, ss. 20(1)(2).

[74] Ibid., ss. 22(1) and 22(2).

but not the same as, a common plan.[75] Whereas criminal liability for common plan (joint commission) arises *only* when the planned or agreed crime has actually been committed (i.e. when the plan has been carried out to fruition), the criminal liability for conspiracy arises by mere conclusion of an *agreement to commit a crime.* Therefore, regardless of whether or not the underlying (planned) crime has been committed, the conspirator's criminal liability remains intact under the Kenyan law.[76]

4.3.1.3.3 Further Evaluation

Given their organized nature, commission of crimes under international law usually involves two groups of perpetrators. The first and bigger group is that of direct perpetrators i.e., those who perform the actual or physical acts of killing, rape, torture, etc. The second and smaller group is that of indirect perpetrators i.e., those who rarely commit the crimes personally, but who, through planning, funding and instigation, do facilitate or contribute substantially to the commission of the crimes. The second group of perpetrators is considered the *most responsible* for the crimes, despite usually being far away from the actual scenes of crime, and it is this group that the ICC normally targets for prosecution.[77] This, in a nutshell, means that if the ordinary-crime approach is used to prosecute such crimes, first and foremost, the rules establishing individual criminal responsibility must, as a matter of principle, be able to connect or link both groups of perpetrators to the crimes and punish them sufficiently.[78] The Kenyan Penal Code is suitable for the task as far as the post-election violence is concerned.

In the Kenyan scenario, the direct perpetrators who committed crimes against the members of "unwanted" communities or perceived "invaders" in their locality, or the police officers who through deliberate omission failed to prevent the

---

[75] Ibid., Chap. XLI; ss. 393–395.

[76] It is also immaterial whether the planned crime is possible of being committed or the conspirator is actually capable of committing the underlying offence. Cf. Meierhenrich 2006, pp. 344–345. NB. The crime of conspiracy is treated slightly differently in the Common Law and Romano-Germanic legal traditions. These differences have been reflected in the jurisprudence of the Ad hoc Tribunals, and have also impacted on the ICC Statute. For a recent in-depth study in this regard, see Okoth 2014.

[77] Accordingly, very often the degree of criminal responsibility for crimes under international law tends to increase (rather than decrease) as the perpetrator's physical distance from the scene of the crime increases. See Judgment, *Tadic* (IT-94-1-A), 15 July 1999, paras 191–2; Werle 2009, p. 166.

[78] Cf. Amnesty International 2000, pp. 5–6. In this regard, Osiel notes that on a case-by-case basis, depending on the structure of the domestic law concerned, several challenges may arise from the use of the ordinary-crime approach, including (i) the failure to link the indirect perpetrators to and hold them responsible for the misconduct of the direct perpetrators; (ii) domestic rules putting more concentration on the actual perpetrators, thereby letting the indirect perpetrators of the crimes go scot free; or (iii) although the scope of domestic rules on individual criminal responsibility could be wide enough to net in the indirect perpetrators, such law may end up apportioning them less criminal liability (e.g. accessorial liability and consequently, a less severe sentence) than the direct perpetrators. See Osiel 2005, pp. 793–795.

attacks on the civilian populations, can be prosecuted as direct perpetrators under section 20(1)(a) of the Penal Code. Falling under this group also are the ordinary followers or sympathizers of the PNU and the ODM, including the members of the affiliated criminal gangs such as the *Mungiki*.

As already shown (supra Sect. 3.2.2), the post-election violence assumed a pattern of coordinated attacks. As such, most of the direct perpetrators mentioned above, although also criminally responsible for their own acts, were knowingly or unknowingly implementing some sort of a plan, or at least acted on some encouragement. In order to avoid the possibility of the domestic prosecutions concentrating only on these "small fish" by relying on direct commission, domestic prosecutors could, when charging these crimes, also rely on the modes of participation entailing indirect commission. In this regard, if the provisions of section 21 of the Penal Code (common plan) were to be applied effectively and genuinely, the liability of the architects of the violence—the planners, buyers and distributors of weapons and the instigators—could be established under the ordinary-crime approach. In the case of *Republic v. Letting and three others,* the High Court of Kenya already took cognisance of the uniqueness of the crimes committed during the post-election violence and highlighted, inter alia, that the doctrine of common plan would have been the most appropriate way of dealing with the crimes as they apparently involved group planning.[79]

Secondly, as the Kenya National Commission on Human Rights has correctly argued that *encouragement* and *assistance* would be two of the most appropriate domestic modes of responsibility to found criminal liability, for "[a] majority of the senior actors, especially political leaders, who might not have been directly involved in the execution of the violence as opposed to the youths on the streets who did the actual killing and destruction of property".[80] This argument is plausible because, by its nature, accessory liability arises upon proof that the accused person was connected to the crime in question but not necessarily by being physically present at the scene of the crime. Under the current common law position, the person who counsels, encourages or otherwise aids and abets another person to commit a crime is considered to be arguably the "actual originator" of the crime.[81] It is notable that even the old requirement that the direct perpetrator must first be found guilty in order for the accessory to also be found guilty is no longer applicable.

Thus, it can be asserted that the practical distinction between principals and accessories to a crime has significantly lost its relevance in the common law legal tradition, thereby making the two parties to crime equal in terms of culpability and

---

[79] See *Republic v. Kiprotich Letting and Three Others (2009) eKLR,* pp. 15–18.

[80] See Kenya National Commission on Human Rights 2008, p 159, para 609.

[81] See LaFave 2003, pp. 666–667.

liability for punishment.[82] The Kenyan Penal Code amply supports this assertion. It clearly provides that regardless of whether the accused person is the direct perpetrator of the crime or otherwise contributed indirectly to its commission through assistance or encouragement, his or her criminal responsibility is the same. In this respect, the chapeau of section 20 of the Code provides categorically that those who directly commit, assist or encourage the commission of a crime are "deemed to have taken part in committing the offence and to be guilty of the offence, and may be charged with actually committing it". Also those who counsel or procure others to commit a crime "*may* be charged *either* with committing the offence *or* with counselling or procuring its commission".[83]

The foregoing explanations suggest that if the Kenyan Penal Code was *genuinely* applied as the basis for charging the crimes associated with the post-election violence, the architects of the violence would not escape liability easily. The most important and challenging task on the part of domestic prosecutors would be to establish the connection or contribution of these individuals to the crimes in terms of the actual planning, instigation, aiding or abetting in the commission of the violence.

At another level, by prosecuting the acts as ordinary Penal Code crimes, Kenyan prosecutors would have an additional practical advantage which they would not have if they prosecuted the acts as crimes against humanity as such. Such advantage relates to the onus of proof. Usually, for ordinary crimes the prosecution's task is mainly to prove the objective and subjective elements of the crime i.e., *actus reus* and *mens rea* for the ordinary crime charged. The prosecution is therefore relieved of the additional burden of proof relating to the contextual elements of crimes against humanity (see infra Sect. 6.4.2.2) which must be proved alongside the individual acts should the crimes must be charged as crimes against humanity as such.[84]

Furthermore, given the lack of expertise in international criminal law in Kenya, especially on the part of the state prosecutors and investigators (see infra Sect. 4.3.1.5), prosecuting the conduct as ordinary crimes is more likely to yield better results. Local prosecutors are much more versed with the crimes in their

---

[82] For example, s. 8 of the English Accessories and Abettors Act of 1861 (amended by the Criminal Law Act 1977) provides: "Whoever shall aid, abet, counsel or procure the commission of any indictable offence whether the same be an offence at common law or by virtue of any act passed or to be passed, shall be liable to be tried and punished as a principal offender". As an exception to this rule, common law retains the distinction between a principal and an accessory in respect of cases relating to strict and vicarious liability offences; as well as in cases where the laws requires that the offence in question can be committed only by a member of a specific class. See LaFave 2003, p. 669. Cf. Allen 2005, p. 199; Hamdorf 2007, p. 218; Smith and Hogan 2005, p. 165.

[83] Kenyan Penal Code, s. 20(1) (emphasis added).

[84] In this regard, Heller notes that the ordinary crimes approach, especially in the developing states, gives more flexibility to domestic prosecutors to select a crime they are conversant with and which they can successfully prosecute and secure maximum conviction easily. Therefore, requiring them to prosecute as "international crimes" as such might make them fail to prove their case due to the requirement to prove not only the criminal conduct charged but also the contextual elements of the crime. See. Heller 2012, pp. 216–218.

Penal Code than crimes under international law or in the ICC statute for that matter. This could be one of the explanations behind the decision that the proposed Special Tribunal for Kenya would have drawn its investigators and chief prosecutor from outside Kenya (see supra 3.5.1.1). In proposing the outsourcing of the prosecutorial function, the contemplators of the special tribunal must have considered, among other factors, the knowledge gap in the domestic institutions vested with investigative and prosecutorial authority in terms of the general understanding and mastery of the core crimes under international law and their sophistications.

Lastly, it is admitted that charging the conduct as "ordinary crimes" may not squarely depict the degree of condemnation or the "moral repugnancy" that attaches to the conduct as the case would seem to be if charges were, for example, for "crimes against humanity" per se. But for the international community, and more importantly for the victims of the post-election violence, it is not necessarily the label of the conduct charged that matters most, but rather the punishment of the perpetrators for the criminal conduct they committed. In this regard, it is now evident that the Kenyan Penal Code is even more punitive than the ICC Statute.[85]

4.3.1.4 To What Extent Has Kenya Utilized the Ordinary-Crimes Approach?

Having established that the ordinary-crime approach is sufficient for Kenya, this section proceeds to examine the extent to which Kenya has utilized the approach to prosecute the crimes committed during the post-election violence. It is worth stating that, 3 years after the violence, in December 2010, Kenya's Attorney-General, who was at that time the head of Kenya's prosecutorial authority, stated as follows:

> I must say there has been some prosecution for the post-election violence, but it was minimal and did not make any impact. The people perceived to have been perpetrators were not investigated and accordingly, were not prosecuted.[86]

---

[85] The ICC cannot impose death penalty. The maximum sentence it can impose is life imprisonment. See ICC Statute, Article 77. In the first two convictions by the ICC against Thomas Lubanga (for war crimes) and Germain Katanga (for war crimes and crimes against humanity), jail sentences of 14 and 12 years were imposed, respectively. See Decision on Sentence, *Lubanga* (ICC-01/04-01/06-2901); TC, 10 July 2012; Decision on Sentence, *Katanga* (ICC-01/04-01/07-3484), TC, 23 May 2014. Similarly, studies of the ITY and CTR sentencing jurisprudence indicate that the two Tribunals are considerably less punitive than national courts of Rwanda and Yugoslavia prosecuting the same conduct as domestic ordinary crimes. See Heller 2012, pp. 226–228. For more details see Drumbl 2007; Harmon and Gaynor 2007, pp. 688 et seq; Meernik and King 2003, pp. 717 et seq.

[86] See Statement of Kenya's Attorney-General Amos Wako during the opening of an workshop on the ICC and complementarity in Nairobi, 3–4 December 2010, p. 13. Available at http://www.africalegalaid.com/news/proceedings-of-icc-complementarity-workshop-in-kenya. Accessed August 2014.

In view of this statement, it is important to analyse what crimes have been charged, who has been prosecuted, who has not been charged, and why.

Initially, the speed with which the security agencies and prosecutorial authority started dealing with the crimes seemed promising, although at first they focused only on minor offences. For example, by 1 June 2008, just 4 months after the end of the violence, a total of 4,690 petty offences related to the post-election violence had been prosecuted and disposed of country wide, while 7,310 cases were pending in courts.[87] The minister responsible for internal security directed the police to speed up the investigations and prosecutions, especially of "those linked to capital and serious offences" and give the various cases priority in accordance with gravity.[88] The crucial question then remained whether the investigative and prosecutorial authorities would ensure that the main architects of the violence were investigated and prosecuted. If these authorities were seriously determined to address this question, they would, as a matter of priority, have taken into consideration the following lists of known suspects.

4.3.1.4.1 Lists of Suspects

At least four lists of suspects have been compiled at different times by different sources, although not all the individual suspects in the lists have been expressly identified by names. In the two cases where names have been expressly mentioned, the lists do overlap greatly.

The first list of suspects was compiled by the Waki Commission. It was a list of 20 names that were enclosed in an envelope and handed over to the African Panel of Eminent Personalities and later to the ICC Prosecutor for further investigations. The envelope not only contained the names of the alleged main perpetrators, but also contained reasons (supporting evidence) for an investigation. However, the identities of the persons named in the envelope were not revealed to the public. The ICC Prosecutor stated that "the content of the envelope will remain confidential, there will be no leaks".[89] Thus, it can only be stated with certainty that the list remains known to the members of the Waki Commission, the members of the AU Panel of Eminent African Personalities and the Office of the ICC's Prosecutor. This is despite the fact that in Kenya it is contended that the list was revealed to President Mwai Kibaki and Prime Minister Raila Odinga; and that the Prosecutor discussed the content of the envelope, including the names therein, with the two principal leaders of the coalition government before the ICC process began.[90]

Another list of suspects is associated with the police. Following the minister's directive to the police to speed up the investigations and prosecutions, the police said that they had already identified a list of 103 "priority cases" against 137

---

[87] Daily Nation, 1 June 2008.

[88] Ibid.

[89] ICC Press Release, ICC-OTP-20090716-PR439, 16 July 2009.

[90] Daily Nation, 5 August 2012.

suspects. Kenyan newspapers reported that the cases in the "priority list" included, for example, the murder of 35 people burnt in the Kiambaa church in Eldoret, 19 people burnt in a house in Naivasha, Catholic Priest, Michael Kamau, an administrative police officer in Kericho, a district officer and Charles Keittany Korir, a former irrigation officer in Koibatek district.[91] It was also reported that the police had drawn up a separate list of 200 "prominent people", including politicians and businessmen, whom they "suspected to have sponsored the violence". Some of these individuals have been charged[92] but not much information about their cases was known at the time of writing. What remains unclear though is whether these two lists by the police were linked, although there is a high possibility that they could be.

The third, long list of suspects was compiled by the Kenya National Human Commission on Human Rights following its thorough and independent inquiry into the violence. This commission is a statutory institution whose mandate is traceable directly to the Kenyan Constitution. As such, its reports on various human rights issues in Kenya have demonstrated that it is an independent and credible body. For that reason, its inquiry into the violence was not done from the perspective of mere "NGO activism". It is on the basis of this background that such reports, including the one containing the list of the suspects accused to have taken part in the post-election violence, must be accorded the weight they deserve.

In order to compile its list of suspects, the Kenya National Human Commission on Human Rights used seven objective criteria based on a "threshold of credible and reliable information" concerning the participation of the various perpetrators in the violence.[93] The following criteria were particularly used:

- Level of information and detail describing the role the alleged person may have played;
- Existence of corroborating or verifying information on the person (including confessions);
- Credibility of the allegations;
- Subjecting "I heard" type of allegations to the preceding three criteria before admission;
- Consideration of the totality of information available, including that obtained through interviews with alleged perpetrators;
- Exclusion of outrageous, preposterous and baseless information; and
- Whether or not, on a balance of probabilities, [the commission] believed that a name should or should not be included based on any or all of the above criteria.[94]

---

[91] Daily Nation, 1 June 2008.

[92] This includes, for example, ODM politician Jackson Kibor, who was charged in Nakuru with incitement; Kapsabet mayor Michael Rono, Councillors Paul Cheruiyot and Johnston Kirua and former councillors Ishmael Choge, Abid Keter, Richard Ruto and George Ruto, who were charged with crimes against property; and former Moi University lecturer and businessman Silas Simatwo, who was charged for allegedly financing the violence. See ibid.

[93] Kenya National Commission on Human Rights 2008, p. 13, para 22.

[94] Ibid.

On the basis of the criteria set out above, the Commission published a list of about 220 alleged perpetrators with a description of their specific role in the organization of the violence. The following important information as regards the perpetrators accompanied the list: (i) "adverse mentions" (i.e. mentioning of their names); (ii) their background information; (iii) the specific allegation(s) against each of them; and (iv) information supporting the allegation(s).[95]

In addition to the list, the Commission developed a "triangle of responsibility" that entailed an attribution of responsibility to the perpetrators according to their alleged degree or level of participation in the violence. Accordingly, the listed alleged perpetrators were classified into three groups, namely (i) "remote perpetrators", namely those who were allegedly the "overall planners, financiers, instigators and organizers" of the violence. This group constitutes the least number forming the apex of the triangle. Notwithstanding their remoteness from the scenes of crime, the perpetrators in this group were classified as being the "most responsible" for the post-election violence; (ii) "mid-level perpetrators", namely those who received instructions or orders from the main perpetrators and oversaw the actual implementation of the plans in the local areas; and (iii) "low-level perpetrators", namely those who physically or directly committed the crimes during the violence. This formed the biggest group of perpetrators.[96]

Furthermore, the Commission included a breakdown in its report which grouped the perpetrators into five categories according to their role or influence in the society. The composition of the categories included (i) 20 MPs or senior politicians, including ministers in the government immediately prior to the 2007 general elections and also those serving in the coalition government; (ii) at least 40 senior public officers or state agents; (iii) five vernacular radio stations; (iv) four religious leaders; and (v) at least 160 other people who do not fall in any of the four groups above.[97]

Interestingly, five out of the six suspects in the "Ocampo six" list, namely Uhuru Kenyatta, William Ruto, Henry Kosgey, Mohammed Ali and Joshua Sang, were adversely mentioned in the list of perpetrators compiled by the Kenya National Commission on Human Rights. The sixth suspect, Francis Muthaura, was not mentioned anywhere in the report. Furthermore, the Commission made it clear that its list of suspects should be a "basis and a good starting point for further investigations".[98] It could not be established the extent to which the list of suspected perpetrators compiled the Kenya National Commission on Human Rights is related to those allegedly compiled by the Kenyan police (if any actually exists).

The fourth and last list of perpetrators was published by the Kenyan Truth Commission in its final report of May 2013 (infra Chap. 5). Save for a few additions, the Truth Commission identified 56 names from the list of perpetrators compiled by

---

[95] See Ibid., pp. 176 et seq. (Annex 1).

[96] Ibid., pp. 12–3, paras 20–21.

[97] Ibid., pp. 176 et seq. (Annex 1).

[98] Ibid., p. 176.

the Kenya National Human Commission on Human Rights and recommended their
further investigation or prosecution.[99] The Truth Commission had a clear statutory
mandate to give binding recommendations, including on prosecutions.

Therefore, in view of all the four lists of perpetrators described above, it is clear
that the investigators and prosecutors had a foundation to build on i.e., the list of
known suspects. The following section examines the available figures and facts
regarding actual investigations and prosecutions by May 2013.

4.3.1.4.2   Figures and Facts on Domestic Investigations and Prosecutions

The figures and facts provided below show that some progress was made between
2008 and 2012 with regard to investigation and prosecution of the crimes linked to
the post-election violence, charges being for ordinary domestic crimes. The question whether this is sufficient for the requirements imposed by the duty to prosecute the core crimes (see supra Sect. 1.2) is addressed at the end of this part.

4.3.1.4.2.1   Attorney-General's Report of 2009

In June 2008, the Kenyan Attorney-General directed the Director of Public
Prosecutions (DPP) to constitute a team to undertake national wide review of the
cases related to the post-election violence. At that time, the Attorney-General was
the Kenya's chief prosecutorial authority, while the DPP was subordinated to the
Attorney-General's Office. The team was constituted accordingly, commenced its
work on 21 June 2008 and submitted its report to the Attorney-General in February
2009.[100] As Table 4.1 shows, the report, contained information of cases which had
already been concluded, those pending in courts and those still under investigation.

The report further indicates that, as of the report date, there were 3,627 cases
under investigation (not yet brought to court) all of which in Rift Valley. The cases
pending in courts were in respect of 33 specific penal code offences, while those
already concluded were in respect of 27 offences.

According to the report, the following number of cases (quantity shown in
brackets) had been concluded in respect of the specified penal code offences: robbery with violence (two); arson (five); attempted arson (two); stealing (six); burglary and stealing (two); malicious damage of property (one); creating disturbance
(one); taking part in riots (five); possession of offensive weapon (one); obstructing
police (one); shop breaking and stealing (eight); stock theft (four); being armed in
public (one); house breaking and stealing (four); breaking into building and committing a felony (five); incitement to violence (six); bar breaking and committing
felony (two); handling stolen property (four); breach of peace (one); conveying
stolen property (three); store breaking and stealing (one); stealing motor vehicle,

---

[99] Kenya Truth, Justice and Reconciliation Commission Report 2013, Vol. IV, Appendix 2.

[100] Republic of Kenya 2009.

Table 4.1 The total number of cases concluded, those pending before courts and those in respect of which the Attorney-General had issued directives to withdraw permanently or to be reinstituted after further investigations as at 27 February 2009

Province	Number of cases concluded		Number of cases pending before courts		AG's directives about action to be taken on the cases pending before courts		
					Proceed to logical conclusion	Withdraw and close file	Withdraw for further investigations
	Cases	Accused	Cases	Accused	Cases	Cases	Cases
Rift valley	28	60	106	504	42	48	16
Western	19	44	23	51	16	7	–
Nyanza	23	112	21	42	11	9	1
Coast	13	51	6	79	–	–	–
Central	–	–	–	–	–	–	–
Eastern	–	–	–	–	–	–	–
Nairobi	–	–	–	–	–	–	–
Total	83	267	156	676	69	64	17

Author's adaptation from the statistical information presented in Republic of Kenya 2009 (AG's report on the post-election violence related cases), pp. 8–37

publishing false rumour, preparing to commit a felony (one); bond to keep peace (one); threatening to kill, threatening violence, setting fire on calculated crop, inquest, riotously interfering with vehicles (two); hotel breaking (two); and being armed in public (one).[101]

As can be discerned from the report, most of the concluded or ongoing investigations and prosecutions had been in respect of relatively "minor" offences, and mostly relating to property. For example, while no single case had been concluded with regard to the crimes of "murder" and "assault causing actual bodily harm", only five cases and one case were pending in court in respect of the two crimes, respectively.[102] What is completely missing in the report is any mention of or information about concluded or pending cases in respect of sexual offences, despite the fact that high number of rapes occurred during the post-election violence and were reported. The report itself expressly observed that until then no subsequent follow-up had been made in respect of the high number of complaints recorded in the internally displaced people's camps, specifically noting that the number of murder cases being investigated or pending in courts was comparatively too small in view of the high number of deaths reported during the violence.[103]

---

[101] See Republic of Kenya 2009, pp. 35–37.

[102] See ibid., Appendix iv.

[103] Ibid., p. 40.

Consequently, the report was quickly dismissed by the ICC Prosecutor as he argued that it was not reflective of a serious willingness to fight impunity.[104]

4.3.1.4.2.2 Attorney-General's Report of 2011

In March 2011, 2 years after the first report was compiled, the Kenyan government through its Attorney-General released another document which was supposedly a "follow-up progress report" to the 2009 report.[105] In this "updated" report, the most prominent chapter was that on gender related violence, which had been completely missing or omitted in the previous Attorney-General's Report. The 2011 report shows that by the date on which the report was published, 399 investigations against 311 persons had been started or concluded in relation to five gender related crimes, namely defilement, attempted defilement, rape, attempted rape and gang rape.[106] A further breakdown regarding sexual offences was as follows: (a) 45 accused persons had been convicted; (b) 41 cases had been withdrawn or acquitted; (c) 25 cases were pending arrest; (d) 72 cases were still pending investigations; (e) 49 cases against unknown accused members of the police force were pending; (f) 105 cases had been forwarded to the Attorney-General seeking his authorization to withdraw; and (g) 62 cases were under trial in court.[107] Table 4.2 provides further statistical information on the status of cases as at March 2011, including those relating to sexual offences.

Table 4.2 The status of cases relating to the post-election violence in Kenya per province in respect of all crimes as at March 2011

Province	Cases still under investigation	Convictions	Acquittals	Withdrawn	Pending arrest of known suspects
Rift valley	3,325	50	40	68	16
Western	51	7	0	3	–
Nyanza	69	25	4	18	1
Coast	14	5	9	90	–
Central	8	–	–	1	–
Eastern	–	–	–	–	–
Nairobi	12	7	4	–	–
Total	3,479	94	57	180	17

Author's adaptation from the statistical information presented in Republic of Kenya 2011 (AG's updated report of post-election violence related cases), pp. 70–72

---

[104] See Prosecutor's Request for Authorisation of an Investigation, *Situation in the Republic of Kenya* (ICC-01/09-3), PTC, 26 November 2009, paras 53–54.

[105] Republic of Kenya 2011.

[106] Ibid., pp. 9–23.

[107] See ibid., pp. 7–8.

One observation to make at this stage is that the 2011 report does not present comprehensive information. In the first place, the report was not an outcome of a thorough exercise. It was compiled in a hurry (only in 10 days)[108] primarily because the Kenyan government wanted to submit it to the ICC to support its admissibility challenge in respect of the two cases before the Court (see infra Sect. 6.5.3.2.2). The report itself states that in that short period of time not all anticipated cases were reviewed and updated.[109] It is further acknowledged that with the exception of the figures on the gender related violence, the rest of the report is a duplication of the information contained in the 2009 report.[110] On these grounds, Human Rights Watch dismissed it as an unreliable report which was "compiled hastily, with little concern for accuracy", and which, as a result, was "riddled with errors".[111] Among flaws which have been identified with regard to the report include, for example, acquittals which were labelled as convictions and the inclusion in the report of cases which were completely not related to the post-election violence, with a view to making numbers impressive for purposes of the above-mentioned admissibility challenge.[112] Moreover, like the 2009 report, it is not clear how the list "priority cases" alleged to have been compiled by the police feature in the 2011 report.

4.3.1.4.2.3   Human Rights Watch Survey of 2011

An independent and comprehensive survey on the status of national investigations and prosecutions of the cases related to the post-election violence was conducted by Human Rights Watch between February and November 2011. The survey covered 13 court jurisdictions in five provinces which were most affected by the violence.[113] Apart from interviews, the research entailed a perusal of 76 court files on selected cases. The selection only targeted cases that could be categorized as "high profile cases". According to Human Rights Watch, two criteria were used in determining whether a particular case passed the high-profile-case test. The first criterion was the official or societal position of the accused persons during the post-election violence. In this regard, the investigations and prosecutions "involving politicians, police, business people, or other influential citizens" were classified as constituting high-profile cases. The second criterion of a high-profile case was the gravity of the offences charged. Falling under this category were cases

---

[108] See the terms of reference in ibid., p. 3.

[109] ibid., p. 73.

[110] ibid., p. 74.

[111] Human Rights Watch 2011, p. 25.

[112] Ibid., pp. 25–27 and 45. Kenya actually invoked this report in its admissibility challenge. See infra Sect. 6.5.3.2.2.

[113] These are Bungoma, Butere, Eldoret, Kakamega, Kericho, Kitale, Molo, Mombasa, Nairobi, Naivasha, Nakuru, Sotik, and Webuye. See Ibid., p. 9.

"involving serious charges, such as murder, robbery with violence, rape, defile-ment and assault causing actual bodily harm".[114]

This survey was an eye-opener. It acknowledged that some progress had up until then been made in the way the domestic courts in Kenya were dealing with the post-election violence cases. It stated that the sweeping allegation that "no one had been convicted in Kenya for the 2007 post-election violence" in respect of high profile cases was not entirely true. Instead it found that by November 2011, there had been at least six convictions in respect of high-profile cases in the domestic courts due to "solid police investigations and assiduous work on the part of the prosecutors".[115] The convictions were for domestic ordinary crimes in respect of the felonies of murder, robbery with violence and causing grievous bod-ily harm.[116] Similarly, there had been seven acquittals in respect of felonies of murder, rape and robbery with violence;[117] while *nolle prosequi*[118] had been entered in respect of three other cases.[119]

In June 2012, subsequent to the publication of the Human Rights Watch Report, three more individuals were convicted by the Kenyan High Court for murder

---

[114] Ibid. For more information about all the researched cases, including the accused, the charges and the outcome of the cases, see pp. 82–92 (Appendix 1).

[115] Ibid., p. 39.

[116] The six cases consulted by the Human Rights Watch are: *Republic v. Robert Kipngetich Kemboi and Kirkland Kipngeno Langat,* Kericho High Court, HCCR 24/08. This judgment was appealed against as *Criminal Appeal 310/09* then pending in the Court of Appeal at Nakuru (charges: murder of two police officers); *Republic v. John Kimita Mwaniki,* Kericho High Court, HCCR 24/08 (now reported as *Republic v. John Kimita Mwaniki [2011] eKLR* (charges: murder of 3 persons); *Republic v. Charles Kipkumi Chepkwony,* Kericho Magistrate's Court, CR 101/08, the judgment appealed against as HCCR A30/09 then pending in the High Court of Kenya at Nakuru (charges: robbery with violence); *Republic v. James Mbugua Ndungu and Raymond Munene Kamau, Naivasha Magistrate's Court. Police file 764/44/08* (charges: sexual offences and robbery with violence; conviction secured only for robbery); *Republic v. Willy Kipngeno Rotich and 7 Others, Sotik Magistrate's Court, CR 8/08* (charges: robbery with violence); and *Republic v. Peter Ochiengo, Nakuru Magistrate's Court, CR 4001/0* (charges: causing grievous bodily harm). For brief facts of these cases, see Human Rights Watch 2011, pp. 40–42.

[117] The cases are: *Republic v. Kiprotich letting & 3 Others (2009) eKLR* (charges: murder of 35 people in Kiambaa, Rift Valley); *Republic v. Edward Kirui* [2010] eKLR (charging police officer for two counts of murder of demonstrators during the violence); *Republic v. Paul Kiptoo Barno, James Yutor Korir, and Isaiah Kipkorir Leting,* Eldoret Magistrate's Court, CR 387/08 (charged only with robbery—although it resulted in killing of District Officer, Benedict Omolo and Chief Inspector of police, Elias Wafula Wakhungu); *Republic v. Francis Kipn'geno and Others, Kericho Magistrate's Court,* CR 86/08 (charges: robbery with violence); *Republic v. Erick Kibet Towett and Simion Kipyegon Chepkwony, Kericho Magistrate's Court, CR 66/08* (rape); *Republic v. Erick Kibet Towett and Simion Kipyegon Chepkwony, Kericho Magistrate's Court, CR 66/08* (rape); *Republic v. Abraham Karonei and Robert Kimaiyo Tanui, Eldoret High Court, HCCR 15'B/2008* (murder). For brief facts of the cases, see Human Rights Watch 2011, pp. 30–39.

[118] For details see infra Sect. 4.4.2.2.4.

[119] *Republic v. Jackson Kibor, Nakuru Magistrate's Court, CR 96/08* (ODM politician charged with incitement to violence); *Republic v. Abraham Karonei and Robert Kimaiyo Tanui,* High Court at Eldoret, HCCR 15'B/2008 (murder). See Human Rights Watch 2011, pp. 32, 37 and 39.

related to the post-election violence. Life imprisonment and death penalty were imposed.[120] Therefore, from 2011, the number of concluded cases in respect of serious crimes was growing steadily.

4.3.1.5 Gaps and Challenges in Respect of the Domestic Prosecutions

As admitted above, the domestic courts have been engaged in prosecuting some of the post-election cases as ordinary crimes. What is evidently missing, however, is any tangible progress in respect of cases involving the architects of the violence, the "big fish". For example, 5 years after the violence, there was still no single record of a case against any of the people mentioned in the report of the Kenya National Commission on Human Rights to be the most responsible for the violence. Interestingly, the DPP said that he was unaware of the so-called "priority cases" that the police claimed to have compiled.[121] Highlighting the impunity with regard to the big fish, in June 2011, the Nairobi-based *Star* newspaper reported as follows:

> More cases related to serious crimes have gone forward (…) but they rarely targeted senior leaders or police use of excessive force. The dozens of convictions for petty crimes are outnumbered by withdrawals or acquittals for petty and serious crimes alike.[122]

Furthermore, for the few cases that have been investigated and prosecuted as ordinary crimes, myriad challenges have been encountered. As already shown, the number of cases completed successfully in respect of serious crimes has, so far, been minimal if compared to the seriousness, magnitude and number of crimes linked to the post-election violence. This is not to suggest that all prosecutions of crimes related to the post-election violence must necessarily result in convictions. But it is to argue that investigations or prosecution of such cases must at least portray the degree of seriousness they deserve.

On the contrary, the investigations and prosecution of some of the few cases that were prosecuted were faced with several limitations; they were devoid of competence and seriousness and were marred by sheer recklessness on the part of the prosecutors. In *Republic v. Kiprotich Letting* et al., for example, the presiding judge lamented about the outrageous "casual manner" in which the investigations and prosecution were handled.[123] He blamed what he referred to as "shoddy investigations" of the case on the police,[124] noting that courts should not be accused of

---

[120] On 11 June 2012, Peter Kipkemboi Ruto was sentenced to life imprisonment by the Nakuru High Court for murder of Kamau Kimani on January 1, 2008. See Capital News, 12 June 2012. On 28 June 2012, the High Court of Kenya in Kitale sentenced two people, Mosobin Sot Ngeiywa and Japheth Simiyu Wekesa, to death for the murder of four people at Kalaha farm in Trans Nzoia district. The motive for the murder was that the victims had not voted for the MP that the accused had preferred. See Kenya Daily Post, 29 June 2012.

[121] Human Rights Watch 2011, p. 17.

[122] The Star, 10 June 2011.

[123] *Republic v. Kiprotich Letting & 3 Others* (2009) eKLR, p. 15.

[124] Ibid., p. 18.

furthering impunity even though it is the investigators and prosecutors who did not bother to do their job competently. In some cases, mostly those prosecuted by the police prosecutors, the biggest weakness is that acts which could have constituted serious crimes were charged as less serious crimes, apparently because the police prosecutors failed to appreciate the correct nature of the crimes.[125] These kinds of challenges can be attributed to the ill-equipped prosecutorial authority in terms of, among other things, inadequacy of human resources as illustrated below.

According to Keraiko Tobiko, Kenya's DPP, by November 2011, there were only 72 trained prosecutors serving in the DPP's office, although the requirement then was 504.[126] This extreme dearth of trained lawyers in the office of the DPP is attributed to factors other than lack or shortage of law graduates in Kenya.[127] As a response to the problem, the 2010 Kenyan Constitution, just like the previous Constitution, provides that the "Parliament may enact legislation conferring powers of prosecution on authorities other than the DPP".[128] It is by virtue of this provision that the task of prosecuting criminal cases has been delegated to lay prosecutors (non-lawyers).

For instance, in all courts subordinate to the High Court (i.e. Magistrates' Courts), criminal cases are still prosecuted by police officers.[129] By virtue of the Kenya Police Force Standing Orders "all police officers of or above the rank of inspector are public prosecutors".[130] There is an exception to this rule which allows for officers of even a subordinate rank to inspector to prosecute in district magistrates' courts.[131] Most (almost all) of these police prosecutors are not lawyers by training. As of November 2011, the number of police prosecutors was 302, but only six of them had a law degree.[132] Although a proposal to phase out the police prosecutors was announced in 2011, its full implementation is yet to be realized.[133]

The challenges highlighted above affect the prosecution of crimes in general; they are not unique to the prosecution of the crimes associated with the post-election violence. But such challenges make it even clearer that, with regard to the criminal acts related to the post-election violence, the current *status quo* speaks

---

[125] Human Rights Watch 2011, pp. 35 and 46–51; Alai and Mue 2011, p. 127.

[126] Daily Nation, 19 November 2011.

[127] This has been associated with the low pay in the public sector i.e., in the government ministries, state law office (including the DPP's office) and the judiciary. As a result, most qualified lawyers are said to prefer employment in the private legal practice, in the corporate sector or in academia. Those who join the public sector are allegedly the least competent law graduates, or if competent, then they quit their jobs after a short time. See Mbote and Akech 2011, pp. 116–167.

[128] Constitution of Kenya of 2010, Article 157(12).

[129] Daily Nation, 6 July 2011.

[130] Kenya Police Force Standing Orders, Chap. 48, s. 7(i).

[131] Ibid., s. 7(ii).

[132] Daily Nation, 19 November 2011.

[133] For more information on police prosecutors in Kenya, see Mbote and Akech 2011, pp. 123–124; Mwalili 1998, p. 222.

more in favour of the prosecution of the conduct as ordinary crimes in the Penal Code with which the lay prosecutors and the trained prosecutors are more conversant. It would be more difficult for them if they were asked to prosecute it as "crimes against humanity" as such, the reason being that the additional task or burden to prove the contextual elements of crimes against humanity would make their job even more challenging, thereby risking letting the masterminds of the post-election violence go scot free.

Way Forward?

Grappling with the challenges highlighted above, and faced with endless calls for fighting impunity by deeds, the Kenyan government continued to act under mounting pressure throughout 2011, thanks to the ongoing ICC process. The pressure to reconsider a new strategy for effective domestic prosecution of those most responsible for the post-election violence was felt after 23 January 2012, the date on which the charges against four of the six Kenyans originally indicted before the ICC were confirmed.[134] Following the ICC's decisions in this regard, Githu Muigai, the newly appointed Kenya's Attorney-General, appointed a "working committee on the ICC", a ten-member panel tasked with advising the government on the "way forward".[135] The Committee comprised legal scholars, including two foreign international criminal law experts, Sir Geoffrey Nice and Mr Rodney Dixon, who acted for the Kenyan government in its unsuccessful admissibility challenge before the ICC.[136]

In what appeared to be an attempt to give domestic prosecutions a new impetus, and apparently this being the only way to keep the ICC away, the working committee advised the Kenyan government to give "immediate consideration" to the formulation of a comprehensive policy to deal with the post-election violence cases, including those before the ICC. It was advised that such policy should entail, inter alia: (i) a "reasonable balance" between retributive and restorative justice; (ii) conducting of a special audit of all the crimes committed during the post-election violence with a view of making an informed decision as to which ones to prosecute or terminate on the basis of the available evidence and the availability and or willingness of the witnesses to testify; (iii) appointment of "a special prosecutor" with a "strict timetable" for the completion of investigation and prosecution of the most serious offenders, regardless of rank or position of the perpetrators.[137]

It was further advised that the envisaged special prosecutor should be assisted by international experts in performing his or her duties, "taking into account the

---

[134] Decision on the Confirmation of Charges, *Muthaura, Kenyatta and Ali* (ICC-01/09-02/11-382-Red), PTC, 23 January 2012; Decision on the Confirmation of Charges, *Ruto, Kosgey and Sang* (ICC-01/09-01/11-373), PTC, 23 January 2012.

[135] VOA News, 24 January 2012. The team was first appointed under GN No. 996 of 2012 which was repealed and replaced by GN No. 3222 (Vol. CXIV-No 20) of 16 March 2012. Formation of the panel was criticized by civil society organisations and the Bar Association as being geared towards undermining the ICC process; serving "narrow and selfish interests"; "an insult to Kenyans"; and "a waste of public resources". African News Online, 26 January 2012.

[136] The Star, 18 March 2012. On the admissibility challenge, see infra Sect. 6.5.3.2.2.

[137] Daily Nation, 20 March 2012.

challenges faced by the current prosecutorial department and the great need to deal with the [post-election violence] expeditiously and on a priority basis".[138] According to the recommendations of the working committee, it was no longer necessary to create a special tribunal to try these cases, given that the judiciary had been reformed and become competent.[139]

In November 2012 the Kenya's new Chief Justice Dr Willy Mutunga stated that Kenya's Judicial Service Commission[140] was "at an advanced stage of setting up an International Crimes Division [ICD] of the High Court"[141] This name created an immediate impression that the envisioned Division would first and foremost prioritize the prosecution of the crimes linked to the 2007–2008 post-election violence in line with the implication of the report by the working committee. But surprisingly, when the establishment of this Division was announced in April 2013, it turned out that it may have nothing to do with the post-election violence. It was made clear by the Attorney-General, who is also a member of Kenya's Judicial Service Commission,[142] that the ICD would have a prospective effect.[143]

4.3.1.6 Interim Conclusion

This section has analysed the ordinary-crime approach as a legal framework for prosecuting the alleged crimes against humanity committed during the post-election violence in Kenya. It has been demonstrated that prosecuting and punishing the crimes as ordinary crimes under the Kenyan Penal Code can achieve the same purposes as prosecuting and punishing them as "crimes against humanity" as such. This argument gives prominence to the *conduct* which is targeted by the punishment rather than to the label or characterization under which that conduct is punished. Consequently, the argument that Kenya did not (or does not) have *any laws* to prosecute the alleged crimes against humanity linked to the post-election violence has been dismissed. It has been shown that Kenya has, to some extent, used its Penal Code to prosecute the crimes committed during the violence, despite the several challenges encountered. But what remains the biggest flaw is that such prosecutions have not targeted those listed as being most responsible for the crimes.

---

[138] Ibid.

[139] Ibid. See infra Sect. 5.3 regarding the reforms implemented in the Judiciary.

[140] See Constitution of Kenya of 2010, Articles 171 and 172.

[141] See remarks by the Kenya Chief Justice on the international justice system, 26 November 2012. http://www.judiciary.go.ke/portal/assets/files/Reports/WAYAMO%20MEETING%20ON%20 THE%20INTERNATIONAL%20JUSTICE%20SYSTEM.pdf. Accessed September 2014. See also The East African, 1 December 2012.

[142] Constitution of Kenya of 2010, Article 171(2)(e).

[143] Capital News, 30 April 2013. See also "CJ Speaks On International Crimes Division" [video] published by Kenya Citizen TV on You Tube, 30 April 2013 http://www.youtube.com/ watch?v=GW4uytJVReU. Viewed August 2014.

4.3.2 Prosecuting as Crimes Against Humanity as Such

Having analysed the ordinary-crime approach and having concluded that the approach provides an adequate legal framework to prosecute the criminal acts committed during the post-election violence, this section explores one more option, namely the possibility of *also* prosecuting the acts as crimes under international law as such i.e., under their label as "crimes against humanity". The section analyses whether it would be possible to do so on the basis of customary international law or the Kenya's International Crimes Act of 2008.

4.3.2.1 Relying on International Customary Law

4.3.2.1.1 Introductory Note

Crimes against humanity had already been established as crimes under customary international law even before the adoption of the ICC Statute[144] or the occurrence of the post-election violence in Kenya. A customary international crime is a prohibited criminal conduct which has acquired a *jus cogens* status, thereby constituting it as *obligatio erga omnes.* Consequently, for such crimes, a non-derogable and a mandatory duty exists for states to prosecute them without *any* restriction.[145]

The preceding paragraph would suggest or imply that, theoretically, the ultimate codification of crimes against humanity into the domestic laws of Kenya in 2008 was merely a "declaration" or "reinstatement" of a pre-existing set of crimes. Arguably, the crimes could, as a result, have been directly enforceable in the domestic courts, whether or not there was an implementing legislation. One of the reasons given for this argument is that in common law countries, such as Kenya, criminality may be based on both written and unwritten laws.[146] However, actual practice from common law countries indicates that domestic courts are not prepared to prosecute and punish individuals charged with crimes *only* envisaged in customary international law but which are not expressly codified in the domestic

---

[144] Cf. *National Commissioner of the South African Police and another v. Southern Africa Litigation Centre and others* (485/2012) [2013] ZASCA 168 (27 November 2013), para 40, in which the South African Supreme Court of Appeal stated that the ICC Statute is "a codification of sorts" of customary international law.

[145] See Bassiouni 1996, pp. 63 et seq. (pointing out, at p. 68, that apart from the four core crimes under international law, the crimes of piracy, slavery, torture and slave-related practices are also *jus cogens*).

[146] See Werle 2009, p. 119. On common law crimes, generally see LaFave (2003), pp. 74–85.

laws.[147] This is without exception to important common law jurisdictions such as the United Kingdom[148] and Australia.[149] It is, therefore, important to find out the position in Kenya.

4.3.2.1.2 Enforceability of Customary Law in Kenya: An Overview

The same reluctance cited above with respect to Australia and United Kingdom is foreseeable in the Kenyan courts. This is true despite the fact that, strictly speaking, the legal system of Kenya is a mixture of common law and customary law. Part of what is usually referred to as "African customary law" is enforceable in the Kenyan domestic courts even though it is uncodified and not uniform as customs differ from one ethnic (tribal) community to another. In fact, this particular category of law, like Acts of Parliament and the Constitution, forms an independent source of law in Kenya. However, the African customary law is enforceable only insofar as it relates to matters of *civil* nature, mostly succession and marriage. The so-called "African customary crimes" are not enforceable in the Kenyan courts for that matter.[150]

There is no record of prosecution of any of the core crimes under international law in the Kenyan domestic courts solely on the basis of its status under customary international law. However, there is evidence of prosecution of the customary crime

---

[147] Cassese 2005, p. 224; Jeßberger and Powell 2001, p. 350; Werle 2009, p. 119. For instance, in the UK the old view that courts had a general residual power to create new crimes (common law crimes) has been dismissed. See *Knuller (Publishing, Printing and Promotions) Ltd. v. Director of Public Prosecutions* [1973] A.C. 435; *R. v. Jones and Others* [2006] UKHL 16 [2006] UKHL 16, p. 42, para 102. In South Africa, too, the practice has ceased. See Maqungo 2000, p. 186.

[148] In the case of *R v. Johns and Others* [2006] UKHL 16, the House of Lords was called upon to address the question whether the crime of aggression formed part of English criminal law in the absence of domestic legislation. It had been argued that since the crime of aggression was recognized as a customary crime under international law, then such crime was directly enforceable in the UK's national courts without a need for any domestic statute or judicial decision. The House of Lords decided that the crime of aggression was not part of the domestic law of England even though there was no doubt that it had acquired a *jus cogens* status. In particular, their lordships stated categorically that "new domestic offences should be debated in Parliament, defined in a statute and come into force on a prescribed date. They should not creep into existence as a result of an international consensus to which only the executive of this country is a party." See p. 29, para 62. For a commentary on this judgment see Bantekas 2010, p. 25, fn 83; Q'Keefe 2006, pp. 473–476.

[149] In *Nulyarimma v. Thompson* (1999) 165 ALR 621, the Australian Federal Court, by majority, ruled that international customary criminal law does not form a basis upon which to base an indictment for genocide. The court ruled that although genocide was recognised as a *jus cogens,* and despite the fact that Australia had ratified the Genocide Convention since 1949, the domestic courts in Australia could not exercise jurisdiction over the crime of genocide or any other international crime, whether created by treaty or customary law, unless legislation had been implemented to apply the crime in domestic law. For more details generally see Triggs 2003, pp. 507 et seq.; Balkin 2005, pp. 114–140. For a critique of the judgment see Douglas 2001, pp. 1 et seq; Mitchell 2000, pp. 15 et seq.

[150] See. Juma 2002, pp. 459 et seq.; Ojienda and Aloo 2011; Reed 1964, pp. 164 et seq.

of piracy on the basis of universal jurisdiction. But as it will be shown shortly, the Kenyan courts were able to exercise jurisdiction over the crime of piracy not solely on the basis of its *jus cogens* character, but on the basis of a clear Penal Code provision.

The Interpretation and General Provisions Act[151] is the law that governs how Kenyan laws should be interpreted. Pursuant to this legislation, the interpretation of the word "offence" as applicable in Kenya does not seem to cover a customary law offence, for it is confined to a "written law". Accordingly, the word "offence" is defined as "a crime, felony, misdemeanour or contravention or other breach of, or failure to comply with, any *written law*, for which a penalty is provided".[152] Furthermore, a "written law" is restrictively defined to include three types of laws, namely: (i) an Act of the Kenyan Legislature; (ii) an applied law; or (iii) a subsidiary legislation which is currently in force in Kenya. And an "applied law" means an Act of a legislature of a foreign country or an Order in Council of the United Kingdom or any subsidiary legislation made under them and which is in force in Kenya.[153]

The preceding paragraph speaks against a possibility of bringing charges in the Kenyan courts solely on the basis of the *jus cogens* nature of a norm, unless there is evidence that such a norm had been codified (written) *domestically* at the time of its breach. It would not matter if the customary norm had already been codified in an international instrument. On this basis, a legal practitioner in Kenya believes that the domestic courts would not be prepared to accept international customary law as a sole basis for charging the crimes under international law allegedly committed during the post-election violence.[154]

In spite of the restrictive definition of the word "offence" as outlined above, the Penal Code of Kenya theoretically retains the enforceability of the "unwritten" common law offences. Particularly, the Penal Code clearly provides that although it codifies individual offences, nothing in it shall affect or prevent "the liability, trial or and punishment of an offence against the common law".[155] But since crimes under international law per se are not common law crimes[156] in the sense of the Kenyan Penal Code, this provision cannot be extended by analogy to include them. Moreover, practice shows that even big common law jurisdictions such as the UK, the USA, Australia and Canada have gone a step further to codify what used to be unwritten common law crimes, the fact which indicates that the enforceability of unwritten (uncodified) crimes (if any) remains largely theorctical.[157]

---

[151] Cap. 2 (R.E 2008).

[152] Interpretation and General Provisions Act, s. 3 (emphasis added).

[153] Ibid.

[154] Views of Mr. Eugene Nyamunga, advocate of the High Court of Kenya and the subordinate courts thereto, a doctoral researcher at the Tanzanian-Germany Centre for Post-graduate Studies in Law, TGCL (interviewed by author on 13 August 2011 at Bayreuth University, Germany). Cf. Fernandez 2006, p. 80 (advancing a similar argument about enforceability of the crime of torture in South Africa).

[155] Kenyan Penal Code, s. 2(a).

[156] Regarding how common law crimes developed, see LaFave 2003, pp. 74–75.

[157] Cf. Ambos 2010, 163–164; LaFave 2003, pp. 74–77.

4.3.2.1.3 Considerations from Specific Jurisprudence of Kenyan Courts

As shown earlier, under the old Constitution (1963–2010), Kenya followed a strictly dualist approach of implementing international law pursuant to *Okunda v. Republic*. As a result, international treaties or customary law would be enforceable in domestic courts only if expressly codified and domesticated. However, from 2002, a new jurisprudential trend, which started to "loosen" the strict dualist practice, specifically with regard to human rights treaties, started to emerge. Thus, from *Rono v. Rono*[158] onwards, various rulings stated that *for purposes of interpretation* of domestic laws, Kenyan courts could rely directly on international customary law embodied in human rights treaties that had been *signed without reservation* "even in the absence of implementing legislation". According to the High Court, this consideration was necessary to ensure that Kenya "was moving intandem with emerging global culture".[159]

A question that arises is whether this reasoning could also be applied with respect to customary international criminal law which entails not merely "an emerging global culture" but a *settled principle* of zero tolerance to impunity for, inter alia, international customary crimes contained in the ratified treaties. This question is yet to be addressed by the Kenyan domestic courts.

One could further consider the often-cited prosecutions of the customary crime of piracy in Kenya, especially the 2009 High Court Judgment in *Hassan M. Ahmed v. Republic*.[160] However, two points must be clarified before proceeding further. First, piracy is not a crime under the ICC Statute, but is one of the earliest *jus cogens* crimes for which universal jurisdiction applies.[161] Second, unlike crimes against humanity, which had not been domesticated in Kenya at the time of the post-election violence, piracy, as charged in *Hassan v. Republic,* had already been codified as a crime in the domestic laws of Kenya at the time of its commission.[162] Therefore, the issue in *Hassan v. Republic* was not whether jurisdiction over the crime of piracy could be founded solely on its *jus cogens* nature. Rather, the issue was whether the trial court was right in exercising universal jurisdiction in respect of pirates arrested in the high seas, for it was argued that Kenya lacked any traditional jurisdictional links to them.

---

[158] Decision on Civil Appeal No. 66 of 2002 (Court of Appeal at Eldoret), reported in (2005) eKLR and also in (2008) 1 KLR (G & F) 803.

[159] See *Rono v. Rono and another* (2008) KLR (G & F) p. 813. See also *Kenya Airways Corporation Ltd v. Tobias Oganya Auma & 5 others* [2007] eKLR p. 15; *Republic v. Minister for Home Affairs & 2 others Ex Parte Sitamze* [2008] eKLR; *Rose Moraa & another V. Attorney-General* [2006] eKLR. For more details see Ambani 2010, p. 30; Viljoen 2007, p. 540.

[160] [2010] eKLR, decision of High Court at Mombasa, 12 May 2009.

[161] See Cassese 2008, p. 28; Cryer et al. 2007, pp. 33; Werle 2009, p. 30, fn. 156.

[162] Piracy was then a crime under s. 69 of the Penal Code of Kenya. Currently it is a crime under the Merchant Shipping Act of 2009, s. 371.

The relevant part of *Hassan v. Republic* for the purposes of this book comes at the end of the judgment. The High Court made a finding by way of an *obiter dictum* (i.e. remarks based on hypothetical facts assumed by the court). It first quoted the Penal Code provision establishing the crime of piracy in Kenya to show that it was indisputably an offence under the existing domestic written law. Having done so, the learned judge went on to opine:

> *Even if the Penal Code had been silent on the offence of piracy*, I am of the view that the Learned Principal Magistrate would have been guided by the United Nations Convention on the Law of the Sea which defines piracy in Articles 101 (…) I would go further and hold that *even if the Convention had not been ratified and domesticated*, the Learned Principal Magistrate *was bound to apply international norms and Instruments* since Kenya is a member of the civilized world and is not expected to act in contradiction to expectations of member states of the United Nations.[163]

If, according to the High Court, the magistrate would have been "bound" to apply the definition of piracy in an international convention "even if the Penal Code had been silent", a question that arises is whether this statement opened the Pandora's box to allow other crimes of the same nature i.e., those that are also *jus cogens* constituting *obligatio erga omnes,* including crimes against humanity, to be directly prosecutable as such in Kenya on the basis of their customary nature. A US-based Kenyan scholar, James Gathii, is of the view that the answer to this question is in the negative. He rightly bases his argument on the common law principle of *stare decisis,* which is also applicable in Kenya, and on English judgments which have expressly rejected a direct enforceability (in domestic courts) of undomesticated international customary crimes.[164] In Kenya, and generally in the common law tradition, the part of a judgment which creates binding law (precedent) is the *ratio decidendi* (i.e. the one that disposes of the issues raised). An *obiter dictum* does not create law, but merely carries a persuasive value.[165]

Therefore, the opinion of the judge quoted above, which was an *obiter dictum*, did not change the *status quo*. Moreover, it cannot be argued with confidence that domestic courts in Kenya would interpret a criminal law treaty in the same way they would do for a treaty on socio-economic human rights. This is because, by its nature, criminal law involves the curtailing of personal liberty of individuals (accused). As a result, whenever doubt or ambiguity exists, courts tend to be very strict in interpreting and applying rules of criminal law, and always to the advantage of the accused person.

---

[163] See *Hassan M. Ahmed v. Republic* [2010] eKLR (emphasis added).

[164] He argues that "Piracy *jure gentium* and other crimes of an international character that are triable in domestic courts cannot be directly created by customary or international law without a domestic statute conferring such jurisdiction". See Gathii 2010, p. 8, fn 28. Note, however, that judgments of English courts are only persuasive (are not binding) to Kenyan courts. See Hussain 2003, p. 16.

[165] See Hussain 2003, p. 16.

4.3.2.1.4 Interim Conclusion

There is no doubt that crimes against humanity had become *jus cogens* crimes before their commission during Kenya's 2007–2008 post-election violence. Thus, if the criminal acts committed during this particular violence were to be charged domestically as crimes against humanity per se by directly relying on customary international law, such charges would not, in principle, violate the principle of legality. However, as it has been shown, practice clearly indicates that domestic courts in common law countries have, in such circumstances, expressly declined to entertain an indictment made solely on the basis customary international law which is not part of their written domestic laws. In addition, at the time of commission of the alleged crimes in Kenya, there was no provision conferring jurisdiction over such crimes on the domestic courts. As such, it may, therefore, not be possible to prosecute crimes against humanity as such solely on the basis of their *jus cogens* status, for the courts might claim not to have jurisdiction.

4.3.2.2 Relying on the International Crimes Act of 2008

4.3.2.2.1 Domestication of the ICC Statute

As already stated, although at the time of the post-election violence Kenya had already ratified the ICC Statute, it had not domesticated it; it was purportedly still "in course with internal procedures for its domestication".[166] The Waki Commission recommended the fast-tracking of the domestication process, expecting that the resulting law would be used by the proposed Special Tribunal for Kenya to prosecute the crimes committed during the violence.[167] This was done through a comprehensive piece of legislation, the International Crimes Act of 2008, which came into force on 1 January 2009.[168] The purpose of this legislation is to "make provision for the punishment of certain international crimes, namely genocide, crimes against humanity and war crimes, and to enable Kenya to co-operate with the International Criminal Court established by the Rome Statute in the performance of its functions".[169]

---

[166] See Statement by Mr. Z.D. Muburi-Muita, Ambassador and Permanent Representative of Kenya to the UN at the 62nd Session of the UN General Assembly, New York, 1 November 2007, p. 1. http://www.iccnow.org/documents/Kenya.pdf. Accessed August 2014.

[167] Republic of Kenya 2008, p. 476.

[168] For its legislative history see Ford 2008, p. 57. Kenya followed the 2004 Commonwealth domesticating model legislation. See Parliament of Kenya 2008, p. 907. This model legislation was revised in 2011. See Commonwealth Secretariat (2011).

[169] International Crimes Act of 2008, Preamble.

4.3.2.2.2 General Overview of the Act

The Act, to which the ICC Statute is annexed as a Schedule, domesticates by reference all the core crimes and *almost* all the general principles of criminal law contained in the ICC Statute.[170] Moreover, it requires that in interpreting the Act Kenyan courts must first "have regard" to the ICC's Elements of Crimes before the Kenyan Penal Code, and that in the case of a conflict between the two, the former prevails. The Kenyan courts can exercise jurisdiction over the crimes mainly on the basis of the territoriality or nationality principles.[171] Universal jurisdiction can also be exercised, but only if the perpetrator is present in Kenya after committing the offence elsewhere.[172]

The Act is slightly broader than the ICC Statute as regards crimes against humanity. It defines crimes against humanity to also include an act defined as such in conventional or customary international law "that is not otherwise dealt with in the Rome Statute".[173] However, the Act has a few inconsistencies with the ICC Statute. For example, it does not domesticate the principle under article 27 of the Statute which outlaws official capacity of the suspect as a justification for non-prosecution for crimes under international law. The relevancy of official capacity is only outlawed in relation to Kenya's exercise of duty to respond to requests for transfer or surrender of an immune person to the ICC or another state.[174] This seems to have been a deliberate omission to make the Act consistent with the then Constitution,

---

[170] Ibid., s. 7(2).

[171] See Ibid., s. 8(i)(a) and (b). For territoriality principle, jurisdiction is exercised when perpetrator of whatever nationality commits the crime on the territory of Kenya. As regards nationality principle, the courts have jurisdiction when the perpetrator himself or the victim is a citizen of Kenya, regardless of where the crime happens. Courts also have jurisdiction if, at the time of commission of the crime, the perpetrator was a national of another state which was engaged in an armed conflict against Kenya, or if the victim was a national of another state which was allied with Kenya in an armed conflict.

[172] Ibid., s. 8(1)(c). Kenya's official position given in 2008 with regard to universal jurisdiction was that it is no longer for national courts of states to exercise such jurisdiction at the current time where the ICC is in place, and that such mandate jeopardises the principles of equality and rule of law as it is being abused by courts in the developed countries against leaders of the developing countries. See pp. 4–5 of the Statement of the Attorney-General of Kenya to the seventh session of the Assembly of States Parties to the ICC, 22 November 2008. http://www.icc-cpi.int/iccdocs/asp_docs/library/asp/ICC-ASP-ASP7-GenDebe-Kenya-ENG.pdf. Accessed August 2014. See also Okuta 2009, p. 1075. Note, however, that: (i) contrary to what is implied in Kenya's position stated above, the ICC does not exercise universal jurisdiction; its jurisdictional powers are limited to the nationality and territoriality principles. See ICC Statute, Article 12; (ii) Kenya's belief that the ICC could, unlike third states abusing universal jurisdiction, stand for "equality and rule of law" changed drastically when the ICC intervened in Kenya. The opinion currently held by Kenya is that the ICC is now being abused by Western countries against the interests of developing (African) countries. See infra Sect. 6.7.4.

[173] International Crimes Act of 2008, s. 6(4).

[174] Ibid., s. 27. Also see Murungu 2011, p. 55 (wondering why this clear provision was not enforced against President Omar Al Bashir of Sudan when he visited Kenya on 27 August 2010, given that there was a pending ICC's arrest warrant against him); Okuta 2009, p. 107.

which granted such immunity to the President.[175] However, this omission has now been cured by Article 143(1) of the Constitution of Kenya of 2010 which, although it extends similar immunity to the President, has introduced an exception that explicitly removes "international crimes" from the scope of such immunity.

Initially when the Act was enacted, two concerns emerged. The first concern was that in view of the existing Constitution, the President could grant pardon to people convicted for the international crimes under the Act pursuant to the President's constitutional prerogative powers of mercy.[176] Although there is abundant literature clearly illustrating the fact that the culture of impunity has previously been entrenched in Kenya, especially with respect to certain types of crimes or perpetrators, there are only a few incidents in which such impunity is said to have resulted from an obvious "abuse" of the prerogative powers of mercy vested in the President.[177] However, the possibility of abuse for political reasons, especially when high-profile political figures are involved, cannot be completely ruled out. It is noteworthy that these powers have been retained in the Constitution of Kenya of 2010, but a check has been introduced to some extent.[178]

Another issue that has raised a concern relates to inconsistencies between the International Crimes Act and the ICC Statute or with other domestic criminal law legislation as far as penalties and the minimum age of criminal responsibility are concerned. While the maximum penalty that can be imposed by the ICC is life imprisonment,[179] the maximum penalty for murder constituting a crime under the Act is death sentence.[180] Similarly, the minimum age of criminal responsibility for

---

[175] See Okuta 2009, p. 1073. Such powers were provided for under Constitution of Kenya of 1963, Article 14(1).

[176] Constitution of Kenya of 1963, Article 28; Okuta 2009, p. 1074.

[177] See Mbote and Akech 2011, pp. 68–69.

[178] See Constitution of Kenya of 2010, Article 133(1). In exercising the prerogative powers of mercy under this constitution, the President is obligated to act in accordance with the advice of the Advisory Committee on Prerogative of Mercy created in the provision cited. Pursuant to Article 133(2) of the same Constitution, the Power of Mercy Act of 2011 sets the criteria to be followed by the said committee in giving advice to the President. Although this law does not have any express provision that outlaws pardon or amnesty in respect of international crimes, its section 22 provides for the "nature and seriousness of the crime" and "interests of the community and the victims" to be among the criteria to be considered before pardon is given. Since there is an international law principle (see infra Sect. 5.2.3.2.4) that discourages the granting of amnesty or pardons for the "most serious crimes" of international character, it is not expected that in normal circumstances the Committee can give advice which defeats the desire to put an end to impunity for such crimes. On the emerging *opino juris* on amnesty in relation to the core crimes, generally see Obura 2011, pp. 11–31.

[179] ICC Statute, Article 77(1).

[180] S. 6(3)(a) of the International Crimes Act 2008 provides that conviction for wilful killing amounting to an international crime shall be punished as for murder. Under section 204 of the Kenyan Penal Code, murder is punishable by death. It seems that the drafters of the Act correctly decided to make it consistent with the Penal Code rather than the ICC Statute, in order to make sure that murder amounting to "a serious crime of concern to the international community" is not treated more leniently than an "ordinary" murder. This provision is likely to remain unchanged as long as Kenya maintains the death penalty.

the core crimes domesticated in the Act is 18 years[181]; it is much higher than the lowest age of criminal responsibility in other domestic crimes.[182]

4.3.2.2.3 Implications of the 2010 Constitution on the Act

The new Constitution of Kenya, adopted on 27 August 2010, introduced a new legal position with regard to enforceability of international law in the domestic courts in Kenya. It officially converted Kenya from its previous strict dualist practice to a monist practice of implementation of international treaties.[183] By virtue of Article 2 of the 2010 Constitution, *both* conventional and customary norms of international law become directly applicable and enforceable in Kenyan domestic courts without necessarily having to be domesticated, provided that they do not conflict with the Constitution.[184] According to Gathii, the *entire series of treaties*, including criminal law treaties, which Kenya had ratified but not domesticated, became enforceable as part of Kenyan law from the date on which the new constitutional provision became operational.[185]

There is a view that the new position above i.e., the change from dualism to monism per se, has created a possibility for the International Crimes Act of 2008 to be applied retrospectively, making it possible to charge the alleged crimes against humanity committed during post-election violence, 1 year before the Act was enacted. The next section outlines such a view and related arguments, and also analyses such a possibility.

---

[181] See s. 7(1) of the International Crimes Act of 2008 (domesticating Article 26 of the ICC Statute). Under Article 26 of the Statute, the minimum age of a perpetrator who can be prosecuted and held criminally responsible for the core crimes in the ICC Statute is 18 years.

[182] Generally, the lowest age of criminal responsibility in Kenya is 8 years. Section 14(1) of the Penal Code completely exonerates a child under the age of 8 years from criminal responsibility. Section 14(2) requires that a child between 8 and 12 can be criminally liable, but only if it is proved that at the time of the act or omission the child had the capacity to know that he or she "ought not to" do the act or make the omission. However, as far as rape is concerned, an exception exists: the minimum age of criminal responsibility is strictly 12 years (see s. 14(3) of the Penal Code). Therefore, 18 years is set as minimum age of criminal responsibility only for purposes of proceedings carried out under the Kenya's International Crimes Act. However, this will not bar prosecution of child perpetrators of the conduct criminalized in the crimes of genocide, crimes against humanity or war crimes as part of "ordinary crimes" under the Penal Code or the Sexual Offences Act, which provide for a lower age of criminal responsibility.

[183] On the monism see Bradley1999, p. 530. Nsereko 2000, p. 174.

[184] Constitution of Kenya of 2010, Article 2(1) and (4). The Constitution provides that "the general rules of international law shall form part of the law of Kenya", and that "any treaty or convention ratified by Kenya shall form part of the law of Kenya under this Constitution". See Article 2(5) and (6), respectively.

[185] See Gathii 2011.

4.3.2.2.4 Evaluation of Retroactivity Vis-a-Vis the International
           Crimes Act

The question whether the International Crimes Act could be used to try the alleged
crimes against humanity relates to the principle *nullum crimen, nulla poena sine lege*
(principle of legality). Among other things, this principle seeks to enhance certainty
of the law and safeguard individuals against arbitrary actions of state, thereby
strengthening the rule of law.[186] To achieve this, the principle embodies, inter alia,
two main prohibitions. Firstly, it prohibits the punishing of a conduct which had not
been clearly defined by the relevant legal order as constituting a criminal offence at
the time of its occurrence. Secondly, it prohibits an imposition of a penalty which
had not been clearly defined, or which is heavier than that which had been defined
by law *at the time of the commission* of the alleged crime.[187] In view of these prohibitions, one question arises: "When an international crime is prosecuted in a national
court, is the law under which the prosecution occurs national or international? For
purposes of legality, which law must be in place at the time of the act?"[188]

   Initially, some commentators noted that it was "not clear" whether Kenyan
domestic courts would agree to apply the International Crimes Act of 2008 retrospectively.[189] Others argued that the Act "cannot be" applied retrospectively.[190]
Okuta, for example, argued that the Act is "merely a tool for the future", implying
that, apparently, its application can only remain prospective.[191] However, later,
when the 2010 Constitution was adopted, the arguments changed slightly because
of Article 50(2)(n) of the Constitution which provides:

> Every accused person has the right to a fair trial, which includes the right not to be con-
> victed for an act or omission that at the time it was committed or omitted was not (i) an
> offence in Kenya; or (ii) *a crime under international law*.[192]

In view of this provision, the Attorney-General's working committee on the ICC
(see supra Sect. 4.3.1.5) advised the Kenyan government as follows:

> As a matter of law, the committee notes that "international crimes" (which include crimes
> against humanity) that were allegedly committed during the [post-election violence] are

---

[186] Bassiouni 2003, pp. 180, 215–256; Cassese et al. 2009, pp. 437–441.

[187] See Bassiouni 2003, pp. 179–226; Cassese 2013, pp. 23–24; Cryer et al. 2007, pp. 13–16;
Schabas 2000, p. 522; Worster 2011, pp. 973–979. Generally on this principle see Gallant 2010;
Hallevy 2010; Kenyans for Peace with Truth and Justice and Kenya Human Rights Commission
2013, p. 21.

[188] See Gallant 2011, p. 30; Spiga 2011, p 10.

[189] See, e.g., Sing'Oei 2010, p. 14, fn 50; Alai and Mue 2011, pp. 1223–1224; Allai and Mue
2010, p. 2; Open Society Foundations 2011, p. 85.

[190] See, e.g., Okuta 2009, p. 1074; International Centre for Policy and Conflict 2009, p. 9.

[191] A. Okuta 2009, p. 1074 (arguing that even if the Special Tribunal for Kenya materialized, this
Act would still only have served "a limited purpose" in addressing the crimes connected to post-
election violence). For a similar view see Sing'Oei 2010, p. 14, fn 50.

[192] Emphasis added. NB. Under the old constitution, the scope of the principle of legality did not
include crimes under international law. See Constitution of Kenya of 1963, Article 77(4).

triable in Kenya despite being committed before the coming into force of the International Crimes Act on 01 January 2009…. The provisions set out in Article 50(2)(n) of the Constitution … permit Kenya to have jurisdiction in respect of crimes that were committed under international law at the time of [the violence].[193]

The Kenyan government put forward the same argument before the ICC.[194] For the reasons given below, it is submitted that the advice in the above-quoted paragraph is sound and could be implemented. However, a minor but crucial amendment to the International Crimes Act of 2008 would be required.

Pursuant to what Bassiouni refers to as "the substantive aspect" of the principle of legality, if, at the time of commission of a crime under international law, a state had ratified a convention establishing the crime, or if the crime had acquired a *jus cogens* status, then such a crime could or should be prosecuted in national courts of that state without the fear of breaching the principle of legality.[195] This view is based on the meaning ascribed to the principle of legality under the provisions of several international instruments, including Article 15 of the International Covenant on Civil and Political Rights (ICCPR)[196]; Article 11 of the Universal Declaration of Human Rights (UDHR)[197]; and Article 7 of the European Convention on Human Rights (UCHR).[198]

According to the Kenyan Interpretation and Application of Laws Act,[199] the date on which a piece of legislation becomes operational in Kenya can be either (i) the day on which the legislation is published in the Gazette; or (ii) a day specified in that legislation to be the date on which it "shall come or be deemed to have come" into operation.[200]

The fact that a piece of legislation in Kenya can be "deemed to have come into operation" suggests that the Kenyan Parliament can assign a retrospective operational date to a piece of legislation, thereby "deeming" it to have come into force on a date earlier than that on which it was passed. However, a caveat must be added here: For criminal law legislation, such retroactivity may (and should) be

---

[193] Quoted in Kenyans for Peace with Truth and Justice and Kenya Human Rights Commission 2013, p. 21.

[194] See, e.g., Application on Behalf of the Government of the Republic of Kenya Pursuant to Article 19 of the ICC Statute, *Situation in the Republic of Kenya* (ICC-01/09-02/11-26), PTC, 26 April 2011, para 58; Open Society Foundations 2011, pp. 85 and 107.

[195] See Bassiouni 2005c, pp. 374–376; Ferstman and Machover 2008, p. 13 There is also the "strict" or "formal" aspect of the application of the principle of legality which is followed in some countries. This requires that a crime can be prosecuted in a national court only if at the time of its commission it had already been codified and published, for example, in an Official Gazette. Cf. Bassiouni 2005c, pp. 372–374; Lattanzi 2001, p. 186. This was the approach taken by the U.K. courts in the Pinochet case *R v. Bow Street Metropolitan Stipendiary Magistrate, Ex parte Pinochet Ugarte* [1999] 2 WLR 827. For more details see Fox et al. 1999, pp. 687 et seq.

[196] Adopted on 16 December 1966 and entered into force on 23 March 1972.

[197] UN General Assembly Resolution No. 217 of 10 December 1948.

[198] Adopted 1950; entry into force 3 September 1953.

[199] Cap. 2 (R.E 2008).

[200] Interpretation and General Provisions Act, ss. 9(1) and 9(3), respectively.

permitted or tolerated only if it does not violate the purposes of the principle of legality. In this regard, it is submitted that retroactivity is justifiable in two scenarios. The first scenario is where it aims at conferring jurisdiction *ratione materiae* or jurisdiction *ratione temporis* on the national courts for crimes already existing under customary international law over which the domestic courts would not have had jurisdiction had it not been so expanded. The second scenario is where such retroactivity entails a retrospective re-labelling (re-naming) of an already criminalized conduct, provided, of course, that the conduct in the "new label" does not carry a punishment which is heavier than that which it would otherwise have carried had it been prosecuted under the "old label".[201]

On the basis of the foregoing, it is submitted that, the Kenya's International Crimes Act of 2008 could be made to apply retroactively, and thereby charge the crimes against humanity committed 1 year before the enactment of the Act. Such legislative amendment would only be retrospective from a *chronological point of view*, but would not otherwise lead to the punishment of non-criminalized conduct at the time of its commission.[202]

There is the argument that since the Kenyan International crimes Act became operational "well after the commission of the crimes in question", the principle against retroactivity is "a feasible defence if raised at the domestic level, even though such a defence would not stand before an international tribunal".[203] The argument implies two things. First, it suggests that because "crimes against humanity" as such were not provided for (codified) anywhere in the Kenyan domestic laws at the time of the post-election violence, then the perpetrators would not have been aware of their prohibition. Second, the argument also suggests that there should be a distinction or dichotomy between domestic courts and international tribunals in the manner in which they apply and interpret the principle of legality.[204]

The argument above is not entirely convincing because, as already shown, irrespective of their legal characterization under international or domestic law, the substantive conduct in the criminality committed during the post-election violence had already been criminalized under the Kenyan Penal Code. The perpetrators could not, therefore, purport to have been unaware of the *prohibited conduct* (or at least the illegality thereof) at the time of its commission.[205] For purposes of the principle of legality, it is enough that the criminalization of the conduct had been established; it does not matter whether the accused knew the legal label or characterization of the conduct under international law.

---

[201] Cf. Bassiouni 2005c, pp. 374–376; Ferstman and Machover 2008, p. 14.

[202] Cf. Kenyans for Peace with Truth and Justice and Kenya Human Rights Commission 2013, pp. 21–23; Spiga 2011, p. 10.

[203] Sing'Oei 2010, p. 14, fn. 50.

[204] This reasoning comes from the seemingly erroneous and much criticized decision of the Economic Community of West African States (ECOWAS) Court in *Hissein Habré Cl Republique Du Senegal Role General* No *Ecw/Ccj/App/07/08* Arret No: *Ecw/Ccj/Jud/06/10* du 18 novembre 2010. For a critical evaluation of this judgment, see Hessbruegge 2010; Spiga 2011, pp. 5 et seq.

[205] For a similar argument see Spiga, 2011, pp. 19–20.

A similar argument pertaining to retroactivity was advanced by the defendants during the Nuremberg trial in respect of crimes against peace and crimes against humanity for which individuals were prosecuted for the first time in history. They claimed that these two categories of crimes were non-existent prior to their alleged commission, and that, prosecuting them before the IMT was, therefore, a violation of the principle of *nullum crimen sine lege*. Rejecting this argument, the IMT indicated that the principle of legality could not be used as an absolute bar to state's sovereignty in punishing criminality. The Tribunal established that the conduct was already "illegal" under the existing international law and arguably criminal. It then justifiably observed as follows:

> The maxim "*nullum crimen sine lege*" is not a limitation of sovereignty, but in general a principle of justice. To assert that it is unjust to punish those who in defiance of treaties have [planned to attack] neighbouring states without warning is obviously untrue, for in such circumstances the attacker must know that he is doing wrong, and so far from it being unjust to punish him, it would be unjust if his wrong were allowed to go unpunished.[206]

Applying the above IMT ruling in the context of Kenya, it could be argued that it is within Kenya's sovereignty if, as has been suggested, it amended its domestic laws retroactively to provide for the alleged crimes against humanity. However, if the crimes are to be prosecuted as crimes under international law *as such,* the definitional criteria as well as the individual acts in respect of which such amendment should cover must be *only* those which had already indisputably acquired a *jus cogens* status at the time of their commission. In that regard, such amendments would not create new crimes as such, but would only be codifying crimes which had already existed under customary international law. The amendment would only play three roles, namely: (i) to put the crimes in a "written law" on the basis of which the charge can be brought; (ii) to prescribe the applicable penalties and (iii) as already stated, to confer jurisdiction on the domestic courts over the crimes. The third role has precisely been described as "retroactive expansion of criminal jurisdiction".[207]

Other common law jurisdictions, particularly Canada and New Zealand, have domesticated the ICC Statute retrospectively to achieve similar goals. According to the Canada's Crimes against Humanity and War Crimes Act of 2000, international crimes committed before the adoption of the ICC Statute can be prosecuted retrospectively, provided they had qualified as *crimes under customary international law at the time of their commission*. This law also provides that genocide, crimes against humanity and war crimes are deemed to have reflected customary law by the time the Statute was adopted. The Act further provides "for greater certainty" that crimes against humanity had already constituted a criminal conduct under customary international law or general principles of law recognized by civilized nations arguably "even prior" to the Nuremberg and the Tokyo Charters of

---

[206] IMT Judgment, p. 445. Cf. Cassese 2013, pp. 25–26.

[207] See Worster 2011, p. 974.

1945 and 1946, respectively.[208] Basing on this legislation, on 22 May 2009, the Superior Court of Quebec convicted Mr. Desire Munyaneza for genocide, war crimes and crimes against humanity committed in Rwanda in 1994.[209]

Similarly, although the ICC Statute was domesticated in New Zealand in 2000, 2 years after its adoption, the domesticating legislation provides that jurisdiction for genocide and crimes against humanity commences retroactively on 28 March 1979 and 1 January 1991, respectively. These are the respective dates on which New Zealand acceded to the 1948 Genocide Convention, and when the jurisdiction of the ICTY for crimes against humanity commenced.[210]

Therefore, if Kenya was to amend and give a retrospective effect to its International Crimes Act of 2008, it would not be setting a new precedent in the common law world. Kenya would not breach the principle of legality or the principle of individual guilt.

4.3.2.2.5   Interim Conclusion

Given that international criminal justice is becoming increasingly important, there should not be room for international or domestic jurisdictions to use technicalities to defeat its purpose, especially in places such as Africa where such atrocities are on the increase. Allowing that to happen would be tantamount to using the law to defeat (instead of promoting) the ends of justice. Thus, domestic jurisdictions must always ensure that their application and interpretation of the principle of legality seeks to promote substantive justice for serious forms of criminality.[211] Since the principle of legality does not prohibit retrospective confirmation of jurisdiction on courts, the Kenyan International Crimes Act of 2008 could be amended if at all the alleged crimes against humanity *must* be prosecuted under that label. However, such amendment would be possible only if there was a political will to genuinely fight impunity with respect to the post-election violence, especially with regard to the main perpetrators.

---

[208] See Canadian Crimes against Humanity and War Crimes Act of 2000, ss. 4(4), 6(4) and (5), and s. 7. See also Cryer et al. 2007, p. 66.

[209] See *R. v. Desire Munyaneza* [2009] QCCS 2201. For more details on this trial, see Lafontaine 2010, pp. 269 et seq. It can be noted that also in 1987 Canada amended its Criminal Code retrospectively to provide for the crimes of genocide, war crimes and crimes against humanity. On the basis of this amendment, crimes committed during the Second World War (so-called "Canadian holocaust") were prosecuted and some convictions were achieved. See Braham 1995, p. 293 et seq.; Matas 1990, pp. 347 et seq.; Namwase 2011, p. 29.

[210] International Crimes and International Criminal Court Act, 2000 (New Zealand), s. 8(4); Cryer et al. 2007, p. 66.

[211] Cf. Cassese 2013, pp. 24–25.

4.4   Issues Relating to Exercise of State Prosecutorial Function

Having analysed Kenya's substantive criminal law and the options it offers for the domestic prosecutions of the alleged crimes against humanity, it is suggested to also highlight issues relating to the exercise Prosecutorial function in Kenya. Such analysis is relevant for one main reason: It is not correct to assume (as most scholars do) that mere availability of adequate substantive criminal law and the existence of a competent judiciary are enough factors to guarantee that the fight against impunity for crimes under international law can be realized by all domestic jurisdictions. The fact of the matter is that these are just two of three equally important pillars to fight impunity for such crimes at the national level. The third pillar is the national prosecutorial authority.[212] In particular, three aspects of such an authority can be used to fight or perpetuate impunity. These are (i) its level of independence; (ii) the amount of discretionary powers it is vested with, and more importantly (iii) the manner in which such discretion is exercised.

This section outlines and comments on the foregoing three aspects in relation to the legal framework governing the prosecutorial function in Kenya. It takes into cognizance the fact that the litigation tradition in Kenya adheres to the common law adversarial system. Pursuant to this tradition, in any proceedings, including those in respect of a criminal trial, the judge, unlike the judge in the Romano-Germanic legal tradition, sits purely as an arbiter: he or she does not play any active role with regard to filing of charges; defining the scope of such charges; identifying the suspect to charge; or even deciding what evidence must be presented to court. These roles are exclusively left within the mandate of the prosecutorial office. Thus, the pivotal role of this office in the fight against impunity for the crimes related to the post-election violence cannot be over-emphasized.

4.4.1   Position Under the 1963 Constitution

Under the Constitution of Kenya of 1963, the state prosecutorial function was vested in the Attorney-General (AG),[213] who was not only a political appointee of the President,[214] but also an overall adviser of the government in all matters pertaining to law. Apart from this advisory role, the office of the AG was also responsible for handling all criminal cases and only those civil matters to which the

---

[212] Cf. Opening speech by Amos Wako, Attorney-General of Kenya, at "the ICC and Complementarity Workshop" held 3–4 December 2010 in Nairobi, p. 13 http://www.africalegalaid.com/news/proceedings-of-icc-complementarity-workshop-in-kenya. Accessed August 2014.

[213] Constitution of Kenya of 1963, Article 26.

[214] Ibid., Article 109.

government was a party. The DPP was subordinated to, and received instructions from, the AG as regards the handling of criminal cases. Thus, the AG had absolute, discretionary and broadly defined powers. Accordingly, if the AG considered it desirable, he had the absolute discretion to: (i) select a case to institute i.e., to decide who the defendant should be and the offence with which to charge him or her; (ii) to take over (i.e. "snatch") and continue any case that had been instituted by a private prosecutor; and (iii) discontinue any case at any stage before judgment, including one which was being privately prosecuted.[215]

4.4.2 Current Position

The Constitution of Kenya of 2010 stripped the AG of the state prosecutorial powers and entrusted them *exclusively* to the DPP. More importantly, the new Constitution severed the link between the offices of the AG and that of the DPP, such that the DPP's office is now an independently established constitutional office under Article 157(1) of the Constitution. Thus, currently, the office of the DPP is statutorily more autonomous than previously. In addition, the new Constitution contains important provisions which *prima facie* are aimed at enhancing the independence of the office of the DPP though minimization of political control. This manifests itself in the DPP's appointment procedure, execution of duties and security of tenure.

4.4.2.1 Independence of the DPP

The DPP is appointed by the President from a list of persons approved by the National Assembly, and who have the qualifications of a High Court Judge. DPP's tenure of office is limited to only one eight-year term with no eligibility for re-appointment.[216] Unlike previously where the DPP would require the consent of the Attorney-General to indict a person, the current Constitution clearly stipulates that the DPP "shall not require the consent of any person or authority for the commencement of criminal proceedings and in the exercise of his or her powers or functions, shall not be under the direction or control of any person or authority".[217]

To enhance independence, DPP's security of tenure is safeguarded under Article 158 of the Constitution, which removes the possibility of arbitrary termination of his

---

[215] Ibid., Article 26(3).

[216] Constitution of Kenya of 2010, Articles 157(2), (3) and (5). Note that under the old Constitution, the AG had neither a term limit nor a security of tenure. Apparently, he could remain in office for as long as he did not interfere with the political interests of the incumbent president or his cronies. E.g., the former Attorney-General, Amos Wako, who controlled state's the prosecutorial authority, stayed in office for 20 years. In this period, he allegedly covered "many scandals" involving politicians. See Capital News, 28 August 2011.

[217] See Constitution of Kenya of 2010, Article 157(10).

or her appointment. Unless he or she resigns, the DPP's appointment can be terminated only on five grounds: mental or physical incapacity leading to failure to perform his or her duties; non-compliance with the tenets of leadership and integrity under the Constitution; bankruptcy; incompetence; or gross misconduct.[218] Even in the event that a matter of removal from office arises, the President cannot remove the DPP arbitrarily; he can only remove him or her upon a recommendation of a tribunal which has looked into the matter.[219]

Thus, under the current constitutional order, the DPP is an independent constitutional office. Given that the first DPP under the new Constitution has only be in office for virtually 1 year, it is too early to make a determination whether practically this independence exists and is being exercised. However, this does not preclude critical observations in relation to the wide range of discretionary powers that the DPP enjoys.

4.4.2.2 Forms of Prosecutorial Discretion

The DPP is empowered to execute three functions. Stated more precisely, there are three forms of prosecutorial discretion which the DPP can exercise legally. These are (i) selection of cases and charges; (ii) interference with private prosecution; and (iii) withdrawal of cases.[220]

4.4.2.2.1 Selection of Cases and Charges

The DPP has the liberty to choose whom to prosecute and with what type of a crime or count to charge. This discretion presupposes two possibilities. One possibility is that the selection of cases may be, as it should rightly be, made on objective grounds. In this regard, selection of who to prosecute for the crimes related to the post-election violence would be informed mainly by the evidence obtained from the domestic investigations. The assumption here is that the DPP's selection

---

[218] Ibid., Article 158(1).

[219] Ibid., Article 158(2) to (5).

[220] Ibid., Article 157(6) provides: The Director of Public Prosecutions shall exercise State powers of prosecution and may:

(a)   institute and undertake criminal proceedings against any person before any court (other than a court martial) in respect of any offence alleged to have been committed;

(b)   take over and continue any criminal proceedings commenced in any court (other than a court martial) that have been instituted or undertaken by another person or authority, with the permission of the person or authority; and

(c)   discontinue at any stage before judgment is delivered any criminal proceedings instituted by the Director of Public Prosecutions or taken over by the Director of Public Prosecutions under paragraph (b).

of cases would be *bona fide*, geared toward achieving the general objectives of criminal law, namely retribution, deterrence, fostering public interest, etc.[221]

However, there is also a possibility that the selection of cases by the DPP could be informed by subjectivity. In a worst-case scenario, this may include *mala fide*, such as achieving a show trial, victors' justice, a witch hunt, shielding of the suspect, etc. Similarly the DPP might decide to charge a less serious offence when the evidence actually points to a more serious offence. Experience shows that, previously, the prosecutorial authority (AG through the DPP) would not institute cases against certain people even where the investigations offered a "watertight case for prosecution".[222] There are indications that this may also be the case with regard to the crimes related to post-election violence.

The "danger" of selective prosecution is not unique to Kenya, and it cannot be avoided completely. It is a common problem in any criminal justice system where absolute prosecutorial discretion is practised. As such, it can affect both national jurisdictions and international criminal tribunals, including the ICC. Some checks, however weak they might seem, have been designed to mitigate its effect in Kenya. One of such checks is private prosecutions.

4.4.2.2.2 Private Prosecution

Private prosecutions are regulated under section 88 of the Kenyan Criminal Procedure Code.[223] A private person, either personally or through an advocate, is allowed to conduct private prosecution, provided a permission *of a magistrate* is obtained. Conceivably, a private prosecution could be triggered when, after the usual police or DPP investigations are done, the DPP, exercising his absolute discretion, decides not to institute proceedings. An individual in his personal capacity, most likely as the victim of the crime, might wish to prosecute the case privately, if for example: (i) the decision of the DPP not to institute proceedings does not seem to be genuine; (ii) there is an indication that the DPP deliberately abused his discretion with an intent to shield the suspect; or (iii) if it appears that the DPP will not be able to prosecute expeditiously due to his overwhelming backlog of cases, lack of requisite expertise, etc.

Therefore, as the High Court of Kenya has noted, private prosecutions can serve as "a constitutional safeguard against capricions, corrupt or biased failure or refusal of police forces and the office of the [DPP] to prosecute offenders against

---

[221] See generally Ashworth 2006, pp. 15–17.

[222] See a detailed discussion in Mbote and Akech 2011, pp. 138–140.

[223] NB. At the time of writing, the provision had not yet been amended (adjusted) to reflect the changes introduced by the new constitution. Thus, the Code still made reference to the Attorney-General instead of the DPP as the chief Prosecutorial authority in Kenya. However, no substantive implication would result by a mere change of terminology.

the criminal law".[224] However, the precedents emanating from the Kenyan old constitutional order indicate that the permission to conduct a private prosecution can be granted only if the court is satisfied that the state prosecutorial authority has been informed and, apparently, has consented to it.[225]

4.4.2.2.3 Power to "Interfere" with Private Prosecution

Even though a private prosecution could be viewed as a check to the prosecutorial discretion relating to selectivity of cases, Article 157(6)(b) of the Constitution indicates that the DPP can still interfere with cases being privately prosecuted. According to the provision, the DPP can take over a case originally instituted as a private prosecution but only "with the permission of the person or authority" which commenced the prosecution, thereby converting it to a public prosecution. Again, the requirement for permission is a check on the DPP's discretion. If it is perceived that the DPP's intention in "hijacking" the prosecution is only to frustrate the proceedings and shield the accused, it is unlikely that the authorized private prosecutor will agree to relinquish the prosecution of the case. Although not clearly stated, it appears that if the two continue "competing" for the same case, the court has the final say as to who should be entitled to proceed with prosecuting the case. When compared to the position in the repealed constitution of 1963, this position is a breakthrough of its own kind.[226]

However, although it may appear that a private prosecution could provide a certain solution to DPP's failure to act with regard to cases related to the post-election violence, it is nevertheless not an easy or a reliable option. Given that a private prosecutor does not have the police at his or her disposal, serious challenges relating to investigations, search and seizure, etc., are bound to arise.[227] Thus, it is not conceivable that private prosecutions can be a panacea for impunity as regards the crimes committed during the post-election violence.

4.4.2.2.4 Discretion to Withdraw Cases: Nolle Prosequi

Article 157(6)(c) of the Constitution gives the DPP the powers to "discontinue" any criminal proceedings which he or she has instituted or taken over. The DPP can do so "at any stage before judgment is delivered". This aspect is further

---

[224] See Mwalili 1998, p. 226 (citing as an example the High Court of Kenya ruling in *Richard Kimani & S. M. Maina v. Nathan Kahara* of 1983).

[225] Ibid.

[226] Under the 1963 Constitution (Article 26), the DPP was not supposed to seek consent of the private prosecutor before he took over.

[227] On the contrary, for a public prosecution, the DPP has the mandate to order the Directorate of Criminal Investigations (the police) to investigate any information or allegation of any criminal conduct. See Constitution of Kenya of 2010, Article 157(4).

regulated by section 82(1) of the Kenyan Criminal Procedure Code, and is referred to as *nolle prosequi*, which simply means the discretion or powers of the DPP to withdraw an already instituted criminal case at will. If *nolle prosequi* is entered after the closure of the prosecution's case, the consequence is that the accused person must be acquitted.[228] However, if it is entered before the prosecution's case is closed, *nolle prosequi* is not a bar to subsequent re-arrest or prosecution.

If not subjected to a check, the DPP's *nolle prosequi* powers could be abused. In fact, Musila reveals that this discretion was often abused in Kenya in the past, as it was in various occasions used as a tool for "political witch-hunt" and, "in some cases, to settle personal scores".[229] It is also possible that the DPP could abuse his discretion in this respect by purporting to be genuinely asking to take over proceedings instituted by a private prosecutor only to terminate them subsequently by entering *nolle prosequi.*

However, Article 157(11) of the 2010 Constitution introduces the much needed check on this discretion by subjecting it to a judicial review. First, the DPP must adhere to the general obligation imposed by the Constitution in that before withdrawing the proceedings, he or she must "have regard to the public interest, the interests of the administration of justice and the need to prevent and avoid abuse of the legal process".[230] Secondly, before entering *nolle prosequi,* the DPP must also obtain the permission of the court.[231] The High Court of Kenya has made it clear that for the courts to grant such permission, the DPP will be obligated to furnish acceptable reasons for the decision to enter *nolle prosequi.*[232]

4.4.3 Interim Conclusion

The critical role of Kenya's DPP in realizing the fight against impunity for the crimes related to the post-election violence must not be underrated. Although the DPP's independence is constitutionally guaranteed, such independence has not so far been exercised robustly to show any tangible progress with regard to investigation and prosecution of especially those who allegedly bear greatest responsibility for the crimes. This has been associated with a lack of institutional and political will to do so; and also with the fact that although significant reforms have been done with respect to the judiciary (see infra Sect. 5.3), the prosecutorial authority itself was not completely reformed.[233]

---

[228] Constitution of Kenya of 2010, Article 157(7).

[229] Musila 2007, p. 31. Also see Mbote and Akech 2011, p. 137.

[230] Constitution of Kenya of 2010, Article 157(11).

[231] Ibid., Article 157(11).

[232] *Republic v. Enock Wekesa & Another* [2010] eKLR.

[233] See Kenyans for Peace with Truth and Justice and Kenya Human Rights Commission 2013, pp. 26–27.

It has been suggested, and rightly so, that perhaps the best solution could be a creation of a Special Prosecution Office which will be independent of the DPP specifically to investigate and prosecute the cases related to the post-election violence in the Kenyan national courts.[234] Although on the face of it this is an attractive idea, just like the idea about the creation of a special tribunal for Kenya, it is unlikely to materialize, as it will obviously not get the prerequisite political support from the Kenyan Parliament that must enact a specific law in that regard.

4.5 Chapter Summary

This chapter has discussed two options for the effective domestic prosecution of the crimes against humanity linked to the post-election violence, namely prosecuting as ordinary domestic crimes or as international crimes per se.

As regard the first option, it has been argued that the alleged crimes against humanity committed in Kenya can be punished effectively even when they are charged as ordinary crimes under the Kenyan Penal Code. In this regard, it has been suggested that the ordinary-crime approach remains the best option for Kenya due to the practical advantages it offers for the domestic prosecutors. It has further been shown that indeed Kenya has de facto chosen to rely on this option. However, the main flaw is that Kenya has not used this option satisfactorily, because the investigations and prosecutions carried out so far have not covered most of those who are alleged to be most responsible for the post-election violence.

As regards the second option, it has been argued that Kenya's International Crimes Act of 2008 could be relied on only if it was first amended. As this legislation was enacted after the commission of the crimes, it would, as a matter of necessity, require the law maker to first give it an *express* retrospective application in order for the domestic courts to apply it on the crimes in question, and most importantly, in order for it to confer retrospective jurisdiction on the domestic courts. It has been shown that this per se would not violate the principle of legality. However, it has been cautioned that since the alleged crimes were committed prior to the enactment of this particular legislation, only the conduct of individual acts which had undoubtedly acquired a *jus cogens* character would be prosecutable under the Act. But, as it stands now, the prospects of the Kenyan Parliament to amend the legislation specifically for purposes of prosecuting the post-election violence remain very slim, because most of the alleged architects of the violence are politicians or their allies who are currently members of Parliament or Senate.

---

[234] Ibid., p. 28.

References

Allai C, Mue N (2010) Kenya: impact of the Rome statute and the International Criminal Court. *ICTJ Briefing*. http://ictj.org/sites/default/files/ICTJ-Kenya-ICC-Impact-2010-English.pdf. Accessed Aug 2014

Alai C, Mue N (2011) Complementarity and the impact of the Rome statute and the International Criminal Court in Kenya. In: Stahn C, El Zeidy M (eds) The International Criminal Court and complementarity, vol II. Cambridge University Press, New York

Allen MJ (2005) Textbook on criminal law, 8th edn. Oxford University Press, Oxford

Ambani JO (2010) Navigating past the Dualist doctrine: the case for progressive jurisprudence on the application of international human rights norms in Kenya. In: Killander M (ed) International law and domestic human rights litigation in Africa. Pretoria University Law Press, Pretoria

Ambos K (2008) Internationales Strafrecht, 2nd edn. Verlag C.H Beck, München

Ambos K (2010) International criminal law at the crossroads: from Ad hoc imposition to a treaty-based universal jurisdiction. In: Stahn C, Van den Herik L (eds) The future perspectives of international criminal justice. T.M.C. Asser Press, The Hague

Amnesty International (2000) The International Criminal Court: checklist for effective implementation, IOR 40/011/2000. http://www.refworld.org/docid/4c7f6e4c2.html. Accessed Aug 2014

Ashworth A (2006) Principles of criminal law, 5th edn. Oxford University Press, Oxford

Balkin R (2005) International law and domestic law. In: Blay S et al (eds) Public international law: an Australian perspective, 2nd edn. Oxford University Press, Sydney

Bantekas I (2010) International criminal law, 4th edn. Hart Publishing, Portland

Bassiouni MC (1996) International crimes: *Jus Cogens* and *Obligatio Erga Omnes*. Law Contemp Probl 59(4):63–74

Bassiouni MC (2003) Introduction to international criminal law. Transnational Publishers, New York

Bassiouni MC (2005a) International crimes: "Jus Cogens" and "Obligation Erga Omnes". Law Contemp Probl 59(4):63–74

Bassiouni MC (2005b) Legislative history of the International Criminal Court, vol 2. Transnational Publishers Inc., New York

Bassiouni MC (2005c) Post-conflict justice in Iraq: an appraisal of the Iraq special tribunal. Cornell Int Law J 38:327–390

Batros B (2011) The evolution of the ICC jurisprudence on admissibility. In: Stahn C, El Zeidy M (eds) The International Criminal Court and complementarity, vol I. Cambridge University Press, New York

Bellelli R (2010) Obligation to cooperate and duty to implement. In: Bellelli R (ed) International criminal justice: law and practice from the Rome statute to its review. Ashgate Publishing Limited, England

Boas G et al (2011) International criminal law practitioner library, vol 3, International criminal procedure. Cambridge University Press, New York

Bradley CA (1999) Our dualist constitution, and the internationalist conception. Stanford Law Rev 51(3):529–566

Braham RL (1995) Canada and the Perpetrators of the Holocaust: the case of *Regina v* Finta. Holocaust Genocide Stud 9(3):293–317

Burchards W (2006) Die Verfolgung von Völkerrechtsverbrechen durch Drittstaaten-Das kanadische Beispiel. Berliner Wissenschafts-Verlag, Berlin

Carter LE (2010) The principle of complementarity and the International Criminal Court: the role of ne bis in idem. Santa Clara J Int Law 8(1):165–198

Cassese A (2005) International criminal law. Oxford University Press, Oxford

Cassese A (2008) International law, 2nd edn. Oxford University Press, New York

Cassese A (2013) International criminal law, 3rd edn. Oxford University Press, Oxford

Cassese A et al (2009) The Oxford companion to international criminal justice. Oxford University Press, Oxford

Commonwealth Secretariat (2011) Report of the Commonwealth Expert Group on review of the implementing legislation for the Rome statute. Commonwealth Secretariat, London

Collier JG (1989) Is international law really part of the law of England? Int Comp Law Q 61:924–935

Cryer R (2005) Prosecuting international crimes: selectivity and the international criminal law regime. Cambridge University Press, Cambridge

Cryer R et al (2007) Introduction to international criminal law and procedure. Cambridge University Press, Cambridge

Damgaard C (2008) Individual criminal responsibility for core international crimes. Springer, Heidelberg

Douglas G (2001) *Nulyarimma v. Thompson*: Is genocide a crime at common law in Australia? Fed Law Rev 29(1):1–37

Dörmann K et al (2003) Elements of war crimes under the Rome statute of the International Criminal Court: sources and commentary. Cambridge University Press, Cambridge

Drumbl MA (2005) Collective violence and individual punishment: the criminality of mass atrocity. Northwest Univ Law Rev 99:539–610

Drumbl MA (2007) Atrocity, punishment and international law. Cambridge University Press, New York

Duffy H, Huston J (2000) Implementation of the ICC statute: international obligations and constitutional considerations. In: Kreß C and Lattanzi F (eds) The Rome statute and domestic legal orders, vol 1. ilSirente, Baden-Baden

Ellis MS (2002–2003) The International Criminal Court and its implication for domestic law and capacity building. Fla J Int Law 15:215–242

Fernandez L (2006) Post-TRC prosecutions in South Africa. In: Werle G (ed) Justice in transition—prosecution and amnesty in Germany and South Africa. Berliner Wissenschafts-Verlag, Berlin

Ferstman C, Machover D (2008) Ending impunity in the United Kingdom for genocide, crimes against humanity, war crimes, torture and other crimes under international law: the urgent need to strengthen universal jurisdiction legislation and to enforce it Vigorously. REDDRESS and Heckman & Rose. http://www.redress.org/downloads/publications/UJ_Paper_15%20Oct%2008%20_4_.pdf. Accessed Aug 2014

Fichtelberg A (2006) Conspiracy and international criminal justice. Crim Law Forum 17:149–176

Fletcher GP (2002) The storrs lectures: liberals and romantics at war: the problem of collective guilt. Yale Law J 111:1499–1573

Ford J (2008) Country study III: Kenya. In: Plessis M and Ford J (eds) Unable or unwilling? Case studies on domestic implementation of the ICC statute in selected African countries Monograph Series No. 141. Institute of Security Studies, Pretoria

Fox H et al (1999) The Pinochet case no. 3. Int Comp Law Q 48(3):687–702

Gallant KS (2010) The principle of legality in international and comparative criminal law. Cambridge University Press, New York

Gathii JT (2010) Kenya's credible commitment to keep its date with the ICC. http://papers.ssrn.com/sol3/papers.cfm?abstract_id=1729813. Accessed Sept 2014

Gathii JT (2011) The pitfalls of adopting international laws. The Nairobi law monthly. http://nairobilawmonthlycom/index/content.asp?contentId=253&isId=6&ar=1. Accessed July 2011

Ginsburg T (2006) Locking in democracy: constitutions, commitment, and international law. Int Law Polit 38(707):707–759

Hallevy G (2010) A modern treatise on the principle of legality in criminal law. Springer, Heidelberg

Halling M (2010) Push the envelope—watch it bend: removing the policy requirement and extending crimes against humanity. Leiden J Int Law 23:827–845

Hamdorf K (2007) The concept of joint criminal enterprise and domestic modes of liability for parties to a crime: a comparison of German and English law. J Int Crimi Justice 5:208–226

Harmon MB, Gaynor F (2007) Ordinary sentences for extra-ordinary crimes. J Int Crimi Justice 5:688–712

Heller KJ (2012) A sentence-based theory of complementarity. Harvard Int Law J 53(1):201–249

Hessbruegge JA (2010) ECOWAS court judgment in Habré v. Senegal complicates prosecution in the name of Africa. Insights 15(4). http://www.asil.org/insights/volume/15/issue/4/ecowas-court-judgment-habr%C3%A9-v-senegal-complicates-prosecution-name-africa. Accessed Aug 2014

Human Rights Watch (2011) "Turning Pebbles": Evading accountability for post-election violence in Kenya. ISBN: 1-56432-836-8. Human Rights Watch, New York

Hussain A (2003) General principles and commercial law of Kenya. East African Publishers, Nairobi

International Centre for Policy and Conflict (2009) Elusive post-election violence justice: a trail of lies and betrayal. http://www.capitalfm.co.ke/eblog/2009/10/18/a-trail-of-lies-and-betrayal/. Accessed Sept 2014

International Center for Transitional Justice (2013) Prosecuting international and other serious crimes in Kenya. ICTJ Briefing. http://www.ictj.org/publication/prosecuting-international-and-other-serious-crimes-kenya. Accessed Aug 2014

Isabirye DM (1980) The status of treaties in Kenya. Indian J Int Law 20:63–82

Jeßberger F, Powell C (2001) Prosecuting Pinochets in South Africa—implementing the Rome statute of the International Criminal Court. S Afr J Crim Justice 14:344–362

Juma L (2002) Reconciling African customary law and human rights in Kenya: making a case for institutional reformation and revitalization of customary adjudication processes. St. Thomas Law Rev 14:459–512

Jurdi N (2011) International Criminal Court and national courts: a contentious relationship. Ashgate Publishing Limited, England

Kenya National Commission on Human Rights (2008) On the brink of the precipice: a [Report on] human rights account of Kenya's post-2007 election Violence. Nairobi

Kenya Parallel Report (2008) Taking these rights seriously: civil society organisations: parallel report to the initial state report of the Republic of Kenya on the implementation of the International Covenant on Economic, Social and Cultural Rights. Nairobi

Kenya Truth, Justice and Reconciliation Commission (2013) Final report, vols I, IIA, IIB, IIC, III and IV. Nairobi

Kenyans for Peace with Truth and Justice and Kenya Human Rights Commission (2013) Securing justice: establishing a domestic mechanism for the 2007/8 post-election violence in Kenya. http://www.iccnow.org/documents/SecuringJusticeKPTJandKHRC.pdf. Accessed Aug 2014

Kleffner JK (2003) The Impact of complementarity on national implementation of substantive international criminal law. J Int Crim Justice 1:86–113

LaFave WR (2003) Criminal law, 4th edn. West Publishing Co, Illinois

Lattanzi F (2001) The International Criminal Court and national jurisdictions. In: Politi M, Nesi G (eds) The Rome statute of the International Criminal Court. Ashgate, England

Maqungo S (2000) Implementation of the ICC statute in South Africa. In: Kreß C , F Lattanzi F (eds) The Rome statute and domestic legal orders, vol I. ilSirente, Baden-Baden

Matas D (1990) Prosecution in Canada for crimes against humanity. N Y Law Sch J Int Comp Law 11:347–355

Mbote PK, Akech M (2011) Kenya: justice sector and the rule of law. The Open Society Initiative for Eastern Africa, Nairobi

Meernik J, King K (2003) The sentencing determinants of the international criminal tribunal for the former Yugoslavia: an empirical and doctrinal analysis. Leiden J Int Law 16:717–750

Megret F (2011) Too much of a good thing? ICC Implementation and the uses of complementarity. In: Stahn C, El Zeidy MM (eds) The International Criminal Court and complementarity: from theory to practice. Cambridge University Press, Cambridge

Meierhenrich J (2006) Conspiracy in international law. Annu Rev Law Soc Sci 2:341–357

Meierhenrich J, Ko K (2009) How do states join the International Criminal Court? J Int Crim Justice 7:233–256

Mitchell AD (2000) Genocide, human rights implementation and the relationship between international and domestic law: *Nulyarimma* v. Thompson. Melbourne Univ Law Rev 24(1):15–49

Musila G (2007) The Office of the Attorney-General in East Africa: Protecting Public interest through independent prosecution and quality legal advice. In: Kindiki K (ed) Reinforcing judicial and legal institutions, Kenyan section of the International Commission of Jurists, Nairobi

Mwalili JJ (1998) The role and function of prosecution in criminal justice. In: UNAFEI, Annual Report for 1997 and resource material series no. 53. Asia and Far East Institute for the prevention of crime and the treatment of offenders (UNAFEI), Tokyo

Namwase S (2011) The principle of legality and the prosecution of international crimes in domestic courts: lessons from Uganda. LL.M Dissertation, University of Pretoria

Nsereko DDN (2000) Implementing the ICC statute within the Southern African region (SADC). In: Kreß C, Lattanzi F (eds) The Rome statute and domestic legal orders, vol 1. ilSirente, Baden-Baden

Nouwen SMH (2011) Fine-Tuning Complementarity. In: Brown BS (ed) Research handbook on international criminal law. Edward Elgar, Northampton

Obura K (2011) Duty to prosecute international crimes under international law. In: Murungu C, Biegon J (eds) Prosecuting international crimes in Africa. Pretoria University Law Press, Pretoria

Ojienda T, Aloo LO (2011) Researching Kenyan law. Hauser global law school program. http://www.nyulawglobal.org/globalex/Kenya.htm. Accessed Aug 2014

Ojwang JB, Otieno-Odek JA (1998) The judiciary in sensitive areas of public law: emerging approaches to human rights litigation in Kenya. Neth Int Law Rev 35:29–52

Okoth JRA (2014) The crime of conspiracy in international criminal law. T.M.C Asser Press, The Hague

Okuta A (2009) National legislation for prosecution of international crimes in Kenya. J Int Crim Justice 7:1063–1076

Olasolo H (2012) Essays on international criminal justice. Hart Publishing, Portland

Open Society Foundations (2011) Putting complementarity into practice: domestic justice for international crimes in DRC, Uganda and Kenya. http://www.opensocietyfoundations.org/reports/putting-complementarity-practice. Accessed Aug 2014

Osiel MJ (2005) Modes of participation in mass atrocity. Cornell Int Law J 38:793–822

Philippe X (2006) The principle of universal jurisdiction and complementarity: how do the two intermesh? Int Rev Red Cross 88:375–398

Q'Keefe R (2006) Crimes, the courts and customary international law: case and comment. Cambridge Law J 63(3):473–476

Reed JS (1964) Crime and punishment in east Africa: the twilight of customary law. Howard Law J 10:164–186

Parliament of Kenya (2008) Official Hansard reports. Doc. Hansard 07.05.08P. Nairobi

Republic of Kenya (2008) Report of the Commission of Inquiry into Post-election Violence (CIPEV). Government Printer, Nairobi

Republic of Kenya (2009) Report to the Kenya Attorney-General on the review of post election violence related cases in Western, Nyanza, Central, Rift Valley, Eastern, Coast and Nairobi Provinces. Nairobi

Republic of Kenya (2011) Progress report to the Kenya Attorney-General on update of post election violence related cases in Western, Nyanza, Central, Rift-Valley, Eastern, Coast and Nairobi Provinces. Nairobi

Sadat LN (ed) (2011) Forging a convention for crimes against humanity. Cambridge University Press, New York

Schabas WA (2000) Perverse effects of the *Nulla Poena* principle: national practice and Ad Hoc tribunals. Eur J Int Law 11:521–539

Schabas WA (2007) An introduction to the International Criminal Court, 3rd edn. Cambridge University Press, New York

Schabas WA (2010) Prosecuting Dr. Strangelove, Goldfinger, and the Joker at the International Criminal Court: closing the loopholes. Leiden J Int Law 23:847–853

Sedman D (2010) Should the prosecution of ordinary crimes in domestic jurisdictions satisfy the complementarity principle? In: Stahn C, Van den Herik L (eds) Future perspectives on international criminal justice. T.M.C. Asser Press, The Hague

Sing'Oei AK (2010) The ICC arbiter in Kenya's post-election violence. Minnesota J Int Law Online 19:5–20

Smith JC, Hogan B (2005) Criminal law, 11th edn. Oxford University Press, Oxford

Spiga V (2011) Non-retroactivity of criminal law: a new chapter in the Hissene Habré Saga. J Int Crim Justice 9:5–23

Swart B (2009) Modes of international criminal liability. In: Cassese A (ed) The Oxford companion to international criminal justice. Oxford University Press, Oxford

Triffterer O (2000) Legal and political implications of domestic ratification and implementation process. In: Kreß C, Lattanzi F (eds) The Rome statute and domestic legal orders, vol I. ilSirente, Baden

Triggs G (2003) Implementation of the Rome statute for the International Criminal Court: a quiet revolution in Australian. Sydney Law Rev 25:507–534

Viljoen F (2007) International human rights law in Africa. Oxford University Press, Oxford

Werle G (2007) Individual criminal responsibility under Article 25 ICC statute. J Int Crim Justice 5(4):953–975

Werle G (2009) Principles of international criminal law, 2nd edn. T.M.C Asser Press, The Hague

Werle G, Jeßberger F (2002) International criminal justice is coming home: the new German code of crimes against international law. Crim Law Forum 13:191–223

Wouters J (2005) The obligation to prosecute international law crimes. The need for justice and requirements for peace and security, Collegium edn. No. 32. College of Europe, Bruges

Chapter 5
Alternatives and Adjuncts to Domestic Prosecutions

Abstract When a country decides to address past human rights violations committed on its territory, it has two options to pursue, namely retributive justice (prosecution) and restorative justice (non-prosecution) mechanisms. However, within the context of so-called "peace versus justice debate", it is settled that whenever both mechanisms are pursued in a given transition, it is important to ensure that both peace and justice are achieved. This chapter focuses mainly on the Kenyan truth commission as one of the restorative justice mechanisms pursued as an integral part of the agreed domestic road map for accountability for the atrocities linked to the post-election violence. The chapter concentrates only on the aspects of the truth commission that have a bearing on criminal accountability for the crimes against humanity allegedly committed during the violence. It reveals that in view of the structure of the commission's legal framework, there are both strong and grey areas with the potential of affecting criminal accountability positively or negatively.

Contents

© T.M.C. ASSER PRESS and the author 2015

S.F. Materu, *The Post-Election Violence in Kenya*,

International Criminal Justice Series 2, DOI 10.1007/978-94-6265-041-1_5

5.1 Introductory Remarks

The recent past demonstrates amply that various states implementing transitional justice[1] schemes have successfully employed non-prosecutorial mechanisms as alternatives, adjuncts or supplements to prosecution. So far the non-prosecutorial approach to transitional justice has involved a diverse range of options, such as truth commissions, reparations, lustrations, granting of amnesties and traditional dispute settlement mechanisms.[2] The decision as to which mechanisms should be utilized always depends entirely on the unique circumstances of the transition itself.

There are three main lessons that can be learned from the past experience of transitional justice arrangements. First, the prosecutorial and the non-prosecutorial mechanisms are not mutually exclusive: they can be pursued simultaneously as complements.[3] Second, whereas the main objective of prosecution is to achieve *retributive justice* i.e. punishment of the perpetrators, the main objective of the non-prosecutorial mechanisms is to achieve *restorative justice* i.e. reconciliation, restitution, compensation, institutional reforms and restoration of rule of law.[4] Third, a proper combination of retributive and restorative justice mechanisms in one transition may lead to better results. For example, a recent study has concluded that more satisfaction is likely to be achieved when a truth commission is used alongside prosecution and amnesty, provided that such a combination strikes a "justice balance". According to the study, a justice balance is achieved when: (i) the prosecution component is included to underscore zero tolerance for impunity for gross violations of human rights; (ii) the amnesty component, especially in cases of negotiated transitions, is included to enhance political stability; and (iii) the truth-finding component is included to lay bare the past systematic abuses in order to, inter alia, prevent future recurrence.[5]

In the light of foregoing, it was agreed domestically in Kenya that both prosecutorial and non-prosecutorial mechanisms should be pursued to respond to, inter alia, the atrocities committed during the post-election violence.[6] In particular, legal frameworks for four non-prosecutorial mechanisms, namely a truth commission,

---

[1] The phrase "Transitional justice" (also "post-conflict justice" or "justice in transition") refers to a set of different mechanisms adopted in the aftermath of a period of conflict, civil strife, repressive regime, etc., that are aimed at dealing with the human rights violations committed during such period. See Roht-Arriaza 2006, p. 2; UN Security Council 2004, para 8. For other comprehensive literature on the subject of transitional justice, see Ambos et al. 2009; Hayner 1994, p. 600; Kritz 1995a; McAdams 1997; Teitel 2000.

[2] See Robertson 2006, p. 283; Kritz 1995b, pp. xix et seq.; Steiner and Alston 2000, p. 1217; Werle 2009, pp. 74–78.

[3] Amnesty International 2007; Bisset 2012, pp. 1–2; Ratner et al. 2009, p. 167; Villa-Vicencio 1999–2000, pp. 165 et seq., 2000, pp. 205 et seq.; United Nations Security Council 2004, p. 9.

[4] Bisset 2012, pp. 11–12 and 25–26; Collins 2010, pp. 12–14.

[5] Olsen et al. 2010, pp. 457–476. See also Bisset 2012, pp. 40–42.

[6] See generally Stahn and Nedelsky 2013, pp. 261–266.

amnesties, reparations and lustration (vetting of judges and magistrates), were adopted. Whereas amnesties and reparations were pegged to the legal framework for the truth commission, a separate legal framework was adopted for the vetting of judges and magistrates.[7]

This chapter deals mainly with the truth commission as the main response to the post-election violence pertaining to restorative justice. The framework for the vetting of judges and magistrates is outlined briefly only for purposes of completeness. In order not to drift away from the main theme of this book, which is criminal accountability for the violence, the chapter focuses more narrowly on the aspects of the truth commission with a direct or indirect bearing on criminal accountability for the crimes related to the violence. However, in order to put the discussion in context, the chapter will start off with a brief outline of the background, objectives and main features of the Kenyan truth commission and of the proposed amnesty.

5.2 Transitional Justice in Kenya Through a Truth Commission

5.2.1 Prelude to Truth Commissions

Truth commissions are fact-finding bodies established to investigate past mass atrocities. Their main objective is to clarify and acknowledge the truth about past occurrence of injustice; and document the same, thereby preserving its memory for future generations.[8] They also seek to bring about a break with the past human rights violations and promote reconciliation between the perpetrators and the victims, in order to create a sustainable environment for future peace, democracy and political stability.[9] They have three specific features: First, they investigate past human rights abuses over a given period. As a result, they are usually *not* event-specific. Second, they are temporary in nature: they exist only for a pre-determined period of time after which they are dissolved, usually having compiled a report about their findings. Third, they operate strictly according to given mandates that are usually defined by their establishing authorities.[10]

---

[7] See Vetting Act of 2011.

[8] Werle 2009, p. 75.

[9] Hayner 1994, p. 604.

[10] Hayner 1994, p. 604, 2011; Freeman 2006, pp. 12–18. See also Cassese et al. 2009, pp. 543–553; Grandin and Klubock 2007. On classification, advantages and disadvantages of the various types of truth commissions see Buergenthal 2006, pp. 105–108.

5.2.2 Introduction to the Kenyan Truth, Justice and Reconciliation Commission

5.2.2.1 Origins

The idea of creating a truth commission in Kenya emerged for the first time after the historic 2002 general elections which saw the Rainbow Coalition ousting the long-ruling dictatorial party (see supra Sect. 2.4.2.2). On 17 April 2003, the Rainbow government appointed the Task Force on the Establishment of the Truth, Justice and Reconciliation Commission (hereafter "Task Force") and directed it to seek opinions of the citizens on whether a truth commission was needed in Kenya in order to inquire into human rights violations committed under the previous governments.[11] The Task Force found that indeed over 90 % of Kenyans were in favour of the creation of a truth commission for that purpose.[12]

However, as the new government consolidated power, the enthusiasm about the truth commission faded drastically. Apparently, this was due to the fact that *most* of the politicians in the new government, including President Mwai Kibaki himself, had served in the previous dictatorial regimes. Thus, politically speaking, the "new regime" was made of "recycled" politicians: the same people in a new government. The fear seems to have been that any investigations of the past atrocities and injustices by the truth commission could become a miscalculation, as it would, most probably, end up linking those serving in the new regime or their close allies to the very atrocities. Consequently, the report of the Task Force on truth commission was archived just like the reports of previous similar bodies (see supra Sect. 2.5.3), thereby putting the desire of the Kenyans to have a truth commission in abeyance.

It took five more years for the creation of the truth commission to materialize, thanks to the 2007–2008 post-election violence. This time the idea was resuscitated by the AU-brokered mediation process (see supra Sect. 3.3), being part of the broad objectives of agendas two and three in the mediation process. These agendas sought to seek ways to address issues relating to promotion of the reconciliation, healing and restoration, and also how to look for lasting solutions for the long-term grievances and other pertinent issues that had until then not been resolved in Kenya. On 4 March 2008, the parties to the mediation process agreed on the immediate establishment of a truth commission for these purposes.[13] Consequently, the commission was established pursuant to the Kenyan Truth, Justice and Reconciliation Commission Act of 2008 (hereafter "TJRC Act").[14]

---

[11] See Kenya G.N No. 2701 of 17 April, 2003.

[12] See Republic of Kenya 2003. For greater detail see Ndung'u 2009, pp. 29–48.

[13] Kenya National Dialogue and Reconciliation 2008.

[14] See s. 3.

5.2.2.2 Objectives

In its Preamble, the TJRC Act started by acknowledging that gross violations of human rights, abuse of power and public office had happened in Kenya since independence in 1963. It stated that the climax of such violations was the post-election violence of 2007–2008.[15] The Parliament therefore resolved to establish the Kenyan TJRC as a "free reconciliatory forum"—a "platform for non-retributive truth telling" where the victims' voice would be heard and their dignity restored, and where the perpetrators' actions would be confessed.[16] To achieve this broad objective, the TJRC Act required the commission to conduct public hearings in all cases except in three circumstances, namely: (i) where a public hearing would be against the interests of justice; (ii) where the hearing would endanger the security of perpetrators, victims and witnesses; or (iii) where, as a result of public proceedings, "harm" could occur to "any person".[17]

5.2.2.3 Composition and Independence

The TJRC was a mixed commission composed of nine members, six Kenyans and three non-Kenyans, who were appointed on 22 July 2009.[18] While the Kenyan members were appointed by the President after undergoing a domestic vetting process, the international commissioners were appointed after being nominated by the African Panel of Eminent Personalities.[19]

The TJRC's independence was guaranteed under section 21 of its legislation, which provided that the commission would "not be subject to control or direction of any person or authority".[20] The Act further required that in performing their duties, the TJRC's commissioners and members of staff had to do so "in their individual capacity, independent of political parties, the government, or other organizational interests, and that they must avoid taking action which could give an impression of partiality or otherwise harm the credibility or integrity of the Commission".[21]

---

[15] TJRC Act, Preamble paras 2 and 5.

[16] Ibid., Preamble para 4; s. 5(h) and (i).

[17] Ibid., s. 25(a).

[18] The six Kenyan commissioners were: Ambassador Bethuel Kiplagat (Chairperson), Tecla Namachanja Wanjala (Vice Chairperson), Major General Ahmed Sheikh Farah, Margaret Shava, and Professor Tom Ojienda. The international commissioners were: Professor Ronald Slye (USA), Judge Gertrude Chawatama (Zambian) and Berhanu Dinka (Ethiopian). See Kenya Gazette Notice No. 8737, Special Issue, Vol. CXI-No. 70 of 14 August 2009 http://www.law.co.ke/KenyaGazette/view_gazette.php?title=3224. Accessed September 2014.

[19] TJRC Act, s. 10, read together with the first Schedule to the Act.

[20] Ibid., s. 21(1).

[21] Ibid., s. 21(2).

5.2.2.4 Mandates

5.2.2.4.1 Temporal Mandate

The temporal mandate of the TJRC was defined very broadly, in order to enable it establish as "accurate and complete" historical record of all the violations as possible.[22] This mandate covered a time frame of 45 years, extending from 12 December 1963, the date on which Kenya obtained independence, to 28 February 2008, the date on which the agreement bringing the post-election violence to an end was signed.[23] But, by virtue of section 5(a) of the TJRC Act, the commission was allowed to even go beyond the 45 years by investigating the "historical antecedents" of the violations where necessary. In this regard, the TJRC later indicated that indeed it had to investigate the pre-independence colonial period in order to understand the context of the post-independence injustices, specifically those related to land.[24]

5.2.2.4.2 Subject-Matter Mandate

The subject-matter mandate of the commission covered two categories of crimes. The first category was broadly described as "gross human rights violations and violations of international human rights law".[25] This formulation meant that any act or omission that could constitute a violation of "a fundamental human right" fell within this category, and this included crimes against humanity and genocide. Other specific violations of human rights which were expressly included under this category were: (i) torture; killing; abduction; severe ill-treatment; (ii) imprisonment or deprivation of physical liberty; (iii) rape and other forms of sexual violence; (iv) enforced disappearances of persons; (v) persecution against an identifiable group or collectivity on political, racial, national, ethnic, cultural, gender or other ground; and (vi) expropriation of private property.[26]

The second category of crimes which the TJRC was mandated to investigate was that of "economic crimes". This included "economic rights violations", such as grand corruption, exploitation of natural or public resources and "irregular" or illegal acquisition of public land.[27]

For both categories of crimes—economic crimes and gross violations of human rights—the TJRC was tasked with looking into, inter alia, the context, causes and circumstances under which the crimes occurred, and to identify the individuals,

---

[22] Cf. Ibid., s. 5(a).

[23] Ibid., ss. 6(a) and 5(a).

[24] See Kenya Truth, Justice and Reconciliation Commission 2011a, p. 44.

[25] TJRC Act, ss. 5(a), (c) and 6(a).

[26] Ibid., s. 2, read together with s. 6(a–e), (h) and (r).

[27] Ibid., s. 6(f), (g), (n) and (o).

institutions, state and non-state actors responsible for such violations, and the victims.[28] Thus, impliedly, the commission could include in its final report the names of persons allegedly responsible for the atrocities and violations it had investigated.

The inclusion of economic crimes in the subject-matter mandate of the TJRC goes beyond the traditional focus of investigations of the "first generation" of truth commissions which concentrated on the violations relating to political and civil rights. Recently, there has been a rising trend that seeks to respond to the increasing need for truth commissions to suit the local contexts of the transition in question. The mandate of the Kenyan TJRC on economic crimes is reflective of this trend, and is welcome. It takes cognisance of the fact that in this particular transition, there was a nexus between the violations of political and civil rights on the one hand and socio-economic rights on the other hand. The Liberian and Indonesian truth commissions, too, had a similar mandate, which included, for example, looking into corruption.[29]

However, it is beyond the scope of this book to discuss the mandate of the TJRC with regard to economic crimes. Rather, the focus is limited to the category "gross violations of human rights", and more narrowly to only the atrocities linked to the 2007–2008 post-election violence.

5.2.2.5   Final Report and Credibility Issues

5.2.2.5.1   Final Report

The TJRC legislation required the TJRC to prepare and submit a final report to the President.[30] It also required the commission to include in the report findings and recommendations on, among other things, *prosecution of individuals* implicated in the violations investigated, and a proposal on the mechanism and framework for the implementation of all its recommendations.[31] In addition, the law further required that the commission must publish its report immediately after submitting it to the President, and that the report must be tabled in Parliament within 21 days following such publication.[32] The report of the commission was handed over to the President on 21 May 2013, and was officially published on the same date.[33]

Furthermore, according to the TJRC Act the implementation of the TJRC report was supposed to commence within 6 months upon its publication. To this end, the Minister of Justice was put under an obligation not only to operationalize an "implementation mechanism", but also to submit bi-annual reports to the National

---

[28]   Ibid., s. 6(b).

[29]   Valji 2009.

[30]   TJRC Act, s. 48(1).

[31]   Ibid., s. 48(2)(b)–(f).

[32]   Ibid., s. 48(3) and (4).

[33]   See Kenya Truth, Justice and Reconciliation Commission Report 2013 (Vols. I–IV).

Assembly concerning the implementation of the recommendations of the commission. If any of such recommendations was not implemented, the Minister was required furnish reasons for non-implementation.[34] In addition, section 49(2) of the TJRC Act provided for the creation of an "implementation committee" to, inter alia, evaluate the "efforts" of the Government to implement TJRC's recommendations and submit quarterly reports "to the public" about its evaluation.

By June 2014, 1 year after the publication of the TJRC's report, there was no talk in Parliament or any commitment from the Kenyan government regarding the implementation of the report. Among the citizens, there was no optimism that the report would ever be implemented fully. In fact, there were indicators already that any attempt to implement the report fully would be faced with enormous political and legal obstacles, as the political elite were already unhappy about the commission's findings.

At this juncture, a few issues pertaining to the credibility of the commission and its report are also worth highlighting before moving to the critical aspects of the commission that have a bearing on the criminal accountability for the post-election violence.

5.2.2.5.2 False Start and Credibility Question

The TJRC was inaugurated in July 2009, and was given 2 years within which to finalize its operations, with a possibility of a six-month extension by Parliament. This is besides a three-month period given to the commission after its inauguration to prepare itself for the commencement of operations.[35] Therefore, going by the strict timelines specified above, the TJRC was supposed to commence its operations officially by November 2009, and if one includes an extension of 6 months, the operations of the commission ought to have been finalized not later than May 2011. However, these strict timelines were not met. The main reason for the delay was a long controversy which arose with respect to the TJRC's chairperson, Ambassador Bethuel Kiplagat. Several revelations that emerged subsequent to his appointment put to question his personal credibility and suitability to serve in the commission.[36] The controversy started when Kiplagat was implicated in three areas of atrocities that fell within the mandate of the TJRC. These were the assassination of Kenya's former minister of foreign affairs, Robert Ouko, in 1990; a notorious massacre (Wagalla massacre) of 1984; and a corruption scandal related to land transactions occurring in 1988.[37]

---

[34] TJRC Act, ss. 49 and 50.

[35] Ibid., s. 20(1)–(4).

[36] Kenya Truth, Justice and Reconciliation Commission Report 2013, Vol. I, Chap. 4, paras 4–85.

[37] Ibid., paras 5–9; Kenya Truth, Justice and Reconciliation Commission 2010, pp. 2–5; Slye 2012–2013.

While Kiplagat strongly denied any wrongdoing[38] and refused to resign voluntarily, the rest of the TJRC commissioners refused to work under his chairmanship
unless he was first "cleared". They feared, reasonably so, that doubts about the
credibility of their chairperson would reverberate as questionable credibility of the
commission itself, including its final report. Thus, the TJRC commissioners
(excluding Kiplagat) jointly petitioned the Chief Justice of Kenya, requesting him
to appoint a tribunal pursuant to section 17 of the TJRC Act, which laid down the
grounds for removal of a TJRC's commissioner from office, "to inquire into the
question of the removal of the TJRC's Chairperson" on grounds of "misbehaviour
or misconduct".[39] Thenceforth, both legal and political "battles" ensued, entailing,
inter alia, a number of court cases.[40] After long hesitation on the part of the Chief
Justice, the tribunal was finally formed in November 2010, and was directed to
inquire into claims that Kiplagat's past conduct "erode[d] and compromise[d] his
legitimacy and credibility" to chair the TJRC.[41] Kiplagat reluctantly stepped aside
to allow these investigations to take place.[42] However, the tribunal could not finalize its task due to yet more legal battles; no decision was rendered.[43] Following a
judicial review application, the High Court of Kenya ruled eventually that even the
Chief Justice had no powers under section 17 of the TJRC Act to order an inquiry
into the said "past conduct" of Kiplagat. This ruling paved the way for Kiplagat to
return to the TJRC. Upon returning, Kiplagat indicated explicitly that he came
back to the commission "to shape the final report".[44] This left the substantially
crucial question of his suitability and credibility unanswered.

The above-mentioned wrangles led to the following outcomes: (i) The Vice
Chairperson of the TJRC Betty Murungi resigned from the Commission. Another
commissioner (American) threatened to resign because he had "lost faith" in the
ability of the TJRC "to fulfil even a small part of its mandate"[45]; (ii) the
Parliament issued an ultimatum threatening to disband the Commission if the
commissioners "did not resolve their differences"[46]; and (iii) the Commission lost

---

[38] See Kenya Truth, Justice and Reconciliation Commission Report 2013, Vol. I, Chap. 4, paras
10–15.

[39] See Kenya Truth, Justice and Reconciliation Commission 2010.

[40] See Kenya Truth, Justice and Reconciliation Commission Report 2013, Vol. I, Chap. 4,
paras 16–60. See also *Republic v Truth Justice & Reconciliation Commission & another Ex-
parte Augustine Njeru Kathangu & Nine others* [2011] eKLR; *Truth Justice and Reconciliation
Commission v Chief Justice of The Republic of Kenya and Bethwel Kiplagat* [2012] eKLR, hereafter "TJRC v. C.J of Kenya & Bethwel Kiplagat".

[41] Daily Nation, 29 October 2010.

[42] BBC News, 2 November 2010.

[43] *TJRC v C.J of Kenya & Bethwel Kiplagat* [2012] eKLR, p. 3.

[44] See Kenya Truth, Justice and Reconciliation Commission Report 2013, Vol. I, Chap. 4. para 47.

[45] See Kenya Truth, Justice and Reconciliation Commission 2011a, p. 39; See also Christian
Science Monitor, 22 October 2010; Daily Nation, 29 October 2010.

[46] Daily Nation, 28 October 2010.

1 year without operations.[47] As a result, when its operations resumed, the TRC had to request the Parliament for the extension of its life for 6 months to the end of 2011.[48] However, further extension was granted, following the amendment of the TJRC Act in 2012, to enable the Commission finalize its report.[49]

5.2.2.6 Interim Conclusion

Despite the false start, the TJRC nevertheless embarked successfully on its operations. Against all odds, it was able to visit all the 47 counties in Kenya and received testimonies of about 40,000 people.[50] In order to enhance the credibility of its final report, the Commission ensured that the controversy about its chairperson was documented in a very detailed manner in the final report. Then the Commission provided the assurance that Kiplagat had been strictly denied any influence or opportunity in the drafting of the parts of the report dealing with the violations to which he had been implicated.[51]

5.2.3 Analysis of TJRC's Mandates Vis-a-Vis Criminal Accountability for the Post-Election Violence

When a truth commission and prosecution operate simultaneously or successively as accountability mechanisms responding to the same atrocities, a regulation of their relationship is very crucial; the reason being that an overlap between the investigations conducted pursuant to the two mechanisms is almost guaranteed. Usually such an overlap gives rise to certain difficulties and challenges for which only a careful and proper coordination can make the two mechanisms operate smoothly, harmoniously and effectively.[52] Schabas and Darcy rightly capture these challenges as "the tension between criminal justice and the search for truth".[53]

---

[47] See Kenya Truth, Justice and Reconciliation Commission 2011a, p. 38; Kenya Truth, Justice and Reconciliation Commission Report 2013, Vol. I, Chap. 4, paras 76–81.

[48] See Kenya Truth, Justice and Reconciliation Commission 2011b.

[49] See Statement by the Minister for Justice, National Cohesion and Constitutional Affairs on the TJRC, 31 July 2012 http://www.tjrckenya.org/index.php?option=com_content&view=article&id=561:statement-by-the-minister-for-justice-national-cohesion-and-constitutional-affairs-on-the-tjrc&catid=1:tjrc-news&Itemid=187. Accessed April 2013.

[50] See Slye 2012–2013.

[51] See Kenya Truth, Justice and Reconciliation Commission Report 2013, Vol. I, Chap 4, paras 72–75. See also Kenya Commission on Administrative Justice 2012, p. 9.

[52] Cf. Bisset 2012, pp. 4–6, 45–73; Valji 2009.

[53] Schabas and Darcy 2004; Lutz 2006, pp. 336–337.

Three institutions, namely the TJRC, national courts and the ICC have, at different levels and degrees, investigated or prosecuted the crimes related to the post-election violence in Kenya. Considering their overlapping mandates, it is very likely that two of or all the three institutions may have handled, are handling, or will have to handle the same individuals or information. This overlap is inevitable due to the fact that the investigations have most likely involved or will involve the same perpetrators, victims, witnesses and, more importantly, same pieces of evidence. This elicits the pertinent question whether in this situation the legal framework adopted in Kenya provides for a *proper* coordination of this multifaceted approach to justice. The incidental question is whether any challenges could arise in the future in the absence of such coordination.

When the Kenyan TJRC legislation was still at a bill stage, Amnesty International published a "constructive critique" of the bill in which four "problematic aspects" of its proposed legislation were identified. The critique raised the concern that the relationship between the envisioned TJRC and the Kenyan national courts was not clearly articulated in the bill, and that this had the potential of affecting negatively the search for criminal accountability for the crimes to be investigated by the commission, including those linked to the post-election violence.[54] Similarly, the Multi-Sectoral Task Force on the Truth, Justice and Reconciliation Process, an umbrella body of Kenyan civil society organisations, identified several "manifest weaknesses" in the bill and proposed its amendment before it became law.[55] Concerns were raised with regard to four uncoordinated or unclear aspects in the TJRC bill that had the potential of affecting criminal accountability during or after the TJRC's investigations. These aspects pertained to: (i) the type and nature of the crimes that the TJRC and the national courts were empowered to investigate; (ii) the mandate of the TJRC to recommend prosecution in national courts; (iii) the mandate (or lack thereof) of the TJRC to grant amnesty; and (iv) information sharing between the TJRC and the national courts and the national investigative and prosecutorial authorities.

Despite the concerns raised by Amnesty International and other commentators, some of the "problematic" aspects of the bill remained unchanged in the text of the TJRC Act which was finally passed by Parliament. The following discussion will make a critical analysis of these aspects, clearly indicating how they could affect criminal accountability for the post-election violence.

5.2.3.1   Nature and Scope of Crimes in the TJRC Act

Of the four core crimes under international law, the TJRC was empowered to investigate genocide and crimes against humanity as such. The TJRC legislation defined these two crimes specifically for purposes of the TJRC's investigations. In this regard,

---

[54] Amnesty International 2008; Asaala 2010, pp. 397 and 398.

[55] See Multi-Sectoral Task Force on the Truth, Justice and Reconciliation Process 2008.

both similarities and discrepancies can be noted between some aspects of the definitions in the TJRC Act and the definitions of the same under the domestic laws of
Kenya and under international law. For example, like the ICC Statute, the definition
of crimes against humanity in the TJRC Act contained two parts: the individual acts
(material elements) and contextual elements. As regards the individual acts, the Act
included the same acts that one finds under Article 7(1) of the ICC Statute as also rep-
licated in section 4(2)(a) of Kenya's International Crimes Act of 2008, except for the
crime of apartheid which was not provided for in the TJRC Act. As regards the contextual elements, the TJRC Act only required that for the individual acts to amount to
"crimes against humanity" they must have been committed as part of a "widespread
or systematic attack directed against a civilian population with the knowledge of the
attack".[56] The fact that the TJRC Act did not require the attack to have been committed "pursuant to or in furtherance of a State or organizational policy" means that, for
purposes of its investigations, the TJRC was required to apply the definition of crimes
against humanity under customary law, which definition is narrower than the definition found in the Kenya's International Crimes Act of 2008 (see supra Sect. 4.3.2.2.2
and infra Sect. 6.4.2.2). Consequently, this gave rise to two *potentially* disharmonious
definitions of crimes against humanity in Kenya. Questions that arise are: How and
why did such discrepancy arise; and what implications might it have?

The afore-mentioned discrepancy is directly traceable to the mediation process
carried out pursuant to the post-election violence (see supra Sect. 3.3). As already
shown, three proposals emerged out of this process, namely: (i) the creation of a special tribunal for Kenya; (ii) the fast-tracking of the domestication of the ICC Statute;
and (iii) the establishment of the TJRC. This is the reason why even the legislative
processes in respect of implementation of each of these three proposals commenced
immediately after the mediation talks, and proceeded concurrently. As a result, the
bill for the Special Tribunal for Kenya was drafted and given *a retroactive effect*
to specifically address the crimes committed during the post-election violence; the
International Crimes Act of 2008 was enacted and given *prospective* applicability to
cater for future eventualities of crimes; and the TJRC Act was enacted specifically to
provide for a framework for investigations pertaining to truth-seeking.

A closer look at the TJRC Act suggests that this legislation never intended to
provide a comprehensive legal framework on which the charges for the atrocities
investigated by the TJRC, including the crimes committed during the post-election violence, would be based. This can be inferred from three features that can be
deduced from the Act. Firstly, although the TJRC Act gave the TJRC the powers
to recommend prosecutions (see infra Sect. 5.2.3.3), it did not specify whether or
not such prosecutions must be based on the Act itself. Secondly, although the Act
enumerated crimes which constituted "gross human rights violations", it did not
define or impose any penalties, nor did it expressly confer criminal jurisdiction on
the Kenyan domestic courts in respect of those crimes. Thirdly, and more importantly, apart from "genocide", "crimes against humanity" and "enforced disappearance of persons", the TJRC Act did not at all define the other specific criminal acts

---

[56] TJRC Act, s. 2.

enumerated therein, such as torture, persecution, deportation, severe ill-treatment, etc.; it only mentioned the crimes and stated that they constituted "gross violations of human rights" for purposes of TJRC's investigations.

Therefore, by not defining all the crimes exhaustively and by not defining penalties or expressly establishing criminal jurisdiction for the domestic courts in the TJRC Act, the Kenya Parliament envisioned an implicit arrangement whereby the prosecution of the atrocities investigated by the TJRC would be done on the basis of domestic legislation other than the TJRC Act. The thinking appears to have been that the charges of those atrocities with a nexus to the 2007/2008 post-election violence would be based on the Special Tribunal for Kenya Act and be prosecuted by the envisioned Special Tribunal for Kenya (see supra Sect. 3.5), while those atrocities without any link to this particular violence would be charged under the Kenyan Penal Code and thereby be prosecuted in the Kenyan ordinary courts.

The foregoing can be the only logical and reasonable explanation as to why, for instance, in terms of the definitions of the core crimes, the TJRC Act was made to be more consistent with the proposed law for the Special Tribunal than with the Kenya's International Crimes Act of 2008. This is true with respect to the contextual elements of crimes against humanity, according to which the drafters made sure that the definition in the TJRC Act and that in the bill for the Special Tribunal for Kenya were substantially the same, as they both adopted the customary law definition. In addition, the same individual acts which were enumerated but not defined in the TJRC Act were defined exhaustively in the proposed law for the Special Tribunal.[57]

Thus, even though it was not stated explicitly anywhere in these pieces of legislation, one can still infer an implicit effort or a plan to create a relationship between the proposed Special Tribunal for Kenya and the TJRC. Such a relationship would have been symbiotic in nature. However, for this arrangement to have succeeded, it was imperative that both institutions materialized. Unfortunately, as already shown (see supra Sect. 3.6), the proposed Special Tribunal for Kenya was blocked by Parliament for political reasons.

Therefore, the fact that the TJRC materialized while the Special Tribunal did not materialize disturbed the implicit original plan for addressing criminal accountability for the crimes in question in a more co-ordinated manner. This fact, which has not received any attention so far, may give rise to several challenges in future. One such challenge could arise in relation to prosecutions recommended by the TJRC after having formed an opinion that certain conduct it investigated amounts to "crimes against humanity" pursuant to the TJRC Act. It is now clear that since the proposed Special Tribunal did not materialize, such prosecutions will have to be conducted by the ordinary courts. In this regard, the following three points are worth reiterating for domestic prosecutors to take note of specifically with regard to crimes against humanity.

First, already shown in the previous chapter, it may not be possible to bring the charges on the basis of the definition in the International Crimes Act of 2008 unless the Act is amended. Second, it is unlikely that the ordinary courts will allow charges to be

---

[57] E.g. torture, deportation and persecution. See Special Tribunal for Kenya Bill of 2009, s. 2.

brought on the basis of customary international law in view of the reluctance of domestic courts to rely directly on customary law. Third, the best solution in this situation is to disregard and avoid the label "crimes against humanity" and charge the conduct as "ordinary crimes" under the Kenyan Penal Code, thereby circumventing the intricacies or challenges relating to retroactivity or the policy element in crimes against humanity. This, as already shown, is the de facto approach so far taken in Kenya, even before the creation of the TJRC, and is likely going to remain the most convenient approach for the domestic prosecutors and the courts. A challenge that could arise in this respect is that some conduct such as "enforced disappearances", which has been investigated by the TJRC, and which clearly constitutes gross violations of human rights under international law, may fail to be captured in the available domestic ordinary crimes.[58] However, this will not affect criminal accountability for the crimes related to the post-election violence per se, as no enforced disappearances were reported.

As regards the crime of genocide, the definition in the TJRC Act was largely consistent with the definitions in the Genocide Convention, the ICC Statute and Kenya's International Crimes Act of 2008. The only discrepancy in this regard is found under section 2 of the TJRC Act which replaced the act (conduct) of "forcibly transferring children of the group to another group" under Article 6(e) of the ICC Statute with "forcibly transferring children of the group from one place to another" place. It is not very clear why this replacement was considered important in relation to the TJRC's investigations. In addition, it is difficult to figure out how, in view of the replacement, the mere *physical* transfer of children of a group "from one place to another place" (within Kenya) would satisfy the *dolus specialis* requirement for the crime of genocide, namely the specific intent to destroy a protected group in whole or in part. Interestingly, the same ambiguity would have been found in the law for the Special Tribunal for Kenya had its bill been passed into law.[59] However, irrespective of the implication this provision has or may seem to have, and whatever the purpose it was meant to serve, it may not be of much concern here, given the conclusion (supra Sect. 3.4.3.1) that no genocide happened in Kenya

5.2.3.2 Powers to Recommend Amnesty

5.2.3.2.1 Procedure for Proposed Amnesty

The TJRC had the mandate to recommend the granting of amnesty to "any person" for "any act or omission" it investigated,[60] but it decided not to utilize this mandate. However, this does not preclude an evaluation of the structure and scope of

---

[58] It appears that the TJRC was given mandate over the act of 'forced disappearances' partly on account of such incidents alleged to have occurred prior to the resumption of multipartysm, as well as during operation *Okoa Maisha* linked to the violence in Mt. Elgon (see infra Sect. 6.3.3).

[59] See the definition of genocide in the STK Bill, s. 2. On specific intent for genocide see Bantekas 2010, p. 47.

[60] TJRC Act, ss. 34(1) and (2), 36(6) and 39.

the amnesty proposed in the TJRC Act. In doing so, the justification for TJRC's decision not to utilize this specific mandate will be identified.

While the law was clear that the amnesty would have followed three procedural steps, the authority that would have been responsible for ultimately *granting* the amnesty cannot be clearly identified. The first step towards the amnesty would have been an application made in a prescribed format.[61] As a second step, upon receipt of the application, the TJRC would have had two options, namely to accept or reject the application forthwith; or to conduct "a hearing for amnesty" before deciding on the application.[62] The third step would have come into play if the applicant qualified for amnesty. In this regard, the TJRC was required to *make a recommendation* for amnesty *to the Attorney-General*, and thereby proceed to gazette the names of the persons *recommended* for amnesty.[63] In these three procedural steps, the right to legal representation would have been availed to the applicants.[64]

5.2.3.2.2   The Unclear Role of the Attorney-General

As indicated above, the TJRC's mandate was merely to *recommend* to the Attorney-General (AG) the granting of amnesty to the applicants who qualified. This is a grey area whose intention raises suspicion. In plain English, the power to *recommend* amnesty is not the same as the power to *grant* amnesty. In this regard, the TJRC Act was not clear about the role of the AG in the amnesty process—whether or not, upon receipt of such a recommendation, the AG would have been the ultimate authority to *grant* amnesty. The law was silent as to whether the AG had powers to *reject* a TJRC's recommendation for amnesty. Similarly, the Act remained silent as to whether the TJRC's publication (gazetting) per se of the names of the people *recommended* for amnesty would have amounted to the *granting* of amnesty.[65]

It was agreed during the mediation process that the TJRC's recommendations would be made to the President.[66] This suggests, therefore, that the mediators envisioned that the ultimate mandate to receive recommendations for amnesty and grant the same would be vested in the President. But the TJRC Act did not provide so. It cannot be argued or assumed that the mandate was subsumed in the presidential prerogative power of mercy. The reason is that while the prerogative power of mercy

---

[61] Ibid., s. 35. This includes a joint application in respect of the same act or omission. See s. 36(6).

[62] Ibid., s. 36(1)–(5). In both scenarios i.e. where a hearing took place and where it did not, the commission was supposed to notify the applicant if he or she qualified to be recommended for amnesty or not. See s. 40.

[63] Ibid., ss. 38 and 39.

[64] Ibid., s. 28.

[65] This grey area had been clearly identified even before the TJRC bill was passed into law, but was not rectified. See Multi-Sectoral Task Force on the Truth, Justice and Reconciliation Process 2008, pp. 6–7.

[66] Kenya National Dialogue and Reconciliation 2008, p. 2.

(pardon) only enables the beneficiary to have his sentence (not criminal liability) expunged or reduced, amnesty absolves the beneficiary from criminal liability.[67]

Perhaps the AG was linked to the proposed amnesty process because of his prosecutorial role under the existing Kenyan Constitution. The TJRC Act made the AG an ultimate receiver of the recommendation for amnesty probably in order for him not to feel that his constitutional authority had been abrogated with regard to the crimes in question.[68] However, the involvement of the AG in this regard created room for potential abuse or politicization of the amnesty process, given that his role in the process was not clearly defined. The fear of politicization emerges because, pursuant to Kenya's 2010 Constitution (under which the TJRC finalized its operations), the AG is not only a political appointee of the President, but also a member of the cabinet by virtue of his position.[69] Therefore, to minimize actual or perceived politicization and give more credibility to the amnesty process, it would have been more prudent if the mandate *to grant* amnesty was vested expressly and exclusively in the TJRC itself as the case was with the South African Truth and Reconciliation Commission.[70]

5.2.3.2.3   Conditional Amnesty

Kenya had the idea to put in place an amnesty regime modelled partly around that of the South African Truth Commission.[71] Consequently, although the Kenyan TJRC had the mandate to recommend the granting of amnesty to "any person" in respect of "any act or omission", no absolute or blanket amnesty would have been recommended. The law imposed a general condition on the applicant for amnesty to make a "full disclosure of all relevant facts" about the act, omission or offence in respect of which amnesty was applied.[72]

Even upon a full disclosure, the decision to grant or not to grant amnesty would have further depended on the following additional conditions: (i) the motive of the perpetrator when he committed the act; (ii) the context of the act; (iii) the legal or factual nature of the act, including its gravity; (iv) the objective of the act—whether it was primarily directed at a political opponent or state property or personal or against private property or individuals; (v) whether the act was committed in execution of an order or on behalf of or approval of a organization, institution,

---

[67] For details, see Lévy 2007, pp. 551 et seq.

[68] But this consideration must have been rendered irrelevant after the adoption the 2010 Constitution which, as already shown (supra Sect. 4.4.2), deprived the Attorney-General of the prosecutorial authority and vested it exclusively in the Director of Public Prosecutions.

[69] Constitution of Kenya of 2010, Articles 156(1) and 152(1)(c).

[70] This mandate was given to the amnesty committee of the Commission. See s. 20 of the Promotion of National Unity and Reconciliation Act No. 34 of 1995 (hereafter "South African TRC Act").

[71] See generally Du Bois-Pedain 2007.

[72] TJRC Act, s. 38(1)(b).Cf. South African TRC Act, s. 3(1)(b).

liberation movement or body of which the perpetrator was a member; and (vi) the relationship of the act with the political objective pursued.[73]

However, one aspect about the amnesty provisions is that the Kenyan law failed to be as precise as that of the South African Truth and Reconciliation Commission. The *specific* criteria for amnesty under provisions of section 38(3) of the Kenyan TJRC Act outlined above are far from clear. For example, paras *a* and *c* of section 38(3) only *mentioned* the "motive" and "objective" of the perpetrator to be among the factors that would have been taken into account in determining whether or not an act, omission or offence qualified for amnesty. Similarly, para *f* of the same provision added in particular that the "political objective" of the act, omission or offence would have been another criterion.[74] However, unlike the South African Truth and Reconciliation Commission, the Kenyan TJRC was not given any guidance as to what "political objective" and "motive" would have been determined. In particular, the TJRC Act did not stipulate what kind of motive or objective with which the act, omission or offence should have been committed in order for it not to qualify for amnesty. Unlike the Kenyan legislation, the legislation establishing the South African Truth Commission explicitly stated that, apart from the condition of "full disclosure", only acts committed or omissions "associated with a *political* objective" were eligible for amnesty.[75] In addition, the South African law went further to define and set out clearly the parameters of what constituted acts "associated with a political objective".[76]

Thus, the conditions for the proposed amnesty in Kenya were unclear and insufficiently explained in the law. If the TJRC had decided to grant amnesty, it would have inevitably adopted its own specific criteria from the general "political objective" criteria given in the legislation.[77] But even so, the considerations in the following sections would have played a clearly significant role in the amnesty process.

5.2.3.2.4   Crimes not Eligible for Amnesty

As shown in Sect. 3.2, almost all the attacks and retaliatory attacks committed during the post-election violence in Kenya were motivated by two closely related factors, namely political and ethnic objectives. If one assumed that *all* the crimes "associated with a political objective" were to qualify for amnesty without having to meet further criteria, and in the absence of a clear definition of a "political

---

[73] TJRC Act, s. 38(3).

[74] NB. Section 2 of the TJRC Act also referred to the "political motive" of the specific acts listed as being a factor that would make such acts qualify as "gross human rights violations". See paragraph *f*. Cf. South African TRC Act, s. 20 (1)(b).

[75] South African TRC Act, ss. 3(1)(b), (4)(c) and 18 (emphasis added).

[76] Ibid., s. 20(2) and (3). See also Bubenzer 2009, p. 11–18; Bhargava 2002, pp. 1304 et seq.; Pedain 2006, pp. 205–210. For an in-depth study regarding the amnesty granted in South Africa see Sarkin-Hughes 2004.

[77] Cf. Pedain 2006, pp. 200–204 (identifying practical challenges in this regard with reference to the South African TRC).

objective", then perhaps almost all criminal acts committed during this violence would have qualified for amnesty under the TJC Act.

However, according to section 38(c) of the TJRC Act, one criterion in the determination of whether or not a crime qualified for amnesty would have been the "legal and factual nature" of that crime, including its "gravity". Although the TJRC Act did not elaborate what the "legal nature" of the crime entailed, it is not difficult to infer its meaning in light of other provisions of the legislation. In this regard, there were provisions which identified specific crimes in the TJRC Act and explicitly disqualified them from amnesty, ostensibly due to, among other things, their "legal nature" under international law. Section 34(3) of the Act provided as follows:

> [N]o amnesty may be recommended … in respect of genocide, crimes against humanity, gross violations of human rights or any act, omission or offence constituting a gross violation of human rights including extra judicial execution, enforced disappearance, sexual assault, rape and torture.

The strict exclusion of acts constituting genocide, crimes against humanity and gross human rights violations such as torture and forced disappearances from the scope of the amnesty is proper; and is welcome. As one can easily note, war crimes are not mentioned in the quoted provision, although they, too, should have been excluded from the scope of the proposed amnesty. However, this omission should not necessarily be construed as an oversight; it ostensibly resulted from the fact that no war crimes had been committed in Kenya falling within the temporal mandate of the TJRC.

The exclusion of the core crimes from the scope of the amnesty is consistent with the earlier recommendation given by the UN High Commissioner for Human Rights on how the amnesty issue should be handled in the proposed Kenyan TJRC Act. The aim of the recommendation was to ensure that the amnesty to be granted in Kenya would remain in conformity with the international customary law according to which the granting of absolute amnesties in respect of such acts is prohibited.[78] Thus, the amnesty proposed in Kenya clearly differed from the initial trend of amnesties, mostly in the South American transitions, such as Peru and Chile. In these transitions, laws were promulgated to grant absolute and blanket self-amnesties to perpetrators of gross violations of human rights, specifically to benefit the ousted dictators and their henchmen. In many instances the Inter-American Court of Human Rights declared these types of amnesties to be against international law.[79]

---

[78] Office of the UN High Commissioner for Human Rights 2008, p. 17. See also Amnesty International 2003; Stahn 2005, pp. 695 et seq.; Meisenberg 2004, pp. 837 et seq.; UN Commission on Human Rights, Resolution 2002/79, 25 April 2002, s. 2. For more information on amnesties generally see Freeman 2009.

[79] See *Barrios Altos v. Peru,* Inter-American Court of Human Rights, Judgment of March 14, 2001 (Merits), paras 41–44 (see also the Concurring Opinions of Judge A.A. Cancado Trindade and Judge Sergio Garcia Ramirez); *Almonacid-Arellano* et al. *v. Chile,* Inter-American Court of Human Rights, Judgment of 26 September 2006 (Preliminary Objections, Merits, Reparations and Costs) paras 105–128. The Special Court for Sierra Leone (SCSL) has followed the same trend. See *Prosecutor v. Morris Kallon and Brima Buzzy Kamara,* SCSL-2004-15-AR72(E) and SCSL-2004-16-AR72(E), Appeals Chamber Decision on Challenge to Jurisdiction: Lomé Accord Amnesty, 13 March 2004, paras 66–74.

5.2.3.2.5 Non-utilization of the Amnesty Mandate

The original TJRC Bill had proposed the exclusion of *only* two categories of crimes, namely crimes against humanity and genocide, from the scope of the amnesty in Kenya. This narrow exclusion elicited strong criticism from various sources, including Amnesty International. The argument was that there was an implicit proposal in the Bill for the granting of an "illegal blanket amnesty" for other atrocities which, even though might fail to meet the legal requirements for genocide or crimes against humanity, they still constituted serious human rights violations.[80] Owing to such criticism, the Bill was amended, and as a result, the formulation adopted in section 34(3) in the TJRC Act required that "gross violations of human rights" or "any act, omission or offence constituting a gross violation of human rights" be *also* strictly excluded from amnesty.

In view of the above-mentioned amendment, the scope of conduct excluded from amnesty became very broad to the extent that almost no crimes would have qualified for amnesty, given that the definitions of "crimes against humanity" and "gross violations of human rights" in section 2 of the TJRC Act were, as already discussed, extremely broad.[81] Therefore, on that basis, and also on the basis of the flawed procedure which only empowered it to *recommend* and not *grant* amnesty, the TJRC deliberately, and justifiably so, decided *not* to utilize its mandate on amnesty.[82]

5.2.3.3 Powers to Recommend Prosecutions

One of the tasks of the TJRC was to identify persons who might have been responsible for or involved in human rights violations and other atrocities and recommend them for prosecution.[83] Truth commissions are not in any respect substitutes for criminal courts.[84] Consequently, although the Kenyan TJRC had the mandate to investigate crimes, such mandate did not confer upon it the ability to determine individual criminal responsibility. Regardless of how broad or thorough the investigations of the Commission may have been, such investigations could only be a cursory pointer as to the nature of the crimes committed; they cannot meet the evidentiary standard that a criminal court trying such crimes would require.

The TJRC's mandate to recommend prosecution must therefore be understood as a corollary of its mandate to recommend further investigations. The reason is

---

[80] See Amnesty International 2008, pp. 4–5; Kenya Truth, Justice and Reconciliation Commission Report 2013, Vol. I, paras 54–56, and 115–121.

[81] See supra Sect. 5.2.2.4.

[82] Kenya Truth, Justice and Reconciliation Commission Report 2013, Vol. I, paras 122–125.

[83] TJRC Act, ss. 5(d), 6(f) and 6(k)(ii).

[84] Cf. Amnesty International 2007, pp. 8–10; Inter-American Commission on Human Rights, Report No. 36/96, case 10.843 (Chile), 15 October 1996, paras 75 and 77; Inter-American Commission on Human Rights, Report No.136/99, case 10.488 (El Salvador), 22 December 1999, paras 229–230.

that even though the TJRC was empowered to "recommend prosecution", legally speaking, its recommendations would not have the effect of overriding the decision of the Kenyan prosecutorial authority which has the ultimate constitutional powers to determine whether or not there is actually a prosecutable case. Thus, although not expressly stated, the TJRC's mandate in this respect only sought to provide the important link between the Commission's investigative roles on the one hand and the investigative and prosecutorial roles of the national criminal investigative and prosecutorial authorities on the other hand. It is submitted that depending on the level of coordination and management put in place, such a link or relationship could profoundly enhance the fulfilment of Kenya's duty to prosecute the alleged crimes against humanity committed during the post-election violence.

Pursuant to its mandate to recommend prosecution, the TJRC identified about 80 names of individuals and recommended further investigations against them, specifically for being criminally linked to the crimes committed during the 2007–2008 post-election violence. Out of this number, 56 individuals, mostly politicians, were directly derived from the list of alleged instigators, planners, sponsors or funders of the violence which had been compiled by the Kenya National Commission on Human Rights following its inquiry into the violence.[85] The rest were names which had emerged during TJRC's hearings, being persons who were adversely mentioned as having participated directly or indirectly in the commission of crimes during the violence.[86] The TJRC insisted that its recommendation for further investigations was binding on the Director of Public Prosecutions (DPP) and that such investigations must be concluded within 1 year after the publication of its final report.[87]

In view of the pivotal role of evidence in any criminal prosecution, and pursuant to the TJRC's recommendation for further investigations and prosecutions, it is now relevant to analyze the manner in which the Kenyan prosecutorial authority and national courts should treat the bulk of information (evidence) already disclosed to the TJRC and which may, at the same time, become relevant for subsequent prosecutions in the domestic courts. It is conceivable that in some cases, this information may have been the very basis upon which the recommendation for prosecution or further investigation has been made by the TJRC. It is notable that the TJRC Act contains some provisions on how such information should be handled by the national courts, but it does not specifically have any clear provisions on the relationship between the TJRC and the domestic prosecutorial authorities. It will be shown subsequently that some provisions in the TJRC Act could either boost or vitiate this relationship and, more specifically, affect prosecutions in the national courts.

But before further examination is done in this respect, the powers of the TJRC with regard to information gathering are first outlined and analysed. This analysis

---

[85] Kenya Truth, Justice and Reconciliation Commission Report 2013, Vol. IV, Appendix 2, S/N 119–175. See also supra Sect. 4.3.1.4.1.

[86] Ibid., Appendix 1.

[87] Ibid., paras 13–14.

is crucial in view of the fact that the manner in which certain information was gathered and handled by the TJRC may, in the future, determine how such information should or can be handled by the courts, and also whether such information will remain "usable" for purposes of a criminal trial.

5.2.3.4 Information Gathering Powers

Most truth commissions rely on voluntary disclosure of information as an inherent method of truth-seeking. Information on the violations or atrocities under investigation is gathered from willing persons, including victims, witnesses or perpetrators, who are responding to a call, persuasion or encouragement by the commission to do so. In some past transitions, this has been the only information gathering method available to the truth commissions.[88]

However, some truth commissions are given powers to also employ non-voluntary methods of information gathering. These methods do not depend entirely on the willingness of the information giver to volunteer information. Rather, they involve elements of compulsion anchored on the commission's quasi-judicial powers, such as powers to issue summonses to appear, subpoena information, conduct search and seizure of documents, etc.[89] The availability of such powers to a truth commission signifies the goal to enable the particular commission gather as much information as is required to accomplish commission's core business, namely finding of the truth.

The Kenyan TJRC had powers to gather "any information" it considered relevant by using "any means it deemed appropriate".[90] As a traditional method, it was required to use the voluntary means of information gathering in the first place.[91] In addition, it was also given powers to use "compulsion" where necessary to gather information. The commission had powers to (i) demand "any information", including documentary evidence from any source, and "to compel the production of such information as and when necessary"; (ii) visit any place without prior notice in order to obtain information, including taking copies of any necessary documents; (iii) "compel the attendance of any person … to appear and to answer questions relevant to the subject matter of the session or hearing"; (iv) "require statements [to] be given under oath or affirmation"; and (v) issue summons to appear to any person, ordering him to "to produce any document thing or information that may be considered relevant to the functions of the

---

[88] See, e.g., Cueva 2006, pp. 78–79, indicating that the Peruvian truth commission only relied on "its own friendly persuasion to obtain information and testimonies it needed".

[89] See generally Freeman 2006, pp. 188–221.

[90] TJRC Act, s. 7(2)(1.a).

[91] See Ibid., s. 20(5)(a) and (b). A special form was designed for voluntary information gathering. See Kenyan TJRC Statement Form at http://www.tjrckenya.org/images/documents/statement-taking-form.pdf. Accessed April 2013.

Commission".[92] To ensure that these "coercive" means worked, the commission had the police at its disposal in order enforce such powers. [93] In addition, any failure to cooperate with the commission in this regard amounted to a criminal offence punishable with a fine of up to 100,000 Kenyan shillings (about USD 1,200) or imprisonment for 1 year, or both.[94]

5.2.3.5 Handling of Information Gathered by the TJRC

Given the TJRC's vast information gathering powers, it is proper to examine how information so gathered must be handled, especially between the commission and the investigative and prosecutorial authorities or the national courts. This includes the handling of information disclosed to or obtained by the TJRC in respect of atrocities for which subsequent investigations or prosecution have been recommended. As Burgess notes, in such instances, the major issue usually becomes "whether information given to the commission must be made available to those bodies responsible for prosecutions, or alternatively, whether it should be privileged".[95] Schabas adds that in such scenarios, the prosecutors and defence lawyers might be tempted to go on "fishing expedition" in the records and archives of the commission with a view to obtaining evidence for their cases.[96]

5.2.3.5.1 Confidentiality Versus Sharing of Information

With the exception of information divulged during the public hearings, the TJRC Act provided clearly that certain type of information gathered by the TJRC must remain confidential. This includes: (i) information or documentation accompanying an application for amnesty (ii) information and evidence obtained by the commission during an investigation; and (iii) deliberations of the commission leading to any decision, including a decision regarding the conducting of an amnesty hearing *in camera*.[97] As to whether this privileged information could be shared

---

[92] TJRC Act, s. 7(2).

[93] Ibid., s. 7(2)(1.i). This model had been used in other transitions prior to Kenya. See, e.g., s. 29(1)(c) of the TRC Act (South Africa); s. 13 of the National Reconciliation Commission Act of 2002 (Ghana); s. 27(d) of the Act to Establish the Truth, and Reconciliation Commission of Liberia of 2005(Liberia:); s. 14(1)(c) of the UN Transitional Administration in East Timor, Regulation 2001/10 (East Timor); and s. 8(1)(g) of the Truth, and Reconciliation Commission Act of 2000 (Sierra Leone).

[94] TJRC Act, s. 7(3)–(7).

[95] Burgess 2004, p. 144.

[96] Schabas 2004, p. 32. See also Cueva 2006, pp. 83–85 (explaining the "friction" and "estrangement" between the Peruvian TRC and the Prosecutor's General Office with regard to sharing of the information gathered by the commission).

[97] TJRC Act, s. 36(9)(a).

depends on who wanted to share it i.e. whether it is a commissioner or employee of the commission or the commission as an institution.

The TJRC Act absolutely prohibited TJRC employees (including the commissioners) from divulging any confidential information in a manner that is inconsistent with their functions as members of staff of the commission.[98] However, the Commission as an institution or entity was not prohibited from sharing its information. Article 36(9)(b) of the TJRC Act is clear that although the information gathered by the TJRC is generally confidential, such confidentiality would lapse "when the Commission decides to release such information".

Therefore, apart from the information published in its final report, the TJRC was, in principle, not prohibited from sharing any other information in its custody at any time and in any manner that it deemed fit. This could include sharing of the information with the Kenyan prosecutorial authorities or national courts. The existence of the possibility to share information in this way heeded to the advice by Amnesty International that had criticized the provision in the TJRC Bill which intended to absolutely prohibit the TJRC from sharing *any* of its information. The advice had hinted that such an absolute prohibition would eventually become an obstacle to both "the transmission of evidence and information to national prosecution authorities and to plaintiff victims and their families in civil proceedings for reparations".[99]

Indeed the liberty to share its information in this regard adds more sense to the TJRC's mandate to recommend further investigation or prosecutions. Any credible evidence in the custody of the Commission pointing to individual criminal responsibility for any conduct, could, in the TJRC's its own initiative, and on a confidential basis, been forwarded to the DPP for further investigations and prosecutions.[100] And if the national courts subpoena information from the commission's archives, such information should be given or retrieved by following a procedure which should have been put in place.[101]

This book was finalized when the TJRC had already been dissolved. Yet there was no indication that the Commission had put in place a mechanism or procedure pertaining to how its information should be shared after its dissolution. According to section 52(1) of the TJRC Act, the TJRC dissolved automatically 3 months after the date of submission of its final report to the President. This means that the Commission dissolved already by September 2013. But before it stood dissolved by law, the TJRC was required to leave in place a clear mechanism regarding how to organize its "archives and records for possible future reference", specific consideration being on

---

[98] Ibid., s. 23.

[99] Amnesty International 2008, p. 6.

[100] Cf. The Peruvian TRC. See also Cueva 2006, pp. 85–89. Previous commissions which had or exercised the authority to share their information this way are those in Uganda, Argentina, Haiti, the Republic of Korea, Peru and East Timor. See Freeman 2006, pp. 172–173.

[101] Cf. Report of the Chilean National Commission on Truth and Reconciliation, Vol. 1 (English Version) 1993, p. 22 (noting that the commission was empowered to submit (and it actually submitted) to the courts any evidence it came across which was relevant for further judicial investigations.).

(i) the information that may be made available to the public "either immediately or when conditions and resources allow"; and (ii) the necessary measures "to protect confidential information".[102]

One critical issue that must be addressed now is the extent to which such information would be useful if it was in fact shared or if is retrieved from the archives of the commission.

5.2.3.5.2 Incriminating Information

According to section 36(9)(c) of the TJRC Act, information embodying any confession or admission made before the TJRC about person's past crimes cannot be used in any subsequent criminal or civil proceedings against the person who made it. Similarly, according to section 24(3), a person who appeared or testified before the TJRC (as victim, witness or perpetrator) cannot be held liable for "any criminal or civil proceedings or to any penalty or forfeiture in respect of any evidence or information he or she [gave] to the Commission". These provisions might have two implications on the post-TJRC prosecutions (if any), including the prosecution of atrocities linked to the post-election violence.

5.2.3.5.2.1 Witnesses' Testimonies Incriminating Perpetrators

The information given to the TJRC by a person (witness) who testified against an alleged perpetrator of a past atrocity cannot form the basis of a subsequent criminal or civil trial against *the giver*. It follows, therefore, that even if such information was false or malicious, the person against whom it was given has no recourse whatsoever against the person who gave it as the former would otherwise have, for example, in cases befitting the common law suits of malicious prosecution. However, there is nothing speaking against such information being used against the perpetrator in a subsequent criminal trial. This, however, does not necessarily mean that this kind of information will be automatically admissible as evidence even if the criminal trial ensues from the recommendation of the TJRC. Rather, the usual procedures of evidence scrutiny, including cross examination must be followed.

One possible challenge is worth noting. If the prosecutors in the subsequent trial will seek to use the same witnesses who gave evidence against the accused before the TJRC, there may be reluctance on the part of these witnesses to testify "again" before a fully constituted criminal court, the main reason being the atmosphere in which such criminal trials will take place, specifically the adversarial nature of the trial. Usually, such atmosphere will differ significantly from that under which the TJRC's hearings took place. While the environment before the TJRC might have been friendlier and more informal, the environment in a court room will always be too formal, confrontational and, sometimes, intimidating for

---

[102] See TJRC Act, Article 52(2).

the witnesses or victims. Thus, to some of the victims, it may be too traumatizing to repeat the narration of their past experiences under cross-examination having previously done so before the TJRC. In the end, the quality of evidence given before the TJRC by the victims and witnesses who also happen to testify in a subsequent trial could be affected. As a result, evidence that appeared to the TJRC to constitute a clear case of, for example, crimes against humanity, may end up not being so clear-cut in a subsequent trial recommended by the TJRC.

Even though no indictment has been instituted pursuant to the recommendations of the TJRC so far, the challenge anticipated in the foregoing paragraph should not be ruled out completely. It is thus important for domestic prosecutors in Kenya to take note of it and figure out ways to mitigate its effect. One such way is to give due priority to documentary evidence, including that collected by the TJRC, to corroborate the oral evidence given by witnesses.

5.2.3.5.2.2 Self-incriminating Information

There is also the issue of self-incriminating evidence which may have been disclosed to the TJRC by the perpetrators through, inter alia, their confessions, admissions or surrendered documents. Priscilla Hayner makes crucial observations with regard to this kind of evidence. She states that in transitions where amnesty is proposed as a "carrot", some perpetrators of past atrocities do disclose information to truth commissions willingly, hoping that their disclosure will eventually earn them amnesty. She also states that in instances where truth commissions are vested with, inter alia, quasi-judicial powers to gather information, perpetrators are sometimes *forced* to disclose *self-incriminating* evidence regarding their own involvement in the commission of the violations under investigation.[103] While Hayner's first point does not apply to Kenya, given that the TJRC decided not to exercise its mandate on amnesty, the second point is relevant and is worth further consideration.

In most jurisdictions, the law on criminal procedure normally requires that in the course of investigating or prosecuting a crime, *before* a suspect records a statement or makes any plea before the court, he or she must be cautioned about the possibility of that statement being used subsequently against him or her in the trial. If the suspect or accused is properly warned but nevertheless proceeds to give self-incriminating evidence voluntarily, then such evidence can be used against him or her in a trial.[104]

There is no provision in the Kenyan TJRC Act requiring that a person disclosing self-incriminating evidence before the TJRC must be forewarned of a possibility of that information being used against him or her in a subsequent trial. It is, therefore, proper that the TJRC Act made it clear that such evidence cannot be used against that person in a subsequent trial against him or her. It appears from this prohibition that it is irrelevant whether or not such a trial ensues from the

---

[103] Hayner 2011, p. 117. Cf. Nerlich 2006, pp. 55–57.

[104] Cf. Kenyan Criminal Procedure Code, Cap 75 (R.E 2009), s. 137 F(a)(iv).

recommendation of the TJRC. This is in line with an established principle of fair trial in criminal cases that generally offers protection to accused persons against self-incrimination.[105] However, nothing speaks against the use of self-incriminating evidence disclosed to the TJRC as a means to locate other key sources of evidence for a subsequent trial, such as the tools of commission of the crimes, remains of victims, if any; or even to identify key prosecution witnesses.[106]

5.2.3.5.2.3 Implications of Absolute Protection Against Self-incrimination

At another level, in transitional contexts such as Kenya, where a combination of mechanisms of justice have been adopted, offering an absolute protection against the use of self-incriminating evidence, including that disclosed *voluntarily* before the truth commission, has both negative and positive implications, first on the truth-seeking process and second, on criminal accountability for the crimes investigated. The experience from the Sierra Leone transition provides clear evidence that a truth commission and criminal prosecutions can co-exist and actually operate in tandem or simultaneously. However, the same experience shows that although such co-existence is possible and actually desirable, the handling of self-incriminating evidence may require a more careful regulation due to its implications on the transition.[107]

As indicated earlier, the reason for the adoption of the strategy of full disclosure in exchange for amnesty in Kenya was to enable the TJRC accomplish its key objective, namely "establishing an accurate, complete and historical record" of the acts it was mandated to investigate. The protection against the use of self-incriminating evidence in a subsequent trial presents itself also as a technique for achieving the same objective. The reason is that this technique is useful in transitional contexts as an incentive for the perpetrators not only to come forward and testify voluntarily before the truth commission, but also to make full disclosure, thereby facilitating the goal of reconciliation.[108] For instance, in 2002, after the Sierra Leonean truth commission and the Special Court had been established, an NGO working with ex-combatants stated that the ex-combatants had said that they would cooperate with the truth commission only if they were assured that whatever testimony (truth?) they gave to the commission would not be used against them in any subsequent prosecutions by the Special Court.[109] Human Rights Watch indicated

---

[105] Cf. Bisset 2012, pp. 129–134 (discussing the dilemmas of incriminating evidence obtained by truth commissions in relation to subsequent trials before the ICC); Constitution of Kenya of 2010, Article 50(2)(l); International Covenant on Civil and Political Rights, Article 14(3)(g). For details on the principle against self-incrimination see Helmholz et al. 1997.

[106] Cf. Report of the Chilean Truth Commission Report 1993 (English Version), p. 22; Freeman 2006, pp. 173–174 (highlighting the critical challenges that may arise if there is no proper mechanism of managing the archives of a truth commission after its dissolution).

[107] Cf. Schabas 2004, pp. 25–41.

[108] Cf. International Centre of Transitional Justice 2002, p. 13; Burgess 2004, p. 145.

[109] Letter from PRIDE to ICTJ as quoted in International Centre of Transitional Justice 2002, p. 8. See also Schabas 2004, p. 28.

that such "truthful testimony" by the ex-combatants could be useful in subsequent prosecutions by the Special Court but only if it was to be used *in favour of* the perpetrators, e.g. to justify a "reduced sentence".[110]

On the other hand, there is a "negative" side of availing total protection or privilege against self-incriminating evidence. Such a protection could end up becoming a "danger" or setback in a transitional justice context. When prosecutions are tied to, or are expected to ensue from, a truth-seeking process, the perpetrators of the violations in question could go before the truth commission voluntarily and make a deliberate revelation of self-incriminating evidence. In doing so, they could be indifferent about whether or not they will eventually be granted amnesty. In fact, they could even be sure that on the basis of the very information they disclose, amnesty will be denied. In adopting such a strategy, the intention of the perpetrator may be to pre-empt the prosecution's evidence in future trials (civil or criminal) against them, since such evidence will, in principle, no longer be admissible.[111]

In view of the "danger" identified in the preceding paragraph, and even before the Kenyan TJRC Act was passed by Parliament, Amnesty International expressed its scepticism about the implication of availing *absolute protection* against self-incrimination in the Kenyan context. It stated that such a protection would hinder subsequent prosecutions instead of facilitating them. It was particularly noted that such a protection would "easily be used by the perpetrators to shield themselves from future prosecutions and civil suits for reparations regarding any crime"; and that it would "create obstacles to the transmission of evidence and information to national prosecution authorities and to plaintiff victims and their families in civil proceedings for reparations".[112]

The East Timor experience reveals that its truth commission did not offer absolute protection in this regard. The self-incriminating evidence revealed before the commission was not protected or privileged; it could be used against the person giving it or other persons, provided it had been given voluntarily.[113] On its part, the Special Court for Sierra Leone prevented the suspects already indicted formally before it from going to testify before the Sierra Leone truth commission, despite the fact that they were willing and wished to do so.[114] It appears that the Special Court acted this way in order to eliminate the possibility of the suspects to pre-empt the criminal trials before the Special Court by deliberately revealing self-incriminating evidence before the truth commission knowing that such evidence would no longer be admissible before the Court. But the Special Court succeeded

---

[110] Human Rights Watch 2002, fn 10.

[111] Cf. Nerlich 2006, pp. 60–61.

[112] Amnesty International 2008, p. 6; Burgess 2004, p. 145.

[113] See Burgess 2004, p. 145; Freeman 2006, pp. 172–173 (noting that information revealed voluntarily to a truth commission must not be privileged, but as a matter of procedural fairness, truth commissions must forewarn the deponents about possible consequences of their testimony, including the possibility that self-incriminating evidence may be used against them in future trials).

[114] See Schabas 2004, p. 30.

in this regard largely because in the Sierra Leonean transitional justice arrangement, the Special Court and the truth commission operated simultaneously, and, luckily, the indictment before the Court had preceded the attempt by the suspects to testify before the commission. In Kenya the scenario is different: prosecutions, if any, will ensue long after the truth commission has finished its work. Thus, the Kenyan courts, unlike the Special Court, no longer have the opportunity to prevent perpetrators from disclosing self-incriminating evidence before the TJRC.

From the final report of the Kenyan TJRC, it cannot be established how much self-incriminating evidence (if any) was revealed by those who appeared before it. For that reason, it cannot be predicted how, in the aftermath of the commission's work, the Kenyan courts will resolve challenges pertaining to the handling of such evidence in connection with subsequent prosecutions (if any) ensuing from the TJRC process.

5.3 Vetting of Judges and Magistrates

One of the major reformative steps taken after Kenya's post-election violence was lustration through the vetting of the judiciary. Vetting refers to a process by which the integrity of individuals is assessed with a view to establishing their suitability for public employment. In a post-conflict or post-dictatorship situation, vetting (also called purging of public service) ordinarily targets public institutions which were complicit or were perceived to be complicit or sympathetic to abuses of human rights during the conflict or dictatorship. The aim of vetting is usually to transform the particular public institutions by excluding from public service individuals with "integrity deficits" in order not only to strengthen the efficiency and independence of the institution in question, but also to re-establish civil trust, public support and confidence in it.[115]

In Kenya, the said vetting was done pursuant to the Vetting of Judges and Magistrates Act (hereafter "Vetting Act")[116] which was enacted in 2011. This law established a mechanism and laid down procedures for vetting of judicial officers, namely judges, magistrates, Registrar of the High Court and Chief Court Administrator.[117] The process aimed at determining whether judicial officers who were serving in the judiciary prior to the adoption of Kenya's Constitution of 2010 were still *suitable* to continue serving in that office.[118] The task of carrying out the

---

[115] For more details see United Nations Development Programme 2006.

[116] Available at http://www.jmvb.or.ke/images/documents/vetting_act.pdf. Accessed May 2013.

[117] Vetting Act, ss. 4 and 20. For greater detail see Imende 2012; UNDP-Kenya 2010.

[118] Vetting Act ss. 2–4, read together with Articles 10, 159 of the Constitution of Kenya of and s. 23 of the sixth Schedule. Two options were given to the judicial officers: (i) Those who did not want to be vetted could retire early from the Judiciary and (ii) Those who wanted to continue working in the judiciary must be vetted. But early retirement benefits were offered to both those who opted for an early retirement as well as those who chose to be vetted but were found unfit to remain in office. See Vetting Act, s. 24.

vetting exercise was vested in the Judges and Magistrates Vetting Board (hereafter "Vetting Board"),[119] which was chaired by Mr. Sharad Rao, an experienced barrister from the UK.[120]

In determining the suitability of a judge or magistrate, the Vetting Board was required to consider a range of criteria, including: (i) whether the judge or magistrate met the constitutional criteria for appointment to such office[121]; (ii) past work record, including his or her previous pronouncements; (iii) if there had been any pending or concluded criminal case or any recommendation to prosecute such a person for involvement in any crime, including corruption; and (iv) if there was any pending complaint against the judge or magistrate.[122] Furthermore, the Vetting Act required that the matters listed in (i) and (ii) above be determined against the bedrock of candidate's (a) competence and intellectual capacity; (b) communication skills; (c) integrity; (d) fairness; (e) temperament; (f) good judgment; and (g) legal and life experience.[123]

The number of candidates for vetting included 58 judges, 352 magistrates, the Registrar of the High Court and the Chief Court Administrator.[124] The vetting process commenced on 23 February 2012.[125] By February 2013, nine of the judges who were serving in the High Court or Court of Appeal, who opted to be vetted, had been declared unsuitable to continue in office for various reasons, including the lack of impartiality; deliberate wrong application of the law with a view to serving the interests of the repressive regime or those of the people accused of grand corruption; lack of integrity; unjustifiable delay of judgments, etc.[126] As of June 2013, the vetting of Magistrates had just commenced. Apart from the vetting process, other structural and administrative reforms were introduced in the judiciary through the new Constitution.[127] These included, inter alia, the appointment of a new Chief Justice and other judges some of whom had never served in the Judiciary before.

In view of the foregoing, one relevant question arises: To what extent may the judicial reforms resulting from the judicial purges have an impact on the criminal accountability for the crimes committed during the post-election violence? It is noteworthy that after the said reforms, public confidence in Kenya's Judiciary increased empirically. For example, in December 2008, a few months after the post-election violence, public confidence in the judiciary was only 31 %. After the

---

[119] For establishment, membership and appointment see Vetting Act, ss. 7–12.

[120] See Judges and Magistrates Vetting Board Members Profile http://www.jmvb.or.ke/index.php/about-us/members-profile. Accessed May 2013.

[121] See Constitution of Kenya of 2010, Article 166(3–5).

[122] Vetting Act, s. 18(1).

[123] Ibid., s. 18(2).

[124] Kenya Judges and Magistrates Vetting Board 2012, para 13.

[125] Ibid., para 36.

[126] Business Daily, 25 January 2013. For detailed reports on the determinations of the vetting process see the announcements of the Vetting Board http://www.jmvb.or.ke/index.php/reports. Accessed September 2014.

[127] See Constitution of Kenya of 2010, Chap. 10.

reforms introduced by the new constitution, and especially after the commencement of the vetting process which was done publicly, surveys show that between December 2012 and January 2013, the Judiciary had regained "unprecedented public confidence" ranging from 75 to 78 %.[128]

Therefore, as at October 2013, the fear that the Kenyan judiciary lacks capacity, integrity, impartiality, independence and public trust to try the masterminds of the post-election violence was lower. However, the practical impact of these judicial reforms on criminal accountability for the crimes associated with the post-election violence can only be measured if the reformed judiciary was "triggered" in this regard by the investigative and prosecutorial authorities. This means that if those crimes are not charged, and thereby impunity is perpetuated, the first institution to bear the blame will not be the Kenyan judiciary but the prosecutorial authority which is vested with responsibility to set the courts (judiciary) in motion (see supra Sect. 4.4). Only when the concrete cases are brought to courts can the willingness, independence, competency and capacity of the reformed judiciary to punish the "big fish" responsible for the post-election violence be assessed effectively. It is to be noted, however, that apart from hiring new top leadership, Kenya's investigative (police) and prosecutorial institutions were not vetted.

5.4 Chapter Summary

This chapter has highlighted alternatives and adjuncts to domestic prosecutions, the main focus being on the Kenyan TJRC. It has also briefly highlighted the ongoing vetting process in Kenya.

The chapter has shown that Kenyans decided to establish a truth commission and gave it vast temporal and subject matter mandates in order to ensure, inter alia, that the truth about atrocities committed in the past is uncovered through an investigative process. In this regard, the commission was given the mandate to recommend the granting of amnesty as well as to recommend prosecutions for those responsible for serious crimes or gross violations of human rights. On the face of it, the proposed amnesty would have complied with international law. However, the commission decided not to exercise its mandate on amnesty due to, inter alia, the extra-ordinarily narrow scope of the proposed amnesty, and also due to the fact that the commission did not have full powers: it could only *recommend* but *not grant* amnesty.

The chapter has also identified strengths and shortcomings of the relationship between the Kenyan TJRC process and national prosecutions, especially the prosecution of the crimes related to the post-election violence. It has been shown that one positive aspect of such relationship is the fact that the TJRC was not barred from sharing its information with national investigative, prosecutorial or courts

---

[128] Kenya National Dialogue and Reconciliation Monitoring Project 2013, paras 38–43.

where necessary. If this is genuinely done, it may tremendously facilitate post-TJRC investigations and prosecutions. However, one critical issue whose improper coordination has the potential of vitiating prosecutions (if any) to be carried out subsequent TJRC process is the handling of self-incriminating evidence which was divulged to the TJRC. Another issue is the potentially disharmonious definitions between the core crimes, specifically crimes against humanity, as investigated by the TJRC and the definitions of the crime as found in other national criminal laws.

Lastly, the Chapter has shown that the judicial reforms brought about by, inter alia, the vetting process significantly boosted the credibility of the Kenyan judiciary. However, since no concrete case has been brought to court in respect of the alleged masterminds of the post-election violence, it is impossible to state conclusively whether or not the reformed judiciary is willing or independent enough to now punish this category of perpetrators. What is clear though is that the judiciary, however competent, independent or credible it may currently seem, will only be able to act on the alleged crimes upon being "triggered" by the prosecutorial authority. Thus, the pertinent question still remains whether this authority will ever take the initiative to charge the political elite who allegedly bear the greatest responsibility for the violence.

References

Ambos K et al (eds) (2009) Building a future on peace and justice: studies on transitional justice, peace and development. Springer, Berlin

Amnesty International (2003) Sierra Leone: Special Court for Sierra Leone: denial of right to appeal and prohibition of amnesties for crimes under international law. AI Index: AFR 51/012/2003. http://www.amnesty.org/ar/library/asset/AFR51/012/2003/en/a0baf42e-d674-11dd-ab95-a13b602c0642/%20afr510%20122003en.pdf. Accessed Aug 2014

Amnesty International (2007) Truth, justice and reparation: establishing an effective truth commission. AI Index: POL 30/009/2007. http://www.amnesty.org/en/library/info/POL30/009/2007/en. Accessed Aug 2014

Amnesty International (2008) Kenya: concerns about the truth, justice and reconciliation commission bill. AI Index: AFR 32/009/2008. http://www.amnesty.org/en/library/info/AFR32/009/2008. Accessed Aug 2014

Asaala EO (2010) Exploring transitional justice as a vehicle for social and political transformation in Kenya. Afr Hum Rights Law J 10(2):377–406

Bantekas I (2010) International criminal law, 4th edn. Hart Publishing, Portland

Bisset A (2012) Truth commissions and criminal courts. Cambridge University Press, New York

Bhargava A (2002) Defining political crimes: a case study of the South African Truth and Reconciliation Commission. Columbia Law Rev 102:1304–1399

Bubenzer O (2009) Post-TRC prosecutions in south africa: accountability for political crimes after the Truth and Reconciliation Commission's amnesty process. Martinus Nijhoff Publishers, Leiden

Buergenthal T (2006) Truth commissions: functions and due process. In: Dupuy P et al (eds) Völkerrecht als Wertordnung: Festschrift für Christian Tomuschat, N.P. Engel, Kehl

Burgess P (2004) Justice and reconciliation in East Timor: the relationship between the Commission for Reception, Truth and Reconciliation and the courts. In: Schabas WA, Darcy S (eds) Truth commissions and courts: the tension between criminal justice and the search for truth. Kluwer Academic Publishers, Dordrecht

Cassese A et al (2009) The Oxford companion to international criminal justice. Oxford University Press, Oxford

Collins C (2010) Post-transitional justice human rights trials in Chile and Salvador. Pennsylvania State University Press, Pennsylvania

Cueva EG (2006) The Peruvian Truth and Reconciliation Commission and the challenge of impunity. In: Roht-Arriaza N, Mariezcurrena J (eds) Transitional justice in the twenty-first century. Cambridge University Press, Cambridge

Du Bois-Pedain A (2007) Transitional amnesty in South Africa. Cambridge University Press, Cambridge

Freeman M (2006) Truth commissions and procedural fairness. Cambridge University Press, New York

Freeman M (2009) Necessary evils—amnesties and search for justice. Cambridge University Press, Cambridge

Grandin G, Klubock TM (eds) (2007) Truth commissions: state terror, history and memory. Duke University Press, Durham

Hayner PB (1994) Fifteen truth commissions—1974 to 1994: a comparative study. Hum Rights Q 16:597–655

Hayner PB (2011) Unspeakable truths: transitional justice and the challenge of truth commissions, 2nd edn. Taylor and Francis, New York

Helmholz RH et al (1997) The privilege against self-incrimination: its origins and development. The University of Chicago Press, Chicago

Human Rights Watch (2002) The interrelationship between the Sierra Special Court and Truth Commission. Policy paper. http://www.hrw.org/news/2002/04/18/interrelationship-between-sierra-leone-special-court-and-truth-and-reconciliation-co. Accessed Aug 2014

Imende GS (2012) Vetting of judges and magistrates in institutional transformation: lessons from Kenya. LL.M Dissertation, University of Nairobi

International Centre of Transitional Justice (2002) Exploring the relationship between the Special Court and the Truth and Reconciliation Commission of Sierra Leone. http://ictj.org/publication/exploring-relationship-between-special-court-and-truth-and-reconciliation-commission. Accessed Aug 2014

Kenya Commission on Administrative Justice (2012) Advisory opinion on the truth, justice and reconciliation commission, Ref. CAJ/MED/04/1/12. http://www.ombudsman.go.ke/index.php?option=com_docman&view=docman&Itemid=465. Accessed Sept 2014

Kenya National Dialogue and Reconciliation (2008) Agreement on the truth, justice and reconciliation commission. http://www.lcil.cam.ac.uk/sites/default/files/LCIL/documents/transitions/Kenya_12_KNDR_Truth_Justice_Reconciliation_Commission.pdf. Accessed Aug 2014

Kenya National Dialogue and Reconciliation Monitoring Project (2013) Kenya's 2013 general election: review of preparedness (report). Nairobi

Kenya Truth, Justice and Reconciliation Commission (2010) Petition [to the Chief Justice] from the commissioners of the TJRC pursuant to section 17 and section 10 of the Truth, Justice and Reconciliation Act no. 6 of 2008, as amended. http://www.tjrckenya.org/images/documents/petition-by-commissioners.pdf. Accessed April 2013

Kenya Truth, Justice and Reconciliation Commission (2011a) Progress report to the national assembly submitted pursuant to section 20(3) of the Truth, Justice and Reconciliation Act no. 6 of 2008. http://www.dhnet.org.br/verdade/mundo/quenia/cv_31_quenia_report.pdf. Accessed April 2013

Kenya Truth, Justice and Reconciliation Commission (2011b) Request for extension of the life of the Truth, Justice and Reconciliation Commission submitted to the national assembly pursuant to section 20(3) of the TJRC act no. 6 of 2008 http://www.tjrckenya.org/images/documents/extention-of-life.pdf. Accessed April 2013

Kenya Truth, Justice and Reconciliation Commission (2013) Final report of the Kenyan Truth, Justice and Reconciliation Commission, vols I, IIA, IIB, IIC, III and IV. Nairobi

Kritz NJ (ed) (1995a) Transitional justice: how emerging democracies reckon with former regimes, vols I–III. US Institute of Peace Press, Washington

Kritz NJ (1995b) The dilemmas of transitional justice. In: Kritz NJ (ed) Transitional justice. US Institute of Peace, Washington

Lévy R (2007) Pardons and amnesties as policy instruments in contemporary France. Crime Justice 36(1):551–590

Lutz E (2006) Transitional justice: lessons learned and the road ahead. In: Roht-Arriaza N, Mariezcurrena J (eds) Transitional justice in the twenty-first century. Cambridge University Press, Cambridge

McAdams AJ (ed) (1997) Transitional justice and rule and the rule of law in new democracies. University of Notre Dame Press, Notre Dame

Meisenberg SM (2004) Legality of amnesties in international humanitarian law: the Lomé amnesty decision of the Special Court for Sierra Leone. Curr Issues Aff 86(856):837–851

Multi-Sectoral Task Force on the Truth (2008) Justice and reconciliation process: memorandum on the proposed amendments to the TJRC Bill, 2008. http://www.africog.org/reports/MEMORANDUM_ON_PROPOSED_AMENDNMENTS_TO_THE_TJRC_BILL.pdf. Accessed Sept 2014

Ndung'u D (2009) An attempt to deal with the past: exploring Kenya's long road to a truth commission. M.A Dissertation, Central European University

Nerlich V (2006) Lessons for the International Criminal Court: the impact of the criminal prosecutions on the South African amnesty process. In: Werle G (ed) Justice in transition—prosecution and amnesty in Germany and South Africa. Berliner Wissenschafts-Verlag, Berlin

Olsen TD et al (2010) When truth commissions improve human rights. Int J Transit Justice 4:457–476

Pedain A (2006) The South African amnesty scheme: a model for dealing with systematic and politically motivated human rights violations. In: Werle G (ed) Justice in transition—prosecution and amnesty in Germany and South Africa. Berliner Wissenschafts-Verlg, Berlin

Ratner SR et al (2009) Accountability for human rights atrocities in international law: beyond the Nuremberg legacy, 3rd edn. Oxford University Press, New York

Robertson G (2006) Crimes against humanity, New edn. Penguin, London

Roht-Arriaza N (2006) The new landscape of transitional justice. In: Roht-Arriaza N, Mariezcurrena J (eds) Transitional justice in the twenty-first century; beyond truth versus justice. Cambridge University Press, Cambridge

Sarkin-Hughes J (2004) Carrots and sticks: the TRC and the South African amnesty process. Intersentia, Antwerp

Schabas WA (2004) A synergistic relationship: the Sierra Leone truth and reconciliation commission and the Special Court for Sierra Leone. In: Schabas WA, Darcy S (eds) Truth commissions and courts: the tension between criminal justice and the search for truth. Kluwer Academic Publishers, Dordrecht

Schabas WA, Darcy S (eds) (2004) Truth commissions and courts: the tension between criminal justice and the search for truth. Kluwer Academic Publishers, Dordrecht

Slye RC (2012–13) Truth, justice and reconciliation: seeking truth and justice for Kenyans. http://www.law.seattleu.edu/news-and-features/features/truth-justice-and-reconciliation. Accessed April 2013

Stahn C (2005) Complementarity, amnesties and alternative forms of justice: some interpretative guidelines for the International Criminal Court. J Int Crim Justice 3:695–720

Stahn L, Nedelsky N (eds) (2013) Encyclopedia of transitional justice, vol 2. Cambridge University Press, Cambridge

Steiner HJ, Alston P (2000) International human rights in context: law politics and morals, 2nd edn. Oxford University Press, New York

Teitel RG (2000) Transitional justice. Oxford University Press, Oxford

United Nations Development Programme (2006) Vetting public employees in post-conflict settings: vetting public employees in post-conflict settings: operational guidelines. http://www.ictj.org/sites/default/files/ICTJ-UNDP-Global-Vetting-Operational-Guidelines-2006-English.pdf. Accessed Aug 2014

United Nations Development Programme (2010) Judicial integrity and the vetting process in Kenya. Amani papers, vol I, No 6. http://www.ke.undp.org/content/dam/kenya/docs/Amani%20 Papers/AP_Volume1_n6_Sept2010.pdf. Accessed Aug 2014

United Nations Office of the High Commissioner for Human Rights (2008) Report from OHCHR fact-finding mission to Kenya, 6–28 Feb 2008

United Nations Security Council (2004) Report of the secretary general on the rule of law and transitional justice in conflict and post-conflict societies, UN Doc. S/2004/616, 23 Aug 2004

Valji N (2009) Trials and truth commissions: seeking accountability in the aftermath of violence. http://www.csvr.org.za/index.php/publications/1656-trials-and-truth-commissions-seeking-accountability-in-the-aftermath-of-violence.html. Accessed Aug 2014

Villa-Vicencio C (1999–2000) The reek of cruelty and the quest for healing: where retributive and restorative justice meet. J Law Relig 14:165–187

Villa-Vicencio C (2000) Why perpetrators should not always be prosecuted: where the International Criminal Court and truth commissions meet. Emory Law J 49:205–222

Werle G (2009) Principles of international criminal law, 2nd edn. T.M.C Asser Press, The Hague

Part III
International Responses

Chapter 6
The Kenya Situation Before the ICC

Abstract As part of the road map for criminal accountability for the post-election violence in Kenya, parties which were involved in the violence agreed categorically that the ICC's intervention would be invoked if the agreed domestic judicial mechanisms failed. This agreement would appear to be evidence of a strong determination to break the "culture of impunity" which had become entrenched in Kenya as far as gross violations of human rights are concerned. However, when the domestic mechanisms actually failed and the ICC intervened, both legal and political "battles" ensued. This chapter addresses the legal issues relating to or arising from the Kenya situation before the ICC, covering four main areas. Firstly, it clarifies and examines the trigger mechanism employed; jurisdictional issues and the scope of the charges and ICC investigations. Secondly, it identifies and analyses contentious legal issues arising in relation to the definition of crimes against humanity and the principle of complementarity. Thirdly, it evaluates Kenya's legal responses as well as political and diplomatic strategies and reactions to the ICC's intervention. Fourthly, it examines the future of the ICC process in Kenya in light of Kenya's 2013 presidential election results and other specific developments at domestic level.

Contents

© T.M.C. ASSER PRESS and the author 2015
S.F. Materu, *The Post-Election Violence in Kenya*,
International Criminal Justice Series 2, DOI 10.1007/978-94-6265-041-1_6

6.1 Introductory Remarks

At the end of 2013, the second phase of proceedings, the trial stage, of one of the two cases derived from the Kenya situation[1] had just commenced at the ICC.[2] But the ICC process with respect to Kenya had commenced officially since 31 March 2010, the date on which the ICC Prosecutor was authorized by the Pre-Trial Chamber to commence an investigation.[3] Following such an investigation, on 8 March 2011, the ICC's Pre-Trial Chamber issued two summonses to appear against six suspects, all of whom Kenyan citizens. The first summons was issued against William Samoei Ruto (then suspended Higher Education Minister), Henry Kiprono Kosgey (then Chairman of the ODM party and former Minister for Industrialisation) and Joshua Arap Sang (a journalist who was then KASS FM radio executive).[4] The second summons was issued against Francis Kirimi Muthaura (then Head of the Public Service, Secretary to the Cabinet and Chairman of the National Security Advisory Committee), Uhuru Muigai Kenyatta (then Deputy Prime Minister doubling as Finance Minister) and Major General Mohammed Hussein Ali (former police chief).[5]

---

[1] The word "situation" as used in the ICC legal regime refers to events suggesting that a crime or crimes under the jurisdiction of the ICC have been or are being committed. It entails a *general* state of affairs defined in terms of temporal, territorial and personal parameters, thus specifying when, where and sometimes who committed or is committing the alleged crime(s). See Decision on the Applications for Participation in the Proceedings of VPRS1, VPRS2, PRS3, VPRS4, VPRS5 and VPRS6, *Situation in the DRC* (ICC-01/04-101-tEN), PTC, 17 January 2006, para 65.

[2] For details on the procedural phases of proceedings before the ICC, i.e. pre-trial, trial and appeal phases, see DeSmet 2009, pp. 405–440; Kress 2003, pp. 606–14.

[3] See Decision on the Authorization of an Investigation, *Situation in the Republic of Kenya* (ICC-01/09-19), PTC, 31 March 2010.

[4] Decision on the Summonses to Appear for William Samoei Ruto, Henry Kiprono Kosgey and Joshua Arap Sang, *Situation in the Republic of Kenya* (ICC-01/09-01/11-01), PTC, 8 March 2011. This decision defines the first case out of the Kenya situation, hereafter cited as *Ruto, Kosgey and Sang.*

[5] Decision on Summonses to Appear for Francis Kirimi Muthaura, Uhuru Muigai Kenyatta and Mohammed Hussein Ali, *Situation in the Republic of Kenya* (ICC-01/09-02/11-01), PTC, 8 March 2011. This decision defines the second case out of the Kenya situation, hereafter cited as *Muthaura, Kenyatta and Ali.*

The Pre-Trial Chamber conducted confirmation of charges proceedings from 1 to 8 September 2011 for the first case and from 21 September to 5 October 2011 for the second case. On 23 January 2012, the Chamber issued a consolidated decision confirming the charges against four of the six accused persons. Charges were confirmed against Ruto and Sang in the first case and against Kenyatta and Muthaura in the second case.[6] These four accused persons were committed to the Trial Chamber for trial that was originally scheduled to commence in April 2013, but was later postponed to September 2013.[7] However, before the trial commenced, the Prosecutor dropped all the charges against Muthaura, thereby leaving Kenyatta as the only accused person in the second case.[8] In addition, while the trial of Ruto and Sang commenced in September 2013 as scheduled, that of Kenyatta was rescheduled to 7 October 2014, but was later postponed indefinitely in view of serious challenges encountered by the Prosecution.[9]

6.2   Issues Relating to Trigger of Jurisdiction

6.2.1   Proprio Motu Investigation

The ICC Statute provides for three modalities, commonly referred to as "trigger mechanisms", through which the jurisdiction of the ICC can be activated. The first mechanism is where a State Party to the ICC Statute refers a situation in its own

---

[6] Decision on the Confirmation of Charges, *Ruto, Kosgey and Sang* (ICC-01/09-01/11-373), PTC, 23 January 2012; Decision on the Confirmation of Charges, *Muthaura, Kenyatta and Ali* (ICC-01/09-02/11-382-Red), PTC, 23 January 2012.

[7] Decision on Prosecution Requests to add Witnesses and Evidence and Defence Requests to Reschedule the Trial Start Date, *Ruto and Sang* (ICC-01/09-01/11-762), TC, 3 June 2013.

[8] See Statement by ICC Prosecutor on the notice to withdraw charges against Muthaura http://www.icc-cpi.int/en_menus/icc/press%20and%20media/press%20releases/Pages/OTP-statement-11-03-2013.aspx. Accessed August 2014.

[9] The commencement date of the *Kenyatta case* was postponed several times on account of the many challenges faced by the Prosecution in preparing their case, including, inter alia, recantation of evidence by key witnesses and allegedly lack of cooperation from the Kenyan government (cf. infra Sects. 6.7.3 and 6.7.5). For the chronology of these postponements see Public Redacted Version of "Decision on Commencement Date of Trial", *Kenyatta* (ICC-01/09-02/11-763-Red), TC, 20 June 2013; Decision Adjourning the Commencement of Trial, *Kenyatta* (ICC-01/09-02/11-847), TC, 31 October 2013; Order Vacating Trial Date of 5 February 2014, Convening a Status Conference, and Addressing other Procedural Matters, *Kenyatta* (ICC-01/09-02/11-886), TC, 23 January 2014; Decision on Prosecution's Applications for a Finding of Non-compliance pursuant to Article 87(7) and for an Adjournment of the Provisional Trial Date, *Kenyatta* (ICC-01/09-02/11-908), TC, 31 March 2014; Prosecution Notice Regarding the Provisional Trial Date, Kenyatta (ICC-01/09/02/11-944), TC, 5 September 2014; Order vacating Trial Date of 7 October 2014, Convening two Status Conferences, and Addressing Other Procedural Matters, Kenyatta (ICC-01/09-02/11-954), TC, 19 September 2014.

territory or in that of another State Party's territory to the Court.[10] The second mechanism is where a situation in a State Party or non-State Party to the Statute is referred to the ICC by the UN Security Council.[11] The third mechanism is where ICC's jurisdiction is triggered by the Prosecutor *proprio motu* (i.e. acting in his or her own initiative).[12] Since the third trigger mechanism, namely *proprio motu* referral, was used in respect of Kenya, it is discussed more fully below.

A *proprio motu* investigation is regulated under Articles 15 and 53 of the ICC Statute, read together with Rules 46–50 of ICC's Rules of Procedure and Evidence.[13] It operates as follows: Different sources such as individuals, NGOs, human rights commissions, etc., which may have knowledge or belief that a crime within the jurisdiction of the ICC is being or has been committed, can send "information" (also known as a "communication") to the ICC Prosecutor.[14] The Prosecutor then assesses this information to decide whether or not it presents a reasonable basis to proceed with an investigation. If it does, the Prosecutor must request the Pre-Trial Chamber to authorize commencement of an investigation into that situation.[15] If the Chamber is satisfied that in fact there is a "reasonable basis to proceed"[16] with an investigation, it will grant Prosecutor's request.[17] Out of such general investigations the Prosecutor identifies individuals to be charged for the alleged crimes.

---

[10] ICC Statute, Articles 13(a) and 14. For details see Marchesi 2008, pp. 575–579. Note that according to Article 12(3) of the ICC Statute, a non-state party can also be referred through this mechanism but only if it has accepted the jurisdiction of the ICC.

[11] ICC Statute, Article 13(b) read together with the UN Charter, Chapter VII, Article 39.

[12] ICC Statute, Articles 13(c) and 15. For greater detail see Bergsmo and Pejic 2008a, pp. 581–593.

[13] Available at http://www.icc-cpi.int/iccdocs/PIDS/legal-texts/RulesProcedureEvidenceEng.pdf. Accessed August 2014.

[14] ICC Statute, Article 15(1).

[15] See Ibid., Article 15(2) and (3), read together with Article 53(1)(a) (b) and (c) and Rule 48.

[16] Four different evidentiary standards are used at different phases of proceedings under the ICC Statute. The lowest standard is "a reasonable basis to proceed with an investigation" (Articles 15 and 53), which is applied to determine whether an investigation should be authorized. The second higher standard is "reasonable grounds to believe" that the suspected person has committed a core crime (Article 58), which is applied to determine whether an arrest warrant or summons to appear should be issued. The third higher standard is "sufficient evidence to establish substantial grounds to believe that the person committed each of the crimes charged" (Article 61(7)), which is applied to determine whether or not to confirm the charges against specific accused persons. The fourth and highest evidentiary standard is "proof beyond reasonable doubt" (Article 63(3)), which is applied to determine the guilt or innocence of the accused person. For more details, see Decision on the Authorization of an Investigation, *Situation in the Republic of Kenya* (ICC-01/09-19), PTC, 31 March 2010, paras 21–35.

[17] Investigation will not be authorized if the request does not disclose a "reasonable basis to proceed". However, it can be authorized subsequently based on new facts and evidence. See ICC Statute, Article 15(4) and (5).

6.2.2 The Waki Commission on Trigger Mechanism

As shown earlier (see supra Sect. 3.4.4), the Waki Commission recommended that the ICC's intervention should be invoked only if Kenya failed to create and put to operation the proposed special tribunal. Even though the inquiry by the Waki Commission was carried out pursuant to a proposal that originated from an externally brokered mediation process, the managers of that process *did not* deprive Kenya totally of its control over matters pertaining to criminal accountability, specifically those which would later lead to the trigger of the ICC jurisdiction. Kenya's control in this regard can be seen in least two ways, both of which linking to its Parliament.

First, the inquiry into Kenya's post-election violence was, for the most part, a Kenyan national process. The reason is that the Waki Commission, which carried out this particular inquiry, was established pursuant to a national piece of legislation, the Commissions of Enquiries Act.[18] Second, the recommendation regarding why, how and when the ICC should be asked to intervene was endorsed by Parliament on 27 January 2009 when it adopted the Waki Report.[19] Thus, these two ways in which the Kenyan Parliament was associated with the process indicate clearly that Kenya was not merely a "consumer" of an externally imposed idea as far as the road map for criminal accountability is concerned, but rather that Kenya became a "co-owner" of that idea and the ensuing processes.

It is due to the foregoing that when the ICC Prosecutor was asked to intervene in Kenya, some of the commentators viewed this invitation more as a self-referral rather than a call for a *proprio motu* investigation. Others, like Professor Kai Ambos, observed that it was "not clear" how exactly to classify the referral of the Kenya situation.[20] The fact that Kenyan Parliament had voted for the "The Hague Option" may have given the impression that Kenya as State Party to the ICC Statute had decided (through the Parliament) to "take" itself to the ICC voluntarily. In addition, the fact that hitherto there is no prescribed format to which a state referral must conform supports the thinking that a self-referral could take *any form* which the referring state deems fit, such as, for example, a parliamentary resolution.[21] Thus, those who opined that Kenya had made a self-referral must have drawn such inference, inter alia, from the domestic agreements and parliamentary deliberations which, as shown above, indicated the Parliament wanted the government to embrace the "The Hague option".

---

[18] Cap. 102 (R.E 2009). Pursuant to this legislation, the Waki Commission was established via the Kenya Gazette Notice No. 4473, Vol. CX-No.41 of 23 May 2008.

[19] See Parliament of Kenya 2008, Doc. Hansard 04.12.08, p. 3874; Parliament of Kenya 2009, Doc. Hansard 27.01.09, pp. 4426 et seq.

[20] Guest lecture delivered on 9 March 2011 at the South African-German Centre for Transnational Criminal Justice, University of the Western Cape, South Africa. The author was in attendance.

[21] So far, States have used simple letters to make self-referrals. See, e.g., ICC Press Release, ICC-OTP-20040419-50, 19 April 2004 (DRC referral) and ICC Press Release ICC-OTP-20050107-86, 7 January 2005 (Central African Republic referral).

However, the Office of the Prosecutor (OTP) treated the receipt of the envelope that contained suspects' names and the accompanying evidence compiled by the Waki Commission not as constituting a referral but rather as a mere communication calling for a *proprio motu* investigation. The Waki Commission had made it clear (supra Sect. 3.4.4) that if circumstances so dictated, its evidence would be transmitted to the ICC Prosecutor for him to "analyze its seriousness" and decide if he should commence investigations and prosecution. From the wording of this recommendation, it is clear that the Commission contemplated making a "communication" and rather than a (self) referral. In any case, on account of Kenya's foreign policy and practice regarding international treaties, it is inconceivable that the Waki Commission would have been able to make a "self-referral" on behalf of the Kenyan government.[22] Thus, the Prosecutor rightly treated the transmission of the envelope and the accompanying materials as a communication just like 30 other communications he had received by November 2009 in respect of Kenya.[23] However, as the following sections reveal, the Prosecutor would have been glad if indeed Kenya had made a self-referral.

6.2.3 Responses of ICC Prosecutor and Kenyan Government to Trigger Mechanism

The Kenyan government and the OTP had different preferences as regards the trigger mechanism. This was among the fundamental issues which seemed to affect the interests of each side. On the one hand, the Prosecutor thought that a *proprio motu* investigation was not the most convenient trigger mechanism for the OTP. He therefore wanted to avoid it at any cost. On the other hand, although the Kenyan government had failed to institute domestic proceedings, it would not easily let the ICC process ensue. But when it eventually became evident that the ICC's intervention was unstoppable, the Kenyan government battled with the dilemma whether it should make a self-referral or let the agreed *proprio motu* route take its course.

6.2.3.1 Prosecutor's Preference for Self-referral

There is no doubt that the then ICC Prosecutor Moreno-Ocampo was aware that a *proprio motu* investigation was the route recommended in the mediation process and that it had been endorsed by the Principals in the Kenyan coalition government.[24]

---

[22] In Kenya, the powers to ratify international treaties (and thus, to officially transact on behalf of Kenya with respect to issues pertaining to Kenya's rights and obligations under such treaties) reside exclusively with the Executive. See infra Sect. 6.6.3.2.

[23] See Prosecutor's Request for Authorisation of an Investigation Pursuant to Article 15, *Situation in the Republic of Kenya* (ICC-01/09-3), 26 November 2009, p. 3.

[24] See, e.g. OTP's statement in relation to events in Kenya. http://www.icc-cpi.int/NR/rdonlyres/1BB89202-16AE-4D95-ABBB-4597C416045D/0/ICCOTPST20080205ENG.pdf. Accessed August 2014. See also "ICC Prosecutor reaffirms that the situation in Kenya is monitored by his office". http://www.icc-cpi.int/NR/rdonlyres/06455318-783E-403B-8C9F-8E2056720C15/279793/KenyaOTPpubliccommunication20090211.pdf. Accessed August 2014.

However, he embarked on a "strategy" to avoid the *proprio motu* route and lobby for a self-referral. For example, in a meeting held on 3 July 2009 between the Prosecutor and the Kenyan government, Ocampo "manipulated" the Kenyan government into signing an undertaking to make a self-referral.[25] Here, a question arises as to why the Prosecutor wanted to avoid the *proprio motu* route in favour of a self-referral? Two main factors must have informed Prosecutor's preference. These are the prosecutorial policy of his Office and the negative perception about the work of the ICC in Africa.

6.2.3.1.1 ICC's Prosecutorial Policy

The prosecutorial policy adopted by the OTP from early days clearly encourages self-referrals more than the other forms of referral apparently on account of the advantages the former offers. A self-referral of a situation may guarantee more cooperation from the referring state as regards the facilitation of investigations, arrest and surrender of suspects (if necessary), witness protection, etc.[26]

This policy echoes the controversy that surrounded the idea of *proprio motu* investigations at the Rome Conference for the adoption of the ICC Statute. According to the *travaux préparatoires*, while many states strongly supported state referrals, the idea of vesting the Prosecutor with *proprio motu* powers was very contentious. On the one hand, a group of so-called "like-minded states" favoured a powerful and independent Prosecutor with absolute prosecutorial discretion. On the other hand, another group of states argued that "excessive" powers would be prone to abuse by the Prosecutor. The second group feared that such an abuse would curtail a widespread acceptance of the Statute, or impair the willingness of States Parties to cooperate with the Court.[27] Given this contention, a compromise had to be reached. Consequently, although *proprio motu* powers were eventually included in Article 15 of the Statute, the Prosecutor can only invoke such powers after having been authorized by the Pre-Trial Chamber.[28]

Therefore, in order to minimize or avoid criticism and to maximize cooperation, rightly, the OTP, through the prosecutorial policy, rightly made *proprio motu* investigations the least of its priorities.

6.2.3.1.2 Negative Perception About the ICC in Africa

The second reason for the Prosecutor's preference of a self-referral in relation to Kenya may have been the strained relationship between the ICC and Africa as a

---

[25] See ICC Office of the Prosecutor 2009, p. 2; UN General Assembly 2009, para 49.

[26] See Office of the Prosecutor 2006, pp. 2, 7; International Criminal Court 2003c. See also Ambos 2007, pp. 55–68; Cote 2012, pp. 408–410.

[27] See Bergsmo and Pejic 2008a, pp. 581–585; Schabas 2011, pp. 176–182 (noting, at p. 177, that there was fear that the position of the prosecutor "might be occupied by an NGO-friendly litigator with an attitude"); William 2008, pp. 343–349. On the role of NGOs in the adoption of the ICC Statute, see Ellis 2011, pp. 146–148; Struett 2008.

[28] Ambos 2007, pp. 55–56; Schabas 2011, p. 178; Decision on the Authorization of an Investigation, *Situation in the Republic of Kenya* (ICC-01/09-19), PTC, 31 March 2010, para 18.

regional bloc. Negative perceptions had emerged in Africa about the ICC's activities in the continent, especially after the issuing of warrants of arrest against President Omar Al-Bashir of Sudan. The ICC had already been accused by the African Union (AU) of being a biased institution, "hunting" or targeting only Africans, while perpetrators of similar crimes from Europe, America and allied countries are not targeted even where there is clear evidence against them.[29]

A strong counter-argument is usually given in response to the foregoing perception. The argument is that in the instances where African states invite the ICC voluntarily, i.e. through self-referrals, to intervene into crimes committed in their territories, the claim that the ICC is targeting African states cannot be sustained.[30] The Prosecutor was aware that this specific argument would not apply to *proprio motu* investigations, hence his preference for a self referral from Kenya. On the one hand, a self-referral would have lent more political legitimacy to the ICC's intervention, both at the domestic and international level, by creating the impression that it was Kenya itself which invited the ICC "voluntarily". On the other hand, the Prosecutor seems to have feared that a *proprio motu* intervention would create more "antagonism" between the ICC on one side and the AU and Kenyan government on the other. The Prosecutor must also have feared that such antagonism would consequently impair Kenya's voluntariness or readiness to cooperate with his Office. Given that Kenya was the first case in which *proprio motu* powers would be exercised, the Prosecutor had foreseen a mammoth challenge of having to justify why he only chose Kenya for *proprio motu* intervention and not any of the other similar situations which had been under preliminary investigations over a considerable period of time even prior to Kenya's post-election violence.[31]

Thus, it was not a surprise that Ocampo tried to promote a self-referral from Kenya. In fact, this was not his first time to do so. In the first two situations before the ICC, namely those of Uganda and the DRC, the Prosecutor had been successful in "encouraging" the respective governments to make self-referrals, although he had also received a number of calls for the initiation of *proprio motu* investigations.[32] He achieved his aim in the Uganda and the DRC situations despite the criticisms that his conduct elicited.[33]

---

[29] See, e.g., Cote 2012, pp. 411–412; Hansen 2013. See Jalloh 2012b, pp. 203 et seq.; NewAfrican 2012, pp. 10–29 (NB. This entails a collection of articles taking a clearly biased perspective (against the ICC) on the work of the Court in Africa); Murungu 2011, pp. 1067 et seq.; Mills 2012, pp. 404 et seq.; Murithi 2012, pp. 4–9, Murithi 2013; Villa-Vicencio 2011, pp. 38–41; Werle et al. 2014. For more details see infra Sect. 6.7.4.

[30] Cf. Ambos 2013, pp. 499 et seq.; Keppler 2011, pp. 1–14; Sriram 2009, pp. 320 et seq.

[31] See International Criminal Court 2011. By the end of December 2013, for instance, the OTP had received a total of 10,470 requests for *proprio motu* investigations. See ICC-OTP, "Preliminary Examinations" http://www.icc-cpi.int/en_menus/icc/structure%20of%20the%20court/office%20of%20the%20prosecutor/comm%20and%20ref/Pages/communications%20and%20referrals.aspx. Accessed September 2014.

[32] See Muller and Stegmiller 2010, p. 1271.

[33] This has, e.g., been described as a "ridiculous love of self-referrals". See Heller 2011.

6.2.3.2 Why Did the Prosecutor Fail to Secure Self-Referral?

Despite his attempt, the Prosecutor could not secure a self-referral from Kenya for obvious reasons. It is noteworthy that in all the self-referrals made so far the primary motivation of the referring governments has been the crimes committed by rebel groups or government opponents.[34] However, the situation in Kenya was completely different: there were no rebels as such. Thus, although, as indicated above, the Kenyan government had agreed with the Prosecutor that it would make a self-referral if it failed to institute domestic proceedings, Kenya was not ready to honour this undertaking at the time it was expected to do so. The argument which emerged was that Kenya was unprepared to relinquish its sovereign right to investigate and try its own nationals.[35]

It is true that no functional state would agree easily to waive its sovereignty over its own nationals through a simple agreement with another state or with a prosecutor of a foreign tribunal. The existence of several bilateral (impunity?) agreements between the USA and other states to ensure that no citizen of the USA will be arraigned before the ICC attests to this fact.[36] Notwithstanding the sovereignty argument, the Kenyan government's reluctance to make a self-referral was influenced more by the prevailing circumstances in Kenya's domestic politics at that particular time. The Kenyan government was, at that time, a coalition between two parties (see supra Sect. 3.3). Both parties to the coalition, the PNU and the ODM, had clearly been implicated in the crimes associated with the post-election violence. It would have been ironical to expect them to "invite" the ICC through a self-referral to investigate and prosecute the alleged crimes, given that up to the time such a self-referral was being sought, the leaders of the coalition government were not aware as to who would be arraigned before the ICC. This being the case, even on political grounds, a self-referral would have been counter-productive from Kenyan government's point of view: It could have indeed been tantamount to inviting serious trouble to oneself.[37]

6.3 Issues Relating to Parameters of ICC's Investigation

Usually, the ICC Prosecutor's investigation into any situation is confined to territorial, temporal and material parameters. The investigation authorized by the Pre-Trial Chamber was confined to the territory of Kenya, since the alleged crimes did not have cross-border character or effect.[38] There are no concerns or issues arising

---

[34] Cf. Akhavan 2005, p. 403 et seq.; Schiff 2008, pp. 198–199.

[35] See Application on behalf of the Government of the Republic of Kenya Pursuant to Article 19 of the ICC Statute, *Ruto, Kosgey and Sang* (ICC-01/09-02/11-26), PTC, 31 March 2011, para 3.

[36] On this see generally Bantekas 2010, pp. 439–440; Hafner 2005, pp. 323 et seq.

[37] Cf. Brown and Sriram 2012, pp. 244 et seq.

[38] Prosecutor's Request for Authorisation of an Investigation Pursuant to Article 15, *Situation in the Republic of Kenya* (ICC-01/09-3), PTC, 26 November 2009, para 50.

in this regard. However, with respect to the temporal and material parameters of the authorized investigation, a few specific legal issues that need more clarification and critical evaluation arise.

6.3.1 Temporal Scope of Investigation

6.3.1.1 Prosecutor's Intention to Conduct Open-Ended Investigation

In the request for authorization of an investigation, the Prosecutor stated that the crimes which occurred in Kenya were "not limited to the time period between 27 December 2007 [and] 28 February 2008".[39] However, in the remedy part of his request, the Prosecutor asked the Pre-Trial Chamber to authorize an investigation "in relation to the post-election violence of 2007–2008".[40] In addition, the Prosecutor based his request on the findings of 11 "reliable" reports, most of which focused *exclusively* on the "alleged crimes committed during the post election violence".[41]

The wording of the Prosecutor's request, as shown above, entails two possible interpretations regarding the temporal scope of the investigation envisioned by the Prosecutor. Both interpretations lead to the conclusion that the Prosecutor envisioned an open-ended investigation that would stretch beyond the 2-month period of active violence.

6.3.1.1.1 First Interpretation of Prosecutor's Request

One interpretation is that the Prosecutor intended not only to focus on the crimes committed *during* the post-election violence, but also on any criminal conduct *incidental* to the violence, namely atrocities which happened outside the 2-month time frame, but which nonetheless had *a direct nexus* with the 2007 general elections. Pursuant to this interpretation, Prosecutor's *proprio motu* investigation would clearly have covered the planning, organization and incitement to commit violence which had started even before the election date. Crimes committed prior to the election date, such as the murder of 70 people and displacement of 2,000 others during the campaign period,[42] would have been covered. Also, the investigation would have covered crimes committed *after* the official "ceasefire" agreement of 28 February 2008, but which crimes could have a retrospective nexus with the elections.

---

[39] Ibid., para 93.

[40] Ibid., para 114.

[41] Ibid., para 3.

[42] See Kenya National Commission on Human Rights 2007, p. 6.

6.3.1.1.2 Second Interpretation of Prosecutor's Request

The second interpretation of Prosecutor's request begins from the premise that the main trigger of the ICC's intervention in Kenya was the crimes associated with the 2007–2008 post-election violence. However, there could also have been other atrocities committed in Kenya which might not have had any clear nexus with the 2007 elections, but which could nevertheless be crimes falling under the jurisdiction of the ICC.

Certainly, the second interpretation is broader than the first. It would view the post-election violence only as a "door way" through which the ICC entered Kenya. It thus would have enabled the ICC to adopt a holistic approach to the fight against impunity in Kenya by also investigating *other* atrocities which had not been prosecuted domestically. As will be shown shortly (infra Sect. 6.3.3), the serious crimes alleged to have been committed in Mount Elgon district would have fallen under this scope.

6.3.1.2 Victims' Views

A close look at the views of the victims reveals that they embraced both interpretations above. Most of the victims wanted a broadly defined temporal scope of investigations, stretching beyond the officially defined 2-month time frame for the post-election violence. Individual victims wanted redress for other past atrocities, irrespective of whether the particular atrocities had occurred in the context of the 2007 elections. For instance, victims variously wanted the investigations to span diverse periods, such as (i) 6 months before and after the elections; (ii) the campaigning period, during election and after election; (iii) from February 2007 "during the establishment and training of militia groups"; (iv) from 2006 to 2008, "as the violence was pre-planned" (v) from 2005 during the constitutional referendum "when the incitement started"; (vi) after February 2008, "because some crimes continue to be perpetrated to date"; (vii) since 1992 onwards; (viii) up to March and April 2008, etc.[43]

6.3.1.3 Pre-Trial Chamber's Decision

The Pre-Trial Chamber noted by a majority that it could not be established clearly from Prosecutor's submission whether he wanted the investigation to be confined to the 2-month period of violence or to go beyond this time frame. However, considering the views of the victims, among other factors, the Chamber confined the temporal scope of the investigation to "the events that took place between 1 June

---

[43] Corrigendum to the Report on Victims' Representations and Annexes 1 and 5, *Situation in the Republic of Kenya* (ICC-01/09-17-Corr-Red), PTC, 29 March 2010, paras 95–105.

2005 (i.e., the date of the Statute's entry into force for the Republic of Kenya) and 26 November 2009 (i.e., the date of the filing of the Prosecutor's Request)".[44] Furthermore, the Chamber was of the view that confining the investigation to the 2-month time frame would have been "inconsistent with (i) the purpose behind investigating an *entire situation* as opposed to subjectively *selected crimes* and (ii) the Prosecutor's duty to establish the truth by extending the investigation to cover all facts and evidence pursuant to article 54(1) of the Statute".[45]

6.3.1.4 Evaluation

The decision to fix 26 November 2009 as the *end date* for the investigation was based on Pre-Trial Chamber's understanding of Article 53(1)(a) of the ICC Statute. This Article requires that a *proprio motu* investigation can be authorized if the available information shows that a crime within the jurisdiction of the Court "has been or is being committed". The Pre-Trial Chamber found that this particular provision prohibits authorization of an open-ended investigation. The Chamber stated:

> It would be erroneous to leave open the temporal scope of this investigation to include events subsequent to the date of the Prosecutor's Request. Article 53(1)(a) of the Statute, by referring to "a crime [which] has been or is being committed" makes clear that *the authorization to investigate may only cover those crimes that have occurred up until the time of the filing of the Prosecutor's Request.*[46]

6.3.1.4.1 Pre-Trial Chamber's Interpretation Questioned

The Chamber's interpretation of Article 53(1)(a) implied that whenever a *proprio motu* investigation is authorized, its temporal scope must always be sealed. It further appears that in setting an end date to the investigation, rather than leaving it completely open-ended, the Chamber wanted to achieve certainty as regards the scope of Prosecutor's investigation. However, concerns have emerged about the practicability of this interpretation. What is particularly questioned is whether the contention that it is "erroneous" for the temporal scope of a *proprio motu* investigation "to include events subsequent to the date of the Prosecutor's request" for authorization of investigation is the most correct and practicable interpretation of Article 53(1)(a).

Rastan opines that promotion of this interpretation will generally have negative implications on *proprio motu* investigations, contending that it will arguably affect all future Article 15 decisions. He further contends that such an interpretation will not be practicable in respect of all *proprio motu* investigations, more specifically

---

[44] Decision on the Authorization of an Investigation, *Situation in the Republic of Kenya* (ICC-01/09-19), PTC, 31 March 2010, para 205.

[45] Ibid. (emphasis added).

[46] Ibid., para 206 (emphasis added).

those initiated in respect of *ongoing crimes*. According to him, this interpretation implies that whenever authorization for initiation of *proprio motu* investigations is requested with respect to a situation where the commission of crimes is still going on, several requests will have to be made serially or sequentially, i.e. each time a need arises to investigate events subsequent to the end date originally fixed, the Prosecutor must again submit a request for fresh authorization of a "new or extended investigation". Rastan acknowledges that requesting for a new or extended investigation in this regard is possible under the Statute, but he rightly notes that it is "impracticable", and that it entails "unnecessary restrictions" of the powers of the Prosecutor to investigate.[47]

Interestingly, the Prosecutor did not bother to contend the Pre-Trial Chamber's demarcation of an end date to the scope of the investigation authorized. This indifference seems to have stemmed from the fact that the demarcation of an end date per se would not have had any negative impact on Prosecution's case in the two Kenyan cases. There is no express or implied indication that the Prosecutor had intended to extend his investigations even close to 26 November 2009 (the date of his request for authorization of investigation), as he did not include any incident beyond 28 February 2008 in the charges against the six suspects. As such, the Prosecutor may have chosen not to contend the demarcation of an end date not necessarily because he agreed to the Pre-Trial Chamber's interpretation of Article 53(1)(a), but merely because such a demarcation did not have any limiting effect on the investigation of incidents or crimes he had resolved to investigate and charge. Thus, if the commission of the crimes had transcended the date of his request to commence an investigation, it is most likely that the Prosecutor would have contended the Chamber's reasoning.

6.3.1.4.2 Is Pre-Trial Chamber's Reasoning Convincing?

The phrase a crime "is being committed" in Article 53(1)(a) refers to ongoing crimes. It is not entirely convincing to argue, as the Pre-Trial Chamber did, that generally a *proprio motu* investigation should be authorized in respect of crimes committed subsequent to the date of Prosecutor's request for authorization thereof. Such an argument is particularly problematic because the phrase "a crime *is being committed*" not only suggests that there could be continuity in the commission of the crime or crimes in question, but also that there could be a link between the crimes already committed, those being committed at the date of Prosecutor's request and those which might be committed subsequent to that date. The Pre-Trial Chamber's reasoning overlooks such possibilities and will definitely not be practicable in all scenarios.

Experience from the other situations before the ICC, especially those that have resulted from state self-referrals and Security Council referrals, reveals that the Prosecutor's investigations have never been sealed. It is noteworthy that even in

---

[47] Rastan 2011, pp. 434–437.

cases where no crimes continued to be committed after referral of the situation, the practice, and apparently, the interest of the OTP has always been to keep the investigations open-ended.[48] This has been Prosecutor's discretion over which the Pre-Trial Chamber has not exercised control, for it does not have any. The question is whether there is any justification for such a control with regard to *proprio motu* referrals.

The negotiators of the ICC Statute were, for various reasons, overly cautious about an "all powerful prosecutor" to the extent that States Parties to the ICC Statute did not want to grant excessive powers to the Prosecutor with regard to *proprio motu* investigations, and that in order to control such powers, they agreed to subject the exercise of *proprio motu* powers to the judicial control of the Pre-Trial Chamber (see supra Sect. 6.2.3.1.1). So, one needs to find out whether by extension those drafters also wanted the Chamber to exercise strict judicial control with regard to temporal scope of investigations commenced *proprio motu*. An affirmative answer to this question would then justify the demarcation of an end date as per the Pre-Trial Chamber's reasoning.

Neither the available commentaries on Articles 15 and 53 nor the *travaux préparatoires* suggest anything to that effect.[49] Instead, literature shows that the manner in which the States Parties wanted to limit the temporal scope of investigations (jurisdiction *ratione temporis*), regardless of the type of trigger mechanism used, was strictly with regard to clearly demarcating the date in respect of which the investigation commences. This is clear under Articles 11(2) and 12(3) of the ICC Statute. These provisions clearly designate the date of entry into force of the Statute for a particular State, or the date on which such State accepts the jurisdiction of the ICC voluntarily, as the case may be, to be the dates prior to which, strictly speaking, the Prosecutor cannot investigate. And in any case, the Prosecutor cannot investigate any crimes prior to the date of entry into force of the Statute, which is 1 July 2002.[50]

Thus, Pre-Trial Chamber II's reasoning that the ICC Statute requires that the date of Prosecutor's request must always be set as an end date for a *proprio motu* investigation is not entirely correct. However, for the reasons started above, as flawed as it may be, this decision will not have any effect on the two cases so far derived from the Kenyan situation. In addition, this flawed reasoning may not necessarily "affect all future" *proprio motu* situations as Rastan contends. Practice shows that rather than relying on previous decisions mechanically, the various

---

[48] E.g. the situation in the Central African Republic was referred to the ICC in 2005 following an attempted coup, and only one person, Jen-Pierre Bemba, was subsequently indicted in 2008. However, the Prosecutor left the investigations open-ended. Seven years later, in March 2013, when another coup happened, the Prosecutor issued a statement *reminding* the warring groups that still the ICC had jurisdiction on the basis of the 2005 referral. See Prosecutor's Statement in relation to Central African Republic, 22 March 2013 http://www.icc-cpi.int/en_menus/icc/structure%20of%20the%20court/office%20of%20the%20prosecutor/reports%20and%20statements/statement/Pages/otp-statement-CAR-22-03-2013.aspx. Accessed August 2014.

[49] See, e.g. Bergsmo and Kruger 2008, pp. 1065–1076.

[50] ICC Statute, Article 11(1).

Chambers of the ICC do consider each situation before them on a case-by-case basis. And in any case, the ICC is not bound by precedent.[51]

In fact, the reasoning of the Pre-Trial Chamber II in the Kenyan cases in this very aspect was departed from shortly later by the Pre-Trial Chamber III in yet another request for *proprio motu* investigation, the Cote d'Ivoire situation. In the latter case, the Prosecutor, apparently having been influenced by the "precedent" in the Kenya situation, requested the Chamber to authorize an investigation into the Cote d'Ivoire situation "up to the date of filing of the request". However, distinguishing the decision of Pre-Trial Chamber II in the Kenya situation, the Pre-Trial Chamber III *declined* to fix an end date for the investigation as requested by the Prosecutor for practical reasons. The Chamber underscored the importance of considering the context of each situation, rightly noting that in the context of the Cote d'Ivoire situation, it was of paramount importance to ensure that:

> Any grant of authorisation covers investigations into "continuing crimes"—those whose commission extends past the date of the application. Thus, crimes that may be committed after the date of the Prosecutor's application will be covered by any authorisation, insofar as the contextual elements of the continuing crimes are the same as for those committed prior to [the date of the filing of Prosecutors Request]. They must, at least in a broad sense, involve the same actors and have been committed within the context of either the same attacks (crimes against humanity) or the same conflict (war crimes). Therefore if the authorisation is granted, it will include the investigation of any ongoing and continuing crimes that may be committed after [the date of the filing of Prosecutor's request] as part of the ongoing situation.[52]

Therefore, as it stands now, there are two positions emanating from the Pre-Trial Chamber with regard to the demarcation of an end date for *proprio motu* investigations. One position was set in the Kenya situation and the other position in the Cote d'Ivoire situation. The position set in the Cote d'Ivoire situation is more convincing and practicable. However, it remains to be seen which position will be taken by the Appeals Chamber if a need arises, especially by determining what "an ongoing situation" precisely entails with reference to a *proprio motu* investigation.

6.3.2   Subject-Matter Jurisdiction

Subject-matter jurisdiction determines which crimes are to be investigated or prosecuted. The victims of Kenya's post-election violence argued that all types of

---

[51] Ibid., Article 21(2).

[52] Decision on the Authorisation of an Investigation, *Situation in the Republic of Cote D'ivoire* (ICC-02/11-14), PTC, 3 October 2011, para 179. This is in line with a ruling of the Pre-Trial Chamber in the DRC situation, which noted that a single situation "can include not only crimes that had already been or were being committed at the time of the referral, but also crimes committed after that time, insofar as they are sufficiently linked to the situation of crisis referred to the Court as ongoing at the time of the referral". See Under Seal Decision on the Prosecutor's Application for a Warrant of Arrest against Callixte Mbarushimana, *Situation in the DRC* (ICC-01/04-01/10-1), PTC, 28 September 2010, para 6.

violations of their rights should be investigated.[53] On his part, the Prosecutor sub-mitted that the available information revealed that only *crimes against humanity* had been committed. However, he stated that this submission was "without preju-dice to other possible crimes within the jurisdiction of the Court which may be identified during the course of an investigation".[54] It appears that by referring to "other possible crimes", the Prosecutor did not want to completely rule out war crimes and genocide, which other sources claimed that had been committed or at least attempted in Kenya.

Eventually, the Pre-Trial Chamber authorized the Prosecutor to investigate only crimes against humanity.[55] This, however, did not *per se* preclude the Prosecutor from subsequently asking the Chamber to broaden the scope of the investigation to include the other crimes in case there are facts pointing to their commission.[56]

6.3.3 Locating Crimes in Mount Elgon Area in the Investigation

There was another wave of violence in Kenya's Mount Elgon district that existed almost independently of the post-election violence.[57] In view of the temporal and material scope of the investigation authorized by the Pre-Trial Chamber, the crimes associated with this particular violence could be and should have been addressed by the Prosecutor. Despite the fact that most of the crimes associated with this specific violence are not wholly part of the defined time frame of the post-election violence, they nevertheless fall within the temporal scope of the investigation authorized by the Chamber. In addition, the nature, magnitude and gravity of the crimes commit-ted during this violence warrant its special consideration.

6.3.3.1 Origins of Violence in Mount Elgon

The violence started in 2006, being a reaction to a three-phase resettlement pro-gramme implemented by the Kenyan government in Mount Elgon district between 1968 and 2005. The Sabot, a pastoralist ethnic community residing in the area, opposed the fact that their land was being allocated to the people of other

---

[53] Corrigendum to the Report on Victims' Representations and Annexes 1 and 5, *Situation in the Republic of Kenya* (ICC-01/09-17-Corr-Red), 29 March 2010, paras 109–113.

[54] Prosecutor's Request for Authorisation of an Investigation Pursuant to Article 15, *Situation in the Republic of Kenya* (ICC-01/09-3), PTC, 26 November 2009, para 93.

[55] Decision on the Authorization of an Investigation, *Situation in the Republic of Kenya* (ICC-01/09-19), PTC, 31 March 2010, para 209.

[56] ICC Statute, Article 15(5).

[57] See also Kenya Truth, Justice and Reconciliation Commission Report 2013, Vol. III, pp. 39–80. See also supra Sect. 3.4.3.3.

communities resettled in the area. In 2002, the Sabot Land Defence Force (hereafter "Sabot militia") was formed with a view to defending the Saboti land. From 2006, the militia, resisting phase III of the resettlement programme, launched attacks targeting those who, among other things, opposed its cause.[58] Heinous crimes were allegedly committed both by the Sabot militia and the Kenyan security forces which, in 2008, carried out an operation, operation *Okoa Maisha* (Save Lives), a "deadly" military campaign against the militia.[59]

6.3.3.2 Gravity and Nature of Resulting Crimes

It is alleged that the Sabot militia killed more than 600 civilians, displaced between 66,000 and 200,000 others, and that it forcibly recruited about 650 child soldiers, mostly boys. It is further alleged that its members abducted, raped, mutilated and tortured many victims; destroyed property; and looted livestock.[60] Similarly, it is alleged that during the operation *Okoa Maisha*, the Kenyan security forces committed serious atrocities, as they arbitrarily arrested almost all men and boys as young as 10 years old, and "screened" them in a nearby military camp. The screening exercise, which Human Rights Watch describes as "systematic torture", resulted in serious bodily injuries and many deaths.[61] It has further been alleged that by July 2008, the Kenyan security forces had caused about 220 enforced disappearances, besides raping women and burning houses and property belonging to the suspected members of the Sabot militia.[62]

Both Human Rights Watch and the Kenya National Commission on Human Rights have concluded that both the Sabot militia and Kenyan security forces violated international human rights law and humanitarian law, specifically the Geneva Conventions of 1949.[63] It has even been claimed that from 2006 to 2008 the Sabot militia was "in effective control" of the Mount Elgon district, because "there was no government in that area".[64] Further documentation suggests that, just like the Kenyan security forces, the structure of the Sabot militia entailed a defined hierarchical chain of command. Accordingly, it is has been argued that the doctrine of command responsibility could also apply in dealing with the crimes of the militia.[65]

---

[58] Human Rights Watch 2008, pp. 11–14.

[59] Ibid., pp. 27–28. See also generally Kenya National Commission on Human Rights 2008a; United Nations Development Programme 2009.

[60] Human Rights Watch 2008, pp. 19–26.

[61] See Kenya National Human Rights Commission 2008b, pp. 23–87 (documenting the medical reports of 26 victims, including pictures showing severe bodily injuries).

[62] Human Rights Watch 2008, pp. 27–34; Human Rights Watch 2011.

[63] Human Rights Watch 2008, pp. 39–42.

[64] Ibid., p. 19.

[65] Ibid., p. 15. See also Kenya National Commission on Human Rights 2008a, p. 20.

After the end of the operation *Okoa Maisha*, about 700 members of the Sabot militia were charged domestically under the Kenyan Geneva Conventions Act with the crime of promoting "war-like activities".[66] However, the crimes alleged to have been committed by the Kenyan security forces were not prosecuted.[67] Prospects of their being investigated and prosecuted domestically remain very slim.

The allegation that war crimes were committed is serious, but cannot be adequately scrutinized here to establish if all the legal requirements for such crimes could actually be established. However, as the Kenyan Truth, Justice and Reconciliation Commission also concluded, the nature of the crimes committed indicates that there could be a reasonable basis to believe that crimes against humanity were indeed committed.[68]

6.3.3.3 Interim Conclusion

Most of the atrocities in Mount Elgon were *not* committed in connection with Kenya's 2007 elections. However, there is no doubt that these crimes clearly fall within the jurisdiction of the ICC given the broader temporal and material scope of investigations as authorized by the Pre-Trial Chamber into Kenya. It is noteworthy that, when authorizing the investigation, the Chamber referred to the violence in Mount Elgon by passing, but the crimes committed in this area are conspicuously missing in the charges subsequently brought before the ICC. This deliberate "omission" seems to have been influenced by the Prosecutor's express statement that the primary reason for his *proprio motu* intervention in Kenya was to deter future crimes *associated with election violence.*[69] Hence, the atrocities committed in Mount Elgon remains one of the areas in which the prosecutorial discretion failed to meet the legitimate expectations of victims of serious crimes in Kenya.

6.4 Issues Relating to Substantive Criminal Law

There are two main issues of substantive law arising from the pre-trial phase of the Kenya situation that merit critical analysis. The first issue relates to the characterization of the facts in the charges. The second issue relates to the contention arising from the definition of crimes against humanity.

---

[66] Human Rights Watch 2008, p. 45.

[67] Kenya Truth, Justice and Reconciliation Commission Report 2013, Vol. IV, p. 68 (specifically see Annex 1, theme/subject no. 16).

[68] See Ibid., para 133.

[69] See Ocampo's statement on Kenya [video], published on You Tube by NTV Kenya, 1 April 2012 http://www.youtube.com/watch?v=Pg4jxfsXT98. Viewed September 2014.

6.4.1 Prosecutorial Discretion Vis-a-Vis Scope of Charges

The indictment in the two Kenyan cases encompassed a total of five individual acts charged as crimes against humanity contrary to Article 7 of the ICC Statute.[70] The acts charged are only those with a direct nexus to the post-election violence, namely murder; deportation or forcible transfer of population; persecution; rape and other forms of sexual violence; and other inhumane acts.[71] However, a contention emerged during the pre-trial proceedings as to how property crimes should have been characterized in the indictment. The main issue was whether, considering the circumstances in which they were committed, such crimes should have been characterized as "persecution"; or as "deportation or forcible transfer of population"; or as "other inhumane acts".

6.4.1.1 Characterization of Crimes Relating to Property

The charge, by either design or oversight, treated the property crimes of looting and destruction of property differently in the two cases.

In the case of *Ruto, Kosgey and Sang*, the Prosecution argued that these acts constituted the crime against humanity of "deportation or forcible transfer of population" contrary to Article 7(1)(d) of the ICC Statute. Accordingly, the Prosecutor alleged that these acts were committed by the "Network Perpetrators" (see infra Sect. 6.4.2.2.1.1) in order to "permanently expel PNU supporters from the Rift Valley".[72] However, in the second case, *Muthaura, Kenyatta and Ali*, the Prosecution argued that the looting and destruction of property allegedly committed by "the Mungiki Perpetrators" (see infra Sect. 6.4.2.2.1.2) constituted the crime of "*other inhumane acts*" under Article 7(1)(k) of the ICC Statute. Accordingly, the Prosecutor submitted that these acts and several others affected the "physical and mental health" of the victims.[73]

6.4.1.1.1 Victims' Arguments

A total of 327 victims indicated that they had suffered theft, looting or destruction of their property during the post-election violence. They raised a concern that the

---

[70] See Document Containing Charges, *Muthaura, Kenyatta and Ali* (ICC-01/09-02/11-257-AnxA), PTC, 19 August 2011, pp. 38–43; Document Containing Charges, *Ruto, Kosgey and Sang* (ICC-01/09-01/11-261-AnxA), PTC, 15 August 2011, pp. 35–38.

[71] See Decision on the Confirmation of Charges, *Muthaura, Kenyatta and Ali* (ICC-01/09-02/11-382-Red), PTC, 23 January 2012, paras 231–280; Decision on the Confirmation of Charges, *Ruto, Kosgey and Sang* (ICC-01/09-01/11-373), PTC, 23 January 2012, paras 223–281.

[72] Document Containing Charges, *Ruto, Kosgey and Sang* (ICC-01/09-01/11-261-AnxA), PTC, 15 August 2011, paras 37 and 101.

[73] Decision on the Confirmation of Charges, *Muthaura, Kenyatta and Ali* (ICC-01/09-02/11-382-Red), PTC, 23 January 2012, para 268–269.

charges brought by the Prosecutor "did not indicate clearly and expressly" whether they would actually cover such property crimes. In particular, the common victims' representative argued that in *both cases*, the Prosecution had characterized the facts in relation to property crimes erroneously. In her view, under the ICC Statute, property crimes committed in Kenya were neither "other inhumane acts" nor "deportation or forcible transfer of population" as characterized in the charges. Rather, the she submitted that these acts constituted a crime against humanity of "persecution" under Article 7(1)(h) of the ICC Statute. Thus, the victims asked the Pre-Trial Chamber to advise the Prosecutor to consider amending the charges accordingly, since the error would adversely affect their individual interests at the end of the trial.[74]

6.4.1.1.2   Reasoning and Decision of Pre-Trial Chamber

In the case of *Ruto, Kosgey and Sang*, the Pre-Trial Chamber approved of the Prosecutor's approach. It ruled that the acts of looting, theft and destruction of property were correctly characterized in the charging document as constituting "deportation or forcible transfer of population" under Article 7(1)(d). The crime of "deportation or forcible transfer of population" is defined as "forcible displacement of the persons concerned by expulsion or other *coercive acts* from the area in which they are lawfully present, without grounds permitted under international law".[75] Pursuant to this definition, the Chamber endorsed the Prosecutor's argument that the acts of burning and looting of property belonging to PNU supporters in Rift Valley could amount to "coercive acts", because they appeared to have been committed with the intention to force such supporters to vacate the area. Accordingly, the charges were confirmed as framed.[76]

However, in *Muthaura, Kenyatta and Ali*, the Pre-Trial Chamber found that there was a mistake in the manner in which the Prosecutor characterized the facts relating to property crimes. The Chamber rejected Prosecutor's characterization of facts which had suggested that the looting and destruction of property belonging to the ODM supporters constituted "other inhumane acts". In particular, the evidence produced by the Prosecutor was insufficient to persuade the Chamber that such conduct met the definitional requirements of "inhumane acts" under Article 7(1)(k) of the Statute. The Chamber noted that the crime of "other inhumane acts", being a "catch-all" category of crimes against humanity, can only cover conduct *which is not covered* by the preceding paras *a* to *j* of Article 7(1). But for such conduct to qualify as "inhumane acts" under the provision, the acts must, inter alia, be capable of "causing great suffering or serious injury to body or mental or

---

[74] See e.g., Request by the Victims' Representative for Authorisation by the Chamber to Make Written Submissions on Specific Issues of Law and/or Fact, *Ruto, Kosgey and Sang* (01/09-01/11-263), PTC, 15 August 2011.

[75] ICC Statute, Article 7(2)(d) (emphasis added).

[76] Decision on the Confirmation of Charges, *Ruto, Kosgey and Sang* (ICC-01/09-01/11-373), PTC, 23 January 2012, para 277.

physical health". Applying this standard, the Chamber rejected the Prosecution's characterization, stating that while the Prosecution had succeeded in showing that such property crimes had actually occurred, it had failed to establish the mandatory link between these acts and "serious injury to body or mental health".[77]

Finally, the Chamber also rejected the victims' views that the proceedings should be adjourned so that the Prosecutor could be requested to amend the charges accordingly. The Chamber noted that in characterizing the facts, however wrongly, the Prosecutor had exercised his prosecutorial discretion. Ultimately, the Chamber concluded that to request for an amendment "would mean to go beyond the factual ambit of the charges, and would therefore be tantamount to requesting the Prosecutor to consider adding a new charge".[78]

6.4.1.1.3 Evaluation

Certainly, the Prosecutor exercised his prosecutorial discretion in framing the charges the way he did with respect to property crimes committed during the post-election violence. However, the fact that property crimes were confirmed in the first case and rejected in the second case will potentially entail different implications for the victims in the two cases.

At the trial stage of a case before the ICC, the Trial Chamber can only adjudicate on charges that have been confirmed by the Pre-Trial Chamber at the end of the pre-trial stage. This is the reason why, for example, Article 61(9) of the ICC Statute provides that if, after confirmation of charges decision and before trial begins, the Prosecutor feels that there is a need to amend the confirmed charges by, for example, adding more charges or substituting more serious charges, a separate confirmation of charges hearing must be conducted in respect of the additional or substituted charges. It is only when these new charges are also confirmed that they can be adjudicated upon by the Trial Chamber, the reason being that during the trial stage, the Trial Chamber cannot "exceed the facts and circumstances described in the charges and amendment to the charges".[79]

In addition, the Regulations of the Court only allow the Trial Chamber to "change the legal characterisation of facts to accord with the crimes under Articles 6, 7 or 8", but strictly speaking, this must "not exceed the facts and circumstances described in the charges and any amendments to the charges".[80] In fact, the Appeals Chamber has stated clearly that such re-characterization "must not exceed

---

[77] Decision on the Confirmation of Charges, *Muthaura, Kenyatta and Ali* (ICC-01/09-02/11-382-Red), PTC, 23 January 2012, para 279.

[78] Ibid., para 286.

[79] ICC Statute, Article 74(2).

[80] Regulation 55 of the Regulations of the Court as amended, ICC-BD/01-02-07.

the factual circumstances that were identified in the confirmation decision as supporting each of the legal elements of the crimes charged".[81]

The implication of the foregoing paragraph is that in *Muthaura, Kenyatta and Ali*, the facts relating to acts of destruction and looting of property, which the Pre-Trial Chamber declined to confirm, can no longer be part of the charges to be adjudicated upon during trial. As a result the victims, who expressed their wish to seek remedy against such acts will no longer be able to claim individual reparation for these acts in case of a conviction. On the other hand, the victims of similar crimes in *Ruto, Kosgey and Sang* will have the property crimes adjudicated upon during trial, because these crimes will remain part of the charges. Thus, the victims in the second case will have the opportunity to claim and be granted reparations for the personal loss they incurred in this regard in line with the ICC reparation principles which have been adopted recently in the *Lubanga case*. According to these principles, "economic harm", such as "loss of, or damage to, property", can be compensated, provided the harm is sufficiently quantifiable.[82]

The above-mentioned mistake regarding characterization of facts in the *Muthaura, Kenyatta and Ali case* could have been rectified, and thereby mitigate the "injustice" which could occur to the victims of the acts in question. Rather than outrightly declining to confirm the wrongly characterized facts, the Chamber should have, pursuant to Article 61(7) of the Statute, and as proposed by the victims' representative, considered requesting the Prosecutor to re-characterize the facts correctly. Article 61(7) provides that during the confirmation of charges hearing, the Pre-Trial Chamber has three mandates. It can (i) confirm the charges wholly or partly; or (ii) decline to confirm all or part of the charges; or (iii) propose or advise an amendment of a charge which would not have otherwise been confirmed so that it can be confirmed. Particularly, on the third mandate, Article 61(7)(c)(ii) further provides that the Chamber "shall adjourn the hearing and request the Prosecutor to consider amending a charge because the evidence submitted appears to establish a different crime within the jurisdiction of the Court". It appears that such amendment may also rectify a wrong characterization or labelling of facts. Moreover, the use of the word "shall" *may*, in this case, be taken to imply that an adjournment is mandatory. Accordingly, whenever the Pre-Trial Chamber notices that certain facts have been wrongly characterized in the charges and that on the basis of such a mistake the facts are unlikely to be

---

[81] Judgment pursuant to Article 74 of the ICC Statute, *Lubanga* (ICC-01/04-01/06-2842), TC, 14 March 2012, para 7. See also Judgment on the appeals of Mr. Lubanga Dyilo and the Prosecutor against the Decision of Trial Chamber I of 14 July 2009 entitled "Decision giving notice to the parties and participants that the legal characterisation of the facts may be subject to change in accordance with Regulation 55(2) of the Regulations of the Court", *Lubanga* (ICC-01/04-01/06-2205), AC, 8 December 2009; Judgment on the appeal of Germain Katanga against the decision of Trial Chamber II of 21 November 2012 entitled "Decision on the implementation of regulation 55 of the Regulations of the Court and severing the charges against the accused persons", *Katanga* (ICC-01/04-01/07 OA 13), AC, 27 March 2013.

[82] Decision Establishing the Principles and Procedures to be Applied to Reparations, *Lubanga* (ICC-01/04-01/06-2904), TC, 7 August 2012, paras 226–230; Moffett 2012, pp. 1 et seq.

confirmed unless they are re-characterized, then the Chamber should not simply decline to confirm such facts before *advising* the Prosecutor to *consider amending* the charge.

It is submitted that while the Pre-Trial Chamber's reasoning is partly correct in that the Prosecutor had the discretion to frame the charges as he deemed fit, two aspects of its decision are questionable regarding what should have been the correct application of Article 61(7)(c)(ii) of the ICC Statute. Firstly, taken plainly, the wording of Article 61(7)(c)(ii), which allows for re-characterization of facts, retains the prosecutorial discretion as it provides that the Pre-Trial Chamber will only "request" the Prosecutor "to consider" amending a charge. This means that even if he had been *requested* to do so, the Prosecutor would not have been obligated to act as per the request of the Chamber.[83] Here, one must draw a distinction from the controversy that emerged from the *Lubanga case* in which the Pre-Trial Chamber "usurped" the prosecutorial powers and purported to re-classify the charges *suo motu* (in its own initiative) instead of requesting the Prosecutor to do so. This tendency was reversed by the Appeals Chamber.[84] Secondly, the count entailing property crimes was already part of the indictment, except that the facts had been wrongly characterized as constituting "other inhumane acts" instead of "deportation or forcible transfer of population" and "persecution", which were also contained in the indictment.[85] Thus, contrary to what the Pre-Trial Chamber suggested, had an amendment to the charge been requested and effected, the result would not have been tantamount to adding a "new charge".

Therefore, the failure to provide an opportunity for the amendment of the charges with respect to property crimes in *Muthaura, Kenyatta and Ali* case was an oversight on the part of the Pre-Trial Chamber. This is despite the fact that it still remains unclear if the Prosecutor would in fact have considered re-characterizing the facts had he been requested to do so. The Prosecutor himself did not take any initiative to have the facts re-characterized so that they could be adjudicated

---

[83] Stahn 2009, p. 255 (noting that this is one of the areas where "Judges are allowed to exercise scrutiny, but are not meant to replace prosecutorial judgment for reasons of institutional independence"). See *generally* Schabas 2009, pp. 227–246,

[84] The Prosecutor had charged Lubanga with enlistment, conscription and active use of child soldiers being crimes committed in the context of an *internal armed conflict* under Article 8(2) (e)(vii) of the ICC Statute. This charge was confirmed. However, the Pre-Trial Chamber argued, having made *suo motu* assessment, that the crimes were *also* committed in the context of an *international armed conflict* under Article 8(2)(xxvi) of the ICC Statute. It then proceeded to also confirm the charges in this regard. The Prosecutor successfully appealed against the confirmation of charges for war crimes in the context of an international armed conflict which he had not presented, arguing that it was an imposition of an additional burden of proof on the Prosecution's case. See Decision on the Prosecution and Defence Applications for Leave to Appeal the Decision on the Confirmation of Charges, *Lubanga* (ICC-01/04-01/06-915), PTC, 24 May 2007. See also Schabas and Shibahara 2008, pp. 1179–1180.

[85] Cf. Renewed Request by Victims' Representative for Authorization by the Chamber to Make Written Submissions on Specific Issues of law and/or Fact, *Ruto, Kosgey and Sang* (ICC-01/09-01/11-333), PTC, 16 September 2011, para 19.

upon during trial.[86] This shows clearly that the Prosecutor became indifferent about the legitimate concerns of the victims. This indifference gives rise to the question whether, in view of the ICC's unique procedure allowing victims' representation, the OTP should always view issues of victims' welfare as an entire responsibility of the victims' representative, or whether such issues should also be viewed as an integral part (a concern) of the Prosecution's case.

6.4.2 Whether Acts Committed During Post-Election Violence Amounted to Crimes Against Humanity

6.4.2.1 Introductory Note

Although the definitions of crimes against humanity under customary international law and under the ICC Statute have many similar elements, the two are not entirely the same. In view of this fact, even before the ICC intervened in Kenya, the Kenya National Commission on Human Rights had already contended that the crimes committed during the post-election violence *might not* qualify as crimes against humanity under the ICC Statute, although they obviously *did* qualify as such under international customary law.[87] This contention per se touches on a crucial question of substantive law which must be examined. The reason is that in view of Article 21 of the ICC Statute, the ICC can try only crimes whose elements meet the definitional criteria set out in its Statute. Indeed there are many overlaps between the ICC Statute and international customary criminal law that make the two not mutually exclusive. However, as Cassese notes, in some aspects, the ICC Statute is either broader or narrower than the customary law.[88] For that reason, in terms of substantive law, the ICC enforces international customary law only to the extent the latter is reflected in the ICC Statute.

One area in which the ICC Statute differs slightly from international customary law is in relation to the definition of crimes against humanity. In view of such difference, a disagreement emerged as to whether crimes against humanity *under the ICC Statute* occurred during the post-election violence in Kenya, or whether what happened could only qualify as crimes against humanity under international customary law. Legally speaking, therefore, the ICC would not have jurisdiction over the criminal acts committed in Kenya if such acts did not meet the criteria for crimes against humanity under the ICC Statute.

The said disagreement gained prominence when the judges who sat in the pre-trial proceedings of the Kenya situation expressed divergent opinions on the matter. The disagreement permeated the entire pre-trial phase, clearly manifesting

---

[86] The Prosecutor could have, for example, requested for an adjournment or could have appealed against the Pre-Trial Chamber's decision on the matter.

[87] Kenya National Commission on Human Rights 2008b, paras 638–648.

[88] Cassese 2008, p. 123.

itself in three important Pre-Trial Chamber's decisions. It emerged for the first time in the decision on the authorization of an investigation. It then recurred in the decisions relating to both issuance of summonses to appear and the confirmation of charges. The main bone of contention was on the contextual requirements of crimes against humanity as provided for in the ICC Statute.

Before outlining and evaluating the disagreement at length, the following section will first outline the definition of crimes against humanity with a view to giving a clear perspective to the subsequent discussion.

6.4.2.2 Outline of the Definition of Crimes Against Humanity

The definition of crimes against humanity in the Statute constitutes the material elements of the crime, namely any of the 11 categories of individual acts (*actus reus*) listed under Article 7(1)*a*–*k*[89] of the Statute "when committed as part of a widespread or systematic attack directed against any civilian population, with knowledge of the attack".[90] Furthermore, "an attack directed against a civilian population" entails "a course of conduct involving the multiple commission of acts referred to in [Article 7(1)] against any civilian population, pursuant to or in furtherance of a State or Organizational policy to commit such attack".[91]

Put more precisely, the above definition contains four main *cumulative criteria*, also known as the "contextual elements", under which the material elements (individual acts) constituting the crime must occur if the individual acts are to qualify as "crimes against humanity" under the Statute. These elements are that: (i) the acts must be part of a widespread or systematic attack[92]; (ii) the attack must be directed against any civilian population[93]; (iii) the perpetrator must have the knowledge of the attack[94]; and (iv) the attack must be pursuant to or in furtherance of a policy of a State or an organization.

---

[89] These are: murder; extermination; enslavement; deportation or transfer of population; imprisonment or other severe deprivation of physical liberty in violation of fundamental rules of international law; torture; rape, sexual slavery, enforced prostitution, forced pregnancy, enforced sterilization, or any other form of sexual violence of comparable gravity; persecution against an identifiable group or a collectivity on political, racial, national, ethnic, cultural, religious, gender or other grounds; enforced disappearances; the crime of apartheid; and other inhumane acts of a similar character intentionally causing great suffering, or serious injury to body or mental or physical health.

[90] See ICC Statute, chapeau of Article 7.

[91] Ibid., Article 7(2)(a).

[92] For more details see Boot et al. 2008, pp. 176–180; Werle 2009, pp. 296–299.

[93] For details see Decision on the Confirmation of Charges, *Bemba* (ICC-01/05-01/08-424), PTC, 15 June 2009, paras 75–81; Boot et al. 2008, pp. 180–181; Werle 2009, pp. 296–299.

[94] For details see Boot et al. 2008, pp. 181–183.

6.4.2.3 "State or Organizational Policy": A Source of Disagreement

There was no any disagreement among the judges of the Pre-Trial Chamber as regards the existence of the first three contextual elements in the definition of crimes against humanity identified above in relation to the criminal acts committed during the post-election violence in Kenya. However, the question whether the fourth element, namely a "State or organizational policy", was present, created a sharp division not only among the judges, but also between the parties to the cases as well as among scholars. On the one hand, a two-judge majority of the Pre-Trial Chamber, constituted by Judges Ekaterina Trendafilova and Cuno Tarfusser, maintained that the acts could qualify as crimes against humanity under the Statute, for they satisfied *all* the contextual elements. On the other hand, Judge Hans-Peter Kaul maintained that the acts would not qualify as such. He expressed a "fundamental disagreement" with the majority, arguing that the acts were not committed pursuant to or in furtherance of a policy of State or an organization.[95] Hence, while the majority affirmed that the ICC had jurisdiction *ratione materiae* over the Kenya situation in general and the two cases in particular, the minority's view was that the ICC lacked such jurisdiction under the ICC Statute.[96]

6.4.2.3.1 Prosecutor's Submission

In each of the two cases, the Prosecution maintained that the crimes had been committed pursuant to an "organizational policy". There was no any explicit allegation that there was a State policy per se to commit crimes, although the Prosecution tried to link individual officials in the government and State agencies, such as the police, to the organizational policy of private entities such as the *Mungiki*.[97] Building its case on organizational policy, the Prosecution argued as follows:

6.4.2.3.1.1 The Network as an "Organization"

In the *Ruto, Kosgey and Sang* case, the Prosecution submitted that the alleged crimes were committed by "the Network", an "organization" which was allegedly in support of the Orange Democratic Movement (ODM) party. This "organization" was allegedly linked to the Kalenjins, having been created already in December 2006.[98] Furthermore, it was submitted that the Network had five identifiable components, namely political,

---

[95] Dissenting Opinion of Judge Hans-Peter Kaul appended to Decision on the Authorization of an Investigation, *Situation in the Republic of Kenya* (ICC-01/09-19-Corr), PTC, 31 March 2010, para 36.

[96] See *generally* Hansen 2011, pp. 1 et seq; Jalloh 2011, pp. 540 et seq.; Kress 2010, pp. 855 et seq.; Werle and Burghardt 2012, pp. 1151 et seq.

[97] See Document Containing Charges, *Muthaura, Kenyatta and Ali* (ICC-01/09-02/11-257-AnxA), PTC, 19 August 2011, paras 36 and 46–48.

[98] Document Containing Charges, *Ruto, Kosgey and Sang* (ICC-01/09-01/11-261-AnxA), PTC, 15 August 2011, paras 65–66.

media, financial, tribal and military components, which acted interdependently during the post-election violence to implement a policy. The objective of the policy under implementation was allegedly twofold: (i) "to punish and expel from the Rift Valley" the civilians from the ethnic groups perceived to be supporters of the Party of National Unity (PNU); and (ii) "to gain power and create a uniform ODM voting bloc".[99]

As to the structure of the Network, the Prosecution alleged that William Ruto and Henry Kosgey were not only the organization's top political leaders, but also acted as its main sponsors and mobilizers. Joshua Arap Sang allegedly headed the media component of the Network, and, as such, he was responsible for spreading propaganda, hate speech and incitement through the Kalenjin radio station KASS FM.[100] It was further alleged that the military component of the Network had a defined chain of command, William Ruto being its ultimate supreme commander. Reporting directly to the supreme commander were allegedly three commanders (generals) in charge of one of the three different "military zones" created in Rift Valley. Each zonal commander was allegedly in charge of subordinates, mainly tribal and local leaders. It was these tribal and local leaders who allegedly mobilized the direct perpetrators (mainly youths), facilitated training, provided weapons and guidance on how the attacks should be implemented.[101]

6.4.2.3.1.2 The Mungiki as an "Organization"

In the *Muthaura, Kenyatta and Ali* case, the Prosecution argued that the crimes were committed under the auspices of the *Mungiki*, an organization that was acting in support of the PNU. It was submitted that this organization implemented an "organizational policy", namely "to keep the PNU in power through every means necessary, including by orchestrating a police failure to prevent the commission of crimes". The policy was allegedly implemented through a common plan to attack ODM supporters "by (i) penalizing them through retaliatory attacks; and (ii) deliberately failing to take action to prevent or stop the retaliatory attacks".[102]

In terms of its organizational structure, the Prosecutor alleged that the *Mungiki* was hierarchically organized, with a known national leadership over which Mr. Kenyatta "had control ... due to his wealth and privileged background".[103] It was further alleged that the *Mungiki* had local and regional branches whose leadership had executive and judicial powers, and that it also had a political wing called

---

[99] Ibid., para 41; Decision on the Confirmation of Charges, *Ruto, Kosgey and Sang* (ICC-01/09-01/11-373), PTC, 23 January 2012, paras 181–182.

[100] Document Containing Charges, *Ruto, Kosgey and Sang* (ICC-01/09-01/11-261-AnxA), PTC, 15 August 2011, paras 45–54.

[101] Ibid., paras 57–64.

[102] Document Containing Charges, *Muthaura, Kenyatta and Ali* (ICC-01/09-02/11-257-AnxA), PTC, 19 August 2011, para 35.

[103] Ibid., paras 37 and 39.

the "Kenya National Youth Alliance" and a quasi-military wing known as the "Mungiki Defence Council".[104]

It was the prosecution's case that the logistical, material and moral support from the six suspects in each respective case, facilitated by the hierarchical structures of the two entities, the Mungiki and the Network "organizations" acquired the *capacity* to organize and implement attacks. The prosecution concluded that these organizations actually utilized that capacity and launched attacks on civilian populations pursuant to and in furtherance of their respective policies.

6.4.2.3.2 Defence Submission: There Were No "Organizations"

The defence teams persistently refuted the submissions by the prosecution on the policy element in the definition of crimes against humanity. Their main arguments revolved around one point: the Prosecutor had failed to establish "even a reasonable basis to believe" that there was the existence of an "organization" which was capable of adopting an "organizational policy". Consequently, the defence argued that there were no crimes against humanity committed in Kenya and, as a result, the ICC lacked jurisdiction over the Kenya situation.[105]

In their submission the defence teams banked on the arguments raised in the dissenting opinions of Judge Hans-Peter Kaul. Notably, when Judge Kaul expressed his dissenting opinion for the first time in response to Prosecutor's request for authorization of an investigation, the defence teams had not been constituted, neither had any suspect been identified yet. This being the case, it is doubtful whether the meaning of "organization" as used in the Statute would have become so controversial had Judge Kaul not stirred the debate in the first place. Subsequent to the first dissenting opinion of Judge Kaul, the defence teams cleverly picked his arguments with a view to capitalizing on the fundamental divide already noticed in the Pre-Trial Chamber.

For that reason, and in order to avoid repetition, the core of the defence's argument regarding "organizational policy" should further be inferred from Judge Kaul's opinion outlined below (infra Sect. 6.4.2.3.4).

---

[104] Ibid., paras 40–41.

[105] Specifically see Ruto and Sang's Defence Challenge to Jurisdiction, *Ruto, Kosgey and Sang* (ICC-01/09-01/11-305), PTC, 30 August 2011; Application on behalf of Henry Kiprono Kosgey Pursuant to 119 of the ICC Statute, *Ruto, Kosgey and Sang* (ICC-01/09-01/11-306), PTC, 30 August 2011; Submissions on Jurisdiction on Behalf of Uhuru Kenyatta, *Muthaura, Kenyatta and Ali* (ICC-01/09-02/11-339), PTC, 19 September 2011; Ali's Defence Challenge to Jurisdiction, Admissibility and Prosecution's Failure to Meet the Requirements of Article 54, *Muthaura, Kenyatta and Ali* (ICC-01/09-02/11-338), PTC, 19 September 2011, For counter arguments by the Prosecutor see Prosecution's Response to the Defence Challenges to Jurisdiction, *Ruto, Kosgey and Sang* (ICC-01/09-01/11-334), PTC, 16 September 2011.

6.4.2.3.3 Pre-Trial Chamber's Majority Opinion

The majority (two judges) of the Pre-Trial Chamber agreed with the Prosecutor's submissions regarding organizational policy. The two judges stated expressly that they were in favour of a *broad interpretation* of Article 7(2)(a) of the ICC Statute, such that both the *Mungiki* and the Network would indeed qualify as "organizations" under that provision.[106] The majority enumerated six factors which they insisted "may assist" in determining whether a certain group or entity qualifies as an "organization" capable of authoring a policy. These factors are whether the entity:

> (i) is under a responsible command, or has an established hierarchy; (ii) possesses, in fact, the means to carry out a widespread or systematic attack against a civilian population; (iii) exercises control over part of the territory; (iv) has criminal activities against the civilian population as a primary purpose; (v) articulates explicitly or implicitly an intention to attack a civilian population; and (vi) is part of a larger group, which fulfils some or all of the above-mentioned criteria.[107]

Furthermore, the majority insisted that the factors enumerated above do not constitute a rigid legal definition, nor must they always be fulfilled exhaustively. Rather, an independent determination and assessment about the nature of the entity has to be made on a *case-by-case basis*. Moreover, they noted that the decisive criterion of whether a group qualifies as an organization should not be its "formal nature" or even "the level of its organization". The criterion, according to them, should be the group's "capability to perform acts which infringe on basic human values". Consequently, the majority concluded that an organization envisioned by Article 7(2)(a) must *not* necessarily be linked to a state, nor must it be a state-like entity.[108]

The majority added that Article 7(2)(a) of the ICC Statute envisions (i) policies of states which may be adopted at the highest level or by regional or even local organs (of the State); or (ii) policies of any non-state actor *capable of* adopting and implementing a policy to commit widespread or systematic attacks against a civilian population.[109] They noted that the policy envisaged under Article 7(2)(a) *must not* necessarily be formal or written: It suffices if the policy can, as the case was in Kenya, be deduced or inferred from an attack that exhibits the characteristics of being "planned, directed or organized, as opposed to spontaneous or (consisting

---

[106] Decision on the Confirmation of Charges, *Ruto, Kosgey and Sang* (ICC-01/09-01/11-373), PTC, 23 January 2012, para 186.

[107] Ibid., para 185; Decision on the Authorization of an Investigation, *Situation in the Republic of Kenya* (ICC-01/09-19), PTC, 31 March 2010, para 93.

[108] Decision on the Authorization of an Investigation, *Situation in the Republic of Kenya* (ICC-01/09-19), PTC, 31 March 2010, paras 89–92.

[109] Ibid., paras 89–90 and 92.

of) isolated acts".[110] Thus, the majority were of the view that in each of the two Kenyan cases a policy to attack a civilian population could be established.[111]

6.4.2.3.4 Dissenting Opinion of Judge Kaul

In his dissenting opinion, Judge Hans-Peter Kaul expounded his "fundamental disagreement" with the majority with regard to how the word "organization" in the definition of crimes against humanity should have been construed. While the majority favoured a "broad" or non-restrictive interpretation, Judge Kaul argued that the word should have been interpreted more narrowly or restrictively. Accordingly, Article 7(2)(a) of the Statute should have been viewed as envisaging *not* just any organization but only *State-like organizations*, of which neither the *Mungiki* nor the alleged Network would qualify.

The dissenting Judge agreed with the majority opinion that an "organization" is fundamentally different from a "State", and that the former can include non-state entities. He also agreed with them that a policy can be simply inferred and need not be formalized.[112] However, he disagreed with the majority as regards the attributes of the organization or entity that can author such a policy. He argued that the mere juxtaposition of the notions of "State" and "organization" under Article 7(2)(a) suggests that the "organization" contemplated by that provision must have one specific attribute: it must "partake of some characteristics of a State". As such, it must be an entity which "may act like a State or has quasi-State abilities".[113] Such characteristics or abilities, according to Judge Kaul, could include, but are not limited to, the following:

(a) a collectivity of persons; (b) which was established and acts for a common purpose; (c) over a prolonged period of time; (d) which is under a responsible command or adopted a certain degree of hierarchical structure, including, as a minimum level, some kind of a policy; (e) with capacity to impose the policy on its members and to sanction them; and (f) which has the capacity and means…to attack any civilian population on a large scale.[114]

---

[110] Decision on the Confirmation of Charges, *Ruto, Kosgey and Sang* (ICC-01/09-01/11-373), PTC, 23 January 2012, para 210.

[111] Note, however, that in *Ruto* et al. the majority found that there was only one policy, namely "to punish and expel from the Rift Valley those perceived to support PNU". The alleged second policy, namely "to gain power and create a uniform ODM voting bloc" was rejected for not being a policy in itself but rather a *motive* of a policy. See Ibid., paras 209–221.

[112] Judge Kaul noted in particular: "I agree with the majority that the policy, if not formally adopted, may be deduced from a variety of factors which, taken altogether, militate in favour of a policy, involving ways and means for the common purpose to attack a civilian population". See Dissenting Opinion of Judge Hans-Peter Kaul appended to Decision on the Authorization of an Investigation, *Situation in the Republic of Kenya* (ICC-01/09-19-Corr), PTC, 31 March 2010, para 41.

[113] Ibid., para 51.

[114] Ibid. See also Dissenting Opinion of Judge Hans-Peter Kaul appended to Decision on the Confirmation of Charges, *Ruto, Kosgey and Sang* (ICC-01/09-01/11-373), PTC, 23 January 2012, para 18.

The dissenting judge also listed the characteristics that in his view make certain groups not to qualify as "organizations" within the meaning of Article 7(2)(a) of the Statute. In other words, these entities or groups are not "State-like". These are:

> groups of organized crime, a mob, groups of (armed) civilians or criminal gangs…[such as those] formed on an ad hoc basis, randomly, spontaneously, for a passing occasion, with fluctuating membership, and without a structure and level to set up a policy [do not qualify], even if they engage in numerous serious and organized crimes.[115]

Applying the above understanding, Judge Kaul concluded that the features of the *Mungiki* and the Network, as alleged by the Prosecutor, simply placed the two groups in the category of "organized armed criminal gangs", and not organizations within the meaning of Article 7(2)(a). He thus flawed the majority decision for holding that the two groups qualified as "organizations". He stated that the majority set a bad precedent which, if not reversed, will have far-reaching implications, such as rendering the ICC an incredible institution that usurps the jurisdiction of the domestic courts over "ordinary serious crimes". To Judge Kaul, the criminal acts that were committed in Kenya during the post-election violence were undoubtedly serious but strictly "ordinary" criminality under the Kenyan domestic laws and cannot be elevated to the status of crimes under international law, particularly "crimes against humanity" under the ICC Statute.[116]

Judge Kaul expressed the view that a restrictive interpretation of the word "organization" is important when applying Article 7(2)(a), in order to avoid a "banalisation" or "trivialization" of the crimes that the ICC is meant to handle.[117] Finally, the judge concluded that the ICC was not the right forum to investigate and prosecute the crimes in Kenya, for it lacked jurisdiction.

6.4.2.4 Evaluation

6.4.2.4.1 Policy Element in Crimes Against Humanity

Four major approaches to the policy element in crimes against humanity can be identified so far. These approaches are that crimes against humanity: (1) do not require a policy at all, (2) require a state policy for their commission; (3) require a

---

[115] Ibid., para 18. See also Dissenting Opinion of Judge Hans-Peter Kaul appended to Decision on the Authorization of an Investigation, *Situation in the Republic of Kenya* (ICC-01/09-19-Corr), PTC, 31 March 2010, para 52.

[116] Dissenting Opinion of Judge Hans-Peter Kaul appended to Decision on the Confirmation of Charges*, Muthaura, Kenyatta and Ali* (ICC-01/09-02/11-382-Red), PTC, 23 January 2012, paras 19–21; See also Dissenting Opinion of Judge Hans-Peter Kaul appended to Decision on the Authorization of an Investigation, *Situation in the Republic of Kenya* (ICC-01/09-19-Corr), PTC, 31 March 2010, para 10.

[117] Dissenting Opinion of Judge Hans-Peter Kaul appended to Decision on the Authorization of an Investigation, *Situation in the Republic of* Kenya (ICC-01/09-19-Corr), PTC, 31 March 2010, para 55.

policy of either a state or a state-like organization; (4) require a policy of a state or any organization (not necessarily state-like), provided such organization has the capacity to carry out widespread attacks against a civilian population.[118] Whereas the first two approaches feature more prominently in the jurisprudence of the ad hoc tribunals, the latter two approaches dominate the debate on the ICC Statute as the foregoing discussion has already shown.

However, there is no dispute that the *explicit* requirement of a policy as part of the legal requirements for crimes against humanity came with the ICC Statute.[119] A policy was not, for example, an express requirement in the definitions in the IMT Charter or in the statutes of the ad hoc Tribunals or even those of the hybrid courts.[120] This notwithstanding, the question whether a policy was required for crimes against humanity still emerged in the jurisprudence of the ad hoc Tribunals, always stirring a heated debate. Initially, some scholars, as well as the early judicial pronouncements of the Tribunals, maintained that a policy was an implicit requirement under the customary law definition of crimes against humanity.[121] Others, however, contested this position, arguing that proof of a policy or plan had no relevance in the customary law definition of crimes against humanity.[122] After several inconsistencies in the pronouncements of the Tribunals, especially the ICTY, it came to be agreed that the existence of a policy was merely a demonstration of the systematic character of an attack directed against a civilian population. As to its legal status, the ICTY's Appeals Chamber settled the controversy by ruling that for the customary law definition of crimes against humanity, "the existence of a policy or plan may be evidentially relevant, but it is not a legal element of the crime".[123]

Therefore, the extent to which the jurisprudence of the ad hoc Tribunals on policy element is relevant to the application of the ICC Statute must be taken cautiously. Indeed the ICC Statute made a radical shift from the position under international customary law applied by the Tribunals on this issue. It follows that the jurisprudence on "State or organizational policy" as a *legal requirement* for crimes against humanity is in its infancy, and evolving. Its shape will be defined largely by the ICC. In this regard, there are several issues which are yet to be completely settled at the ICC.

---

[118] See Cupido 2011; Robinson 2011a.

[119] See Chella 2004, p. 185; DeGuzman 2000, p. 368.

[120] See the definitions of crimes against humanity under Articles 6(c), 3 and 5 of the IMT Charter, ICTR Statute and ICTY Statute, respectively. Generally see Badar 2004, pp. 73–144.

[121] See, e.g. Judgment, *Kayishema and Ruzindana* (ICTR-95-1-T), 21 May 1999, para 124; see also Opinion and Judgment, *Tadic* (IT-94-1-T), 7 May 1997. At para 644, the ICTY's Trial Chamber confirmed that for there to be an attack directed against any civilian population under the ICTY Statute, the attack must be committed pursuant to "some form of a governmental, organizational or group policy to commit these acts". Further, The Chamber clarified, at para 655, that "although a policy must exist to commit these acts, it need not be the policy of a State". For greater detail see Badar 2004, pp. 113–114; Robinson 1999, pp. 43 et seq.

[122] Cupido 2011; Mettraux 2002, pp. 281–282.

[123] See Judgment, *Kunarac, Kovac and Vukovic* (IT-96-23/1–A), 12 June 2002, para 98; Badar 2004, p. 113; Chella 2004, p. 187; Footnote 334.

One such issue is whether a "State or organizational policy" in the ICC Statute is an independent contextual element for crimes against humanity, or whether it is simply an indicator of a systematic attack.[124] Regarding this issue, the Pre-Trial Chamber III stated in the *Bemba case* that "the existence of a State or organisational policy is an element from which the systematic nature of an attack may be inferred".[125] However, when the Prosecutor adopted this line of reasoning in the request for authorization of an investigation into Kenya,[126] the Pre-Trial Chamber II, in a unanimous decision, adopted a slightly different position: It decided that an organizational policy is a separate contextual element independent of a systematic attack.[127] Interestingly, two of the Pre-Trial judges in the Kenya situation, Trendafilova and Kaul, were present in the bench for the *Bemba case*.

Another issue which is yet to be completely settled is the one that divided the Pre-Trial Chamber judges in the Kenyan cases, i.e. the meaning of "organization" in the definition of crimes against humanity in the ICC Statute. In the *Bemba case*, Judge Kaul agreed with the other two judges that an "organization" under Article 7(2)(a) of the ICC Statute can be "*any organization* with the capability to commit a widespread or systematic attack against a civilian population".[128] Yet when the Prosecutor adopted this line of reasoning before the Pre-Trial Chamber in the Kenya situation, only the majority, excluding Judge Kaul, upheld the reasoning of the Chamber in *Bemba*. Kaul no longer aligned himself with that reasoning, arguing that the meaning of "organization" that was adopted in the *Bemba* decision was apparently too broad. He thus wrote his dissenting opinion in favour of "State-like organizations". Justifying a change of the position he had previously endorsed in *Bemba*, Judge Kaul said that the *Bemba case* concerned "military-like organized groups in the context of an armed conflict" while the Kenyan scenario was of a different context.[129]

6.4.2.4.2 Key Factors Towards Interpretation of "Organization"

6.4.2.4.2.1 Article 21 of the ICC Statute

Article 21 of the ICC Statute contains a hierarchical order of law applicable before the ICC, which is a self-contained legal regime.[130] It provides that the ICC "shall

---

[124] Hansen 2011, p. 9; May 2010.

[125] Decision on the Prosecutor's Application for an Arrest Warrant, *Bemba* (ICC-01/05-01/08-14-tENG), PTC, 17 July 2008, para 33.

[126] See Prosecutor's Request for Authorisation of an Investigation Pursuant to Article 15, *Situation in the Republic of Kenya* (ICC-01/09-3), PTC, 26 November 2009, para 79.

[127] See Decision on the Authorization of an Investigation, *Situation in the Republic of Kenya* (ICC-01/09-19), PTC, 31 March 2010, para 93.

[128] See Decision on the Confirmation of Charges, *Bemba* (ICC-01/05-01/08-424), PTC, 15 June 2009, para 81 (emphasis added).

[129] See Decision on the Authorization of an Investigation, *Situation in the Republic of Kenya* (ICC-01/09-19), PTC, 31 March 2010, para 48. See also Hansen 2011, p. 13, Footnote 57.

[130] See Werle and Burghardt 2012, p. 1154.

apply" (i) the ICC Statute itself, Elements of Crimes, and its Rules of Procedure and Evidence; (ii) applicable treaties and the principles and rules of international law, including those of armed conflict; (iii) principles derived from national laws of legal systems that would normally try the crimes in the ICC Statute, provided they are consistent with the laws listed in i and ii above; and (iv) principles and rules created in previous decisions of the ICC (precedents). As a common denominator, it the Statute requires that any law applied according to the order above must be, inter alia, consistent with internationally recognized human rights.[131]

6.4.2.4.2.2 Other Factors to Consider

Being a treaty, the ICC Statute must be interpreted according to the Vienna Convention on the Law of Treaties.[132] The Convention requires, inter alia, that when interpreting a treaty, its terms must, first and foremost, be given their "ordinary meanings", unless there are justifiable reasons not to do so.[133] In this regard, it is noteworthy that although the word "organization" is not defined in the Statute or in the Elements of Crimes,[134] resort could be taken to dictionaries. The Black's Law Dictionary defines "organization" as "a body of persons (such as a union or corporation)".[135] Non-legal dictionaries define it more broadly. For example, according to the Shorter Oxford English Dictionary, contextually, the verb "organize", from which the noun "organization" is derived, means to "form into a whole with mutually connected and dependant parts; give a definite or orderly structure to [something]; frame and put into working order (an institution, enterprise, etc.); arrange (something involving united action); become a systematic whole; become coordinated; attain orderly structure or working order". Accordingly, the noun "organization" is defined as "an organized body, system or society".[136]

---

[131] For further details see DeGuzman 2008, pp. 702–712.

[132] Adopted on 23 May 1969 and entered into force on 27 January 1980. Cf. Dissenting Opinion of Judge Hans-Peter Kaul appended to Decision on the Authorization of an Investigation, *Situation in the Republic of Kenya* (ICC-01/09-19-Corr), PTC, 31 March 2010, paras 33–70.

[133] There are only three circumstances (exceptions) under which the ordinary meaning can be dispensed with. These are (i) when the ordinary meaning would defeat the object and purpose of the treaty (Article 31(1)); (ii) when it is clear that the parties to the treaty intended to give a "special meaning" to a term over and above its ordinary meaning (Article 31(4)); and (iii) when the ordinary meaning would lead to ambiguity, obscurity, absurdity or unreasonableness. In the latter case, the *travaux préparatoires* can be consulted as a "supplementary means of interpretation" to resolve the problem (Article 32). A comparable approach is followed in the common law legal tradition. See, e.g., Costello 2006; Hall 1998, pp. 38 et seq.; Scott 2010, p. 346.

[134] See Elements of Crimes http://www.icc-cpi.int/NR/rdonlyres/336923D8-A6AD-40EC-AD7B-45BF9DE73D56/0/ElementsOfCrimesEng.pdf. Accessed September 2014. The Elements are an aid to the interpretation and application of the crimes in the Statute. See ICC Statute Article 9.

[135] Garner 1999, p. 1126.

[136] Stevenson 2007, p. 2033.

6.4.2.4.2.3 Observation

The word "organization" as used in Article 7(2)(a) is not a term of art. It is thus important to give it its ordinary meaning, but which is nevertheless consistent with the *main* intent and purpose of the States Parties to the ICC Statute. As Werle and Burghardt rightly observe, neither the ordinary meaning of the word "organization" nor the grammatical context of the phrase "State or organizational policy" in which the word has been used supports the conclusion that the word envisioned a state-like entity. They further rightly note that the disjunctive "or" juxtaposes "state" and "organization" as equals. Thus, it is grammatically incorrect to infer from the formulation "State or organizational policy" that the "organization" must share the definitional characteristics of a "state" such that the former is necessarily a "state-like" organization.[137]

An analogy could also be drawn from the chapeau of the Article 7(1) of the ICC Statute. This provision defines a crime against humanity as a "widespread *or* systematic" attack on a civilian population. Here, too, the disjunctive "or" has always been understood to indicate that the attack can either be widespread or systematic, and more importantly, a systematic attack need not share the characteristics of a widespread attack. Hence, the two attributes of the attack and could exist independently of each other.[138]

This leads to the conclusion that even on grammatical grounds, the minority's interpretation of the word "organization" cannot stand.

6.4.2.4.3 Teleological Approach of the Dissenting Opinion

At another level, in his dissenting opinion, Judge Kaul Judge attempted to give a "teleological" justification of his restrictive interpretation of the word "organization". His main arguments revolved around four points, but which were followed by contradicting conclusions.

6.4.2.4.3.1 Main Arguments

Firstly, Judge Kaul noted that the earliest definition of crimes against humanity in the IMT Charter was adopted to respond to the crimes committed by the Nazis during the Second World War.[139] As he rightly noted, from the context in which the Nazi crimes happened, the acts were indisputably mass atrocities committed by a "sovereign state against the civilian population … according to a State plan or policy, involving large segments of the State".[140] Secondly, he argued that subsequent

---

[137] See Werle and Burghardt 2012, pp. 1154–1156.

[138] Cf. Werle 2009, pp. 297–299.

[139] Cf. Schabas 2008, p. 974.

[140] Dissenting Opinion of Judge Hans-Peter Kaul appended to Decision on the Authorization of an Investigation, *Situation in the Republic of Kenya* (ICC-01/09-19-Corr), PTC, 31 March 2010, para 59.

to the Nazi crimes experience, crimes against humanity committed in other parts of the world again proved that crimes of such nature and magnitude were possible only "by virtue of an existing State policy". Thirdly, he asserted that by expressly including "State policy" as part of the definition of crimes against humanity, the ICC Statute clearly "embraces" all the historic considerations referred to above.[141] Fourthly, and more importantly, he admitted the fact that, despite the historical role of the State in the commission of crimes against humanity, the definition of the crime under Article 7(2)(a) of the ICC Statute focuses beyond that role mainly for one reason: "to accommodate new scenarios of threats" which, although might not have links to a state, "may equally shake the very foundations of the international community and deeply shock the conscience of humanity".[142]

The notion of "new threats", as referred to by Judge Kaul, was given consideration for the first time by the International Law Commission (ILC) in its 1996 Draft Code of Offenses against the Peace and Security of Mankind.[143] The ILC proposed an express inclusion of "State or organizational" policy in the definition of crimes against humanity as a response to "new developments after Nuremberg".[144] In this regard, therefore, the ICL recognized the dynamic nature of crimes against humanity (i.e. its form and manner of commission) from when they were defined for the first time in history.

6.4.2.4.3.2 Weaknesses and Contradictions

Despite acknowledging the important facts above, especially the emergence of "new threats", it is difficult to comprehend why the dissenting Judge came to the assertion that only the "historic origins *are decisive* in understanding the specific nature and fundamental rationale of this category of international crimes".[145] This assertion further led him to a flawed conclusion that in interpreting the policy element in the ICC Statute, absolute reliance should be placed on the "historic experience", which, he argued, is the only "logical lesson" that influenced the drafters when adopting the definition of crimes against humanity in the ICC Statute.[146]

---

[141] Ibid., para 66.

[142] Ibid.

[143] For origins and mandate of the ICL see Schiff 2008, pp. 26–27 and 38; Bassiouni 1987, pp. 3–11.

[144] The ILC Draft Code of Offenses against the Peace and Security of Mankind of 1996 proposed that for individual acts to qualify as crimes against humanity, they should be committed contextually in a systematic manner or on a large scale "directed by a Government or by any organization or group." See Article 18 of the Draft Code. Although at the Rome conference the word a "group" was dropped and the rest of the wording retained, the ILC's commentary on the provision stated clearly that the definition was intended "to take into account subsequent developments in international law since Nurnberg." See UN International Law Commission 1996, p. 47.

[145] Dissenting Opinion of Judge Hans-Peter Kaul appended to Decision on the Authorization of an Investigation, *Situation in the Republic of Kenya* (ICC-01/09-19-Corr), PTC, 31 March 2010, para 65 (emphasis added).

[146] Ibid., para 60–64.

Of course, Judge Kaul is not alone: his views on "state-like organizations" resonate with those of prominent scholars.[147] However, such views sharply contradict those of other prominent scholars.[148] But these divergent views aside, Judge Kaul's approach contains intrinsic contradictions which make it flawed. Kaul's reasoning is internally inconsistent, for it partly disregards the "new threats" that the judge expressly acknowledges to have kept emerging even after the experience of the Nazi criminality. His approach exhibits too much obsession with the definitions of crimes against humanity prior to the inception of the ICC Statute to the point of overlooking the need for a dynamic interpretation and application of the ICC Statute.[149] This (dynamic interpretation) should have been an important consideration, given the fact that the crime itself and the techniques of committing it are equally dynamic.

---

[147] See, e.g. Bassiouni 1992, pp. 248–249 (arguing that "crimes against humanity" are collective crimes which cannot be committed unless they are part of a given state's policy because their commission requires the use of the state's institutions, personnel and resources in order to commit, or refrain from preventing the commission of, the specific crimes described in Article 6(c) [of the IMT Charter].... The rationale for this requisite of "state action or policy" is that "crimes against humanity," like other international crimes such as genocide and apartheid, cannot be committed without it because of the nature and scale of the crime"); Schabas 2008, pp. 972–974. For more literature in support of the restrictive interpretation see Dissenting Opinion of Judge Hans-Peter Kaul appended to Decision on the Authorization of an Investigation, *Situation in the Republic of Kenya* (ICC-01/09-19-Corr), PTC, 31 March 2010, footnotes 52 and 54.

[148] E.g. Halling 2010, pp. 827 et seq. (suggesting, at p. 829, that the policy requirement for crimes against humanity in the ICC Statute should be removed altogether; or that if not, the word "organization" in Article 7(2)(a) of the Statute should be scribed "the widest definition" possible e.g. by relying on the definition in Article 2(a) of the UN Convention against Transnational Organized Crime of 2000 in which the word "organization" is defined as "a structured group of three or more persons, existing for a period of time and acting in concert with the aim of committing one or more serious crimes", with a "structured group" defined in Article 2(c) as being "not randomly formed...and that it does not need to have formally defined roles for its members, continuity of its membership or a developed structure"); Hansen 2011, p. 37; Sadat 2012; Werle 2009 p. 302 (arguing, inter alia, that "threats to values protected by international law … can certainly arise from non-state actors or private persons .... As with genocide, in crimes against humanity participation of states or state-like organizations is the rule in practice, but not a legal requirement" Consequently, he argues that "in order to classify the attacks on the New York World Trade Centre and the Pentagon [and one could add the crimes perpetrated by the *Boko Haram* in Nigeria or the *Al Shabaab* in Somalia] as crimes against humanity, it does not matter whether the acts can be ascribed to a terrorist organization alone or also to a state-like entity"). For more literature with similar views see footnote 53 in the Dissenting Opinion of Judge Hans-Peter Kaul appended to Decision on the Authorization of an Investigation, *Situation in the Republic of Kenya* (ICC-01/09-19-Corr), PTC, 31 March 2010.

[149] See Eskridge 1987, pp. 1479 et seq. (generally proposing a dynamic model for statutory interpretation, though not specifically for criminal law statutes). On how dynamic interpretation is relevant for international crimes, see Robinson 2010, pp. 145–147 (indicating that the dynamic interpretation approach is human rights-oriented. As such, it requires that "terms must be given meanings relevant to contemporary society" (p. 145), as "crimes appear to be growing broader in case after case" (p. 146)). Also see *generally* Schabas 2006b, pp. 93 et seq (critically discussing the "dynamism and radical evolution" of the interpretation of the crime of genocide by the ad hoc Tribunals); Watson 2003, pp. 871 et seq.; Askin 2002, pp. 903 et seq.

It is submitted that one could still rely on the historical evolution of crimes against humanity to counter-argue the historical–phenomenological justifications on which Judge Kaul based his dissenting opinion. The following section does just that.

6.4.2.4.4 To What Extent Is the Historic Experience Relevant to the ICC?

6.4.2.4.4.1 Evolution of the Definition of Crimes Against Humanity

Of all the definitions of the core crimes under international law, that of crimes against humanity has been most dynamic, having undergone a clear chronological metamorphosis since its first formulation. Such evolution is evident in terms of both the material and contextual elements of the crime.[150] For example, as regards the original definition in the IMT Charter, contextually, crimes against humanity would only result if the material elements were committed "in execution or in connection with" crimes against peace and war crimes.[151] The immediate subsequent definition in the Control Council Law No. 10 dispensed with the requirement for a nexus with the other crimes, thereby effectively treating crimes against humanity as an independent crime.[152]

Then, while the ICTY Statute expressly required that crimes against humanity be committed in the context of an "armed conflict, either of internal or international character", the Statutes of the ICTR and the Special Court for Sierra Leone dispensed with this requirement. Instead, the latter two Statutes required that the material elements of the crime be "committed as part of widespread or systematic attack", and the ICTR Statute further required that the attack be made "on national, political, ethnic, racial or religious grounds".[153] Thus, from the IMT Charter to the ad hoc Tribunals and hybrid courts, there has always been a new element in the definition of crimes against humanity, and this has been not a mere accident.

For example, the definition of crimes against humanity in the IMT Charter responded to the atrocities committed by the Germans alongside the aggression war they waged. For that reason, it required a *nexus with the war or the acts of aggression*. The definition in the ICTY Statute was crafted to respond to the armed conflict which had taken place in the former Yugoslavia. For that reason, it specifically required a *nexus with an armed conflict*. The definition in the ICTR Statute was crafted to respond broadly to the 1994 Rwandan genocide in which close to one million people had been murdered. For that reason, it focused mainly on the

---

[150] See generally Cassese 2013, pp. 84–108; Hwang 1998–1999, pp. 457 et seq.; Ratner et al. 2009, pp. 48–81.

[151] IMT Charter, Article 6(c).

[152] CCL No. 10, Article II(i)(c).

[153] ICTR Statute, Article (3), SCSL Statute, Article 2.

widespread and systematic nature of the atrocities and dispensed with the need for a nexus with an armed conflict which the ICTY Statute had required. The definitions in the ICTY and ICTR Statutes differed in this fundamental way despite the fact that both Statutes were adopted at about the same time (1993 and 1994, respectively) and by the same body, the UN Security Council.

One clear thing from the foregoing paragraph is that *all* the definitions of crimes against humanity prior to the adoption of the ICC Statute were *retrospective* in nature; they were backward looking.[154] They responded to crimes which had already been committed, namely crimes whose specific circumstances and contours were clearly known even before their definitions were adopted. Thus, in all these cases, it was the known characteristics of the already-committed acts that shaped or determined the content and scope of the definitions of the crimes against humanity. But as the following two sections demonstrate, the ICC Statute entails a completely different paradigm.

6.4.2.4.4.2 The Prospective Nature of the ICC Statute

Unlike the IMT Charter and the Statutes of the ad hoc Tribunals, the ICC Statute is *prospective*; it is forward looking.[155] This is not to argue that the historic experiences that underpin the foundations of crimes against humanity have no relevance today as far as the ICC is concerned. Rather, it is to agree with Sadat that *over-reliance* on the Nuremberg precedent today is counter-productive; it amounts to retrogression to almost seven decades ago. Similarly, agreeing with Judge Kaul's argument that "organization" means "military-like organized groups" will in effect "reverse nearly two decades of progressive development by effectively re-linking the commission of [crimes against humanity] to a finding of armed conflict (which requires organized fighting forces)".[156]

The fight against impunity for "serious crimes of concern to the international community" can be more efficient if the ICC Statute is applied progressively, i.e. in a manner that responds to or takes into consideration the new or contemporary experiences. Such experiences include the emergence of organized entities, permanent and ad hoc in nature, which are neither states nor state-like, but which have got the capacity to commit very serious crimes.[157] Indeed, as Sadat rightly puts it, regardless of "the canonical status of the Nuremberg precedent in international criminal law", and even if it may seem "heretical" to object it, Judge Kaul's

---

[154] Cf. Ambos 2010, pp. 161–162 (labelling this as a "congenital defect" of the ad hoc tribunals).

[155] ICC Statute, Article 24(1) read together with Article 126, provide that the ICC has jurisdiction only over crimes committed on or after the Statute came into force i.e. 1 July 2002.

[156] Sadat 2012a, p. 6.

[157] Cf. Damgaard 2008, pp. 83–85.

argument "does not [adequately] respond to the terrible suffering of today's victims of [crimes against humanity], nor does it accurately describe the modern law".[158]

Moreover, unlike the ICTR and ICTY, which were created as ad hoc institutions, the ICC was established with a view to being be a "permanent court".[159] As such, no "completion strategy" was contemplated for the ICC. Logically, therefore, it is expected that this institution will be able to render international criminal justice effectively and adequately for an *indefinite future*. Given that the procedure for the amendment or review of the ICC Statute is long and cumbersome,[160] it is illogical if the ICC Judges were to start introducing untenable restrictions in the application or interpretation of the Statute even *where the Statute itself does not warrant* such restrictions.[161]

6.4.2.4.4.3 Interim Conclusion

The Pre-Trial Chamber's majority view on the interpretation of the word "organization" under Article 7(2)(a) is welcome, for it largely responds to the reality of crimes under international law today. This was another area and opportunity in which the Chamber adopted a pragmatic view in relation to a contentious legal issue involving the interpretation of the ICC Statute.[162] In the circumstances of (or similar to) the crimes committed in Kenya, placing more reliance on the capacity of the entity to organize and implement attacks rather than on the organizational structure of the entity is a correct approach; it is not a mere judicial activism as critics might think or argue. Indeed to the international community, whose interest is to ensure that serious crimes of international concern do not go unpunished, and more importantly, to the victims of the post-election violence in Kenya, justice does not depend on the strict organizational structure of the entities which may have orchestrated the commission of the crimes.

6.5 Issues Relating to Complementarity

6.5.1 Meaning of Complementarity

Legally speaking, the ICC and national courts have concurrent jurisdiction over the core crimes in the ICC Statute. Such a jurisdictional relationship required further regulation in order to avoid competition for cases between the two legal

---

[158] Sadat 2012b, p. 6.

[159] ICC Statute, Article 1.

[160] On the amendment procedure, see Article 121 of the ICC Statute which requires that any amendment to a provision in the Statute must follow a similar procedure of ratification of the Statute. For the procedure of review of the Statute, see Article 123.

[161] Cf. DeGuzman 2000, p. 340.

[162] Others include, e.g., issues of self-referrals and also "inaction" as a ground for admissibility of a case.

regimes. The principle of complementarity[163] was agreed upon to serve this purpose, and also to safeguard States' sovereignty and increase their willingness to accept the jurisdiction of the ICC.[164] Both the Preamble and Article 1 of the ICC Statute, in a similar wording, stipulate that the ICC "shall be complementary to national criminal jurisdictions". It is clear from this formulation that precedence is given to national courts over the ICC as far as the prosecution of the core crimes is concerned. The national courts are the primary jurisdictions while the ICC remains a secondary jurisdiction—a court of last resort. Therefore, the complementarity model clearly differs from the primacy model that governs the relationship between the ad hoc Tribunals and the national courts.[165]

The content of the principle of complementarity is embodied in the provisions of Article 17 of the ICC Statute which deals with "issues of admissibility". The Article enumerates circumstances in which a case becomes *inadmissible* before the ICC. Accordingly, the ICC can admit a case on complementarity grounds if the state with primary jurisdiction is inactive, unwilling or unable to prosecute in good faith.[166] Before analysing complementarity in relation to the Kenya situation, the relevant parts of Article 17 are quoted *verbatim*

1. Having regard to para 10 of the Preamble and Article 1 [of the ICC Statute] the Court shall determine that a case is inadmissible where:

   (a) The case is being investigated or prosecuted by a State which has jurisdiction over it, unless the State is unwilling or unable to genuinely carry out the investigation or prosecution;
   (b) The case has been investigated by a State which has jurisdiction over it and the State has decided not to prosecute the person concerned, unless the decision resulted from unwillingness or inability of the State genuinely to prosecute;
   (c) The person concerned has already been tried for conduct which is the subject of complaint, and a trial by the Court is not permitted under Article 20, para 3.[167]...

2. In order to determine unwillingness in a particular case, the Court shall consider... whether one or more of the following exist, as applicable:

   (a) The proceedings were or are being undertaken or the national decision was made for the purposes of shielding the person concerned from criminal responsibility;

---

[163] For comprehensive literature on complementarity see Stahn and El Zeidy 2011.

[164] See Batros 2011, pp. 589–592; Bekou 2011, pp. 833–835.

[165] See Articles 9(2) and 8(2) of the ICTY and ICTR Statutes, respectively. For more details see El Zeidy 2008b, pp. 403 et seq.; Bekou 2011, p. 833.

[166] See Nouwen 2011, pp. 206–220. See also Bushnell 2009, pp. 77–89; El Zeidy 2008a; Gioia 2006, pp. 1099–1102; Pichon 2008, pp.185 et seq.

[167] Article 17 provides for "complementarity" and "gravity of offence" as two main grounds or tests on the basis of which the admissibility of a case before the ICC is determined. The two tests are independent of each other. However, as the analysis in this part only concerns complementarity, the provision that deals with the gravity-of-offence test (Article 17(1)(d)) is omitted from the quoted text.

(b) There has been an unjustified delay in the proceedings which in the circumstances is inconsistent with an intent to bring the person concerned to justice;

(c) The proceedings were not or are not being conducted independently or impartially, and they were or are being conducted in a manner, which, in the circumstances, is inconsistent with an intent to bring the person concerned to justice...

3. In order to determine inability in a particular case, the Court shall consider whether, due to a total or substantial collapse or unavailability of its national Judicial system, the State is unable to obtain the accused or the necessary evidence and testimony or otherwise unable to carry out its proceedings.

As the following discussion will show, the ICC's exercise of jurisdiction over the Kenyan cases was not, legally speaking, due to Kenya's unwillingness or inability to investigate or prosecute, but was rather due to Kenya's "inaction".

6.5.2 Evaluation of "Unwillingness" and "Inability" in Relation to Kenya

The post-election violence in Kenya *per se* did not have any direct effect on the functioning of the country's judicial system. After the violence, Kenya's ability to arrest, investigate and prosecute those involved in the violence remained the same as it was prior to the violence.[168] The allegations and perceptions that Kenya's judiciary continued lacking independence or being corrupt[169] do not change this reality.

Although the judicial system remained functional, Kenya, as already shown, did not show any political will to investigate or prosecute those who bear the greatest responsibility for the crimes. Yet, as also shown earlier, some of the suspects had been identified in various commission reports, and also the available domestic legal framework could sufficiently be used to prosecute them. Although it has been argued that this state of affairs per se could be taken as constituting "unwillingness" or "inability" to prosecute on the part of the Kenyan government,[170] such an argument cannot meet the threshold of unwillingness or inability if tested against the provisions of Article 17 reproduced above, for reasons explained below.

According to Nouwen, in determining the admissibility of a case before the ICC, examination of state's unwillingness or inability to prosecute is, strictly speaking, a secondary question or step. The primary step, as Article 17 above

---

[168] Cf. Alai and Mue 2011, p. 1233. In this regard, Kenya was completely different from Rwanda whose judicial system could be described as "unavailable" immediately after the 1994 genocide, because most professionals, including prosecutors, judges and lawyers, had died or fled the country. Cf. Nash 2007, p. 79.

[169] See supra Sect. 3.7. As the ICC Prosecutor rightly indicates, these allegations or perceptions per se do not play a role in assessing State's "inability" for purposes of admissibility of a case at the ICC. See Moreno-Ocampo 2011, p. 23.

[170] See, e.g., Sing'Oei 2010, pp. 11–15.

presupposes, is to establish an existence of tangible "proceedings", namely concluded or ongoing investigations or prosecutions in respect of the case. It is only if such proceedings do not pass the genuineness test—e.g. if they were or are intended for shielding the perpetrator(s), or if they lack independence or impartiality—can the state concerned be said to be unwilling or unable to investigate or prosecute.[171]

As already shown, and will be explained below, Kenya did not even initiate proceedings. This is to say that even the first step that would have paved way for the legal assessment of unwillingness or inability was not reached at the domestic level. The mere non-existence of proceedings in this regard, therefore, renders irrelevant a determination of unwillingness or inability for purposes complementarity with regard to the Kenya situation. However, since it was Kenya's failure to initiate proceedings (inaction) which was the basis of admissibility of the situation and the cases before the ICC, it (inaction) merits further evaluation.

6.5.3 Inaction as a Component of Complementarity

6.5.3.1 Meaning of Inaction

The notion of inaction (also "inactivity") is not mentioned explicitly under Article 17 of the ICC Statute. However, it is now settled that inaction is implicit in this provision, being a third ground (in addition to unwillingness and inability) which makes a situation or a case admissible before the ICC for complementarity purposes. The fact that "inaction" is part and parcel of Article 17 was raised for the first time in 2003 by a group of prominent scholars (experts) in a paper commissioned to them by the ICC.[172] Their argument was endorsed by the ICC's OTP[173] and later by both the Pre-Trial Chamber[174] and the Appeals Chamber.[175] Accordingly, "inaction" as a ground for admissibility of situations and cases before the ICC comes into play in circumstances where unwillingness or inability cannot practically or legally apply, namely where there are no national

---

[171] Nouwen 2011, pp. 208–212; Cf. Decision on the Admissibility of the Case, *Gaddafi and Al-Senussi*, (ICC-01/11-01/11-466-Red), PTC, 11 October 2013, paras 24–27.

[172] See Office of the Prosecutor 2003a. For concurring views see Robinson 2011b, pp. 460–502. For dissenting views see Arsanjani and Reisman 2005, pp. 385 et seq.

[173] See Office of the Prosecutor 2003b.

[174] See Decision on Prosecutor's Application for a Warrant of Arrest, *Lubanga* (ICC-01/04-01/06-Corr), PTC, 10 February 2006.

[175] See Judgment on the Appeal of Mr. Germain Katanga against the Oral Decision of Trial Chamber on the Admissibility of the Case, *Katanga and Chui* (ICC-01/04-01/07-1497), AC, 25 September 2009.

proceedings at all encompassing *the same person and the same conduct* forming the subject of the case before the ICC.[176]

Inaction occurs in two scenarios. The first scenario is where the state with jurisdiction is doing nothing as regards investigations or prosecutions, even though, for example, *prima facie*, such a state appears able to do so. The second scenario where inaction comes into play is in a case of a self-referral, i.e. where the state of commission relinquishes or waives its primacy of jurisdiction voluntarily in favour of the prosecution before the ICC believing that, due to specific circumstances, justice will be delivered or rendered more effectively by the ICC. As a practice, the second scenario is now embedded in the ICC's legal regime[177] despite facing a strong criticism when it was first endorsed.[178] In cases of inaction, the ICC intervenes in order to fill the impunity gap that could have resulted if it (the ICC) did not do so.[179]

6.5.3.2   Analysis of Inaction in Relation to Kenya

Complementarity assessment in investigations triggered *proprio motu*, like the case of the Kenya situation, takes place at two levels, i.e. the situation and case levels. Each level entails different thresholds and contexts in which the assessment is done.[180] For example, complementarity requires a higher degree of specificity when assessed at a case level than when it is assessed at a situation level. This being the case, Kenya had an opportunity to claim its primacy of jurisdiction at each level with

---

[176] Decision on Prosecutor's Application for a Warrant of Arrest, *Lubanga* (ICC-01/04-01/06-Corr), PTC, 10 February 2006, paras 31, 37 and 41; Judgment on the Appeal of Mr. Germain Katanga against the Oral Decision of Trial Chamber on the Admissibility of the Case, *Katanga and Chui* (ICC-01/04-01/07-1497), AC, 25 September 2009, paras 75–79.

[177] See Reasons for the Oral Decision on the Motion Challenging the Admissibility of the Case (Article 19 of the Statute), *Katanga and Chui* (ICC-01/04-01/07-1213-tENG), TC, 16 June 2009, paras 76–80; Judgment on the Appeal of Mr. Germain Katanga against the Oral Decision of Trial Chamber on the Admissibility of the Case, *Katanga and Chui* (ICC-01/04-01/07-1497), AC, 25 September 2009, para 86. For more details see Akhavan 2010, pp. 110–111; Akhavan 2011, pp. 299–302; Office of the Prosecutor 2003a, pp. 19–20 and Footnote 24; William and Schabas 2008, p. 614, para 22.

[178] Critics argued that the practice is a clear contravention of the complementarity principle, as it encourages states which are able to prosecute to neglect and shift their duty to the ICC. See e.g., Document in Support of Appeal of the Defence for Germain Katanga against the Decision of the Trial Chamber, *Katanga and Chui* (ICC-01/04-01/07-1279), AC, 8 July 2009, paras 62–72; Arsanjani and Reisman 2005, p. 397; Schabas 2006a, p. 32; Akhavan 2010, pp. 103 et seq.

[179] Office of the Prosecutor 2003a, paras 17–20; Office of the Prosecutor 2003b, p. 5; Judgment on the Appeal of Mr. Germain Katanga against the Oral Decision of Trial Chamber on the Admissibility of the Case, *Katanga and Chui* (ICC-01/04-01/07-1497), AC, 25 September 2009, paras 79–86; Batros 2011, p. 600; Benvenuti 2008, pp. 63–65.

[180] Olasolo and Cernero-Rojo 2011, pp. 393 et seq. (discussing the admissibility of a "situation" and a "case" in view of the differences ascribed to the two notions by the ICC). See also Decision on the Authorization of an Investigation, *Situation in the Republic of Kenya* (ICC-01/09-19), PTC, 31 March 2010, para 43.

different implications. Although Kenya did not bother to invoke complementarity at the situation level, the Pre-Trial Chamber did a *suo motu* assessment. Kenya tried to invoke complementarity only at the case level, albeit unsuccessfully.

6.5.3.2.1 Inaction at Situation Level: The Notion of "Potential Cases" and Deferral of Investigations Under Article 18

Article 18 of the ICC Statute covers complementarity at the level of a situation. It provides that even when the Prosecutor has a reasonable basis to commence a *proprio motu* investigation into a situation, he or she cannot embark on it immediately. The Prosecutor shall first *notify* all the States which could have jurisdiction over the alleged crimes, including the state of commission.[181] Then, a State so notified is given up to 1 month to assert its primacy of jurisdiction by: (i) *informing* the Court if "it is investigating or has investigated" the crimes relating to "the information provided in the notification"; and (ii) *requesting* the Prosecutor to defer to that state's investigation of those persons. In fact, this is not a "request" per se; it is a demand to which the Prosecutor must comply, unless he or she justifies before the Pre-Trial Chamber as to why he or she should be authorized to continue with investigations despite the demand. One such justification could be that the deferral was asked for in bad faith.[182]

Therefore, Article 18 makes it possible for a state with any jurisdictional link with a situation to prevent the Prosecutor from initiating an investigation, "because even initiation of an investigation might interfere with the exercise of national jurisdiction".[183]

6.5.3.2.1.1 Kenya's (Lost) Opportunities Under Article 18

Had Kenya invoked Article 18, it would have got several advantages. At this particular stage, complementarity applies vaguely or generally, since no specific suspects have been identified yet. The basis of its assessment is "possible or potential cases" as opposed to "specific cases". So all Kenya had to do at this stage was to show genuinely that it was *generally* investigating the "group of persons" and "incidents" which were likely to form Prosecutor's future "potential cases".[184] There would not have been a strict requirement to show a high degree of specificity as regards the identity of the persons or the crimes or conduct being

---

[181] ICC Statute, Article 18(1). The notification must contain basic information about acts that may constitute crimes under the Statute, but the notified state may still request for more information from the Prosecutor. See also Rules 52–57.

[182] ICC Statute, Article 18(2). See also Nsereko 2008, p. 632.

[183] Nsereko 2008, pp. 628–629 and footnote 4.

[184] See Decision on the Authorization of an Investigation, *Situation in the Republic of Kenya* (ICC-01/09-19), PTC, 31 March 2010, paras 50–52.

investigated. For example, it would have been sufficient for Kenya to prove that it was investigating "events", such as "the massacre in a certain village or a campaign in a particular geographic area during a particular time period" with regard to the post-election violence.[185]

Even if Kenya had not yet started "actual investigations" at this level, it would still have been possible to argue that it "intended" to do so because the Prosecutor's notification that he wanted to intervene, together with any additional information furnished by the OTP, had been the motivation to trigger such domestic investigations. Such arguments would have been sufficient for a deferral under Article 18 in view of the *general* nature of applicability of the complementarity principle at this (situation) stage.[186] In this regard, Kenya could have presented its plan for domestic investigations and prosecutions. As it will be shown shortly, Kenya attempted to present such a plan at a later stage, but this was already too late.

Lastly, had Kenya requested and obtained a deferral under Article 18, it would have got a period of up to 6 months before the Prosecutor could review the deferral again, provided that it continued to show constant genuineness in its investigations.[187] However temporary this "grace period" might seem, it would have enabled Kenya to commence or continue with investigations while continuing to put its house in order with regard to prosecutions.[188] Thus, there would have been time, for example, to re-engage Parliament with regard to the creation of the proposed local tribunal or the designing of any other domestic forum, such as a special division of the judiciary, where the cases linked to the post-election violence could be tried.

6.5.3.2.1.2 Reasons for Kenya's Failure to Invoke Article 18

Of all the situations he handled, the former ICC's Prosecutor Moreno-Ocampo is said to have acted, arguably, most transparently with regard to Kenya.[189] For example, the Prosecutor did not hasten the ICC's intervention in Kenya even when matters so dictated. Even prior to the official notification of his intention to commence investigations into Kenya, the Prosecutor had insisted that "if the Kenyan authorities [carried] out genuine judicial proceedings against those most responsible, the OTP [would] not have ground to intervene".[190] This suggests that even before the ICC's intervention, the Kenyan authorities were already aware, or at least had a clue, of the "potential cases" that the Prosecutor had in mind. In any case, it must have been clear that the main source of the Prosecutor's potential

---

[185] See Office of the Prosecutor 2003a, paras 24–26 and footnote 10; Olasolo and Cernero-Rojo 2011, p. 405.

[186] Cf. Nsereko 2008, p. 632.

[187] ICC Statute, Article 18(3).

[188] Cf. Bantekas 2010, p. 433 (describing this as a "first (last minute) pick" given to a state before the ICC process commences).

[189] See Seils 2011, p. 1011.

[190] See ICC Press Release ICC-CPI-20090703-PR431, 3 July 2009; Office of the Prosecutor 2009.

action would be, among others, the publicly available reports of the Waki Commission and that of the Kenya National Commission on Human Rights, and that the Prosecutor's main list of suspects would, first and foremost, be derived from the twenty names in the famous Waki envelope.

A question that arises at this juncture is why then did Kenya forgo the opportunity under Article 18, while, as it will be shown shortly, it did not like the ICC's intervention? It is interesting that 2 years after losing this opportunity, the Kenyan government argued in retrospect that it would "not [have been] possible" to invoke Article 18 "before the adoption of the new Constitution and the legislative and other reforms".[191] However, this argument is not convincing since, as already stated, even before the claimed reforms, Kenya's judicial system had by all domestic standards remained functional. Hence one fails to see why investigations, let alone prosecutions, should have been completely "impossible". One could even go further to ask: What if the adoption of these particular reforms (mainly constitutional) failed to materialize? Would it then have remained forever "impossible" for Kenya to investigate and prosecute?

Considering the prevailing Kenyan domestic political situation at that time, there are several reasons that contributed to Kenya's failure to ask the Prosecutor to defer to its investigations at the situation stage. One such reason is that Kenya underestimated the opportunity available under Article 18, given that there had not been any previous precedent where this provision had been invoked. Another reason is that the ICC was still perceived by the Kenyan political elite as a remote threat, especially because until then the names of the specific suspects to be charged by the ICC had not been revealed by the Prosecutor. Lastly, the two main political parties in the coalition government, PNU and ODM, might have failed to agree on a common position as regards the immediate response or reaction to the Prosecutor's notification of his intention to open an investigation. This seems to be the case is in view of the fact that even after the Prosecutor had intervened officially, the two sides of the coalition government opposed each other openly with regard to Kenya's request to the Security Council asking for a deferral of investigation under Article 16 of the ICC Statute.[192]

6.5.3.2.1.3 Assessment by Pre-Trial Chamber

Assessing admissibility *suo motu*, the Pre-Trial Chamber asked the Prosecutor to submit additional information on, inter alia, "admissibility within the context of the situation in the Republic of Kenya", specifically in relation to: (i) the incidents that [were] likely to be the focus of an investigation; (ii) the groups of persons involved that [were] likely to be the target of an investigation for the purpose of identifying the potential cases under consideration; and (iii) domestic

---

[191] Application on behalf of the Government of the Republic of Kenya Pursuant to Article 19 of the ICC Statute, *Ruto, Kosgey and Sang* and *Muthaura, Kenyatta and Ali* (ICC-01/09-02/11-26), PTC, 31 March 2011, para 3.

[192] See infra Sect. 6.6.1.

investigations, if any, with respect to those potential cases as constituted by the previous two elements.[193]

On the basis of this information, the majority of the Pre-Trial Chamber ruled that neither Kenya nor third states were "active" with regard to investigating elements that were likely to shape the Prosecutor's "potential cases" to be derived out of the situation. The Chamber further ruled that although Kenya submitted a report supposedly showing that some domestic prosecutions had taken place, these prosecutions were only in respect of "minor cases". More importantly, it found, as a bigger flaw, that even these minor cases themselves did not cover the potential cases against "senior business and political leaders" related to the two political parties involved in the violence, the PNU and the ODM.[194] Consequently, the Chamber concluded that there was "inaction" at situation level which made the Kenya situation admissible. But after the situation had been declared admissible, the question of "inaction" emerged again at *case level*.

Unlike a situation, a "case" refers to "specific incidents during which one or more crimes within the jurisdiction of the Court seem to have been committed by one or more identified suspects".[195] Thus, a case arises out of an admitted situation. It comes into being when an arrest warrant or a summons to appear has been issued against a specific suspect. Complementarity (admissibility) has to be determined again at this stage by specifically assessing both the *individual* and *conduct* charged.[196] Kenya invoked complementarity at this stage by filing an admissibility challenge pursuant to Articles 19 and 17 of the ICC Statute.

6.5.3.2.2 Kenya's Admissibility Challenge

Read together, Articles 19(2)(b) and 17 of the ICC Statute allow a state to challenge the admissibility of a "case" before the Pre-Trial Chamber by showing, inter alia, that it is investigating or prosecuting the same case.[197] On 31 March 2011, Kenya invoked these provisions by filing an admissibility challenge, being the first admissibility challenge ever by a State Party to the ICC Statute since the Court became operational. Kenya's main argument was that it had the *ability* and *willingness* investigate the charged persons in view of the accomplished or ongoing constitutional and other domestic legislative processes, all of which entailed

---

[193] Decision Requesting Clarification and Additional Information, *Situation in the Republic of Kenya* (ICC-01/09-15I), PTC, 18 February 2010, paras 11 and 14.

[194] Decision on the Authorization of an Investigation, *Situation in the Republic of Kenya* (ICC-01/09-19), PTC, 31 March 2010, paras 53–54 and 182; see also Olasolo 2012, pp. 51–59.

[195] Decision on the Applications for Participation in the Proceedings of VPRS1, VPRS2, PRS3, VPRS4, VPRS5 and VPRS6, *Situation in the DRC* (ICC-01/04-101-tEN), PTC, 17 January 2006, para 65.

[196] Cf. Jalloh 2012a, p. 273.

[197] ICC Statute, Article 19(2)(b).

extensive judicial, prosecutorial and police reforms.[198] In view of these reforms, Kenya submitted, notably using the *future tense*, that: (i) the "investigations of crimes will continue over the coming months"[199]; (ii) "the Government will be in a position to submit [the timetable for the] implementation of the reforms and investigative actions to the Pre-Trial Chamber" if a deadline is set[200]; (iii) "the investigation of all cases, including those presently before the ICC, will be most effectively progressed once the new DPP [Director of Public Prosecutions] is appointed"[201]; (iv) a report "will" be submitted to the Pre-Trial Chamber showing how the investigations "extend upwards to the highest levels and to all cases, including those presently before the ICC"; and (v) that such report will be based on a "bottom-up" investigation and prosecution strategy, which will first target the "lower level perpetrators [and then]...those at the highest levels who may have been responsible".[202]

In addition, Kenya filed 22 documents[203] purportedly "proving" that "the government was investigating the two cases presently before the ICC". Among the documents filed were (1) a letter from Kenya's Attorney General to the Director of Public Prosecutions, directing the recipient to investigate "all persons" alleged to have been involved in the post-election violence, "including the six persons who are subject of the proceedings currently before the ICC"; (2) a copy of the progress report on the post-election violence cases—the March 2011 "updated" report (see supra Sect. 4.3.1.4.2.2); (3) a report on piracy cases prosecuted in Kenya. This report was submitted purportedly to "prove" that "Kenya clearly [had] the capacity and capability to investigate and prosecute serious crimes, and [had] the full backing of the international community in doing so on its behalf"; (4) a copy of Kenya's 2010 (new) Constitution and six other pieces of legislation already enacted or to be enacted to be evidence of the legislative reforms; and (5) various Statements, Reports and Presentations, expressing the *optimism* that local trials were still possible.[204]

---

[198] Application on behalf of the Government of the Republic of Kenya Pursuant to Article 19 of the ICC Statute, *Ruto, Kosgey and Sang* and *Muthaura, Kenyatta and Ali* (ICC-01/09-02/11-26), PTC, 31 March 2011; see also Jalloh, 2012a, pp. 271–272.

[199] Application on behalf of Kenyan Government Pursuant to Article 19, *Situation in the Republic of Kenya* (ICC-01/09-02/11-26), PTC, 31 March 2011, para 13.

[200] Ibid., para 14.

[201] Ibid., para 69.

[202] Ibid., para 71.

[203] See Filing of Annexes and Materials to the Application of the Government of Kenya Pursuant to Article 19 of the Rome Statute, *Ruto, Kosgey and Sang* (ICC-01/09-01/11-64), PTC, 21 April 2011.

[204] Application on behalf of Kenyan Government Pursuant to Article 19, *Situation in the Republic of Kenya* (ICC-01/09-02/11-26), PTC, 31 March 2011, paras 6–33.

6.5.3.2.2.1 *Responses of the Prosecutor and Victims*

Kenya's submission in the future tense had negative implications on its admissibility challenge. Both the Prosecutor and victims' common representative pointed out that the future tense indicated a mere "promise" or "commitment" to investigate, and that Kenya completely failed to reveal that at the time the admissibility challenge was filed any domestic investigations or prosecutions had been instituted by in respect of the same six suspects and for the same conduct which was the subject of the cases facing them before the ICC.[205]

6.5.3.2.2.2 *Majority Decision on the Admissibility Challenge*

The Pre-Trial Chamber dismissed Kenya's admissibility challenge, one ground being that it did not pass the complementarity test. Kenya appealed to the Appeals Chamber, arguing that the decision of the Pre-Trial Chamber contained factual, legal and procedural errors. This appeal, too, was dismissed by a majority of four judges, one judge dissenting.

In short, the majority of Appeals Chamber agreed with the Pre-Trial Chamber, the Prosecutor and the victims' representative, that Kenya was "inactive", for it failed to prove that *at the time of filing* the admissibility challenge there had been concluded or ongoing domestic investigations encompassing "the same individual[s] and *substantially* the same conduct as alleged in the proceedings before the Court".[206] In particular, the Appeals Chamber noted that to invoke complementarity successfully at the case level, Kenya was duty-bound to prove the existence of a "concrete investigative step". This could include, for example, proving that it was "interviewing witnesses or the suspects, collecting documentary evidence, or carrying out forensic evidence" in respect of the same six persons.[207] It was concluded eventually that Kenya's submission as a whole constituted an

---

[205] Prosecution Response to "Application on behalf of the Government of the Republic of Kenya pursuant to Article 19 of the ICC Statute", *Ruto, Kosgey and Sang* (ICC-01/09-01/11-69), PTC, 28 April 2011, paras 16–29; Prosecution Response to "Application on behalf of the Government of the Republic of Kenya pursuant to Article 19 of the ICC Statute", *Muthaura, Kenyatta and Ali* (ICC-01/09-02/11-71), PTC, 28 April 2011, paras 22–29; Observations on behalf of victims on the Government of Kenya's Application under Article 19 of the Rome Statute, *Ruto, Kosgey and Sang* (ICC-01/09-01/11-70), PTC, 28 April 2011, paras 8–46. See also Jalloh 2012a, pp. 272–274.

[206] See Decision on the Application by the Government of Kenya Challenging the Admissibility of the Case Pursuant to Article 19(2)(b) of the Statute, *Ruto, Kosgey and Sang* (ICC-01/09-01/11-101), PTC, 30 May 2011, paras 43–69; Decision on the Application by the Government of Kenya Challenging the Admissibility of the Case Pursuant to Article 19(2)(b) of the Statute, *Muthaura, Kenyatta and Ali* (ICC-01/09-02/11-96), PTC, 30 May 2011, paras 59–70; Judgment on the Appeal of the Kenyan Government against PTC II's Decision on the Admissibility of the Case, *Ruto, Kosgey and Sang* (ICC-01/09-01/11-307), AC, 30 August 2011, para 39; Judgment on the Appeal of the Kenyan Government against PTC II's Decision on the Admissibility of the Case, *Muthaura, Kenyatta and Ali* (ICC-01/09-02/11-274), AC, 30 August 2011, paras 33–46.

[207] Cf. Stigen 2008, p. 203.

expression of "mere preparedness to take steps or the investigation of other suspects", which was *not sufficient* to render the cases inadmissible.[208]

6.5.3.2.2.3 Dissenting Opinion of Judge Anita Usacka

Judge Anita Usacka of the Appeals Chamber wrote a dissenting opinion. She opined that in rejecting Kenya's submission entirely, the Pre-Trial Chamber had failed to "fully balance all relevant interests as required by the principle of complementarity". In particular, she noted that the Pre-Trial Chamber had failed to "give sufficient weight" to the fact that the Court was handling the first admissibility challenge ever brought by a State, and therefore, that the challenge was surrounded by "many legal and factual uncertainties". More importantly, the dissenting judge opined that instead of hastily dismissing Kenya's admissibility challenge on the ground of non-existence of a "concrete case" in respect of the six suspects, some consideration should have been given to *assessing the genuineness* of Kenya's plan. She noted that even though Kenya's plan was clearly a "promise to investigate", Kenya appeared to be acting in good faith, because the plan showed that "within a short period of time, Kenya would reach the level of an investigation that would satisfy the standards". Thus, the dissenting judge found that the Pre-Trial Chamber, inter alia, "did not completely account for the sovereign rights of Kenya and the principle of complementarity". She concluded that if these factors were sufficiently pondered, the Pre-Trial Chamber and the majority of the Appeals Chamber would have reached a different decision on Kenya's admissibility challenge.[209]

6.5.3.2.2.4 Analysis

The Kenyan government's conception of complementarity in its submission was deliberately too broad, a fact which makes it flawed.[210] It sought to oversimplify and overstretch the notion of complementarity by suggesting that the application of the principle must always favour national jurisdictions even where their claim that they are able or willing to investigate is clearly vague. For example, Kenya submitted to the Pre-Trial Chamber that the two Kenyan cases were *inadmissible* before the ICC, arguing that for a case to be declared inadmissible under Article 17 of the ICC Statute, "there is no ground [that the] persons being investigated [by

---

[208] Prosecutor Judgment on the Appeal of the Kenyan Government against PTC II's Decision on the Admissibility of the Case, *Ruto, Kosgey and Sang* (ICC-01/09-01/11-307), AC, 30 August 2011, para 40.

[209] Judge Anita Usacka's Dissenting Opinion on Kenya's Appeal against PTC's Decision on Kenya's Admissibility Challenge, *Muthaura, Kenyatta and Ali* (ICC-01/09-02/11-342), AC, 20 September, 2011, paras 20–32; Judge Anita Usacka's Dissenting Opinion on Kenya's Appeal against PTC's Decision on Kenya's Admissibility Challenge, *Ruto, Kosgey and Sang* (ICC-01/09-01/11-336), AC, 20 September 2011, paras 20–32. See also Jalloh 2012a, p. 274.

[210] Cf. Asaala 2012, pp. 132–134.

a national jurisdiction] must necessarily always be the same as those the ICC Prosecutor has named [or charged]".[211] Rather, Kenya continued to argue, under the same-person test, it is sufficient if the national investigation covers "the persons at *the same level in the hierarchy* being investigated by the ICC". For that reason, Kenya claimed that there were ongoing national investigative processes, which extended "*to the highest levels* for all possible crimes, thus covering the ... cases before the ICC".[212]

Jalloh rightly notes that such a wide interpretation "swings the pendulum too far", as it suggests that "mere expression of an intent to proceed against an amorphous group of unidentified suspects that may or may not include the suspects presently before the Court" is enough.[213] Had this erroneous interpretation been upheld, it could have probably been used by Kenya as a leeway or loophole to eventually shield some of the Ocampo six from prosecution. It could also have been used to shield other persons who might bear major responsibility for the post-election violence by deliberately not specifically targeting them but rather targeting others "at the same level".[214]

More importantly, Kenya's argument was misplaced simply because it was raised at the case level. As already shown above, the general applicability of complementarity criteria as suggested by Kenya in its submission only applies when admissibility is being assessed *generally* at a situation level, namely when no specific suspect has been identified yet. As that stage had passed, it is obvious that the Kenyan government woke up too late.

On the other hand, Jalloh, like Judge Usacka, suggests that the ICC acted too strictly and hastily with regard to Kenya, and thereby failed to strike a pragmatic balance between the role of states and that of the ICC in relation to complementarity. The argument is that the Pre-Trial Chamber should not have made an outright rejection of *all* arguments by the Kenyan government, especially the *self-imposed strict timetable* for ensuring that domestic investigations would be carried out. Jalloh further argues that in this way, the ICC not only wrongly implied that complementarity is akin to primacy, but also discouraged Kenya's seemingly "legitimate national attempts to prosecute". In this regard, he asserts that both the Pre-Trial Chamber and Appeals Chamber missed an opportunity to "breath life" into positive complementarity.[215]

Jalloh's argument is valid only to the extent that the core of the notion of positive (or proactive) complementarity is that the ICC should *actively encourage* states which show a willingness to carry out genuine investigations and

---

[211] Document in Support of Appeal of the Government of Kenya against the Decision on the Application by the Government of Kenya Challenging the Admissibility of the Case, *Muthaura, Kenyatta and Ali* (ICC-01/09-02/11-130), AC, 20 June 2011, para 82 (emphasis added).

[212] Application on behalf of Kenyan Government Pursuant to Article 19, *Situation in the Republic of Kenya,* (ICC-01/09-02/11-26), PTC, 31 March 2011, para 32 (emphasis added).

[213] Jalloh 2012a, pp. 277–278.

[214] Ibid., p. 279.

[215] Ibid., p. 278.

prosecution of the core crimes under international law.[216] This notion is also envisioned by the prosecutorial policy adopted by the ICC's OTP.[217] Kenya attempted to "enforce" it through two requests for "assistance and cooperation" made subsequent to its unsuccessful admissibility challenge. In these requests Kenya asked the Pre-Trial Chamber to "order" the OTP to send "all statements, documents and other evidence" in its possession to Kenya to "assist ... and obviate any unnecessary delays with its national investigation".[218]

However, the notion of positive complementarity is policy-based. As a result, it does not create any legal obligation on the part of the OTP to assist or conduct investigations on behalf of national jurisdictions. It follows that the request by the Kenyan government that the OTP be "ordered" to transmit its independently gathered evidence to the Kenyan authorities lacked a legal foundation. In addition, the request that the OTP should be "ordered" to send its evidence to the Kenyan authorities weakened Kenya's position even more. It must in effect have created the (wrong?) impression that Kenya had already failed (was unable) to conduct investigations on its own.

Interestingly, after losing its admissibility challenge, and after the requests for "assistance and cooperation" had been dismissed, Kenya did not pursue its purported self-imposed time table for domestic investigations and prosecution. This confirms the theory that the plan was only geared towards "rescuing" the Ocampo six, and that it was not necessarily intended as a genuine plan to address impunity with respect to *all* main perpetrators of the crimes linked to the post-election violence.

At another level, assuming that Kenya was able to satisfy the same-person test, i.e. could establish that it was investigating the six suspects, it appears that Kenya would still be faced with another herculean task of proving that any alleged domestic proceedings satisfied the *same-conduct test*. Up until now the ICC has declined to set out the parameters of this test.[219] Even though in the Kenyan case the Appeals Chamber changed its formulation slightly from "same conduct" to be "*substantially* same conduct", the precise scope of the test still remains a matter of

---

[216] For details see Hall 2011, pp. 1014 et seq.

[217] See Moreno-Ocampo 2011, pp. 21–32.

[218] See Requests for Assistance on behalf of the Government of the Republic of Kenya pursuant to Article 93(10), Article 96 and Rule 194, *Situation in the Republic of Kenya* (ICC-01/09-58), PTC, 21 April 2011 and (ICC-01/09-79), PTC, 16 September 2011.

[219] See, e.g. Judgment on the Appeal of Mr. Germain Katanga against the Oral Decision of Trial Chamber on the Admissibility of the Case, *Katanga and Chui* (ICC-01/04-01/07-1497), AC, 25 September 2009, para 81; Decision on the Application by the Government of Kenya Challenging the Admissibility of the Case Pursuant to Article 19(2)(b) of the Statute, *Muthaura, Kenyatta and Ali* (ICC-01/09-02/11-96), PTC, 30 May 2011, para 53; Judgment on the Appeal of the Kenyan Government against PTC II's Decision on the Admissibility of the Case *Muthaura, Kenyatta and Ali* (ICC-01/09-02/11-274), AC, 30 August 2011, para 33; Reasons for the Oral Decision on the Motion Challenging the Admissibility of the Case, *Katanga and Chui* (ICC-01/04-01/07-1213-tENG), PTC, 16 June 2009, para 95. See also Boas et al. 2011, pp. 76–77.

speculation. Since the Prosecutor was not prepared to trust the Kenyan government, given the way it had conducted itself until then, the Prosecution would have probably used this limb of the test to cling to the cases, because the position of the Prosecutor (shown below) as regards the precise scope of the same-conduct test has been equally unpredictable.

For example, in *Katanga and Chui* the Prosecutor argued that "same conduct" means the "precise conduct", meaning that it must entail not only the same *actus reus*, but also the same "specific incidents" sought to be prosecuted at the ICC; and that it must not be merely "similar" or "other conduct".[220] When applying for authorization of investigation into Kenya, the Prosecutor argued that the phrase "same conduct" must *also* encompass a "serious offence" under domestic law and not merely "minor offences".[221] He did not give any criterion as to how the "seriousness" of the offence should be measured. But scholars have, in the same way, suggested that the same-conduct test must consider the *gravity* of the offence charged by the domestic jurisdiction, such that the offence must necessarily be in respect of a "serious ordinary crime". In this regard, it has been argued that the test cannot be said to have been met if the offence charged domestically was, for example, a simple assault, while such a conduct would have contextually amounted to genocide at the ICC.[222] It seems that in view of this argument, gravity of the offence could also be determined on the basis of the maximum sentence that the charged offence attracts domestically.[223]

6.6 Other Responses to ICC's Intervention

Apart from the challenging the admissibility of the two cases, Kenya explored other legal responses and strategies (outside of the ICC's courtroom) to try to halt the trial of the suspects. In addition to the legal responses, some political and diplomatic strategies were also employed. This part identifies and analyses these responses.

Immediately after the six suspects were named, Kenya, through its then Vice President Kalonzo Musyoka embarked extensively on so-called "shuttle

---

[220] See Prosecution Response to Motion Challenging the Admissibility of the Case by the Defence of Germain Katanga, *Katanga and Chui* (ICC-01/04-01/07-1007), PTC, 30 March 2009, paras 64–69; Prosecution's Response to the "Appeal of the Government of Kenya against the Decision on the Application by the Government of Kenya Challenging the Admissibility of the Case, *Muthaura, Kenyatta and Ali* (ICC-01/09-02/11-168), AC, 12 July 2011, para 95; Nouwen 2011, p. 211.

[221] See Prosecutor's Request for Authorisation of an Investigation, *Situation in the Republic of Kenya* (ICC-01/09-3), PTC, 26 November 2009, para 54 (stating that "there are no domestic prosecution [sic] for the crimes against humanity allegedly committed in Kenya", and that there had only been "a limited number of proceedings for less serious offences in connection to the crimes allegedly committed during the post-election violence").

[222] See, e.g. Broomhall 1999, p. 149; Benzing 2003, p. 616; Carter 2010, p. 194.

[223] Cf. supra Sect. 4.3.1.2.

diplomacy". This entailed diplomatic visits and talks with other states aimed at achieving one main broad objective, namely to solicit the support of individual states, the AU and that of the UN Security Council in respect of Kenya's bid for deferral of investigations in respect of the two cases.[224] By 9 February 2011, a total of Kenyan Shillings 31.5 million (about 40,000 US Dollars) had already been spent on lobbying the African states in this regard, and more money was expected to be spent on the lobbying of the members of the UN Security Council.[225]

6.6.1 Attempts to Have the Cases Deferred Under Article 16

In terms of Article 16 of the ICC Statute, the UN Security Council has powers to adopt a resolution under Chapter VII of the UN Charter to suspend ICC's investigations or prosecution in respect of a situation or case can be suspended for a renewable period of 1 year. The Chapter VII mandate confers exclusive and unlimited powers on the UN Security Council with respect to issues of international peace and security. Consequently, the Security Council can request the ICC to defer (postpone) an investigation or prosecution of a situation or a case if the Council is of the view that the continuance of such an investigation or prosecution poses a threat to the international peace and security.[226]

On 4 March 2011, the Kenyan government submitted an official request to the Security Council, asking it to defer the ICC's investigations pursuant to Article 16.[227] In this endeavour, Kenya managed to receive a strong backing of the AU as a regional bloc.[228] This notwithstanding, chances of Kenya succeeding in its deferral bid remained very slim from the onset. Initial indicators that Kenya would fail came even before its request was officially made, when the US Ambassador and British High Commissioner to Kenya declared publicly that their respective countries would veto such a request should it make its way to the Security Council.[229] In the end, Kenya's deferral request was rejected by the Security Council in April 2011.[230] Almost 2 years after this rejection, on 18 January 2013, the Security

---

[224] Daily Nation, 4 March 2011.

[225] See The Standard Digital, 9 February 2011.

[226] For details, see Bergsmo and Pejic 2008b, pp. 595–604.

[227] See the Letter of the Permanent Representative of Kenya to the United Nations to the President of the Security Council on Kenya's deferral request, S 2011/201, 29 March 2011 http://www.securitycouncilreport.org/atf/cf/%7B65BFCF9B-6D27-4E9C-8CD3-CF6E4FF96FF9%7D/Kenya%20S%202011%20201.pdf. Accessed September 2014.

[228] See African Union, Decision on the Implementation of the Decisions on the International Criminal Court (ICC), Doc. Ex.CL/731(XXI) para 4. See also The Standard, 5 February 2011; Sunday Nation, 28 January 2011.

[229] See Kuperstein 2011, p. 56.

[230] Daily Nation, 9 April 2011.

Council published a report which, among other things, discussed Kenya's request and gave the reasons for the rejection.[231]

As indicated above, the Security Council would have adopted a deferral resolution under Chapter VII of the UN Charter in favour of Kenya only if it was convinced that continuing with the ICC judicial process in respect of Kenya posed *a threat* to national or international peace and security. However, even before the Security Council received Kenya's request for deferral, the situation was already pointing to the fact that it would be impossible for Kenya to establish its case convincingly. The main reason is that the Security Council had previously expressed a view that sharply contrasted what Kenya was advancing as a reason for deferral. While Kenya believed that the ICC process per se posed a threat to its internal unity, peace and stability, the Security Council believed that the prosecution of international core crimes by international tribunals per se can be a means of restoring and maintaining peace and security.[232] Hence, it is not surprising that the Security Council members decided to dispose of Kenya's request quickly through a simple "informal interactive dialogue" held with Kenya's Ambassador to the UN and attended by the AU members sitting in the Security Council at that time (Gabon, Nigeria and South Africa). As anticipated, the Security Council members agreed that "the situation in Kenya did not amount to a threat to international peace and security; therefore, it was not an issue for the Council to decide upon".[233]

Kenya's bid for deferral was bound to fail also because Kenya was wrong in seeking to utilize the powers of the Security Council under Article 16 to achieve the ends of complementarity.[234] Having realized that it had a weak case in trying to justify its deferral request on grounds of threat to peace and security, Kenya cited (in its deferral request) the ongoing domestic judicial reforms and its ability and willingness to conduct domestic prosecutions as *other grounds* on the basis of which the Security Council should consider deferring the ICC's investigations.[235] Clearly, these arguments were misplaced, for they pertained to complementarity (see supra Sect. 6.5) and not to deferral of investigations. The two concepts differ in the way they apply under the ICC Statute. That is why the members of the Security Council "advised" Kenya, and rightly so, that the preferable venue where such grounds could be advanced was before the ICC itself, as they pertained to admissibility of a case under Article 19 (read with Article 17) of the ICC Statute; and that such issues fell outside the scope of the Security Council envisioned by Article 16 of the Statute.[236]

---

[231] UN Security Council 2013a, pp. 30–32.

[232] See, for example, Preamble para 6 of the UNSC Resolution S/RES/827 (1993) of 25 May 1993 on the establishment of the ICTY; and Preamble para 7 of the UNSC Resolution 955 (1994) of 8 November 1994 on the establishment of the ICTR; Bergsmo and Pejic 2008b, p. 599.

[233] UN Security Council 2013a, p. 31.

[234] See Gevers and Du Plessis 2011.

[235] See All Africa, 8 March 2011.

[236] UN Security Council 2013a, p. 31.

Also, it was expected from the onset that two aspects of the Darfur situation before the ICC would play a role at the Security Council's deliberations on the Kenya's deferral request. One such aspect is that when the ICC issued arrest warrants against the Sudanese President Omar Al-Bashir,[237] the AU made efforts similar to those made by Kenya to have Al-Bashir's case deferred.[238] The argument then was that if the case against Al-Bashir proceeded, or if the arrest warrants against him were executed, there would be a likelihood of a bigger threat to peace and security than if a deferral was granted to avail the AU an opportunity to mediate in the conflict. As far as the peace-and-security argument is concerned, the argument by the AU regarding Sudan is comparatively more convincing and weightier than the similar argument advanced in relation to Kenya. This is for the simple reason that when the arrest warrants were issued against Al-Bashir, he was a serving Head of State. This being the case, the possibility that his arrest could lead to instability or pose a threat to peace and security cannot be dismissed lightly, neither can it be considered to be a trivial argument. But this notwithstanding, the Security Council declined to defer the case against Al-Bashir.[239]

In fact, when dismissing Kenya's deferral request, the Security Council made a brief but explicit reference to the Al-Bashir case. The members of the Council were of the view that allowing Kenya's deferral request for the reasons advanced would be a "loose reading" of Article 16, and that it would "set a precedent for a similar decision regarding the indictment of President Al-Bashir of Sudan, another deferral case backed by the AU". They further noted that if the Security Council was not at all prepared to defer the case against Al-Bashir, whose case was referred to the ICC by the Council itself,[240] and whose country was not even a State Party to the ICC Statute, then it (the Council) had even better reasons not to interfere with ICC's investigation in respect of Kenya which is a State Party to the ICC Statute and whose referral to the ICC was not done by the Council.[241]

There is yet another aspect of the *Al-Bashir case* that can be directly linked to Kenya, and which, although not explicitly referred to by the Security Council, might have worked negatively against Kenya when the Council was deliberating on its deferral request. This is the fact that previously Kenya had intentionally acted in defiance of its obligation under the ICC Statute, and the UN Charter specifically, in relation to Al-Bashir. On 27 August 2010, Kenya invited Al-Bashir to attend the promulgation of Kenya's new Constitution freely (without arresting him), despite there being pending ICC arrest warrants against him. By doing so, Kenya defied not only the ICC but also the Security Council, given that the situation in Darfur had been referred to the ICC by the Security Council. The ICC

---

[237] See First Warrant of Arrest, *Al Bashir* (ICC-02/05-01/09-1), PTC, 4 March 2009 and Second Warrant of Arrest, *Al Bashir* (ICC-02/05-01/09-95), PTC, 12 July 2010.

[238] See e.g., African Union, Decision on the Meeting of African States Parties to the Rome Statute of the International Criminal Court (ICC), Doc. Assembly/AU/13(XIII), 3 July 2009.

[239] See generally Ciampi 2008, pp. 885 et seq.; Weldehaimanot 2011, pp. 208 et seq.

[240] See UN Security Council Res. 1593 of 31 March 2005.

[241] UN Security Council 2013a, p. 32.

reported Kenya's defiance to the Security Council for the Council to take any action it deemed fit.[242] Although the Council did not take any measures against Kenya in this respect, it is clear that this aspect of the *Al-Bashir case* already militated against Kenya, for Kenya did not have clean hands when it was making its deferral bid.

The last factor which weakened Kenya's deferral request was the contradictions that emanated from the Kenyan coalition government itself. Seven days subsequent to Kenya's filing of its deferral request, the ODM side of the coalition government (see supra Sect. 3.3) sent a letter to the Security Council enumerating "sixteen reasons why the cases must not be deferred". The ODM claimed that the deferral request had been made by one side of the coalition government, the PNU. More importantly, the letter confirmed what has already been mentioned above: It stated that it was not the continued prosecution of the Kenyan cases by the ICC which constituted threat to international peace and security, but rather it was the absence of domestic prosecutions that posed a threat to internal peace and security.[243] This contradiction (two different positions/arguments from the same government) was a clear indication that the Kenyan coalition government itself was not very serious about the deferral request.[244]

Kenya made another (second) deferral request to the Security Council after two of the ICC suspects were elected Kenya's President and Deputy President. The request was inspired mainly by the AU's efforts to fight what it perceived to be a continual "mistreatment" of African leaders by "Western" judicial institutions. This deferral request, which was also unsuccessful, will be examined in detail under Sect. 6.7.4.

6.6.2 Attempts to Resort to Regional Criminal Jurisdictions

As alluded to above, the ICC's intervention in Kenya came at the time when the relationship between the AU and the ICC was already strained.[245] Kenya tried to capitalize on this "hostility" in order to halt the ICC process. In particular, Kenya placed its hope in the ongoing AU's project of extending criminal jurisdiction to the African Court of Justice and Human and Peoples' Rights that is intended to enable that court to, inter alia, prosecute crimes under international law committed by Africans in Africa. This particular project is arguably part of AU's drastic

---

[242] Decision Informing the United Nations Security Council and the Assembly of the States Parties to the Rome Statute about Omar Al-Bashir's Presence in the Territory of the Republic of Kenya, *Al Bashir* (ICC-02/05-01/09-107), PTC, 27 August 2010.

[243] See Letter by Prof. Peter Anyang' Nyong'o, Secretary-General of the ODM, to the President of the UN Security Council, 11 March 2011 http://newmedia-pirate.blogspot.com/2011/03/letter-by-odm-to-un-security-council.html. Accessed September 2014.

[244] UN Security Council 2013a, p. 31.

[245] Cf. Werle et al. 2014.

reaction to the increasing activity of the ICC in Africa against African politicians.[246] But if viewed from a broader perspective, and more positively, the
essence of extending the jurisdiction of this court could also be situated within the
recent AU's political ideal of "African solutions to African problems", which ideal
has largely informed most of AU's recent policies.[247]

However, it soon became clear that the creation and putting into effect of the
contemplated criminal chamber in the AU court would require a process involving
not only the drafting and adoption of a protocol, but also an attainment of a minimum number of ratifications.[248] This means that the completion of such a lengthy
process would definitely have been overtaken by events at the ICC as far as the
Kenyan cases were concerned. To avoid this, the AU, in its May 2012 Summit, recommended that efforts be made to ensure that the cases against the Kenyan suspects
were "transferred" from The Hague to the East African Court of Justice (EACJ), a
regional court operating under the auspices of the East African Community
(EAC),[249] based in Arusha, Tanzania, of which Kenya is a Member State.[250] The
recommendation of the AU was made in line with a preceding Resolution of the
EAC to *also* expand the jurisdictional mandate of the EACJ so that it could try
criminal cases, including the ones facing the Kenyans at the ICC.[251]

The question that therefore crops up is this: Assuming that the proposed criminal chambers in the AU and EAC courts were successfully established, would this
have affected the Kenyan cases already at the ICC? Before answering this question, two important *general* observations are worth making.

First, that there is no any provision in the ICC Statute that provides for a *transfer* of cases from the ICC to national or regional courts. It follows that the ICC
would not have been bound to transfer the Kenyan cases even if the envisioned
criminal chambers in the AU or EAC courts were created.[252] Second, the ICC
Statute is clear that ICC's jurisdiction is "complementary to national [not regional]

---

[246] Generally see Abass 2013a, pp. 933 et seq.; Abass 2013b, pp. 27 et seq.; Ambos 2013,
pp. 499 et seq.; Murungu 2011, pp. 1067 et seq.

[247] See generally Dersso 2012.

[248] The Protocol for the Court was adopted in June 2014. See Protocol on the Amendment to
the Protocol on the Statute of the African Court of Justice and Human Rights, Assembly/AU/
Dec.529(XXIII)—Doc. Assembly/AU/8(XXIII), Twenty-Third Ordinary Session of the AU
Assembly, 26–27 June 2014, Malabo, Equatorial Guinea.

[249] The EAC is presently constituted by 5 States, Tanzania, Kenya, Uganda, Rwanda and
Burundi.

[250] Radio Netherlands Worldwide, 24 May 2012.

[251] See Resolution of the Assembly Seeking the EAC Council of Ministers to Implore the
International Criminal Court, EA Legislative Assembly, 26 April 2012 (on the Transfer of the
Case of the Accused Four Kenyans Facing Trial in Respect of the Aftermath of the 2007 Kenya
General Elections to the East African Court of Justice and to Reinforce the Treaty Provisions).
This Resolution was subsequently endorsed by the EAC General Assembly. See Joint
Communiqué of the 10th Extraordinary Summit of EAC Heads of State, 28 April 2012, para 20.

[252] Cf. Ngari 2012.

criminal jurisdictions".[253] Accordingly, there is nothing in principle that can render a situation or a case *inadmissible* before the ICC, even when the particular situation or case is being investigated by a regional (not national) criminal court.

Despite the general observations above, the use of regional criminal courts to achieve the ends of complementarity is not expressly prohibited or discouraged by the ICC Statute.[254] This could therefore be one of the areas in which flexibility is necessary when interpreting and applying the ICC Statute. It is submitted that properly functioning regional criminal courts, just like national courts, have a great potential in the fight against impunity, given the ever growing number of referrals and a very limited number of cases that the ICC can prosecute. More importantly, in line with the Statute's underlying objective of zero tolerance to impunity for the core crimes under international law, nothing would be wrong from a policy point of view if a tripartite formal or informal relationship were forged between the ICC, national courts and an effective regional criminal court, such that the ICC remains complementary to the regional court as it is currently to national courts. This would be a new catalyst in the fight against impunity, especially where the state of commission or third states are not willing to participate in the fight or where their participation is not genuine. Thus, even though under the current arrangement regional criminal jurisdictions are not expressly contemplated in the complementarity regime of the ICC, it is difficult to imagine the ICC blatantly disregarding proceedings carried out by a regional criminal jurisdiction, if such proceedings have been or are being conducted in good faith and with the degree of genuineness in accordance with Article 17 of the ICC Statute, i.e. with no intention to shield the suspect from criminal responsibility.[255] In any case, Article 20 of the ICC Statute would, in principle, bar the ICC from re-prosecuting a suspect for the same crime or conduct which has already been prosecuted by "another court". A regional criminal court would definitely qualify as "another court" within the meaning of this provision.

Similarly, it is further submitted that the proposal to extend criminal jurisdiction to the EACJ per se was not a bad idea. Assuming that the proposal materialized and that such jurisdiction was exercised robustly in respect of the crimes committed during the post-election violence in Kenya, the EACJ would have probably been able to minimize the impunity gap created by Kenya's failure to institute proceedings at national level against main suspects other than those officially indicted by the ICC.

However, it is doubtful if the proposal to extend the jurisdiction of the EACJ in this regard was informed by good faith. In fact, it was alleged that although the resolution to do so was initiated by a member from Uganda, it was sponsored by Kenya whose President was then chairing the EAC General Assembly. It is no

---

[253] ICC Statute, Article 1.

[254] Cf. Abass 2013a, pp. 941–943. This is contrary to the contention (see Murungu 2011, pp. 1075 et seq.) that such regional courts would be incompatible with the ICC Statute.

[255] Cf. Murungu 2011, p. 1081.

wonder, therefore, that commentators dismissed the proposal as yet another tactic of the Kenyan government to "rescue" the suspects facing trial at The Hague.[256] Indeed this appears to have been the case, given that when it became clear that the ICC would not "transfer" the cases to the EACJ, firstly because there was no legal basis to do so and secondly, because the ICC did not seem have any trust in the move, the speed and vigour to create the said criminal chamber faded and the whole idea was abandoned altogether.

In conclusion, the prospects of Kenya being able to rely on the anticipated African regional criminal jurisdictions thereby "avoiding" the ICC remained hard to realize as the ICC cases proceeded to trial. However, the regional jurisdictions would not have been completely useless if they materialized, since they would still help to address the impunity gap already created by Kenya's failure to hold criminally accountable the main suspects of the crimes linked to the post-election violence. They would also provide useful forums for addressing similar crimes committed elsewhere in Africa.

6.6.3 Threats to Withdraw from the ICC Statute

Another domestic response to the ICC process emanated from Kenya's Parliament which, using its legislative mandate, tried to exert pressure on the Executive to withdraw from the ICC Statute. On 16 December 2010, 1 day after the six suspects were named, Mr. Isaac Ruto (MP) presented a motion to Parliament asking it to pass a resolution to the effect that Kenya should "undomesticate" the ICC Statute, and consequently withdraw from it. The motive of this drastic measure was expressly stated in the motion as being to ensure that Kenya was "immediately released from any obligation" it had committed herself to under the Statute. In addition, the Parliament was asked to also resolve that the government must "suspend any links, cooperation and assistance" to the ICC.[257] Ironically, the MP who moved this particular Motion and most of the other MPs who supported his motion were from the group of MPs who, before the six suspects were named, had campaigned vigorously in favour of the "The Hague option", and who blocked the efforts to create the proposed local special tribunal.[258] It is therefore relevant to briefly outline the basis and consequences of a state's withdrawal from the ICC Statute before proceeding to evaluate the implications that would have resulted from Kenya's withdrawal.

---

[256] Al Shahid, 1 May 2012.

[257] Parliament of Kenya 2010a, pp. 30–45; and Parliament of Kenya 2010b, pp. 66–83.

[258] See supra Sect. 3.5.3.

6.6.3.1 Basis and Consequences of Withdrawal from the ICC Statute

The ICC Statute, just like any other treaty, is subject to the Vienna Convention on the Laws of Treaty. States are free to sign, ratify or accede to the Statute just like they are also free to withdraw from it. On this basis, Article 127 of the Statute provides that a State Party can withdraw from the Statute any time it wishes to do so. The provision also lays down the procedure and consequences of such a withdrawal. It indicates that the withdrawal does not take effect immediately; it only becomes effective *at least* 1 *year after* the withdrawing state has given a written notice.[259] Also, the withdrawal does not relieve the withdrawing State from its obligations arising when the State was still party to the Statute. In particular, the withdrawing State will remain duty-bound to cooperate with the ICC with regard to any proceedings as long as such proceedings "were commenced prior to the date on which the withdrawal became effective". In addition, such a withdrawal does not bar the ICC from continuing to consider any matter which was already under the ICC's consideration "prior to the date on which the withdrawal becomes effective".[260]

6.6.3.2 Response by Kenya's Executive: No Withdrawal

Despite the above-mentioned parliamentary resolution, Kenya did not withdraw from the Statute. The Executive chose to take a wiser and less drastic approach to this matter by making a rational exercise of its exclusive powers to enter into and withdraw Kenya from treaties. Under Kenya's constitutional legal order which existed then, the Parliament did not have much say as regards ratification of, accession to, or withdrawal from, treaties.[261] Even though the motion to withdraw from the Statute was endorsed by Parliament, the Executive refused to align itself with the whims of Parliament. The official position taken by the government (Executive) was that instead of withdrawing from the Statute, it would rely on the other options available under Articles 19 (admissibility challenge) and 16 (deferral

---

[259] ICC Statute, Article 127(1).

[260] ICC Statute, Article 127(2). This is in line with Article 70(1)(a) of the Vienna Convention on the Law of Treaties which provides that unless the parties otherwise agree, termination of a treaty "does not affect any right, obligation or legal situation of the parties created through the execution of the treaty prior to its termination".

[261] But currently under Kenyan Treaty Making and Ratification Act No. 45 of 2012, Part III, ss. 7–12, both Parliament (lower house) and Senate (Upper House) clearly have a say in the ratification of international treaties, such that if the two Houses do not approve ratification of a treaty proposed by Executive, such a treaty cannot be ratified. However, this legislation is not clear as regards the role of the two Houses in relation to withdrawal from treaties.

request) of the Statute, respectively.[262] As shown above, these were the means pursued by the Kenyan government, although both means were unsuccessful.[263]

6.6.3.3   Practical Implications of Withdrawal from the Statute

It might appear that the Kenyan Parliament did not appreciate fully the implications of withdrawal from the Statute. One could think that it was naive or even stupid for the MPs to believe that such a withdrawal per se would have "immediately" released Kenya from "any obligation" under the Statute, or that it would have "immediately suspend[ed] any links, cooperation and assistance" to the Court. This is because, the *assumption* under Article 127 of the Statute is already that Kenya would have remained duty-bound to cooperate with the Court with regard to the two cases, and also with regard to any other cases that the Prosecutor might have derived from the situation within the 1-year period pending Kenya's withdrawal notice to take effect.[264]

However, going beyond the face value of the provisions of Article 127, one will agree to the submission that had Kenya withdrawn from the Statute, such a withdrawal would have had serious negative practical implications on the ICC process. By and large, this is what the Kenyan MPs wanted to achieve. They were aware that Kenya's obligation to continue to cooperate with the ICC would have remained more theoretical than practical after such a withdrawal, since that the ICC would not have sufficient means to enforce cooperation. Given that the Kenya situation emanated from a *proprio motu* investigation and not a Security Council referral, after such a withdrawal from the Statute, the ICC's activities in Kenya would have continued to depend entirely on Kenya's willingness to cooperate with the ICC *voluntarily* and *in good faith*. However, voluntary cooperation from the existing Kenyan government would have remained a mere fallacy. Such a "protest withdrawal" in itself would have been an unequivocal gesture that Kenya was officially unwilling to cooperate with the ICC. This could result in a complete paralysis or frustration of the ICC's activities in Kenya, especially with regard to in situ investigations, witness protection, arrest and surrender of the suspects (if necessary), etc.

---

[262] See Statement of the Government of Kenya on the ICC Process in Parliament of Kenya 2010a, pp. 23–45. Although this was the official position of the Kenyan government, it was still reported that subsequently, Kenya attempted to solicit a mass withdrawal of African countries from the Statute. See Akande 2011; The Standard, 10 January 2011.

[263] NB. In September 2013, immediately prior to the original date set for the commencement of trials in respect of the Kenyan President and Deputy President at the ICC, the Kenyan Parliament and Senate passed another resolution to withdraw Kenya from the Statute. However, this move, too, did not result in a withdrawal.

[264] Cf. Heller 2010. For greater detail see Clark 2008, pp. 1178–1179.

Experience from other areas in Africa already indicates that when the position of the states in which the crimes were committed clashes with that of an international tribunal prosecuting the crimes and with which the states are expected to cooperate, such states tend to take deliberate efforts to frustrate the activities of the respective tribunal. There are clear precedents with regard to the activities of the ICTR in Rwanda[265] and those of the ICC in Darfur, Sudan.[266]

To sum up, it can be reiterated that any thinking that Kenya's withdrawal from the Statute would not have affected the ongoing ICC process is not entirely correct.

6.7 The Future of the Kenyan Cases at the ICC

Upon the confirmation of the charges against four out of the six suspects on 23 January 2012, the prospects that the ICC's process in Kenya could be halted through legal means faded drastically. The last attempt to halt the process was lost on 24 May 2012 when the four appeals filed by the four accused challenging the confirmation of charges against them were unanimously rejected by the Appeals Chamber.[267] However, as the preparations for their trial were underway, new developments with both obvious and potential implications on the ICC process emerged and introduced more complications and (potential) challenges to the process.

---

[265] E.g., on 3 November 1999 the Appeals Chamber of the ICTR dismissed the indictment of Jean-Bosco Barayagwiza on procedural grounds thereby ordering his "immediate release". See Decision, *Barayagwiza* ICTR, Appeals Chamber, 3 November 1999. The government of Rwanda, which was interested in having Barayagwiza punished for his alleged role in the 1994 genocide, was infuriated with this decision. It stated expressly that unless Barayagwiza was tried by the Tribunal, Rwanda would no longer cooperate with the ICTR. The Appeal Chamber's decision was reinstituted 4 months later upon review by the Appeals Chamber on the basis of "new facts". See Decision, *Barayagwiza* (ICTR-97-19-AR72), 31 March 2000. However, the period between the dismissal of the indictment and the reinstitution of the case was hard for the ICTR Prosecutor as regards in situ investigations of other cases. The Prosecutor told the Appeals Chamber that in view of Rwanda's express unwillingness to cooperate, she had been denied visa to enter Rwanda, and that 16 witnesses in other cases pending before the ICTR were stopped by Rwandan authorities from testifying before the Tribunal. See Jalloh 2010.

[266] After the indictment of Al Bashir, the Sudanese government is alleged to have told the ICC Prosecutor that "if you send an investigation team, you may already prepare a second one because the first one will not survive". See Ambos 2007, p. 68.

[267] Decision on the Appeals of Ruto and Joshua Sang against the Pre-Trial Chamber's decision on the Confirmation of Charges, *Ruto, Kosgey and Sang* (ICC-01/09-01/11-414), AC, 24 May 2012; Decision on the Appeal of Muthaura and Kenyatta against the Pre-Trial Chamber's Decision on the Confirmation of Charges, *Muthaura, Kenyatta and Ali* (ICC-01/09-02/11-425), AC, 24 May 2012.

6.7.1 Election of the ICC Suspects to Presidency

The most important domestic development came with Kenya's March 2013 presidential election. In this election, two of the ICC suspects, Uhuru Kenyatta and William Ruto, were elected Kenya's President and Deputy President, respectively. The early indications that Kenyatta and Ruto might ascend to power had been seen since the end of 2012 when the two formed separate political parties, The National Alliance (TNA) and the United Republican Party (URP), respectively. Initially, both of them were endorsed by their respective parties as presidential candidates. However, later, the two parties formed a pre-election coalition (alliance) and named it "the Jubilee Alliance". Eventually, the Jubilee Alliance nominated Uhuru Kenyatta as its presidential candidate and William Ruto as Kenyatta's running mate (deputy presidential candidate) for the 2013 elections.[268]

The coming together of Kenyatta and Ruto, who in the 2007 presidential election were in opposing camps, has been described, and correctly so, as "an opportunistic alliance of convenience".[269] It has been argued that had it not been for the common plight facing them at the ICC, the two would not have allied together. The reason is that the relationship between their respective ethnic communities, Kikuyus and Kalenjins, was still sour, given that these are the two communities whose members unleashed attacks against each other during the post-election violence, and that the two communities have since then not been reconciled.[270]

The Kenyatta–Ruto alliance could also be described as a "marriage of convenience" in the light of the ethinicized nature of the Kenyan politics. It has been shown in Chap. 2 that many people in Kenya vote almost "blindly" for a candidate as long as such candidate is from the voter's ethnic community, and that based on the ethnic composition of Kenya's population, there is no possibility of any single ethnic group or tribe to determine decisively the outcome of a presidential election, even if all votes from members of the respective tribe were to be cast in favour of one candidate (see supra Sect. 2.4.2). On the basis of this state of affairs, formal and informal ethno-political alliances have become increasingly inevitable. It is agreed widely that the Kenyatta–Ruto alliance, which brought together mostly Kenyatta's Kikuyu and Ruto's Kalenjin communities, was an important strategy in this regard, as it assured the duo of what newspapers in Kenya commonly referred to as a "tyranny of numbers". This simply refers to a number of voters which is big enough to guarantee an outright victory in the first round of the presidential election or in the run-off, if any. It is on this basis that upon its creation, opinion polls described the Kenyatta–Ruto alliance as a "firm" and "formidable force" that was poised to win the election. The polls placed Uhuru Kenyatta neck to neck to

[268] Daily Nation, 23 December 2012.

[269] See Mueller 2014, p. 25.

[270] See Daily Nation, 28 January 2012; Daily Nation, 24 November 2012; The Star, 23 February 2013.

Raila Odinga, who was also a presidential candidate of yet another ethno-political alliance, the Coalition for Reforms and Democracy (CORD).[271]

These developments gave rise to many questions ahead of the presidential election. These questions entailed uncertainties and speculations about the fate of the Kenyan cases before the ICC in the event that Kenyatta and Ruto were elected to office.[272] In particular, the following questions emerged:

1. Would Kenyatta as president and Ruto as deputy president continue to appear voluntarily before the ICC?
2. Would their government cooperate with the ICC, for example, with regard to investigations and witness protection?
3. If one or both of them were convicted, what implications would this have domestically?
4. What would happen if, for any reason, the ICC replaced the summonses to appear with arrest warrants?
5. What implication would a Kenyatta–Ruto government have on Kenya's diplomatic and international relations?

Again, the answers that the ICC Statute provides for some of the questions above seemed to be more theoretical than realistic in light of the political context of Kenya. For example, it is clear that Article 27 of the ICC Statute provides that the official capacity of a person as, for example, president or deputy president, does not bar the ICC from prosecuting such a person. But this provision in and of itself is not a guarantee that such official capacity will not be used to impair or frustrate the ICC process, especially by creating a difficult environment for the Prosecutor to, among other things, conduct a successful in situ investigation. Already the Al-Bashir precedent amply proves this. Thus, although the new ICC Prosecutor Fatou Bensouda reiterated the principle under Article 27 by stating that "the trials [against Kenyatta and Ruto would] go on irrespective of the outcome of the [upcoming] political process",[273] she could not have been oblivious to the fact that the Kenyatta–Ruto presidency would have the potential of complicating or even negatively affecting her case in such circumstances.

On their part, Kenyatta and Ruto confirmed repeatedly that even if they won the presidential election, they would want to continue cooperating with the ICC voluntarily by, inter alia, attending the trial sessions as scheduled and required, in order

---

[271] E.g. see, Ipsos Synovate 2013, International Crisis Group 2012, pp. 13–16; Kenya Citizen Tv, Dissecting the Opinion Polls, video published on You Tube, 19 February 2013 http://www.youtube.com/watch?feature=player_embedded<&v=ROyf9H929eY#. Viewed September 2014.

[272] See, for example, Kenya National Dialogue and Reconciliation Monitoring Project 2013, para 77; International Crisis Group 2013, pp. 17–19; International Commission of Jurists et al. 2012; The Standard, 20 December 2012.

[273] The Standard, 20 December 2012.

"to clear their names".[274] Despite this "assurance", commentators speculated that Kenyatta and Ruto would continue to cooperate with the ICC only if they were convinced that the trials were in their favour.[275] In general, the "fear" that their government would or could frustrate the cases at the ICC was real. This kept the ICC and other stakeholders of international criminal justice also worried. Moreover, their presidential bid elicited different reactions from the ICC Presidency, Western countries and Kenyan civil society.

For example, pursuant to the unfolding political developments in Kenya, Judge Sang-Hyun Song, President of the ICC, was almost certain that the ICC was heading towards a huge dilemma with regard to the Kenyan cases. He is on record having desperately stated: "We don't know what is going to happen. At the moment, I must admit that the logistic aspect of the Kenya case … is not necessarily easy".[276] On his part, Johnnie Carson, the US Assistant Secretary of State for African Affairs, stated that the duty to elect leaders in Kenya rested with the Kenyan electorate. However, he "reminded" Kenyans that "choices have consequences".[277] Similarly, the French Ambassador to Kenya stated that, as a matter of policy, France and the European Union as a whole would only maintain "essential contact" with the ICC suspects in case they were elected.[278] Some commentators interpreted these statements as "blackmail" from the respective Western countries whose favourite candidate was allegedly Raila Odinga.[279]

The anxiety above made civil society groups in Kenya to take a legal action. They filed a constitutional petition in the Kenyan High Court challenging the constitutionality of the endorsement by the Kenya Independent Electoral and Boundaries Commission (IEBC) of Kenyatta and Ruto to stand for elective positions in the 2013 presidential election irrespective of the serious charges facing them at the ICC. This case is popularly known as "the integrity case".

6.7.2 The Integrity Case

The case, which was decided on 15 February 2013, emanated from four petitions by two individuals and four NGOs filed at the end of 2012. Among other things, the petitioners wanted the High Court to bar Kenyatta and Ruto from standing for elective positions in the upcoming (2013) general elections, because they allegedly lacked the required *integrity* on account of the serious criminal charges facing

---

[274] See, e.g. Standard Group, Kenya Presidential Debate 2013 [Full Video], published on You Tube, 12 February 2013 http://www.youtube.com/watch?v=i89bSa88dOE. Viewed September 2014; International Crisis Group 2013, p. 17.

[275] International Crisis Group 2013, p. 17.

[276] Daily Nation, 13 February 2013.

[277] Daily Nation, 7 February 2013.

[278] Daily Nation, 8 February 2013.

[279] See, New Vision, 10 April 2013.

them before the ICC.[280] The basis of the petition was the "leadership and integrity" provisions under Chapter 6 of Kenya's 2010 Constitution, which require, among other things that the exercise of authority granted to State officials be done in a manner that "brings honour to the nation and dignity to the office"[281]; that the exercise of such authority must promote "public confidence in the integrity of the office"[282]; and that the selection of State officials be entrusted with such authority must be done "on the basis of personal integrity, competence and suitability".[283]

The petitioners argued before the High Court that the ICC had confirmed the charges against Kenyatta and Ruto because there were reasonable grounds to believe that the two had been either "contributors or co-perpetrators" of crimes against humanity. As a result, their election to office of president or deputy president would "not bring honour to the nation or integrity to the office".[284] It was argued that following the confirmation of charges and committal of Kenyatta and Ruto to trial, the duo would have, as a matter of requirement under the ICC Statute, to attend the hearings of their cases at the ICC in person and on "a full-time basis".[285] This, it was argued, would make the duo unable to discharge their constitutional duties (if elected) properly, especially due to their physical absence from the country when attending trial.[286] In addition, it was argued that if for any reason the ICC decided to issue warrants of arrest against the two after being elected to office, Kenya's sovereignty would be greatly undermined.[287] On these grounds, the petitioners asked the court for, inter alia, the following reliefs:

- A declaration that the presumption of innocence in favour of Kenyatta and Ruto did "not override or outweigh the overwhelming public interests" to uphold the Kenyan Constitution[288];
- A declaration that for individuals committed to trial for such heinous international crimes to be allowed to hold public office, it would be "a recipe for anarchy and perpetuate the culture of impunity" in Kenya[289]; and
- An order that Kenyatta and Ruto be permanently barred from being nominated for elections for "engaging in acts of violence, other crimes and strife contrary to the Constitution".[290]

---

[280] *The International Centre for Policy and Conflict and 7 Others v. The Hon. Attorney General and 4 Others, [2013] eKLR* (hereafter "Integrity Judgment").

[281] Constitution of Kenya of 2010, Article 73(1)(a)(iii).

[282] Ibid., Article 73(1)(a)(iv).

[283] Ibid., Article 73(2(a).

[284] Integrity Judgment, paras 13 and 41.

[285] ICC Statute, Article 63.

[286] Integrity Judgment, paras 15, 38 and 39.

[287] Ibid., para 16. For petitioners' arguments on sovereignty see para 40.

[288] Ibid., para 17.

[289] Ibid.

[290] Ibid., para 23.

As expected, Kenyatta and Ruto opposed the petition vigorously, arguing that they had the right to be presumed innocent unless they were proven guilty.[291] Agreeing to their argument, a bench of five High Court judges held unanimously, and correctly, that the end of a confirmation of charges hearing at the ICC was not in and of itself the end of the cases against the two, and for that reason, the final outcome of the trial could not be predicted; that despite the very serious nature of the charges confirmed against the respondents, the presumption of innocence worked in their favour no matter what the end result of the trial might be; and that the Kenyan judiciary did not have the mandate to interfere with the right of Kenyan citizens to choose freely whoever they wanted as their leaders, just as the judiciary also could not rely on speculations as regards the outcome of the cases at the ICC to deny or deprive Kenyatta and Ruto of their constitutional right to seek political leadership at the domestic level.[292] The Kenyan High Court thus cleared Kenyatta and Ruto to stand for the elective positions they desired.

Given the key role they played during the adoption of the ICC Statute, there is no doubt that NGOs are still important stakeholders in pushing for the realization of the ICC agenda, i.e. fighting impunity for the international core crimes. The integrity case should therefore be viewed partly in this context. This was a second time that NGOs in Kenya tried to persuade the domestic courts to uphold certain constitutional values and practices taking into consideration Kenya's commitment to international criminal justice envisaged by the ICC Statute. The first time this happened was when an NGO successfully asked the High Court to issue order that the Kenyan authorities must make sure that they arrest the Sudanese President Omar Al-Bashir if he ever sets his foot in Kenya again in view of the pending ICC arrest warrants against him.[293] The case was filed after Kenya had invited and hosted President Al-Bashir during the promulgation of Kenya's new Constitution in blatant defiance of its obligations under the ICC Statute and the UN Charter.

However, as NGOs continue to spearhead the ICC agenda, it is important to keep in mind that the fundamental individual rights accruing to those suspected to have violated the ICC Statute cannot be extinguished or dispensed with. It is on this basis that the petition seeking to bar Kenyatta and Ruto from vying for elective positions merely on account of the charges facing them at the ICC lacked a firm legal foundation. The presumption of innocence is a fundamental right that even the ICC itself has to uphold.[294] Similarly, at Kenya's domestic level, the presumption of innocence is one of the rights that constitute the elements of a fair trial, and according to Article 55(c) of the 2010 Kenyan Constitution, such rights cannot be subjected to any limitations whatsoever. The petitioners' argument suggesting that the ICC's evidentiary standard for confirmation of charges should

---

[291] Ibid., paras 59 and 60.

[292] Ibid., paras 154–156 and 168(d).

[293] See *Kenya Section of the International Commission of Jurists v. Attorney General* and *Another [2011] eKLR.*

[294] ICC Statute, Article 66.

have overridden the presumption of innocence is not legally tenable, given that even at the ICC level, a confirmation of charges hearing is not a result of a trial or even a mini trial.[295] The presumption of innocence can only be rebutted if the charges have been proved "beyond reasonable doubt" pursuant to a full trial.[296]

However, if viewed from another angle, namely from a perspective which is not purely legal, the integrity case was not completely without merit. It clearly falls under the general question of moral integrity which, even though it did not pass the legal thresholds under the Constitution, cannot or should not be ignored completely. In most mature democracies, a person facing criminal charges already confirmed by such a reputable court like the ICC would usually be relieved of (or resign from) public or official duties (if he or she holds any), or cannot be entrusted with any such duties until his or her name is cleared. This does not have to wait for a total rebuttal of his or her presumption of innocence. However, in most cases, this is usually not a legal requirement or process, but a practice based purely on moral standards or principles of good governance. But in Kenya this was not the case: the respective political parties of Kenyatta and Ruto decided to close their eyes to this fundamental practice and went on to endorse the duo to run for the highest public office. At this stage, the hands of the judiciary were tied: it did not have any powers to deny them their democratic right to vie for elective positions. It remained entirely up to the Kenyan electorate to use their power through the ballot box to bar Kenyatta and Ruto from ascending to presidency, if at all they (voters) felt that the duo were too "tainted" to become their top leaders.[297] But it is the opposite which happened.

Against all odds, on 4 March 2013, Kenyatta won the presidential election by garnering 50.07 % of all the votes cast. Subsequently, the validity of his victory was endorsed by the Supreme Court after being legally challenged by his main opponent.[298] Ultimately, Kenyatta and Ruto were sworn in on 9 April 2013 as Kenya's President and Deputy President, respectively.[299] This intensified the concerns about the fate of the cases at the ICC, especially with regard to the issues of state cooperation.

---

[295] Decision on the Confirmation of Charges, *Katanga and Chui* (ICC-01/04-01/07-717), PTC, 30 December 2008, para 64.

[296] ICC Statute, Article 66(3).

[297] Cf. See Decision on Ruto's Request for Excusal from Continuous Presence at Trial, *Ruto and Sang* (ICC-01/09-01/11-777), TC, 18 June 2013, para 96 (in which the Trial Chamber stated that "it is not…a valid legal proposition that a person charged with a crime may neither run for public office nor be elected as such, even as he enjoys the presumption of innocence until found guilty beyond a reasonable doubt …. Such a proposition requires a clear and solid basis in the law. The Chamber is unaware of any norm of international law that supports such a bar").

[298] See *Raila Odinga v. the Independent Electoral and Boundaries Commission and Three Others,* Petitions No. 5, 4 and 3 of 2013, Supreme Court at Nairobi, [2013] eKLR.

[299] BBC News, 9 April 2013.

6.7.3 Cooperation from the Kenyan Government

Several concerns about Kenya's willingness to cooperate with the ICC had already arisen even before Kenyatta and Ruto were elected to presidency. At the end of 2012, the new ICC Prosecutor Fatou Bensouda visited Kenya where she met with the leaders of the then coalition government to discuss issues pertaining to cooperation with the Court. However, subsequent to her visit, she constantly expressed frustrations, claiming that the Kenyan government was not giving "full cooperation" to her Office. In particular, she claimed that Kenya had denied her Office the required access to key documentary evidence and witnesses. She further alleged that key witnesses that the Prosecution expected to use during trial had been killed, intimidated, or bribed.[300]

On 11 March 2013, barely a month before the date originally set for the commencement of the trial of the two Kenyan cases, the Prosecutor withdrew all charges against Francis Muthaura,[301] because "a critical witness [had] recanted a significant part of his incriminating evidence after the confirmation decision was issued, and [had] admitted accepting bribes from persons allegedly holding themselves out as representatives of [Muthaura and Kenyatta]".[302] As a result of this withdrawal, the case to which Muthaura was a party remained with Kenyatta as the only accused person.

Many more witnesses in both cases withdrew their evidence, especially after the election of Kenyatta and Ruto to presidency. By 15 May 2013 a total of 13 witnesses on whose testimony the Prosecution had expected to rely during trial had withdrawn their evidence.[303] In what suggested that the situation was becoming more complicated, one of the trial judges, Judge Christine Van den Wyngaert, withdrew from the Trial Chamber for the Kenyan cases.[304] Before withdrawing, the judge had complained, inter alia, about "the Prosecution's negligent attitude towards verifying the trustworthiness of its evidence" from witnesses.[305] Another development in this regard occurred on 2 October 2013. On this date, the Pre-Trial Chamber unsealed an arrest warrant issued under seal on 2 August 2013 against Walter Barasa, a Kenyan journalist, accusing him of being part of "a network of people" allegedly operating a "wide scheme" to "sabotage" the *Ruto and Sang* case. Barasa has been indicted officially under Article 70 of the ICC Statute with "corruptly

---

[300]   Daily Nation, 8 February 2013; Daily Nation, 27 February.

[301]   The Guardian, 11 March 2013.

[302]   Prosecution Notification of Withdrawal of the Charges against Francis Muthaura, *Muthaura and Kenyatta* (ICC-01/09-02/11-687), TC, 11 March 2013, para 11 and Decision on the Withdrawal of Charges against Muthaura, *Muthaura and Kenyatta* (ICC-01/09-02/11-696), TC, 18 March 2013.

[303]   Daily Nation, 11 May 2013; Capital News, 5 April 2013.

[304]   See also Aljazeera, 27 April 2013.

[305]   Concurring Opinion of Judge Christine Van den Wyngaert (annexed to Decision on Defence Application pursuant to Article 64(4) and Related Requests) *Kenyatta* (ICC-01/09-02/11-728-Anx2), TC, 26 April 2013.

influencing" or "attempt to corruptly influence" prosecution witnesses so that they withdraw from the case.[306] More recently, in May 2014, there was an assassination attempt on Maina Njenga, the former leader of the *Mungiki* gang, the "organization" which is at the centre of the *Kenyatta case* (see supra Sect. 6.4.2.3.1.2). Subsequent to this assassination attempt, Njenga claimed before a press conference that the police (government) were behind his shooting, as they had discovered that he had recorded a statement with the ICC and that he could have been lined up as one of the Prosecution's witnesses at the ICC. He even claimed that he had previously been approached by a senior politician who urged him not to testify before the ICC.[307]

6.7.4 ICC's Relationship with the AU in View of the Kenyatta and Ruto Cases

Another interesting issue concerning the Kenya situation before the ICC emerged 6 months after Kenyatta and Ruto were sworn in as Kenya's President and Deputy President, respectively. On 12 October 2013, the AU Assembly (Heads of State and Government) convened in Addis Ababa, Ethiopia, for an Extraordinary Session to discuss "Africa's relationship with the ICC", and in particular, to articulate the "AU's position" with regard to the trial of Kenya's President and Deputy President. This meeting was preceded by a meeting of the AU's Executive Council (Foreign Ministers) held on 11 October 2013. This development came exactly 1 month before 12 November 2013, the date on which Kenyatta's trial was expected to commence and almost 1 month after the trial of Ruto and Sang had commenced.

Although it had been speculated initially that the issue of "mass withdrawal" of African states from the ICC would be discussed, it became clear after the Session that such a topic was not on agenda.[308] Instead, two main issues were discussed with regard to the ICC. The first issue generally concerned the manner in which the UN Security Council had hitherto dealt with the concerns raised by the AU in relation to the ICC and particularly with respect to the previous deferral requests by Sudan and Kenya that had been fully backed by the AU (see supra Sect. 6.6.1). The second issue was similar to the first: it concerned the manner in which the ICC had hitherto treated Africa and Africans in general and Kenya in particular.

As regards the second issue above, the AU expressed serious "disappointment against the ICC and its selective approach vis-a-vis Africa". It further condemned the manner in which the ICC has arguably continued to "treat Africa and Africans in

---

[306] See Warrant of Arrest, *Walter Barasa* (ICC-01/09-01/13-1-Red2), PTC, 2 August 2013. Up until August 2014, Barasa, who had been arrested by Kenyan authorities, had not been transferred to the ICC. His transfer was still a subject of legal contestation before the Kenyan Courts.

[307] See "Former Mungiki Boss Links Attempt on His Life to ICC Ties" [video] K24TV, published 30 May 2014 http://www.youtube.com/watch?v=bpe3sZ2R5Pk. Viewed September 2014. See also The Star, 31 May 2014.

[308] See Sudan Tribune, 12 October 2013.

a condescending manner".[309] This particular argument was given an impetus by President Kenyatta, who delivered a strong-worded speech at the AU Extraordinary Session.[310] Kenyatta stated that the "Western powers are the key drivers of the ICC", because 70 % of the Court's budget is currently "being funded by the EU". He consequently argued that "the threat of prosecution" by the ICC is being used as a tool to make "pliant states execute policies favourable to these [Western] countries". Kenyatta also referred contemptuously to how the ICC Prosecutor had even proposed "undemocratic and unconstitutional adjustments to the Kenyan Presidency" on account of the ongoing proceedings against him (Kenyatta) and his Deputy.[311]

In line with Kenyatta's sentiments, the AU lamented about the ICC's lack of concern about Kenya's "legitimate argument" that, given their role as leaders of the Kenyan government, Kenyatta and Ruto must be excused from attending all their trial sessions in person. Kenya's and the AU's argument was that such excusal was necessary for the duo to be able to balance, on the one hand, their obligations towards the ICC and, on the other hand, their constitutional obligations towards the people of Kenya who elected them as their leaders through a democratic process. However, the AU Chairman claimed that by putting forward certain arguments and demands, the goal of the AU was neither to support impunity in Africa nor to mount a "crusade against the ICC". Rather, he insisted, the AU was only making "a solemn call for the [ICC] to take Africa's concerns seriously".[312] It was in this context that at the end of the Extraordinary Session, the AU Assembly came up with a Decision[313] embodying, inter alia, the following controversial pronouncements and demands that:

---

[309] See Opening and Closing Remarks of Tedros Adhanom Ghebreyesus, Minister for Foreign Affairs of the Federal Democratic Republic of Ethiopia and Chairperson of the Executive Council of the African Union at the 15th Extraordinary Session of the Executive Council of the African Union, 11 October 2013 http://www.au.int/en/content/extraordinary-session-assembly-african-union. Accessed September 2014.

[310] See Daily Standard, 13 October 2013 (reproducing fully Kenyatta's speech at the Extraordinary Session of the African Union).

[311] Three weeks before Kenyatta's speech, during the ongoing trial of William Ruto, the Prosecution had suggested, through an oral submission to the Trial Chamber, that Mr. Ruto's functions of Deputy President of Kenya should be delegated to "an appropriate person" so that his trial at the ICC could continue uninterrupted i.e. so that he would not have an excuse to ask for frequent adjournments. The Prosecution was responding to Mr. Ruto's request for a 1-week adjournment so that he could go back to Kenya to assist the President to attend to an urgent matter, a deadly terrorist attack that had happened in Nairobi.

[312] See Remarks by Mr. Hailemariam Dessalegn, Prime Minister of the Federal Democratic Republic of Ethiopia and Chairperson of the African Union at the Extraordinary Session of the Assembly of Heads of State and Government of the African Union, 12 October 2013, p. 7 http://www.au.int/en/content/extraordinary-session-assembly-african-union. Accessed September 2014.

[313] See African Union, Decision Ext/Assembly/AU/Dec.1(Oct. 2013).

- The indictment of African leaders by the ICC is a result of the politicization and misuse of the Court[314];
- Continuing with the indictment against Kenyatta and Ruto while they are serving Head of State and Deputy Head of State, respectively, can undermine, inter alia, the sovereignty, stability, peace and reconciliation in Kenya, and that such indictment per se contravenes the customary international law principle that avails them immunity on the basis of their official positions. Consequently, the AU demanded that the trial against Kenyatta and Ruto be "suspended until they complete their terms of office"[315];
- Since Kenya was at the frontline in the fight against terrorism at the national, regional and international levels, the criminal proceedings against its top leaders would "distract and prevent them from fulfilling their constitutional responsibilities, including national and regional security affairs". Consequently, the AU *instructed* Kenya to make another deferral request to the UN Security Council subsequent to which an AU's high-profile delegation would be sent to the Security Council to lobby in favour of Kenya[316]; and
- Pending the Security Council's consideration of the deferral request, the ICC must postpone the upcoming trial against Kenyatta and suspend the ongoing trial of Ruto. The AU Assembly agreed that if this specific demand was not granted, then President Kenyatta would "not appear" before the ICC until the AU's concerns were "adequately addressed by the UN Security Council and the ICC".[317]

On 21 October 2013, Kenya filed its second deferral request to the Security Council as "guided" by the AU. The request was accompanied by several supporting documents from the AU, including the above-mentioned AU's decision. In its request, Kenya made reference to "the threat to peace, breach of the peace or act of aggression likely to transpire in light of the prevailing and continuing terrorist threat in the Horn of Africa and Eastern Africa". So Kenya requested that the situation be deferred so as "to prevent the aggravation" of the threat.[318] The new argument, namely terrorism as a threat to peace and security, was triggered by the terrorist attack carried out on the Westgate mall in Nairobi on 21 September 2013 by the *al-Shabaab* in which 67 people were killed.[319]

The Security Council met on 15 November 2013, but failed to adopt a resolution in favour of Kenya's request. Although no member of the Council voted against the request, only seven members[320] voted in favour, while eight mem-

---

[314] Ibid., para 4.

[315] Ibid., paras 5, 9 and 10 (ii).

[316] Ibid., paras 6 and 10 (iii) and (ix).

[317] Ibid., paras 10(x) and (xi).

[318] See UN Security Council 2013c.

[319] See Mail Online, 22 September 2013.

[320] Azerbaijan, China, Morocco, Pakistan, Russia, Rwanda and Togo.

bers[321] abstained from voting. This resulted in the lack of the requisite nine affirmative votes to adopt such a resolution.[322] It had been anticipated that Kenya's second deferral bid, just like the first bid, would fail. It had not been foreseen, however, that the failure would result from abstentions. Three out the five permanent members of the Security Council, namely the USA, the UK and France, had already indicated expressly that they were opposed to Kenya's request even before the Security Council convened to deliberate on it.[323] This had given indication that Kenya's deferral request would most probably fail as a result of the use of the veto powers. Prospects of success had been such slim because the core of Kenya's argument, namely terrorism, is generally a global threat which is not necessarily unique to Kenya. Indeed terrorism had become a problem to Kenya before the indictment of Kenyatta and Ruto and more particularly even before their election to office. So it was clear the effort to "capitalize" on the Westgate terrorist attack might convince members of the Security Council to sanction a deferral.

On the other hand, the AU's argument that the ICC should postpone the trial of Kenyatta and Ruto until they finish their term of office was not legally tenable. As argued elsewhere,[324] Article 27 of the ICC Statute, which Kenya has ratified and domesticated, states clearly that immunity for heads of state is not a bar (permanent or temporary) from prosecution for the core crimes under international law. In fact, even Kenya's own Constitution categorically deprives the Kenyan President of such immunity. Although the Kenyan Constitution generally grants immunity from criminal prosecution to "the President or a person performing the functions of that office",[325] such immunity does "not extend to a crime for which the President may be prosecuted under any treaty to which Kenya is a party and which prohibits such immunity".[326] In addition, postponing the trials on the basis of the Kenyatta-Ruto presidency would have been unfair from the point of view of the victims of the post-election violence. The reason is that although the first term of Kenyatta-Ruto presidency will end in 2017, they are still eligible for, and will most likely seek, re-election for another 5-year term to end in 2023. By the year 2023, some witnesses will have either died or their memories about what occurred during the post-election violence will have faded. This will ultimately affect the Prosecution's case, considering the high evidentiary standard required for criminal cases.

As indicated above, one of the decisions reached during the Extraordinary Session of the AU Assembly urged the AU members who are States Parties to the ICC Statute to use the forthcoming meeting of the ICC's Assembly of States Parties (ASP) to propose "relevant amendments" to the ICC Statute that would address the

---

[321] Argentina, Australia, France, Guatemala, Luxembourg, Republic of Korea, UK and USA.

[322] See UN Security Council 2013b.

[323] Daily Nation, 2 November 2013.

[324] See Materu 2014.

[325] Constitution of Kenya of 2010, Article 143(1).

[326] Ibid., Article 143(4).

AU's demands and concerns.[327] One concern that had particularly troubled both Kenya and the AU revolved around Article 63 of the ICC Statute which provides, inter alia, that "the accused shall be present during trial". Upon their election as Kenya's President and Deputy President, it became increasingly concerning that Kenyatta and Ruto's physical absence from the country while attending the trial at the ICC would distract them from performing their constitutional obligations effectively. In trying to address this concern, their defence teams had, before the abovementioned AU Session, strived to have the *presence requirement* under Article 63 interpreted in a manner that would have excused their clients from being required to always be "physically present" in the courtroom during trial. They had argued for an interpretation that would have allowed either attendance via video link or attendance through counsel.[328] The Trial Chamber rejected the idea of trial or attendance via video link, but agreed to grant a conditional excusal to both Kenyatta and Ruto from continuous physical presence during trial on account of their "domestic public duties". According to the Chamber, it was only mandatory for Kenyatta and Ruto to attend physically *some* of the sessions specifically identified in the decision.[329] However, this victory was short-lived. The Appeals Chamber overturned the Trial Chamber's decision by ruling that the physical presence of the accused at the trial is mandatory during *all sessions,* save for strictly exceptional circumstances none of which applied to Kenyatta or Ruto.[330] The Appeals Chamber judgment caused more frustration to Kenya and infuriated the AU.

According to Section 162 of Kenyan International Crimes Act of 2008, the ICC "may sit in Kenya for the purpose of performing any of its functions under the ICC Statute and under the ICC Rules, including (a) taking evidence; (b) conducting or continuing any proceedings; (c) giving judgment in any proceedings". In addition, Section 163 of the same legislation provides that while sitting in Kenya, the ICC "may exercise its functions and powers as provided under the Rome Statute and under the ICC Rules". In view of these provisions, it has been suggested that if the physical absence of Kenyatta and Ruto from the country was truly the main concern of the Kenyan government, the ICC could be asked, as a response to the concern, to consider conducting its proceedings from Kenya, "so that the government [could] keep functioning".[331] However, given the fact that the Kenyan government

---

[327] See African Union, Decision Ext/Assembly/AU/Dec.1(Oct.2013), para 10 (iv) and (vii).

[328] See e.g., Defence Request for Mr Kenyatta to be Present during Trial via Video Link, *Muthaura and Kenyatta* (ICC-01/09-02/11-667), TC, 28 February 2013.

[329] See Decision on Ruto's Request for Excusal from Continuous Presence at Trial, *Ruto and Sang* (ICC-01/09-01/11-777), TC, 18 June 2013; Decision on Defence Request for Conditional Excusal from Continuous Presence at Trial, *Kenyatta* (ICC-01/09-02/11-830), TC, 18 October 2013.

[330] See Judgment on the Appeal of the Prosecutor against the Decision of Trial Chamber on Ruto's Request for Excusal from Continuous Presence at Trial, *Ruto and Sang* (ICC-01/09-01/11-1066), AC, 25 October 2013; Decision on the Prosecution's motion for reconsideration of the decision excusing Mr Kenyatta from Continuous Presence at Trial, *Kenyatta* (ICC-01/09-02/11-863), TC, 26 November 2013.

[331] See Kemp 2014, Sect. 6.6.1.

had already adopted a clear antagonistic stand towards the ICC, it is sufficient to say that this suggestion was (and still is) simply impracticable.

However, it is noteworthy that the efforts by Kenya and the AU were not completely futile in every aspect. On 27 November 2013, amidst the mounting pressure from the AU, the ASP adopted a resolution that amended the Rules of Procedure and Evidence of the ICC.[332] Among other things, the amendments addressed the strict presence requirement under Article 63 and responded directly to some of the AU concerns, particularly those arising in relation to Kenyatta and Ruto trials. The new Rules not only allowed "presence through the use of video technology",[333] but also made it possible for an accused person who has "extraordinary public duties at the highest national level" to be excused from physical presence at trial.[334] On the basis of these new Rules, the Trial Chamber had to issue a fresh decision in respect of Ruto, whose trial had already commenced, excusing him from continuous physical appearance at the trial.[335]

Although the ASP did not address all the concerns raised by Kenya and the AU, the amendment to the Rules was received positively by the AU Assembly in its Ordinary Session of January 2014.[336] The amendment was clearly a diplomatic (and political) compromise which was made to "save" the ICC process in Kenya. It sought to appease both Kenya and the AU by partly accommodating, albeit indirectly, their interests. For that reason, the amendment can also be viewed as some sort of "victory" for both Kenya and the AU. However, given the political environment that led to the adoption of the amendment, these questions arise: Where shall the ASP stop? How often will similar compromises have to be made in future, namely amendments that respond directly to specific political demands? It remains to be seen whether such compromises are healthy for the future of the ICC, especially as regards the exercise of its judicial mandate.

6.7.5 Interim Conclusion

The trend of events analysed above suggests that despite Kenya's and the AU's discontentment about the ongoing ICC process in Kenya, Kenyatta and Ruto will continue to comply with the conditions imposed on them by the ICC, as they are fully aware that they have been indicted in their personal capacities. The same

---

[332] See Resolution ICC-ASP/12/Res.7, 27 November 2013: Amendments to the Rules of Procedure and Evidence, adopted at the 12th Plenary Meeting of the ICC Assembly of States Parties.

[333] See Ibid., Rule 134 *bis*.

[334] See Ibid., Rules 134 *ter* and 134 *quarter.*

[335] See Reasons for the Decision on Excusal from Presence at Trial under Rule 134 *quarter, Ruto and Sang* (ICC-01/09-01/11-1186), TC, 18 February 2014.

[336] See African Union Decision Assembly/AU/Dec.493 (XXII), January 2014, On the Progress Report of the Commission on the Implementation of the Decisions on the International Criminal Court, para 10.

trend of events suggests that Kenyatta and Ruto are not prepared to run the risk of having their summonses to appear replaced with arrest warrants on account of defiance of orders or conditions imposed on them by the ICC.

As the trials continue, evidence will continue to occupy a centre stage in the whole ICC process. But even before the trial of the two cases commenced at the ICC, the Prosecution's case had already started facing enormous challenges with regard to key witnesses.[337] The allegations raised by the Prosecutor regarding bribery, intimidation and killing of witnesses are not trivial at all. Apart from casting doubt on the effectiveness the witness protection measures taken by the OTP, such allegations are an embodiment of the frustrations and helplessness facing that office. So far there are indicators that unless there is strong documentary evidence for the Kenyan cases at the ICC, and unless the current trend of recantation of evidence by witnesses is abated, the Prosecution's case will continue weakening gradually o even completely fall apart, especially with regard to the *Kenyatta trial.* The mere fact that in less than 2 months about 13 witnesses declared withdrawing their evidence could be a pointer to some coordinated or deliberate efforts to accelerate a "natural death" of the cases. The allegations that such efforts emanate from, or are sponsored by, some sources within Kenya cannot be verified here neither can they be ruled out completely.

6.8 Impact of the ICC's Intervention in Kenya

It has been stated that the ICC's intervention in Kenya has already had both negative and positive impact at the domestic level, especially with regard to deterrence.[338] When announcing the decision to open a *proprio motu* investigation into Kenya, the ICC Prosecutor contended particularly that indeed the ICC's intervention was "the only way to prevent the commission of new crimes during the next [2013] elections".[339] One notes that the 2013 general elections in Kenya were unprecedentedly peaceful. The cycle of election violence (see supra Sect. 2.5.2) was broken in these elections, even though the presidential seat was, like in the 2007 election, highly contested by two major ethno-political alliances. A question that arises is whether this peaceful election could, as the Prosecutor hoped, be truly attributed to the ongoing ICC process.

Indeed there could be many factors which contributed to this "breakthrough", but the contribution of the ongoing ICC process in this regard cannot be overstated. The ICC process per se made both ordinary citizens and the political elite in Kenya appreciate the fact that any commission of crimes under international law in Kenya, regardless of the motivation, is no longer an exclusive domestic affair of

---

[337] Cf. Mueller 2014, pp. 33–35.

[338] See Wanyeki 2012, pp. 15–19.

[339] ICC Press Release ICC-OTP-20090716-PR439, 16 July 2009. See also "Ocampo's statement on Kenya" [video] published by NTV Kenya on You Tube, 1 April 2012 http://www.youtube.com/watch?v=Pg4jxfsXT98. Viewed September 2014.

Kenya, and that the fight against impunity for such crimes is now the interest of the international community as a whole. This realization is partly evident in the overwhelming general support and confidence of ordinary Kenyan citizens, including the victims of the 2007–2008 post-election violence, in the ongoing ICC process (see supra Sect. 3.7). In addition, the fact that the ICC judicial process had continued despite numerous efforts to derail it served as a clear and practical lesson to many that even the Kenyan political elite or their allies, who are usually considered to be too powerful for the domestic judicial system to hold accountable, are no longer "safe" as long as the "watchdog", the ICC, exists. Given this realization, the Kenyan political elite, media houses and individual citizens behaved differently and more "decently" during the 2013 election period. Most of them exercised restraint and avoided any thing that could incite ethnic violence before, during or after the elections. It is in this regard that subsequent to the elections, the USA validated Prosecutor's hypothesis by stating that the ICC process in respect to Kenya had indeed *contributed* to the peaceful 2013 elections.[340]

In spite of the foregoing, it is impossible to conclude with certainty that the ICC process in Kenya has achieved *general* deterrence as regards commission of crimes under international law or gross human rights violations generally. In addition, is also impossible to state with absolute certainty that the breakthrough that appears to have been made in 2013, namely deterrence of election violence, will remain true in Kenya's future or whether it will remain only a specific attribute of the 2013 general elections. There are two reasons for this uncertainty. The first reason is that the underlying issues and grievances, especially those pertaining to land and negative ethnicity, which catalysed election violence in the past (supra Sect. 2.5), have not yet been addressed comprehensively.[341] The second reason for the uncertainty is the recurring moves (threats) of Kenyan political elite to withdraw Kenya from the ICC Statute. Assuming this retrogressive goal, namely withdrawal from the Statute, is ultimately achieved, the ICC will cease to be an "immediate danger" to the political elite.[342] This, in effect, could make them revert to their "old ways", namely capitalizing negatively on the existing societal differences and grievances to achieve their political ends.

6.9   Chapter Summary

The chapter has analysed the Kenya situation and cases before the ICC, more specifically its legal and political aspects. It has shown that Kenya was discontented with the ICC's intervention, and that it unsuccessfully tried to use political, legal and diplomatic means to halt the ensuing process. However, as the trial per se was

---

[340] See Daily Nation, 5 April 2013.

[341] Cf. Wanyeki 2012, pp. 16–17.

[342] Of course, this would not abate the "danger" that even after withdrawal from the Statute a situation in Kenya could still be referred to the ICC by the UN Security Council. However, this could be dealt with more easily by political means, including through lobbying.

underway, the cases shrank from the original six suspects to three suspects, and more signs of Prosecution's case weakening are increasingly becoming more evident by day, especially after two of the accused persons were elected as President and Deputy President of Kenya. Besides, a new argument (or challenge), largely political in nature, was introduced by the AU, which came up with several legally untenable demands after the election of Kenyatta and Ruto to office.

The chapter has further shown that due to the prosecutorial discretion of the ICC Prosecutor, the focus of the investigations in the Kenya situation has been only on the crimes which have a direct nexus with the post-election violence, although, in principle, on the basis of the material scope of the authorized investigation, the Prosecutor could have gone beyond the violence. Consequently, the crimes alleged to have been committed in the Mount Elgon area, have escaped the attention of the ICC Prosecutor.

From the jurisprudential point of view, the Kenya situation has been shown to occupy a special place so far. Apart from being the first laboratory from which the jurisprudence on the ICC's *proprio motu* investigation emerges, the situation has triggered a heated debate over an important issues of procedural and substantive criminal law. The most prominent issue is how to interpret an "organizational policy" in the definition of crimes against humanity per Article 7(2)(a) of the ICC Statute. The chapter has clarified and analysed the arising legal issues and debate, and has concluded that in interpreting the said provision of the ICC Statute, the prospective nature of the ICC should play a role, and that in so doing the main spirit of the Statute, namely the fight against impunity for the core crimes, should override any unjustifiable restrictions.

References

Abass A (2013a) Prosecuting international crimes in Africa: rationale, prospects and challenges. Eur J Int Law 24(3):933–946

Abass A (2013b) The proposed international criminal jurisdiction for the African Court: some problematical aspects. Neth Int Law Rev LX:27–50

African Union, Decision Ext/Assembly/AU/Dec.1 (Oct. 2013) on Africa's relationship with the International Criminal Court (ICC), adopted at the extra-ordinary session of the Assembly of African Union, Addis Ababa, Ethiopia, 12 Oct 2013

Akande D (2011) Is Kenya pushing a mass African withdrawal from the ICC. EJIL Talk. http://www.ejiltalk.org/is-kenya-pushing-for-a-mass-african-withdrawal-from-the-icc/. Accessed Sept 2014

Akhavan P (2005) Developments at the International Criminal Court: the Lord's Resistance Army case: Uganda's submission of the first state referral to the International Criminal Court. Am J Int Law 99:403–421

Akhavan P (2010) Self-referrals before the International Criminal Court: are states the villains or the victims of atrocities? Crim Law Forum 21:103–120

Akhavan P (2011) International criminal justice in the era of failed states: the ICC and the self-referral debate. In: Stahn C, El Zeidy M (eds) The International Criminal Court and complementarity, vol I. Cambridge University Press, New York

Ambos K (2007) Prosecuting international crimes at national level: between justice and realpolitik. In: Kalek W et al (eds) International prosecution of human rights crimes. Springer, Berlin

Ambos K (2010) International criminal law at the crossroads: from *ad hoc* imposition to a treaty-based universal jurisdiction. In: Stahn C, Van den Herik L (eds) The future perspectives of international criminal justice. T.M.C Asser Press, The Hague

Ambos K (2013) Expanding the focus of the African Criminal Court. In: McDermott Y et al (eds) Ashgate research companion to international criminal law: critical perspectives. Ashgate Publishing Company, Aldershot

Alai C, Mue N (2011) Complementarity and the impact of the Rome Statute and the International Criminal Court in Kenya. In: Stahn C, El Zeidy M (eds) The International Criminal Court and complementarity, vol II. Cambridge University Press, New York

Arsanjani MH, Reisman W (2005) The law-in-action of the International Criminal Court. Am J Int Law 99(2):385–403

Asaala EO (2012) The International Criminal Court factor on transitional justice in Kenya. In: Ambos K, Maunganidze OA (eds) Power and prosecution: challenges and opportunities for international criminal justice in Sub-Saharan Africa. Universitätsverlag, Göttingen

Askin KD (2002) Reflections on some of the most significant achievements of the ICTY. New Engl Law Rev 37(4):903–914

Badar ME (2004) From the Nuremberg Charter to the Rome Statute: defining the elements of crimes against humanity. San Diego Int Law J 5(73):73–144

Bantekas I (2010) International criminal law, 4th edn. Hart Publishing, Portland

Batros B (2011) The evolution of the ICC jurisprudence on admissibility. In: Stahn C, El Zeidy M (eds) The International Criminal Court and complementarity, vol I. Cambridge University Press, New York

Bassiouni MC (1987) A draft international criminal code and draft Statute for an international criminal tribunal. Martinus Nijhoff Publishers, Dordrecht

Bassiouni MC (1992) Crimes against humanity in international criminal law. Martinus Nijhoff Publishers, Leiden

Bekou O (2011) In the hands of states: implementing legislation and complementarity. In: Stahn C, El Zeidy M (eds) The International Criminal Court and complementarity, vol II. Cambridge University Press, New York

Benzing M (2003) The complementarity regime of the International Criminal Court: international criminal justice between states sovereignty and the fight against impunity. Max Plank Yearb U N Law 7:591–632

Bergsmo M, Kruger P (2008) Article 53: Initiation of an investigation. In: Triffterer O (ed) Commentary on the Rome Statute of the International Criminal Court: observers' notes article by article, 2nd edn. Verlag C.H Beck oHG, München

Bergsmo M, Pejic J (2008a) Article 15: Prosecutor. In: Triffterer O (ed) Commentary on the Rome Statute of the International Criminal Court: observers' notes article by article, 2nd edn. Verlag C.H Beck oHG, München

Bergsmo J, Pejic J (2008b) Article 16: Deferral of investigation or prosecution. In: Triffterer O (ed) Commentary on the Rome Statute of the International Criminal Court: observers' notes article by article, 2nd edn. Verlag C.H Beck oHG, München

Boas G et al (2011) International criminal law practitioner library. International criminal procedure. Cambridge University Press, New York

Boot M et al (2008) Article 7: Crimes against humanity. In: Triffterer O (ed) Commentary on the Rome Statute of the International Criminal Court: observers' notes article by article, 2nd edn. Verlag C.H Beck oHG, München

Broomhall B (1999) The International Criminal Court: a checklist for national implementation. Nouvelles Etudes Penales 13:113–159

Brown S, Sriram CL (2012) The big fish won't fry themselves: criminal accountability for post-election violence in Kenya. African Aff 111(443):244–260

Bushnell D (2009) Re-thinking international criminal law: re-connecting theory with practice in the search for justice and peace. Aust Yearb Int Law 28:57–89

Carter LE (2010) The principle of complementarity and the International Criminal Court: the role of ne bis in idem. Santa Clara J Int Law 8(1):165–198

Cassese A (2008) International law, 2nd edn. Oxford University Press, New York

Chella J (2004) Persecution: a crime against humanity in the Rome Statute of the International Criminal Court. LL.M Dissertation, University of Bond

Ciampi A (2008) The proceedings against President Al Bashir and the prospects of their suspension under Article 16 ICC Statute. J Int Crim Justice 6:885–897

Clark RS (2008) Article 27: Withdrawal. In: Triffterer O (ed) Commentary on the Rome Statute of the International Criminal Court: observers' notes article by article, 2nd edn. Verlag C.H Beck oHG, München

Costello G (2006) Statutory interpretation: general principles and recent trends, CRS Report for Congress, updated 30 March 2006. Congressional Research Service, Library of Congress

Cote L (2012) Independence and impartiality. In: Reydams L et al (eds) International prosecutors. Oxford University Press, Oxford

Cupido M (2011) The policy underlying crimes against humanity: practical reflections on a theoretical debate. Crim Law Forum [Online] 22(3). file:///C:/Users/Materu/Downloads/SSRN-id1959777.pdf. Accessed Sept 2014

Damgaard C (2008) Individual criminal responsibility for core international crimes. Springer, Heidelberg

DeGuzman MM (2000) The road from Rome: the developing law of crimes against humanity. Hum Rights Q 22(2):335–403

DeGuzman MM (2008) Article 21: Applicable law. In: Triffterer O (ed) Commentary on the Rome Statute of the International Criminal Court: observers' notes article by article, 2nd edn. Verlag C.H Beck oHG, München

Dersso SA (2012) African solutions to African problems should be more than just a Cliché. Institute of Security Studies. http://www.polity.org.za/article/african-solutions-to-african-problems-should-be-more-than-just-a-clich-2012-03-30. Accessed Sept 2014

DeSmet S (2009) A structural analysis of the role of the Pre-Trial Chamber in the fact-finding process of the ICC. In: Stahn C, Sluiter G (eds) The emerging practice of the International Criminal Court. Martinus Nijhoff Publishers, Leiden

Ellis MS (2011) The contribution of non-governmental organizations to the creation of international criminal tribunals. In: Brown BS (ed) Research handbook on international criminal law. Edward Elgar, Cheltenham

El Zeidy MM (2008a) The principle of complementarity in international criminal law: origin, development and practice. Martinus Nijhoff Publishers, Leiden

El Zeidy MM (2008b) Form primacy to complementarity and backwards: (re)-visiting Rule 11 bis of the ad hoc tribunals. Int Comp Law Quart 57(2):403–415

Eskridge WN (1987) Dynamic statutory interpretation. Univ Pa Law Rev 135:1479–1555

Garner BA (1999) Black's law dictionary, 7th edn. West Group, St Paul

Gevers C, Du Plessis M (2011) Another stormy year for the International Criminal Court and its work in Africa. http://papers.ssrn.com/sol3/papers.cfm?abstract_id=1870965. Accessed Sept 2014

Gioia F (2006) State sovereignty, jurisdiction and "modern" international law: The principle of complementarity in the International Criminal Court. Leiden J Int Law 19(4):1095–1123

Hafner G (2005) An attempt to explain the position of the USA towards the ICC. J Int Crim Justice 3:323–332

Hall GR (1998) Statutory interpretation in the Supreme Court of Canada: the triumph of a common law methodology. Advocates Q 21:38–65

Hall CK (2011) Positive complementarity in action. In: Stahn C, El Zeidy MM (eds) The International Criminal Court and complementarity, vol II. Cambridge University Press, New York

Halling M (2010) Push the envelope—watch it bend: removing the policy requirement and extending crimes against humanity. Leiden J Int Law 23:827–845

Hansen TO (2011) The policy element in crimes against humanity: lessons from and for the case of Kenya. George Wash Int Law Rev 43:1–41

Hansen TO (2013) Africa and the International Criminal Court. In: Murithi T (ed) Handbook of Africa's international relations. Routledge, New York

Heller KJ (2010) Kenya moves closer to withdrawing from the ICC. Opino Juris. http://opinioj uris.org/2010/12/23/kenya-moves-closer-to-withdrawing-from-the-icc/. Accessed Sept 2014

Heller KJ (2011) The irritating ICC prosecutor. Opino Juris. http://opiniojuris.org/2011/04/09/. Accessed Sept 2014

Human Rights Watch (2008) All the men have gone. In: War crimes in Kenya's Mount Elgon conflict. Human Rights Watch, New York. ISBN:1-56432-363-3

Human Rights Watch (2011) "Holding Your Hear": waiting for justice in Kenya's Mount Elgon Region. Human Rights Watch, New York. ISBN 1-56432-818-X

Hwang P (1998–1999) Defining crimes against humanity in the Rome Statute of the International Criminal Court. Fordham Int Law J 22:457–504

International Commission of Jurists-Kenya et al (2012) Report on the implications of a Kenyatta/Ruto Presidency in Kenya. http://kenyastockholm.files.wordpress.com/2013/02/kenyatta-ruto-report.pdf. Accessed Sept 2014

International Criminal Court (2003a) Informal expert paper: the principle of complementarity in practice. http://www.iclklamberg.com/Caselaw/OTP/Informal%20Expert%20paper%20The%20principle%20of%20complementarity%20in%20practice.pdf. Accessed Sept 2014

International Criminal Court (2003b) Paper on some policy issues before the office of the prosecutor. http://www.icc-cpi.int/NR/rdonlyres/1FA7C4C6-DE5F-42B7-8B25-60AA962ED8B6/143594/030905_Policy_Paper.pdf. Accessed Sept 2014

International Criminal Court (2003c) Second assembly of states parties to the Rome Statute of the International Criminal Court Report of the Prosecutor of the ICC, Mr Luis Moreno-Ocampo, 8 Sept 2003. http://www.icc-cpi.int/NR/rdonlyres/C073586C-7D46-4CBE-B901-0672908E8639/143656/LMO_20030908_En.pdf. Accessed Sept 2014

International Criminal Court (2011) Report on preliminary examination activities. http://www.icc-cpi.int/NR/rdonlyres/63682F4E-49C8-445D-8C13-F310A4F3AEC2/284116/OTPReportonPreliminaryExaminations13December2011.pdf. Accessed Sept 2014

International Crisis Group (2012) Kenya: impact of the ICC Proceedings. Africa briefing No. 84. http://www.crisisgroup.org/~/media/Files/africa/horn-of-africa/kenya/B084%20Kenya%20—%20Impact%20of%20the%20ICC%20Proceedings. Accessed Sept 2014

International Crisis Group (2013) Kenya's 2013 elections. Africa report No. 197. http://www.crisisgroup.org/~/media/Files/africa/horn-of-africa/kenya/197-kenyas-2013-elections. Accessed Sept 2014

Ipsos Synovate (2013) Presidential race too close to call—an inevitable runoff? http://www.rich.co.ke/rcfrbs/docs/Ipsos%20Synovate%20Polls%20_President_Alliances%20Support%20Levels_January%202013.pdf. Accessed Sept 2014

Jalloh CC (2010) Kenyan parliament endorses Ruto Motion calling for withdrawal from ICC Statute. International criminal law in ferment blog. http://iclferment.blogspot.com/2010/12/kenyan-parliament-endorses-ruto-motion.html. Accessed Sept 2014

Jalloh CC (2011) International decision: situation in the Republic of Kenya No. ICC-01/09-19, decision on the authorization of an investigation. Am J Int Law 105:541–547

Jalloh CC (2012a) Kenya vs. The ICC Prosecutor. Harv Int Law J Online 53:269–285

Jalloh CC (2012b) Lecture. Africa and the International Criminal Court: collision course or cooperation? N C Cent Law Rev 34:203–229

Kemp G (2014) The implementation of the Rome Statute in Africa. In: Werle G et al (eds) Africa and the International Criminal Court. T.M.C Asser Press, The Hague

Kenya National Commission on Human Rights (2007) "Still behaving badly" second periodic report of the election-monitoring project. KNCHR, Nairobi

Kenya National Commission on Human Rights (2008a) "The Mountain of Terror": a report on the investigations of torture by the military at Mount Elgon. KNCHR, Nairobi

Kenya National Commission on Human Rights (2008b) On the brink of the precipice: a [Report on] human rights account of Kenya's post-2007 election violence. KNCHR, Nairobi

Kenya National Dialogue and Reconciliation (KNDR) Monitoring Project (2013) Kenya's 2013 general election: review of preparedness (Report). Nairobi

Kenya Truth, Justice and Reconciliation Commission (2013) Final report of the Kenyan Truth, Justice and Reconciliation Commission, Volumes I, IIA, IIB, IIC, III and IV. Nairobi

Keppler E (2011) Managing setbacks for the International Criminal Court in Africa. J Afr Law 1–14

Kress C (2003) The procedural law of the International Criminal Court in outline: Anatomy of a unique compromise. J Int Crim Justice 1:603–617

Kress C (2010) On the outer limits of crimes against humanity: the concept of organization within the policy requirement: some reflections on the March 2010 ICC Kenya decision. Leiden J Int Law 23:855–873

Kuperstein S (2011) Updates from the international criminal tribunals. Human Rights Brief 18(3):56–57

Marchesi A (2008) Article 14: Referral of a situation by a state party. In: Triffterer O (ed) Commentary on the Rome Statute of the International Criminal Court: observers' notes article by article, 2nd edn. Verlag C.H Beck oHG, München

Materu SF (2014) A strained relationship: reflections on the AU's stand towards the ICC from the Kenyan experience. In: Werle G et al (eds) Africa and the International Criminal Court. T.M.C Asser Press, The Hague

May L (2005) Crimes against humanity: a normative account. Cambridge University Press, Cambridge

May L (2010) A note on state policy and crimes against humanity. In: Oxford transitional justice research working paper series. http://www.csls.ox.ac.uk/documents/May_StatePolicy_Final_OTJR.pdf. Accessed Sept 2014

Mettraux G (2002) Crimes against humanity in the jurisprudence of the international *criminal tribu*nals for the Former Yugoslavia and for Rwanda. Harv Int Law J 43:237–316

Mills K (2012) "Bashir is dividing Us": Africa and the International Criminal Court. Human Rights Q 34(2):404–417

Moreno-Ocampo L (2011) A positive approach to complementarity: the impact of the office of the prosecutor. In: Stahn C, El Zeidy MM (eds) The International Criminal Court and complementarity: from theory to practice, vol I. Cambridge University Press, New York

Mueller SD (2014) Kenya and the International Criminal Court (ICC): politics, the election and the law. J East Afr Stud 8(1):25–42

Muller AT, Stegmiller I (2010) Self-referrals on trial: from panacea to patient. J Int Crim Justice 8:1267–1294

Murithi T (2012) Africa's relationship with the ICC: a need for restoration? Perspectives 1(12). http://www.boell.de/sites/default/files/2012-08-Perspectives_Africa_1_12.pdf.   Accessed Sept 2014

Murithi T (2013) The African Union and the International Criminal Court: an embattled relationship? Policy brief No. 8, March 2013. Institute for Justice and Reconciliation. http://ijr.org.za/publications/pb10.php. Accessed Sept 2014

Murungu CB (2011) Towards a Criminal Chamber in the African Court of Justice and Human Rights. J Int Crim Justice 9:1067–1088

Nash K (2007) A comparative analysis of justice in post genocidal Rwanda: fostering a sense of peace and reconciliation? Africana 1(1):59–100

NewAfrican (2012) ICC versus Africa: the scales of injustice. http://www.exacteditions.com/read/new-african/march-2012-30589/3/3. Accessed Sept 2014

Ngari A (2012) Kenya's ongoing battle with complementarity at the ICC. http://www.icckenya.org/2012/05/kenyas-ongoing-battle-with-complementarity-at-the-icc/. Accessed Sept 2014

Nouwen SMH (2011) Fine-Tuning Complementarity. In: Brown BS (ed) Research handbook on international criminal law. Edward Elgar, Northampton

Nsereko DDN (2008) Article 18: Preliminary rulings regarding admissibility, In: Triffterer O (ed) Commentary on the Rome Statute of the International Criminal Court: observers' notes article by article, 2nd edn. Verlag C.H Beck oHG, München

Office of the Prosecutor (2003a) Informal paper: the principle of complementarity in practice. http://www.iclklamberg.com/Caselaw/OTP/Informal%20Expert%20paper%20The%20principle%20of%20complementarity%20in%20practice.pdf. Accessed Sept 2014

Office of the Prosecutor (2003b) Paper on some policy issues before the office of the prosecutor. http://www.icc-cpi.int/nr/rdonlyres/1fa7c4c6-de5f-42b7-8b25-60aa962ed8b6/143594/030905_policy_paper.pdf. Accessed Sept 2014

Office of the Prosecutor (2006) Report on the activities performed during the first three years (June 2003–June 2006). http://www.icc-cpi.int/NR/rdonlyres/D76A5D89-FB64-47A9-9821-725747378AB2/143680/OTP_3yearreport20060914_English.pdf. Accessed Sept 2014

Office of the Prosecutor (2009) Agreed minutes of the meeting between Prosecutor Moreno-Ocampo and the Delegation of the Kenyan government. http://www.icc-cpi.int/NR/rdonlyres/1CEB4FAD-DFA7-4DC5-B22D-E828322D9764/280560/20090703AgreedMinutesofMeetingProsecutorKenyanDele.pdf. Accessed Sept 2014

Olasolo H (2012) Essays on international criminal justice. Hart Publishing, Portland

Olasolo H, Cernero-Rojo E (2011) The application of the principle of complementarity to the decision of where to open an investigation: the admissibility of "situation". In: Stahn C, El Zeidy MM (eds) The International Criminal Court and complementarity, vol I. Cambridge University Press, New York

Parliament of Kenya (2008) Official Hansard reports. Doc. Hansard 04.12.08. Nairobi

Parliament of Kenya (2009) Official Hansard reports. Doc. Hansard 27.01.09. Nairobi

Parliament of Kenya (2010a) Official Hansard reports. Doc. Hansard 16.12.10P. Nairobi

Parliament of Kenya (2010b) Official Hansard reports. Doc. Hansard 22.12.10P. Nairobi

Pichon J (2008) The principle of complementarity in the cases of Sudanese nationals *Ahmed Harun* and *Ali Kushaby* before the International Criminal Court. Int Crim Rev 8:185–228

Rastan R (2011) Situation and case: defining the parameters. In: Stahn C, El Zeidy MM (eds) The International Criminal Court and complementarity, vol I. Cambridge University Press, New York

Ratner SR et al (2009) Accountability for human rights atrocities in international law: beyond the Nuremberg Legacy, 3rd edn. Oxford University Press, New York

Robinson D (1999) Crimes against humanity at the Rome Conference. Am J Int Law 93(1):43–57

Robinson D (2010) The two liberalisms of international criminal law. In: Stahn C, Van den Herik L (eds) Future perspectives on international criminal justice. T.M.C. Asser Press, The Hague

Robinson D (2011a) Essence of crimes against humanity raised by challenges at ICC. EJIL: Talk (The blog of the European Journal of International Law). http://www.ejiltalk.org/essence-of-crimes-against-humanity-raised-by-challenges-at-icc. Accessed Aug 2014

Robinson D (2011b) The inaction controversy: neglected words and new opportunities. In: Stahn C, El Zeidy MM (eds) The International Criminal Court and complementarity, vol I. Cambridge University Press, Cambridge

Sadat LN (2012a) Emerging from the shadow of Nuremberg: crimes against humanity in the modern age. http://works.bepress.com/cgi/viewcontent.cgi?article=1000&context=leilasadat. Accessed Sept 2012

Sadat LN (2012b) Crimes against humanity in the modern age. In: Washington University in St. Louis egal Studies Research Paper Series Paper No. 11-11-04. file:///C:/Users/Materu/Desktop/SSRN-id2013254.pdf. Accessed Sept 2014

Schabas WA (2000) Perverse effects of the *Nulla Poena* principle: national practice and ad hoc tribunals. Eur J Int Law 11:521–539

Schabas WA (2006a) First prosecutions at the International Criminal Court. Hum Rights Law J 27(1–4):25–40

Schabas WA (2006b) The "Odious Scourge" evolving interpretations of the crime of genocide. Genocide Stud Prev 1:93–106

Schabas WA (2007) An introduction to the International Criminal Court, 3rd edn. Cambridge University Press, New York

Schabas WA (2008) State policy as an element of international crimes. J Crim Law Criminol 98(3):953–982

Schabas WA (2009) Prosecutorial discretion and gravity. In: Stahn C, Sluiter G (eds) The emerging practice of the International Criminal Court. Martinus Nijhoff Publishers, Leiden

Schabas WA (2010) Prosecuting Dr. Strangelove, Goldfinger, and the Joker at the International Criminal Court: closing the loopholes. Leiden J Int Law 23:847–853

Schabas WA (2011) An introduction to the International Criminal Court, 4th edn. Cambridge University Press, New York

Schabas WA, Shibahara K (2008) Article 61: confirmation of charges before trial. In: Triffterer O (ed) Commentary on the Rome Statute of the International Criminal Court: observers' notes article by article, 2nd edn. Verlag C.H Beck oHG, München

Schiff BN (2008) Building the International Criminal Court. Cambridge University Press, New York

Scott J (2010) Codified cannons and common law of interpretation. Georgetown Law J 98(341):341–431

Seils PF (2011) Making complementarity work: maximizing the limited role of the prosecutor. In: Stahn C, El Zeidy MM (eds) The International Criminal Court and complementarity, vol II. Cambridge University Press, New York

Sing'Oei AK (2010) The ICC Arbiter in Kenya's post-election violence. Minnesota J Int Law Online 19:5–20

Sriram CL (2009) The International Criminal Court Africa experiment—The Central African Republic, Darfur, Northern Uganda and the Democratic Republic of the Congo. In: Sriram CL, Pillay S (eds) Peace versus justice? The dilemma of transitional justice in Africa. University of KwaZulu-Natal Press, Cape Town

Stahn C (2009) Judicial review of prosecutorial discretion: five years on. In: Stahn C, Sluiter G (eds) The emerging practice of the International Criminal Court. Martinus Nijhoff Publishers, Leiden

Stahn C, El Zeidy M (eds) (2011) The International Criminal Court and complementarity, vol I. Cambridge University Press, New York

Stevenson A (ed) (2007) Shorter Oxford English dictionary, 6th edn. Oxford University Press, Oxford

Stigen J (2008) The relationship between the International Criminal Court and national jurisdictions: the principle of complementarity. Nijhoff Martinus Publishers, Leiden

Struett MJ (2008) The politics of constructing, the International Criminal Court: NGOs, discourse and agency. Palgrave Macmillan, New York

United Nations Development Programme (2009) Mount Elgon conflict: a rapid assessment of the underpinning socio-economic, governance and security factor. In: Amani Papers. http://www.ke.undp.org/content/kenya/en/home/operations/projects/peacebuilding/amani-papers-/. Accessed Sept 2014

United Nations General Assembly (2009) Report of the International Criminal Court to the United Nations for 2008/2009, UN Doc. A/64/356, 17 Sept 2009

United Nations International Law Commission (1996) Yearbook of the international law commission, vol II, Part 2. United Nations, New York

United Nations Security Council (2013a) The rule of law: the Security Council and accountability, cross-cutting report No. 1, 18 Jan 2013

United Nations Security Council (2013b) Security Council resolution seeking deferral of Kenyan leaders' trial fails to win adoption, with 7 voting in favour, 8 abstaining. http://www.un.org/News/Press/docs/2013/sc11176.doc.htm. Accessed August 2014

United Nations Security Council (2013c) Identical letters dated 21 October 2013 from the Permanent Representative of Kenya to the United Nations addressed to the Secretary-General and the President of the Security Council, S/2013/624, 22 October 2013. http://www.securitycouncilreport.org/atf/cf/%7B65BFCF9B-6D27-4E9C-8CD3-CF6E4FF96FF9%7D/s_2013_624.pdf. Accessed Sept 2014

Villa-Vicencio C (2011) The ICC in Africa. Think 26:38–41

Wanyeki LM (2012) The International Criminal Court's cases in Kenya: origin and impact. In: Institute of Security Studies, paper no 237. http://www.issafrica.org/uploads/Paper237.pdf. Accessed Sept 2014

Watson G (2003) The changing jurisprudence of the International Criminal Tribunal for the Former Yugoslavia. N Engl Law Rev 37(4):871–885

Weldehaimanot SM (2011) Arresting Al-Bashir: the African Union's opposition and the legalities. Afr J Int Comp Law 19(2):208–235

Werle G (2009) Principles of international criminal law, 2nd edn. T.M.C Asser Press, The Hague

Werle G, Burghardt B (2012) Do crimes against humanity require the participation of a state or a "State-Like" organization? J Int Crim Justice 10(5):1151–1170

Werle G et al (eds) (2014) Africa and the International Criminal Court. T.M.C Asser Press, The Hague

Williams SA (2004) Cambodian extraordinary chambers—a dangerous precedent for international justice. Int Crim Law Q 53:227–245

William SA (2008) Article 13: Exercise of Jurisdiction. In: Triffterer O (ed) Commentary on the Rome Statute of the International Criminal Court: observers' notes article by article, 2nd edn. Nomos Verlagsgesellschaft, Baden-Baden

William SA, Schabas WA (2008) Article 17—Issues of admissibility. In: Triffterer O (ed) Commentary on the Rome Statute of the International Criminal Court: observers' article by article, 2nd edn. Verlag C.H Beck oHG, München

Chapter 7
Conclusion

Abstract This chapter carries a comprehensive summary of the book. It brings together the main conclusions made in the preceding chapters. It also embodies author's recommendations.

The study has analysed the historical background and domestic and international responses to the 2007–2008 post-election violence in Kenya. Its main focus has been on the criminal accountability for the crimes against humanity committed during the violence. The study was based on two legal premises. The first premise is that crimes against humanity, like the other core crimes under international law, namely war crimes, genocide and aggression, has acquired a jus cogens status, which has elevated it to a level above that of "ordinary" crimes that are usually found in most domestic criminal codes. Consequently, commission of a core crime is no longer a concern of one individual state (e.g. the state of commission) but of the international community as a whole. The second premise, which flows directly from the first, is that there is a clear consensus, a principle under international customary law, which requires that impunity for the core crimes must not be tolerated. The state on whose territory a core crime has occurred has a duty to investigate and prosecute those who bear major responsibility for the crimes. If the state of commission does not perform its duty, for example by remaining inactive, or when it is unable or unwilling to conduct genuine investigations and prosecutions in its domestic courts, then the ICC can justifiably intervene, in order to minimize the looming impunity gap (supra Sect. 1.2). Kenya associated itself with this global consensus by signing, ratifying and domesticating the ICC Statute.

The main objectives of the study were framed in terms of four specific questions. The first objective was to locate and analyse the link between Kenya's post-election violence and the country's previous socio-political history with a view to understanding prospects and challenges that could be faced when trying to address criminal accountability for the crimes committed during the violence. The second objective was to outline and analyse the structure and implementation of the road map for criminal accountability that was agreed upon at the domestic level. This includes identifying and examining other domestic legal options (frameworks) for

S.F. Materu, *The Post-Election Violence in Kenya*,
International Criminal Justice Series 2, DOI 10.1007/978-94-6265-041-1_7

the prosecution of the core crimes under international law with a view to examining the extent to which Kenya has utilized the options to hold the perpetrators of the post-election violence criminally accountable. The third objective was to locate the link or interplay between retributive and restorative justice mechanisms implemented in Kenya subsequent to the post-election violence, with a view to establishing how such interplay could foster or impair the search for criminal accountability for the crimes in question. The last objective was to evaluate the ICC's intervention in Kenya, particularly providing an extensive critical analysis of the main legal issues linked to or so far arising out of such intervention. The following are the main conclusions.

The background to the 2007–2008 post-election violence in Kenya can clearly be traced to the country's post-colonial history. Throughout the four decades in which Kenya was under dictatorial regimes (1963–2002), the political leadership was an imperial presidency based on a single party system. These successive regimes deliberately used both tyranny and negative ethnicity, originally encouraged by the British colonialists, to consolidate power. During the dictatorial regimes of the first two presidents, Jomo Kenyatta and Daniel Arap Moi, feelings of ethnic and economic marginalization grew very strong among various communities and individual citizens who perceived or believed that people from the president's community had more privileges than those from other communities (supra Sects. 2.2 and 2.3).

Since the re-establishment of multi-party democracy in 1991, the emerging political parties resorted to the formation of political (party) alliances which were (still are) mere tribal outfits and which, in most cases, were (still are) expected to champion interests of specific ethnic communities (supra Sect. 2.4). On the basis of these unhealthy trends in the local politics, both the state and individual politicians developed a culture of creating, sponsoring or exploiting exiting criminal gangs to perpetuate ethno-political agendas. This constituted a catalyst and recipe for recurring electoral violence in 1992, 1997 and 2002. During such kind of violence, atrocious crimes were always committed but no one was held criminally accountable, even though various commissions of inquiry recommended so. The culture of impunity for crimes, especially those involving the political elite, became an entrenched feature (culture) in the Kenyan politics (supra Sect. 2.5). The same factors were responsible for the 2007–2008 post-election violence which was, therefore, not a total surprise.

With the help of the AU mediation team, it was agreed in the aftermath of the 2007–2008 violence that the resulting crimes could only be dealt with meaningfully if addressed together with the historical factors that had previously divided Kenyans and which had constituted a recipe for recurring election violence (supra Sects. 3.2–3.4). So it was considered important that a multifaceted approach involving a combination of various transitional justice mechanisms is taken. Due to the fact that the atrocities committed seemed to have amounted to crimes against humanity, and also because they occurred at the time when the international community as a whole was against impunity for such crimes, a promising road map was put in place to ensure that perpetrators, especially those who bear major criminal responsibility for the crimes, were investigated, prosecuted and punished primarily by Kenya itself or secondarily by the ICC if Kenya failed to do so (supra Sects. 3.4.3 and 3.4.4).

Criminal accountability at the domestic level in respect of the alleged main perpetrators has been bedevilled by politics, and has largely remained a myth— a subject of mere talk. Kenya has failed to prosecute this group of perpetrators, not because it lacks a sufficient domestic legal framework, but because it lacks the political will to do so. Even though the attempts to create the agreed Special (local) Tribunal to try the perpetrators failed, their conduct could still be punished sufficiently if prosecuted under the Kenyan Penal Code as "ordinary crimes". Alternatively, the atrocities could even be prosecuted as "crimes against humanity" as such under customary international law or Kenya's International Crimes Act of 2008 if some necessary legislative amendments were done (supra Sects. 4.3.1 and 4.3.2). However, given the knowledge gap among domestic prosecutors in Kenya, it has been contended that the ordinary-crime approach remains the best way to prosecute the crimes at the domestic level. Domestic courts in Kenya have prosecuted many cases involving minor offences and a few other involving serious offences, such as murder, under this approach. However, the main flaw with regard to these prosecutions is that their primary target has been the direct (low-level) perpetrators, while the main (high-level) perpetrators, who are accused in various official reports to have been the architects and masterminds of the violence, have hitherto remained untouched (supra Sects. 4.3.1.4.2 and 4.3.1.5).

As part of the domestic road map to peace, reconciliation and accountability, the TJRC was created and given very broad temporal and subject-matter mandates, which covered, but purposely went beyond, the 2007–2008 post-election violence (supra Sect. 5.2.2). In particular, the TJRC was given three mandates which link directly to criminal accountability for the post-election violence, the fact which makes them thematically relevant for purpose of this book. These are broad powers to gather information; to recommend prosecution; and to propose the granting of amnesty. As regards information gathering powers, the TJRC had broad quasi-legal powers, such as powers to subpoena information and to compel witnesses. As regards amnesty, the TJRC justifiably decided not to utilize its mandate mainly because that mandate was rendered nugatory by the TJRC Act which over-narrowed the scope of the proposed amnesty in terms of qualifying acts. As regards the mandate to recommend prosecution, the TJRC indeed recommended further investigation and prosecution of 56 individuals who had been named by other official reports as masterminds of the post-election violence (supra Sects. 5.2.3.2–5.2.3.4).

No prosecutions have so far flowed directly from the TJRC recommendations. But regarding the handling of TJRC's information for purposes of possible future trials, if any, the vast information gathered by the TJRC has the potential of either facilitating or impairing domestic criminal accountability for the post-election violence depending largely on how that information has been (or is) handled. On the one hand, criminal trials conducted subsequent to TJRC's dissolution, whether or not they result from TRJC's recommendations, can greatly benefit (in terms of evidence) from the information in the archives of the TJRC, if (and only if) the Kenyan judicial authorities are given access to such information and are willing to utilize it. On the other hand, such future trials, if any, could also be badly impaired or frustrated if too much self-incriminating information (e.g. through admissions and confessions) was revealed to the TJRC. The reason is that such information per se will no longer be admissible in court as evidence against the person who gave it. The only useful part of the self-incriminating information, if any, is that it can still be a good means for the Kenyan prosecutors and courts to locate further (other) sources of evidence (see supra Sect. 5.2.3.5). However, whether or not the Kenyan authorities will implement the TJRC's report, particularly its recommendation on prosecution, remains very doubtful.

The ICC's intervention in Kenya is of historical significance as it was the first time the ICC Prosecutor utilized his *proprio motu* powers to trigger the jurisdiction of the Court. However, the then Prosecutor Moreno-Ocampo had preferred a self-referral to a *proprio motu* intervention. However, for Kenya a self-referral would have been a political miscalculation (see supra Sect. 6.2.3). Subsequent to the ICC's intervention, and more specifically from the time the ICC identified and indicted part of the Kenyan political elite, Kenya started behaving in a manner that clearly showed that it was discontented by the ICC's intervention. The ICC's intervention was solely motivated by Kenya's failure (inaction) to carry out its duty to prosecute. It was for the same reason that Kenya's admissibility challenge, which was part of its efforts to keep the ICC away, was unsuccessful (supra Sect. 6.5). Therefore, despite Kenya's discontentment, the ICC process unfolded, giving rise to other legal issues.

The charges preferred were for crimes against humanity of murder, forcible transfer of population, persecution, rape and other inhumane acts (supra Sect. 4.3.1.3.1). However, at the end of the pre-trial phase, the Pre-Trial Chamber declined to confirm charges in respect of two of the six suspects. More importantly, the Chamber declined to confirm charges relating to property crimes in the *Kenyatta and Muthaura case* but confirmed similar charges in the *Ruto and Sang case*. The Chamber's decision and the Prosecutor's indifference about the exclusion of property crimes in the *Ruto and Sang case* have been flawed, for it jeopardizes the victims' genuine expectations to get reparations (in case of a conviction) for the property lost during the violence (supra Sect. 6.4.1). The ICC's intervention was motivated solely by Kenya's failure (inaction) to carry out its duty to prosecute. Despite this fact, Kenya tried, albeit unsuccessfully, to keep the ICC away by challenging admissibility of the cases (supra Sect. 6.5).

The most crucial legal question which emerged at the ICC during the pre-trial phase of the Kenya situation was whether in terms of their legal threshold, crimes against humanity could have been committed in Kenya during the post-election violence (supra Sect. 6.4.2.3). This controversial question emerged particularly in relation to the contextual elements of the definition of crimes against humanity under Article 7(2)(a) of the ICC Statute requiring such crimes to be committed pursuant to "State or organizational policy". Like the judges of the Pre-Trial Chamber, scholars remain divided to date as to whether, when interpreting the word "organization" from the formulation "State or organizational policy", the main focus should be on the *nature* or on the *capacity* of the entity that was involved in the commission of the crimes, i.e. whether the entity must be a "state-like organization" or it could be any "organization" provided it has the *capacity* to carry out a systematic or widespread attack on a civilian population.

The majority of the Pre-Trial Chamber held that in order to establish whether an entity qualifies as an "organization" capable of adopting a policy for purposes of Article 7(2)(a) of the Statute, the primary focus should not be on the nature or structure of the entity, but rather on its capacity to carry out an attack on a civilian population. The minority opinion, however, was that the nature of the entity, including its permanency, should be the primary focus. Based on the capacity criterion, the majority of the Pre-Trial Chamber concluded that two entities in Kenya, namely Mungiki and The Network, qualified as "organizations", and that they had adopted separate policies pursuant to which there were reasonable basis to believe that crimes against humanity had been committed during the post-election violence. The minority opinion, on the other hand, opined that from their nature as mere "criminal gangs", the two entities could not have qualified as "organizations" capable of adopting such policies, and, therefore, no crimes against humanity could have been committed in Kenya.

The position taken by the majority of the Pre-Trial Chamber has been endorsed in this book, for it is in line with the underlying objective of the ICC Statute to fight impunity for serious crimes of concern to the international community (supra Sect. 6.4.2.3). It entails a more convincing and pragmatic approach to the interpretation of the ICC Statute, and accommodates the fact that the ICC, unlike the ad hoc Tribunals, is forward-looking. Furthermore, such position underscores the importance of interpretation the ICC Statute with a prospective (as opposed to retrospective) outlook, with a view to accommodating the dynamic techniques employed by perpetrators in committing heinous crimes. One of such techniques is to use loosely organized entities which, although may not be state-like, have the *capacity* to carry out widespread and systematic attacks on civilian populations. On the other hand, the position taken by the minority embodies a retrospective outlook. Such outlook has been flawed for not fully appreciating the dynamism with which crimes against humanity are committed, including by entities, such as criminal gangs and terrorist groups, whose capacity to commit heinous crimes is evident in their acts, but whose formal structure may not necessarily be very clear.

Other incidental issues arising in relation to the Kenya situation before the ICC have also been legally analysed. These include Kenya's efforts and attempts to have the cases deferred by the UN Security Council, as well as its attempts or efforts to have the cases transferred to African regional courts. Although in these two endeavours Kenya was fully backed by the AU, its efforts were unsuccessful because they lacked a firm legal foundation (supra Sects. 6.6.1 and 6.6.2). A similar issue which has also been addressed is Kenya's threats to withdraw from the ICC Statute claiming that the ICC's intervention per se constituted an interference with its sovereignty. It has been shown that although withdrawal per se would not have stopped the cases, it definitely would have aggravated the challenges already facing the ICC regarding cooperation from Kenyan government (supra Sects. 6.6.3 and 6.7).

The election of Uhuru Kenyatta and William Ruto, both ICC indictees, as Kenya's President and Deputy President, respectively, became a huge challenge to the ICC. This has contributed to the most recent tension between the ICC and the AU. Both Kenya and the AU have argued that the cases facing the duo must be suspended in view of, inter alia, the immunity from prosecution that heads of state enjoy under customary international law. However, this argument does not hold water in terms of the ICC Statute to which Kenya is a State Party (supra Sect. 6.7.4). On the other hand, the ongoing ICC process in Kenya contributed significantly in deterring crimes during the 2013 general elections, which were comparatively peaceful. However, whether such deterrence will be sustainable in the future remains uncertain (supra Sect. 6.8).

Finally, out of the 8 situations currently before the ICC, the Court indicted an average of only 5 persons per situation. In the case of Kenya, only 6 suspects were originally charged. Out of these, only 4 were found triable, and only 2 were standing trial at the time of writing. This confirms the fact that the ICC is indeed not necessarily a panacea to impunity for the core crimes under international law, but only an important ingredient. Irrespective of the impact that the ICC may have in a given intervention, the fight against impunity cannot be won without the support of national courts. Therefore, despite the ICC's intervention in Kenya, the Kenyan domestic judicial organs still remain indispensable in ensuring that impunity is addressed genuinely with regard to the other alleged perpetrators of the crimes committed during the post-election violence. This is the form of justice that the victims still deserve and seek 6 years after the violence. Kenya subscribes to the adversarial tradition of litigation, as well as to absolute prosecutorial discretion. It follows that if the suspected perpetrators against whom there is enough evidence are not prosecuted, the blame will be shouldered by the Kenyan national prosecutorial authority in the first place. However, whatever the situation, the political will of the Kenyan government as a prerequisite for addressing impunity for the crimes is indispensable.

Index

© T.M.C. ASSER PRESS and the author 2015
S.F. Materu, *The Post-Election Violence in Kenya*,
International Criminal Justice Series 2, DOI 10.1007/978-94-6265-041-1

Printed by Printforce, the Netherlands